SPIRITUALITY WITHOUT GOD

ALSO AVAILABLE FROM BLOOMSBURY

Writing the Self, Peter Heehs
Becoming Atheist, Callum G. Brown
Capitalizing Religion, Craig Martin

SPIRITUALITY WITHOUT GOD

A global history of thought and practice

Peter Heehs

BLOOMSBURY ACADEMIC
LONDON • NEW YORK • OXFORD • NEW DELHI • SYDNEY

BLOOMSBURY ACADEMIC
Bloomsbury Publishing Plc
50 Bedford Square, London, WC1B 3DP, UK
1385 Broadway, New York, NY 10018, USA

BLOOMSBURY, BLOOMSBURY ACADEMIC and the Diana logo are trademarks of
Bloomsbury Publishing Plc

First published in Great Britain 2019

Copyright © Peter Heehs 2019

Peter Heehs has asserted his right under the Copyright, Designs and Patents Act, 1988,
to be identified as the Author of this work.

Cover image: Kenji Yoshida (Japan), *La Vie*, 1993. Metals and oil on canvas, 92 x 73 cm.
Estate of Kenji Yoshida. Photo: Jonathan Greet. Image Courtesy October Gallery, London.

All rights reserved. No part of this publication may be reproduced or
transmitted in any form or by any means, electronic or mechanical,
including photocopying, recording, or any information storage or retrieval
system, without prior permission in writing from the publishers.

Bloomsbury Publishing Plc does not have any control over, or responsibility for,
any third-party websites referred to or in this book. All internet addresses given in
this book were correct at the time of going to press. The author and publisher regret
any inconvenience caused if addresses have changed or sites have ceased to exist,
but can accept no responsibility for any such changes.

A catalogue record for this book is available from the British Library.

Library of Congress Cataloging-in-Publication Data
Names: Heehs, Peter, author.
Title: Spirituality without God : a global history of thought and practice / Peter Heehs.
Description: London : Bloomsbury Academic, 2018. |
Includes bibliographical references and index.
Identifiers: LCCN 2018009114 | ISBN 9781350056206 (hbk.) |
ISBN 9781350056190 (pbk.) | ISBN 9781350056220 (ePDF) |
ISBN 9781350056213 (ebk.) | ISBN 9781350056206 (Hpod)
Subjects: LCSH: Spirituality–History.
Classification: LCC BL624 .H3828 2018 | DDC 201/.4–dc23
LC record available at https://lccn.loc.gov/2018009114

ISBN: HB: 978-1-3500-5620-6
PB: 978-1-3500-5619-0
ePDF: 978-1-3500-5622-0
eBook: 978-1-3500-5621-3

Typeset by Newgen KnowledgeWorks Pvt. Ltd., Chennai, India
Printed and bound in Great Britain

To find out more about our authors and books visit www.bloomsbury.com
and sign up for our newsletters.

CONTENTS

Prologue: A religion is born 1

1 Introduction: Religion and spirituality, gods and godlessness 5

2 Theistic and nontheistic religions in the ancient world 33

3 Defending and debating tradition 71

4 The triumph of theism 101

5 The coming of modernity and the decline of God 139

6 Secularizing the sacred 169

7 The death and afterlife of God 201

Epilogue: Spiritual but still religious? 233

Notes 239
Bibliography 257
Index 273

PROLOGUE: A RELIGION IS BORN

I live in a town in southern India. My building stands midway between a Hindu temple and an ashram. I've never been inside the temple but I walk by its entrance a couple of times a day and am familiar with its routine. A little before six in the morning, a thundering of drums and a blare of conch-trumpets announce the start of daily worship. The presiding deity is Ganesha, the elephant-headed god who is the Remover of Obstacles. A real elephant, Lakshmi, has visiting hours in the evening and she never fails to attract a crowd. But the crush to take selfies in front of this much-loved pachyderm is nothing compared to the chaos on Wednesday and Friday evenings. That's when people bring motorbikes and cars to be blessed.

The ceremony, called *vandi puja* or vehicle worship, is one of the temple's specialties. It consists of a series of ritual acts that have to be performed in just the right way: The owner drives the vehicle, which is draped with garlands, to a spot on the road outside the temple. A priest waves a plate with a piece of lighted camphor, a lemon, and a few other items while chanting the necessary mantras. Then he puts the lemon on the ground. The driver inches the vehicle forward, squashing the lemon, and then puts an offering on the plate. The purpose of the ritual is to ward off accidents. I can understand the drivers' anxieties. Indian roads are among the most dangerous in the world. Part of the problem is widespread laxity in regard to traffic rules. The idea that certain vehicular actions have to be performed or avoided to avert accidents hasn't really caught on.

In the opposite direction is the gate of the ashram. I've been inside it thousands of times because I am a member. Here too I know the routine. In the morning women place floral decorations on the *samadhi* or tomb of the founders. People sit quietly on the perimeter of the courtyard or chat with friends near the entrance. During the day some sit in meditation, others approach the tomb with flowers or incense, still others walk through the courtyard on their way to the administrative offices. A few pause in a room where there is a photograph of one of the founders. It has been there for more than eighty years. Its original purpose was to give visitors an idea of what he looked like because he did not meet visitors or even his own disciples. Later some people began to prostrate before the photograph. He tried to discourage this, writing in a letter that he didn't want the room to become a place of public worship. During the time I have been here, acts of public worship have become more and more common.

When I go to the ashram, I sit near the *samadhi* and meditate or just look around. When I was younger I sometimes put flowers on the tomb but the ritual didn't feel right. I received no religious training when I was a child and have never regretted it. Here mothers teach their children how to bow and make offerings when they can scarcely walk. When I see this, the word "indoctrination" comes to mind but the kids seem to enjoy being told what to do.

I became interested in the teachings of the founders during the 1960s, when Eastern religions were enjoying a moment of vogue in the United States. Lots of swamis were setting up shop in New York, and yoga and meditation became part of the countercultural mix. I too began to meditate, starting with a mantra technique that was popular at the time. I also learned some *hatha-yoga* postures, which I practiced desultorily without getting really proficient. (I still envy people who can do the *purna shalabhasana* or full locust.) Then some friends introduced me to an American teacher who ran a yoga center on the Upper West Side. I ended up staying a couple of years, looking after the business, doing a good deal of meditation, and reading a lot of books, especially those by the founders of my ashram. One of the things I liked about their teachings was their insistence that yoga was not a religion. The phrase "spiritual but not religious" became current around that time and I was one of those who trotted it out when asked whether yoga wasn't some sort of cult.

After three years of study and practice in and around New York I decided to go to India. A few days after landing in Bombay, I arrived in the town where the ashram is located. A week or so later I began working under a man who had been there since the 1930s. He was looking for someone to help him publish a complete edition of the works of one of the founders and asked if I wanted to help. I was thrilled to accept. After a year of apprentice work I began preparing his uncollected writings for publication. I also went to different parts of India looking for material. The founder had been a revolutionary politician before becoming a yogi, and records of his speeches, transcribed by British spies, were lying in government archives. Dusty books in libraries contained uncollected prose pieces and letters. But by far the most copious source of new material was his handwritten manuscripts. Piled up in his secretary's room since his death twenty years earlier, they had never been systematically catalogued. Hundreds of pages remained unpublished. It was up to me and my colleagues to transcribe them and send them to the press. Other people were learning how to microfilm and preserve his manuscripts. In time our little office became an archive.

When I asked the director about the founders of the ashram he would lapse into silence or just say quietly that he thought their work was very important.

This low-key approach was typical of those of his generation. When I spoke with people who came a decade or two later, they were likely to elevate the founders to the heavens—and themselves along with the founders. This hyperbole had two sources: the ancient tradition of devotional poetry and modern mythologizing. I learned about the myths from a guy I used to work out with in the gym. His parents came to the ashram when he was just a child and he grew up listening to stories about its incredible past and still more incredible future. There was a widespread belief that the spiritual work of the founders was going to transform the world and that the people of the ashram would be the first to feel the effects.

The founders had more modest aspirations in regard to the members of the ashram. They hoped that individuals would overcome their problems and make some inner progress and that the community as a whole would function harmoniously and serve as a model for others. Many people in the ashram did make some progress, and the community grew and prospered. Then the founders died. The community survived and many of its members held on to their millennial expectations. My exercise buddy did not. After a while he left the ashram and made a life for himself elsewhere. I felt no urge to leave. I had always taken seriously the founders' affirmation that yoga was a matter of individual effort. However much one depends on the guidance of teachers and the support of friends, one has to do it oneself. With this in mind I settled down to a routine of meditation, work, study, writing, and sports.

The disciples who took charge of the running of the ashram were firm in their faith but open-minded. As time went by, and the first generation passed away, the atmosphere became more stilted and the devotionalism more ostentatious. For a while I was too busy to notice. I had begun to publish articles and books on the Indian freedom struggle and the founder's contribution to it. These were more appreciated by readers outside the ashram than within. The fact that I adhered to normal historiographical methodology was taken by some as a slap in the face. Things came to a head in 2008 when I published a biography of the founder with an American university press. A couple of hardliners picked through the book and found grounds for filing four cases against me and one against the ashram trustees, who were deemed unfit to serve because they refused to expel the author of a "blasphemous" book that was "deliberately and maliciously intended to insult religious beliefs of millions of Indians."[1] This case was dismissed by the Supreme Court of India after five-and-a-half years of costly hearings.

At that time I was working on a history of the idea of the self as told through first-person literature. I found that people in early cultures did not have a sense of self of the sort that most of us take for granted today. The self-idea emerged over the course of many centuries and recently has begun to decline. As I went through my sources, I saw that the history of the idea of self ran parallel to the history of the idea of God. People who played leading roles in the history of the self—Plato, Augustine, Rousseau—also were important in the history of God. People who had doubts about the idea of self—the Buddha, Nagarjuna, David Hume—were skeptical about the God-idea.

The search for spiritual wisdom unfettered by the gods goes back thousands of years. From the days of the Upanishads up to the present there have been traditions of nontheistic spiritual thought and practice that flourished alongside religions based on the worship of spirits, gods, or God. This book is a history of these nontheistic traditions. After looking briefly at the religions of the ancient world, I turn to the therapeutic philosophies of India, China, and Greece. Some of these survived during the thousand-year heyday of theistic religion, which ended around 1600. The rise of materialistic science and atheistic philosophy during the Age of Reason did not mean the end of spiritual seeking. Since the mid-nineteenth century, secular substitutes for religion—literature, art, philosophy, psychotherapy, and so forth—have for many taken the place of God-centered religions. More recently millions of people have taken up practices associated historically with religious traditions, such as yoga and mindfulness meditation, but discarded the religious packaging.

Theistic religions are useful for many but they have a built-in weakness. All of them have different conceptions of God and these differences can never be resolved because they are based on revelations that believers are forbidden to question. To protect divinely revealed certainties, people are willing to persecute and even kill those who accept other revelations. We see this all around us now. One way to prevent religious violence is to encourage spiritual ideas and practices that are not dependent on irreconcilable ideas about the gods.

Many people today reject all religions but still believe there is more to life than mindless consumption and obsessive communication. For such people this brief study of the history of godless spirituality may serve as an introduction to a very large field and provide a basis for further exploration.

1 INTRODUCTION: RELIGION AND SPIRITUALITY, GODS AND GODLESSNESS

For thousands of years almost everyone has believed in the existence of supernatural beings: spirits, demons, ghosts, gods, God. Such beings are the central figures of most of the systems of belief and practice we call religions. Most but not all. Some ancient religions downplayed the importance of supernatural beings; some modern systems of belief and practice have got rid of them altogether. Since the end of the nineteenth century, many people have used the word "spirituality" to describe systems of thought and practice that cover much of the ethical, intellectual, and experiential ground of religion but reject religious dogmas and institutions. Some forms of spirituality admit supernatural beings, others ignore or reject them. When a spiritual approach to life is combined with disbelief in the supernatural, the result is what I call spirituality without God.

Most histories of religion focus on the founders, scriptures, and practices of nine or ten religions that have had a major influence on the history of the world. The authors give much of their attention to beliefs and practices that are connected with God or other supernatural beings. In this book I focus on religions and spiritualities that do not require belief in the supernatural. I also examine secular philosophies and cultural expressions that for many have replaced religions as vehicles of truth and value. As a historian I am not interested in whether the beliefs of these religions and assumptions of these philosophies are true. My aim is to chart their development over time, trying to view them as they were viewed by their contemporaries, but giving none the final word.

In this introductory chapter I lay the structural foundations for the chronological account in Chapters 2–7. In the first section I explain what I mean by terms I use throughout the book, in particular "religion" and "spirituality." Although familiar to everyone, the word religion is hard to define. The religions of the world differ so much from one another that it is impossible to identify their essence, but all the religions I speak of acknowledge the existence of a superhuman principle or order of being, and most make room for supernatural beings such as spirits, gods, or God. The word spirituality has a 600-year history in English. For most of this time it was closely connected with religion. A century or so ago it began to shake itself free from religious connotations, and for many people today it means something that is virtually the opposite of religion. The defining characteristics of spirituality in its modern sense are subjectivity, rejection of religious dogmas and rituals, and individual practice.

Disbelief in God is now widespread, but in most parts of the world it is still a minority view. In the beginning of the second section of this chapter I examine philosophical arguments that support the God-idea. After showing their insufficiency, I look at treatments by social scientists and psychologists. They demonstrate that the case for God is weak, but neither they nor the philosophers have the last word, because the idea of God is, by its very nature, not open to logical proof or disproof.

Even if the existence of God cannot be proved, the idea of God may be required if life is to have any value or language to have any meaning. For millennia people have turned to religion for answers to fundamental questions: What is existence? What is consciousness? What is the basis of ethical and aesthetic value? Since the eighteenth century, materialistic science and naturalistic philosophy have assumed the authority religion once had but have failed to provide answers to these questions. For a number of scientists, philosophers, and scholars, whose thought I examine at the end of the second section, this failure is a sign that the materialistic/naturalistic view of life may be missing out on something.

Nontheistic spirituality began to take shape toward the end of the nineteenth century but came into its own only during the last few decades. In the third section I discuss the ideas of a few contemporary thinkers who promote a spiritual approach to life but deny the existence of God. They show that it is possible to ask difficult questions and wrestle with the great problems of life without invoking the supernatural.

Religion, irreligion, and spirituality

On January 23, 1891, Horace Traubel, a young newspaper editor from Philadelphia, paid a visit to his friend Walt Whitman. The poet, then 71 and in poor health, seemed "more at ease than for some days," Traubel wrote in his diary. For a while the two talked shop. Then Whitman mentioned a pamphlet by agnostic lecturer Robert Ingersoll that he had read several times that day. Its "passionate frank words," he said, "go to the ends of the earth." Traubel pulled out the latest issue of his paper, *The Conservator*, and showed Whitman a piece by Unitarian minister John Chadwick, who declared that Ingersoll, along with English-American pamphleteer Thomas Paine, had no trace of the "spiritual mind." Whitman read the article, looked steadily at Traubel and said: "What Chadwick means by spirituality is his spirituality. But what a little part of the world he is! Here is a world of individuals, each with some fresh, peculiar demonstration of it. Whose is to count—or *all?*" When he considered such matters, Whitman always thought back to Quaker minister Elias Hicks, who said that the Inner Light was more authoritative than the Bible. "Elias would say that we are *all* spiritual," Whitman remarked, "we can no more escape it than the hearts that beat in our bosoms." This gave Traubel an opening to read out his reply to Chadwick. The key sentence was this: "If to refuse to say 'god' and 'heaven' and 'immortality' bars the door 'spiritual' against manhood and individuality, then I say, this house is too small—" Here Whitman broke in: "Yes! Yes!" he exclaimed, "That hits it: I could think of nothing better. I say amen to it, every word."[1]

The idea that spirituality is different from religion is about a century and a quarter old. Before the end of the nineteenth century, the word spirituality meant concern for the things of the spirit rather than those of the body. The idea that someone who was completely unreligious could still be spiritual was new. Since then the meaning of spirituality has been in dispute. When Traubel challenged Chadwick to say what he meant by the term, Chadwick replied that he knew spirituality when he saw it but when he tried to put it into words it came out sounding like a "kind of a sort of something."[2] The situation is around the same today: "spirituality" is used by more and more people, but most would have a hard time saying exactly what they meant by it.

One thing is certain: in the early twenty-first century many people view spirituality *in contrast to* religion, which of course raises the question: What is religion? We all have an idea of what we mean by this word, but when authorities in various fields—theology, philosophy, anthropology, sociology, psychology, and religious studies—try to define it, they sound like they are talking about completely different things. The religions of the world are far too diverse for all of them to share a defining essence of "religiousness." But all the systems of belief and practice that are generally considered religions acknowledge the existence of a superhuman order of being. This order may or may not include spirits or gods or invisible forces, but it must be larger than the physical and social worlds we spend our lives in. (It is possible to speak of a religion of football, and certain players do seem to have greater-than-human abilities, but in the end football does not require the assumption of a superhuman order.) When I speak of religions in this book, I mean systems of belief and practice that are directed toward a superhuman order of being.

Across the millennia, human beings have done many different things to establish or acknowledge relationships with the supernatural. In the course of this book I will speak of five main types of religious activity: magic, sacrifice, worship, rational inquiry, and psychophysical practices. Magic is the use of rituals, spells, and other techniques to gain control over spirits or other supernatural beings and forces. In sacrifice humans give offerings to gods or spirits to establish a reciprocal relationship. Worship, as I use the term, means the adoration of gods or spirits who respond to prayer and bestow their favors through grace. Rational enquiry, in the religious context, means the study of scriptures and the construction of theological systems. The psychophysical practices associated with religion include meditation, prayer, breathing exercises, and other regulated actions of the mind and body.

There were and are remarkable similarities between the religious activities of people in different parts of the world: blood sacrifice in Mesopotamia was a lot like blood sacrifice in Rome; some Indian meditation techniques are almost identical to techniques current in Japan. But there were and are significant differences between the practices of religious people in different cultures. This is illustrated by the divergent ways that practitioners understand religion. The word is European—it comes from the Latin *religio*—and it has a number of connotations that are typical of Western faiths, such as the veneration of God or gods, the mandatory acceptance of a set of beliefs and practices, and a more or less centralized ecclesiastical hierarchy. Judaism, Christianity, and Islam all count as religions in this sense.

As we move further east, the suitability of the term religion diminishes. In India the word normally used to translate "religion" is *dharma*. This is a complex concept with many different meanings, but Hindus, Jains, Buddhists, and Sikhs all use it to cover their beliefs and practices. When speaking English they rarely hesitate to use religion as an equivalent of *dharma*, but there are significant differences between West Asian religions and South Asian *dharmas*. Hinduism does not have a fixed set of beliefs or a central ecclesiastical hierarchy; Jainism and some forms of Buddhism are atheistic or at any rate indifferent about the gods.

When we reach China things get even more difficult. There is no word in classical Chinese that corresponds to our "religion," and Chinese systems of belief and practice such as Confucianism and philosophical Daoism lack most of the characteristics of Western religions. They do, on the other hand, propose ways of living in harmony with a higher order of being—Heaven (*tian*) or the Way (*dao*)—and this is something that all religions and *dharmas* do in one way or another. I therefore use "religion" throughout this book as a rough-and-ready term for beliefs and practices centered on the superhuman among people in China, India, western Asia, and the West.

In Europe before the sixteenth century, the word religion was sufficient to cover all religious activities and beliefs. The rediscovery of the religions of ancient Greece and Rome, the confrontation with the religions of Asia, Africa, and the Americas, and the appearance of philosophies that seemed completely unreligious made it necessary for European scholars to coin new terms. The familiar creeds of the Middle East were termed "monotheistic" because they accepted only one God. The creeds of classical Greece and Rome and modern India were "polytheistic" because they accepted many. The ideas of philosophers who seemed to deny God were called "atheistic" or "pantheistic." Later, as the field of belief and disbelief became increasingly muddled, other neologisms were introduced, among them "deism" and "agnosticism."

"Atheism" comes from the Greek word *atheos*, which originally meant "godless" or "impious." The sense "one who does not believe in the gods recognized by the state" came later. Socrates, accused of being *atheos* in this sense, denied the charge but was convicted and executed in 399 BCE. When the French *athéisme* and English atheism appeared in the sixteenth century they were used primarily to mean "impiousness" or "immorality." It was hardly possible for Europeans of that age to imagine a world without God. After Dutch philosopher Baruch Spinoza published his *Theologico-Political Treatise* in 1670, some of his critics called him an atheist. He denied this, and there is little in the book to suggest that he was, but in a later work he equated God and Nature. A scholar of the time invented the word "pantheism" to describe this view. Another coinage of this period was "deism," which went through several changes of meaning before arriving at its modern sense: belief in a God who created the universe but does not intervene in its workings. In the mid-nineteenth century English biologist Thomas Henry Huxley coined the term "agnostic" to mean a person who believes that knowledge of God, the afterlife, and so forth is impossible.

In current use atheism means disbelief in gods or God, in particular the creator God of the West Asian monotheisms. Agnosticism is the conviction that there is no way to arrive at knowledge about God or other supernatural entities. Agnostics make no claims in regard to the existence or nonexistence of God, gods, the soul, or immortality. Atheists do not believe in such things. But there are different sorts of atheism: positive (or strong or hard) and negative (or weak or soft). Positive atheists assert that God or gods do *not* exist; negative atheists say that they do not happen to believe in God, gods, and so forth. Negative atheism comes close to agnosticism and most agnostics are negative atheists. (As an agnostic I do not hold the belief "God exists." I therefore am a negative atheist.) Despite such clarifications, "atheism" has never lost the connotations of impiousness and immorality that have dogged it since the time of Socrates. In the nineteenth century, some writers introduced the neutral synonym "nontheism," and in recent years this has begun to elbow out "atheism" in scholarly discussions.

So much for religion and the various forms of irreligion. What about spirituality? Before I go into the history of the term and the development of the concept, I have to remove a possible cause of confusion. So far I have spoken of religion and spirituality as though they were a dichotomy: religion on the one side, spirituality on the other. But there is a lot of overlap between the two. Most religions, even the most hidebound, have a spiritual side; many spiritual paths incorporate religious practices. The distinction between them is recent and has more to do with the current meaning of the words than the nature of the things themselves. During the nineteenth century, some people who felt they had to abandon their religions but still were interested in developing their inner capacities hit on the word spirituality as an untarnished alternative to religion. But neither spirituality nor religion cover every possible approach to personal development. Take *xiushen*, which means self-cultivation in Chinese. This term is of central importance in Confucianism, where it is connected with learning and efforts at moral perfection. Does *xiushen* belong to religion or spirituality? In fact it fits neither of these Western categories but its importance to the religio-spiritual culture of China is undeniable. Greek philosophers such as Plato and Epictetus acknowledged the importance of religion (the Greek *thréskeia* corresponds to the Latin *religio*) but they were more interested in cultivating the art or craft of living (*tekhné tou biou*) than in conventional religious practices. Was *tekhné tou biou* a sort of spirituality? I don't think the terms match up very well. Modern psychotherapists perform many of the functions that until recently were the province of religious professionals, but this does not make psychotherapy a religion, and few psychotherapists would be happy to call their profession a form of spirituality.

It would be convenient if there was an English word that subsumed religion, spirituality, *dharma*, *xiushen*, *tekhné tou biou*, psychotherapy, and related concepts but as far as I know there is none. (The term religio-spiritual culture I used earlier was a clumsy attempt to make up for this lack.) The problem is a long-standing one. In *First Alcibiades*, which was written some 2,350 years ago, the author (traditionally thought to be Plato) has Socrates speak about *tekhnés* or crafts that are concerned with the care of the body or things belonging to the body, such as gymnastics, shoemaking, and weaving. Socrates then asks Alcibiades to name the craft by which "we take care of ourselves." Alcibiades has no answer.[3] Today some people might say "self-culture" or "cultivating human potential," but these terms are as much products of the modern West as *dharma* is of ancient India, *xiushen* of ancient China, and *tekhné tou biou* of ancient Greece.

Lacking an umbrella term, I will fall back on the familiar words religion, which I spoke of earlier, and spirituality, which I turn to now. The English word spiritual was coined in the twelfth century on the model of the French *spirituel* or medieval Latin *spiritualis*. All three words look back to the classical Latin *spiritus*, which meant "breathing," "breath," "inspiration," "life," and many other things. In the Latin Bible *spiritus* was used to translate the Hebrew *ruah* and Greek *pneuma*, both of which referred to a nonmaterial principle in human beings. For most of its history in English, "spiritual" was understood to be the opposite of "carnal," "material," or "temporal."

Clearly the religious roots of "spiritual" go very deep. But for many people today "spiritual" is not just distinct from "religious" but virtually its opposite. This semantic shift happened because the European idea of religion underwent massive changes during and after the sixteenth century, to the point where a new word was needed for its inner, noninstitutional, self-reliant aspects. This need was filled by "spirituality," which over the same 500-year period gradually lost its connection with the outer or institutional side of religion.

During the sixteenth and seventeenth centuries, the Protestant Reformation broke the monopoly of the Catholic Church on Christian dogma in Western Europe. This opened the door to a slew of new approaches. Some, like pietism, quietism, and evangelicalism, gave special importance to subjective practices. French quietist Jeanne Guyon and English evangelical John Wesley used the adjectives *spirituel* or spiritual when speaking of inward as opposed to outward devotion. Around the same time, the philosophers Spinoza and Thomas Hobbes distinguished "true religion"—a matter of inner conviction—from outer religion or "superstition." This inner/outer distinction was controversial. In the mid-eighteenth century Swiss writer Jean-Jacques Rousseau proclaimed that true religion was a matter of inner feeling. He was run out of the country for his trouble. A few decades later German theologian Friedrich Schleiermacher wrote that the signs of true religion were inner faith and experience. He was forced to revise the book in which he made that claim. The European Romantic poets of the early nineteenth century, and the American Transcendentalists of a few years later, made inner experience the touchstone of spiritual practice, but they rarely used the term spirituality, which remained for most a virtual synonym of religion.

In the second half of the nineteenth century the cord connecting religion and spirituality began to fray. In 1866 English critic Walter Pater wrote that the spiritual side of life was simply "the passion for inward perfection," which had no necessary connection with religion. (A detractor howled that Pater was promoting "spirituality without God.") This brings us back around to Whitman, who wrote in 1876 that "only in the perfect uncontamination and solitariness of individuality may the spirituality of religion positively come forth at all."[4]

By the turn of the twentieth century, "spirituality" was coming into use in the United States in the sense of the inner or—as philosopher George Santayana put it—the "aspiring" side of religion.[5] Another part of the English-speaking world where the word was catching on was colonial South Asia. Taking their cue from British scholars who wrote that Indian scriptures were troves of spiritual wisdom, Indian and Ceylonese religious leaders based claims of cultural superiority on their ancient spiritual heritage. Hindu reformer Keshab Chandra Sen spoke of the "spirituality of true worship" he found in the Vedas. Buddhist reformer Anagarika Dharmapala wrote of "the psychology of spiritual growth" he found in the Tripitaka. Western practitioners of Eastern religions followed suit. Sister Nivedita, an Irish disciple of an Indian guru, wrote that "spirituality comes to one soul at a time" by means of personal discipline. Henry Steel Olcott, an American Theosophist, encouraged young Buddhists to strive for "spiritual enlightenment," that is, "the development of that Buddha-like faculty which is latent in every man."[6]

Despite their growing popularity, the words spiritual and spirituality remained ill defined. In a 1907 article, British scholar and Theosophist G.R.S. Mead observed: "It is a curious fact that though the terms 'spirit,' 'spiritual,' and 'spirituality'" were in common use, there was no general agreement about their meaning. Defining spirituality as "the manifestation of spirit in man," and spirit as "the attitude of the inmost man, the Divine Spark, towards the daily surroundings of the life of the outer man," Mead distinguished spiritual from religious concerns: "People who think 'heaven and hell' can be named at once as the unspiritual." A California Theosophist was even more severe in his condemnation of conventional religion: "The impartial observer may be pardoned for believing that if there is one place on earth where spirituality is not to be found it is in the organized churches."[7] Still, for most people "spirituality" and "religion" remained virtual synonyms. One of the first to distinguish them explicitly was Indian philosopher Sri Aurobindo. "Spirituality is a wider thing than formal religion," he wrote in 1910. "Spirituality is a single word expressive of three lines of human aspiration towards divine knowledge, divine love and joy, divine strength."[8]

Before long the spiritual/religious distinction was common currency throughout the English-speaking world, and by 1926 the now ubiquitous catchphrase appeared: "Spiritual but not religious?" mused an American journalist. "That is a nice distinction. But is it quite sound?"[9] Whether or not it was, within forty years it was taken for granted by millions. By the beginning of the twenty-first century, three out of ten people polled in the United States said they were "spiritual but not religious." Among younger Americans, the proportion was seven in ten.[10]

For all its popularity, the word spirituality remains vague in meaning. Seeking clarity, a number of recent writers have tried to identify its features.[11] Each writer emphasizes different things, but almost all of them mention three characteristics, which I will call subjectivity, autonomy, and individual effort:

> *Subjectivity.* Spiritual people cultivate inner feelings and experiences and are comparatively indifferent to outward standards of thought and behavior. They try to find what they are looking for (truth, harmony, love, fulfillment, peace) within themselves and not by accepting the ideas of other individuals or groups.
>
> *Autonomy.* In their relations with the communities they belong to, spiritual people insist on personal freedom and are wary of doctrines, scriptures, and institutions. If they choose to join a group or follow a teaching, they do so freely and reject the idea that commitment implies exclusiveness.

Individual effort. Because they are focused on personal experience and suspicious of outward authority, spiritual people see their practice in terms of individual effort. They give more importance to self-discipline, meditation, and private study than congregational rituals and other group activities.

Along with the three main characteristics of spirituality there are a number of others—let's call them secondary characteristics—that are more or less important to particular individuals and groups. Among those mentioned most frequently are universality, empiricism, and corporality.

Universality. Many people believe that the experiences on which spirituality is based are the same in all cultures and periods. They find striking similarities between the teachings of mystics of different times and places, and therefore are open to inspiration from various traditions.

Empiricism. Many modern spiritual teachers have tried to bring spirituality and science together. They treat spirituality as an empirical science, with its own hypotheses and experimental procedures.

Corporality. This experimentation must, according to many people, involve not only the mind and heart but also the life and the body. Hence the popularity, among spiritual practitioners, of yoga, tai chi, and other forms of physical exercise, as well as Ayurveda, massage therapy, and other healing systems. This marks a rejection of the old religious dichotomy between spirit and body.

These are the chief characteristics of modern spirituality. But what is its raison d'être and aim? What is spirituality *about?* This book is a historical and cross-cultural exploration of this question. We will see that people in different eras and cultures have found ways to achieve freedom from suffering and perplexity and to develop their inner and outer capacities without relying on religions.

This is, I think, what most people mean by spirituality at the beginning of the twenty-first century. Others would define the term differently or point out factors I have missed. Still others would scoff at the very idea that there is something called spirituality as distinct from religion at all. One Catholic writer, in a 2003 article, classed the spiritual-but-not-religious phenomenon as a cultural problem of the same severity as "inclusivity, addictions, and family breakdown." Other religious writers have tried to recapture the term. A recent history of spirituality published by an English scholar turns out to be a historical survey of Christian thought, cheered up by passages like this: "'spirituality' implies some kind of vision of the human spirit and of what will assist it in achieving full potential."[12] Unobjectionable in itself, this has more to do with the ideas of twentieth-century secular writers such as Abraham Maslow and

Aldous Huxley than with the doctrines of Saints Augustine, Aquinas, and Ignatius of Loyola. Of course Christian writers have every right to use the word spirituality in its religious sense. It emerged, after all, in a Christian context and even today has technical meanings in Christian theology. But for most people today these meanings are unimportant. Spirituality in its twenty-first-century sense has no necessary connection with religion, just as spiritual practices have no necessary connection with religious beliefs. Spirituality is an imperfect term but it is the only one we have for an increasingly important area of human experience. Rather than worrying about its shortcomings it will be better to accept it and move on.

God: Yes, No, Maybe

In 1899 psychologist and philosopher William James took a sabbatical from Harvard and went to Europe to visit health resorts and write a series of lectures on religion. His health did not improve but he managed to finish the first ten lectures and deliver them in May and June 1901. His primary assumption, he explained, was that "the mother sea and fountain-head of all religions lie in the mystical experiences of the individual." Because they belonged to "a region deeper, and more vital and practical, than that which the intellect inhabits," these experiences were "indestructible by intellectual arguments." But, as he clarified the next year, subjective experiences had nothing to say about the objective existence of God. As a philosopher James was very well acquainted with the arguments put forward in support of the God-idea. In a lecture of April 1902 he dismissed them in two paragraphs. The cosmological argument (there must be a First Cause) assumes we know what causality is when in fact we don't. The argument from design no longer stood up after Darwin. The common consent and moral arguments were too clearly contradicted by experience to be taken seriously. Turning to philosophical demonstrations of God's perfections, he asked: "what vital difference can it possibly make to a man's religion whether they be true or false?" Yet in his concluding lecture James suggested that religion was not altogether useless: When we commune with the spiritual world, "work is actually done upon our finite personality, for we are turned into new men, and consequences in the way of conduct follow in the natural world."[13]

Most religions and many spiritual teachings give central importance to the idea of God. Others treat it as a distraction. In this book I am concerned mainly with godless religions and spiritualities, but it will be useful, before proceeding, to see how the God-fearing majority have defended their beliefs and how others have argued against them.

Most people believe in God because their parents taught them to. If it wasn't their parents, it was other family members or friends or teachers or religious professionals or the collective suggestion of society. Since the beginning of recorded history, and doubtless long before, almost everyone has believed in gods, spirits, or other supernatural beings simply because almost everyone else did. Philosophers call this acceptance of general opinion the common consent argument for God. It has a distinguished pedigree. Plato and Cicero were among its proponents. In recent years it has been treated more as an embarrassment than as an argument because it is clear that "almost everyone" has believed many untrue things—for instance that the sun and planets move around a motionless earth.

Closely related to the common consent argument is the argument from scripture. People accept Upanishadic statements about Brahman or Biblical statements about God or Quranic statements about Allah because they believe that the Upanishads or Bible or Quran come from superhuman sources. Since the sources are superhuman what they say about superhuman beings and forces is true. This begs the question, but it is good enough for billions of people, who believe that the scripture they accept is infallible and that all other scriptures are false or incomplete.

There's no point trying to argue for or against the assertions of a given scripture. Either you believe them or you don't. But some religious thinkers have felt the need to support their belief in God by rational arguments. Dozens have been proposed over the last two millennia, but according to German philosopher Immanuel Kant only three are worth looking into: the ontological, cosmological, and teleological arguments. A believer himself, Kant refuted all three, and most later thinkers have agreed that the arguments have little value. Nevertheless I summarize them and their refutations here because they still turn up in technical and popular literature.

The ontological argument is an attempt to show that God is a necessary being. It goes something like this: It is possible to conceive of a being, namely God, beyond which nothing greater can be conceived. If this being exists in concept, it must also exist in reality, because existence in reality is greater than existence in concept. Therefore God must exist. Today most people find it hard to understand how anyone ever took this seriously. One can see why German philosopher Arthur Schopenhauer called it a "sleight-of-hand trick" and "a charming joke."[14] Kant was a bit more kind, devoting a section of his major work to showing why it fails. The main problem is that existence is not a property. You can say that Mary is and that Mary is or is not tall, but you can't say that God is and that God is or is not existent. So it makes no sense to say that God's actual existence is greater than his conceptual existence.

The cosmological and teleological arguments have also inspired wordy debate but they are not mere wordplay. Both start from observations about the way things are in the world and use inductive reasoning to move from the observations to something or someone that is supposed to lie beyond. The cosmological argument is based on the idea of causality. When we trace a chain of causes and effects back as far as we can go, we are left with the problem of what caused the whole thing to start. Since, according to the argument, nothing is self-caused, there must be an uncaused cause, and this is God. This argument has had a long and distinguished history in Indian, Greco-Roman, Islamic, and European philosophy. During the European Enlightenment the idea of the First Cause persisted even as belief in God declined. Today some think that the Big Bang theory of the origin of the universe implies a creative God, but few contemporary scientists and philosophers think that God is the answer to the question of causation. The problem with all versions of the cosmological argument can be summed up in a question: If God is the Creator, who created God? If God is uncreated, couldn't the same be said of the universe itself?

The cosmological argument is based on speculations about how things begin, the teleological argument on speculations about their purposes or ends. Wherever we look we see indications that the world was created by a designer who had certain ends in mind: the eye was made for seeing, the hand for holding, the feet for running, and so forth. Since no human being designed these things, it is easy to conclude that they were the work of a divine designer. Classic statements of this argument are found in the works of ancient Indian and Greek philosophers. In modern Europe it was memorably set forth by English theologian William Paley, who wrote in 1802 that anyone who examines the mechanism of a watch must conclude it was designed for keeping time. Likewise when we examine the natural world we find that "every manifestation of design, which existed in the watch, exists [also] in the works of nature." It therefore is clear the natural world is the creation of a divine designer.[15] When, three decades later, Cambridge student Charles Darwin came across Paley's argument, he found it satisfactory, but after years of biological research he concluded that all instances of apparent design in living things could be explained by natural selection.

After Kant had disposed of the three rational arguments, he fell back on ethics to prove the existence of God. His argument, roughly, was this: humans are rational, moral beings, and as such must will the highest good, namely perfect virtue and happiness. To rationally will the highest good, we must believe that the fabric of the universe is moral and that justice will prevail in this world or the next. A moral universe can exist only if it is maintained by God. By believing that the fabric of the universe is moral and acting in accordance with that belief, human beings affirm in practical terms the existence of God. So summarized, Kant's argument looks rather lame, but it has parallels in almost every religion. In India, the belief that the universe is moral is bound up with the idea of *karma* (action and its inevitable consequences). In Jainism and Buddhism, the law of karma works automatically without the need of God, but in the theistic philosophies of Nyaya and Vedanta, God is required to make it work. As the eighth-century Vedanta philosopher

Shankara put it, there has to be a conscious agent, namely God, to "ordain the fruits of works for the people according to their merit."[16]

The problem with all moral arguments is that there is no compelling reason to believe that the universe has a moral basis. If anything, the opposite seems true. There is a huge amount of suffering in the world and it is hard to reconcile this with any sort of moral order. An innocent child is kidnapped, confined, repeatedly raped, and murdered. How do we explain this in ethical terms? The popular Christian notion that she will enjoy an afterlife in heaven and the popular Hindu notion that she must have done something terrible in her last life to merit such suffering are puerile and repugnant. But the underlying issues are serious, and philosophers have grappled with them for thousands of years.

Indian thinkers see suffering as the inevitable result of karma but add that karma alone is not enough to insure that people get what they deserve. A single life is too short for this, as simple observation confirms: some evil-doers prosper until they die, some virtuous people suffer their whole lives. Indian religions therefore assume that the karmic drama plays out in a series of rebirths, ending only with final liberation. This provides a neat solution to the problem of moral accountancy but relies on assumptions that cannot be proved. Karma and rebirth are discussed in many scriptures and upheld by Indian philosophy and folklore but there is no hard evidence to support them.[17]

Western theists do not deny the reality of suffering, but they say we have to view it from God's perspective. According to traditional Christian theology, God gave free will to human beings so they could participate consciously in the joys and challenges of existence. With free will came the possibility of sin, with sin the certainty of suffering but also the possibility of redemption. In the eighteenth century German philosopher Gottfried Leibniz coined the word "theodicy" to signify an explanation of evil by appeal to God's justice. He argued that since the world was created by God it was, necessarily, the best of all possible worlds. For humans to understand this, they had to look at it from the divine and not the human point of view. The French writer Voltaire skewered Leibniz's ideas in his 1759 satire *Candide*, and the phrase "best of all possible worlds" has never recovered.

In the twentieth century English theologian John Hick developed a theodicy of "soul-making": virtues won by making correct decisions in the face of difficulty are more valuable than those that come "ready made and without any effort."[18] Like other theodicies, Hick's is circular. It starts with the assumption that God is good and explains the apparent existence of evil by saying that, despite all appearances, God is good. The actual arguments are of course more sophisticated, but even the best of them have satisfied few who are not predisposed to accept them. The problem of evil remains, in the words of contemporary theologian Hans Küng, "the rock of atheism."[19] For thousands of years, it has been the solid basis of moral arguments against God, and a stumbling block for those who have tried, with indifferent success, to argue in God's favor.

Few people turn to moral philosophy to justify their belief in God but many rely on a vernacular moral argument that might be phrased like this: If people didn't believe in God they would have no moral standards. People without moral standards would have no reason not to go around cheating, raping, and killing everybody else. Therefore people should believe in God. This argument, such as it is, assumes that moral standards must be based on theistic beliefs, that people who believe in God always behave well, and that people who do not believe in God always behave badly. All these assumptions are invalid. The available evidence, from ancient history to modern statistics, shows that theistic texts are often unethical, that religious people often behave badly, and that many unbelievers lead virtuous lives. Hebrew scriptures took slavery for granted and slave-owners used them to defend their right to human property right down to the modern era. The same scriptures depict God ordering acts of genocide: "Now go, attack the Amalekites and totally destroy all that belongs to them," God told his chosen people. "Do not spare them; put to death men and women, children and infants, cattle and sheep, camels and donkeys."[20] Hindu law books took the caste system for granted and some high-caste Hindus still use these books to defend the enormities that developed around the system, such as untouchability and honor killing.

A supporter of religion might say that such examples are atypical and that people who believe in God are much more moral than those who don't. Social-science research suggests this is not true. Many countries ranking high in unbelief, such as Denmark, Sweden, Iceland, and the Czech Republic, enjoy excellent societal health, with low levels of homicide, divorce, teenage pregnancy, drug addiction, and so forth. On the other hand, many countries that rank high in belief, among them the United States, have comparatively high levels of these indicators of social breakdown. This is not to suggest that there is an invariable connection between belief in God and immorality. Many studies show high correlations between religious belief and many aspects of physical and psychological well-being. All that can be said for sure is that there is no *necessary* correlation between belief in God and morality and no inevitable link between atheism and immorality.

Despite the problems with religion-based morality, many people still insist that ethical standards must be rooted in God: some actions are good because God commands them, others are bad because he forbids them. There is a refreshing simplicity to this approach, especially if you think you know what God's commandments are. But there are also serious philosophical problems, with serious practical consequences, in thinking that morality is just what God approves. In the Western philosophical tradition, these problems were first discussed by Plato in the *Euthyphro*. In this dialogue, Socrates meets Euthyphro, a conceited young man who is on his way to bring a case of murder against his father on behalf of someone else. In the course of conversation, Socrates asks Euthyphro what is and what is not holy. Euthyphro replies: "What is dear to the gods is holy, and what is not dear to the gods is unholy." Socrates, as is his habit, presses Euthyphro to think carefully about what he said. A question emerges: "Do the gods love the holy because it is holy or is it holy because the gods love it?" Euthyphro rushes off before they can resolve the problem. Philosophers have grappled with it ever since. Nowadays they state the dilemma in more general terms: Is an action good because God wills it, or does God will it because it is good? Neither alternative helps the idea of a moral God. If something becomes good just because God wills it, what if he should will that women must live in perpetual enslavement? Or that everyone must wear pink suspenders on Thursdays? God would come out looking like an arbitrary monster or a joker. If, on the other hand, God wills what is good because it already is good, we don't need God to determine moral behavior. What's good is good just because it is.

The idea that morality is based on human standards has been part of the traditional wisdom of China for millennia. A century before Plato, the philosopher Confucius commented on a situation similar to the one in the *Euthyphro*. Told that a man in a certain village was so straight that he gave evidence against his father, Confucius replied: "In our village those who are straight are quite different. Fathers cover up for their sons, and sons cover up for their fathers." This grounding of morality in the virtue of humanness remained central to Chinese culture well into the twentieth century. The scholar Lin Yutang noted in 1935 that just as Westerners found it strange that morality "could be maintained without reference to a Supreme Being," so the Chinese found it amazing that people could not behave decently with one another without referring to an invisible "third party."[21]

Over the last century, as the rational and moral arguments for God lost their appeal, an empirical alternative emerged: the argument from religious experience. In its most basic form, it goes like this: "I am having an experience of God. Therefore God exists." This is of little interest to those not having the experience. A less restricted version is: "X [a respected saint, mystic or avatar] said that she had experiences of God. Therefore God exists." This adds the weight of authority but in the end differs little from the argument from scripture discussed above. True arguments from experience are attempts to demonstrate that God exists starting from the premise that a great many people have had experiences they took to be experiences of God.

The religious lives of human beings have always had an experiential side. The religious and spiritual literature of the world is filled with descriptions of supernormal experiences—visions, raptures, voyages to higher spheres—that were viewed by those who had them in terms of their religious beliefs. But the category "religious (or mystical or spiritual) experience" is surprisingly modern. It came to the front in Europe during the seventeenth and eighteenth centuries when religious movements such as pietism, quietism, and evangelicalism encouraged personal engagement with God. Nineteenth-century Romantic writers put subjective experiences in the foreground of their work whether or not they connected them with religion. Some European scholars of the same period wrote about the experiential side of Hinduism and Buddhism. Later, defenders of these traditions, such as Swami Vivekananda and D.T. Suzuki, proposed that universal spiritual experiences are the basis of the world's religions.

William James absorbed all these influences and made subjective religious experience the linchpin of his study of the religious life. In his enormously influential *Varieties of Religious Experience* (which comprised his lectures of 1901–1902) he wrote that "the *founders* of every church [or other religious institution] owed their power originally to the fact of their direct personal communion with the divine." This did not mean that the founders, much less their followers, had the right to insist that we accept their experiences as true. "The utmost they can ever ask of us," James wrote, "is to admit that they [their experiences] establish a presumption." Neither did he suggest that religious experiences proved the existence of God. "The whole interest of the question of God's existence," he wrote, "seems to me to lie in the consequences for particulars which that existence may be expected to entail."[22] In other words, the importance of the idea of God lay in the practical effects it had on our lives.

Subsequent philosophers tried to go farther, putting forward theories of knowledge based on religious experience. One of the first to do so was C.D. Broad, who wrote in 1939 that the belief of mystics that their experiences are veridical was not fundamentally different from our everyday belief that sense-perceptions are reliable. Both sorts of perception-based knowledge should be "provisionally accepted as veridical unless there be some positive ground for thinking that they are not." Broad concluded that there was no good reason to believe that "the whole religious experience of mankind" was "a gigantic system of pure delusion," but he said nothing definite about whether religious experiences should be taken as proofs of God's existence.[23]

Over the last eighty years this approach has been refined by other thinkers trained in analytic philosophy, such as William Alston and Richard Swinburne. Alston wrote that mystics who say that they are perceiving God are in the same *sort* of position as people who say they are perceiving everyday objects such as tables and chairs. Therefore the beliefs that mystics have about God have the same sort of value as the beliefs that ordinary people have about furniture. His cautious conclusion was that if God-experience was a valid mode of perception *and* if God in fact existed there was no reason to think that perceptions of God were not "sometimes veridical rather than delusory."[24]

Alston's work in the epistemology of God-perception did not constitute an experiential argument for the existence of God, as he himself admitted.[25] Swinburne was more ambitious. He asserted that the religious experience of a sane individual constituted "*prima facie* reason for all to believe in that of which the reported experience was purportedly an experience." More plainly: if a generally reliable person has an experience of God then everybody else has reason to believe that

God exists. The basis of Swinburne's argument was his Principle of Credulity: we normally believe in the reliability of knowledge based on sense experience unless we have good reason to reject it. It is innocent until proven guilty. In the same way we ought to believe in the reliability of knowledge based on religious experience unless it obviously is unreliable.[26] Swinburne's argument has impressed few people who are not already convinced believers. In fact few people in the modern world turn to philosophers to justify their religious beliefs and few critics of religion even bother to engage with them.

All philosophical arguments for God begin with the assumption (generally unstated) that God in fact exists. Many rely on analogical reasoning: Physical things (smoke) have causes (fire); it follows that the universe itself has a cause, which is God. Or: We assume that sensory experience is reliable; it follows that we should assume that religious experience is reliable, and religious experience is experience of God. These analogies don't really hold up. It is not certain that the universe has a cause (it may be self-existent) or that religious experiences provide knowledge of God in the way that sensory experiences provide knowledge of the physical world. If a supernatural being exists, it is *ipso facto* unknowable by natural instruments. It therefore is futile for believers to try to prove the existence of supernatural beings using arguments based on natural evidence. By the same token, it is futile for atheists to try to prove the *non*existence of supernatural beings using the same sort of arguments.

Since the middle of the nineteenth century the most influential discussions of the roots of religion have been put forward not by philosophers but by social scientists, psychologists, and neuroscientists. Karl Marx, Émile Durkheim, Edward Tylor, James Frazer, Sigmund Freud, and their modern descendants undermined the foundations of religion by treating it as a human invention rather than a divine creation. I discuss their work in Chapters 6 and 7. Briefly, sociologists such as Marx and Durkheim described religion as a function of human society. (To Durkheim religion was simply society writ large.) Early anthropologists such as Tylor and Frazer tried to trace religion back to its origins in primitive human cultures. Freud wrote that the religious impulse grew out of emotions such as fear and the desire for security, while contemporary psychologists and neuroscientists reduce the religious life to patterns of behavior or pulses of neurochemical activity. Yet neither psychological experiments nor social-science data rule out the possibility that there is something beyond the material world or that this something is what gives meaning to our lives.

Rational enquiry has helped us understand the structure of the universe, the functions of the brain, and the varieties of human cultures, but has little to say about the great existential questions that have puzzled human beings since the beginning of time: What is the purpose of existence? What is the nature of consciousness? What is the basis of ethical and aesthetic value? For the most part, scientists, philosophers, and cultural critics give little thought to such questions. They have quite enough to do collecting and analyzing empirical data. Nevertheless a few researchers have looked into these questions and offered some tentative conclusions. In the paragraphs that follow I look very briefly at the work of four contemporary thinkers—two scientists, one philosopher, and one critic—who have tried to enlarge the range of their disciplines while grappling with the problems of existence, consciousness, and value. I also give room to other thinkers who dispute their conclusions.

In *The Mind of God* (1992), English physicist Paul Davies writes that he has come to believe that "the physical universe is put together with an ingenuity so astonishing" that it is impossible "to accept it merely as a brute fact." He also suggests that "even the most optimistic biologists admit that they are baffled by the origin of life," and asserts that "mind—i.e. conscious existence in the world—is not a meaningless and incidental quirk of nature, but an absolutely fundamental facet of reality." Davies' arguments are technical and, on the whole, not terribly convincing. He ends his book on the unsolved problems of physics with this unsupported metaphysical conclusion: "Through conscious beings the universe has generated self-awareness. This can be no trivial detail, no minor byproduct of mindless, purposeless forces. We are truly meant to be here."[27]

The "ingenuity" that impresses Davies has to do with the values of certain physical constants, for example, those governing gravity and electromagnetism, that had to be just right for the universe to come into being, and certain chemical properties, for instance the energy states of carbon atoms, that had to fall in a very narrow range for life to be able to emerge. The physics, chemistry, and mathematics of these "fine-tuning" arguments are exceedingly complex and I will not try to summarize or criticize them here. I will however note that many if not most scientists are not impressed by them. Nobel-Prize-winning biologist Jacques Monod wrote in his 1970 classic *Chance and Necessity*: "Among all the occurrences possible in the universe the *a priori* probability of any particular one of them verges upon zero. Yet the universe exists; particular events must take place in it, the probability of which (before the event) was infinitesimal." However unlikely it was for all the conditions needed for universe-formation to come together, evidently they did at least once. It does not follow that human beings are "meant to be here." Monod's conclusion was more bleak: "Man knows at last that he is alone in the universe's unfeeling immensity, out of which he emerged only by chance. His destiny is nowhere spelled out, nor is his duty." The best humans can hope for is an authentic life free from material want and delusory beliefs.[28]

Most neurobiologists and psychologists believe that consciousness is the product of neurochemical activities, though none know how we get from these activities to the awareness of beauty or the sense of self. Recently however a few scientists have questioned the doctrine that mental activity is wholly reducible to cerebral function. Nobel-Prize-winning neurobiologist R.W. Sperry theorized that conscious awareness was a "dynamic emergent property of cerebral excitation" that was greater than "the sum of the neuro-physico-chemical events" on which it is built. This hypothesis represented, he wrote, "a mid-way compromise between the older extremes of mentalism on the one hand and materialism on the other." He admitted that the available evidence was not probative but felt that new approaches were called for given "the supreme importance of the problem for all kinds of human value, as well as scientific matters."[29]

Sperry's work was an unusual attempt by a front-rank scientist to examine a problem that was thought by many to lie beyond the range of science and even to suggest that human values had something to do with it. Other scientists remain unconvinced. Admitting that biology had not yet fully accounted for subjectivity and consciousness, Monod wrote that he was confident that attempts to fill the gap with "vitalist speculation" would remain unfruitful. Biologists have been able to account for the origin of species and the structure of the genetic code. There was no reason they shouldn't eventually be able to crack the riddle of consciousness.[30]

In the half-century since Sperry and Monod wrote, there has been an explosion of interest among philosophers and cognitive scientists in the problem of consciousness. Most of them remain naturalistic, proposing ever more complicated theories to explain consciousness away. (They leave out of consideration their own conscious activities, such as writing philosophical papers.) But a few face up to the seeming irreducibility of conscious experience. In 1995 Australian philosopher David Chalmers distinguished what he called the "easy" and "hard" problems of consciousness. The easy problems involve functions such as discrimination, categorization, and attention. They are not really easy, Chalmers admits, but they at least can be studied in the laboratory. The hard problem is experience, that is, the subjective side of consciousness. Even if we succeed in explaining how the brain performs its functions, the question remains: "Why is the performance of these functions accompanied by experience?" It is possible to imagine a humanlike being that performed all its biological and neurological activities without being conscious of them or of itself. One approach to a solution, Chalmers suggests, would be to take experience "as a fundamental feature of the world, alongside mass, charge and space-time" and then try to discover any fundamental laws or principles that might be connected with it.[31]

By proposing that consciousness differs fundamentally from matter (which consists of mass, charge, space–time, and so forth), Chalmers broke from the reigning nondualistic model of philosophical naturalism. Supporters of that model were quick to criticize his proposal. "Until Chalmers gives us an *independent* ground for contemplating the drastic move of adding 'experience' to mass, charge, and space-time, his proposal is one that can be put on the back burner," wrote philosopher and cognitive scientist Daniel Dennett.[32] Still, the issues that Chalmers raised remain of great interest to many researchers.

The problem of consciousness is linked with the problem of value, because most of what we regard as valuable (beauty, integrity, unselfishness, and so forth) depends on the existence of conscious experience. Up till the end of the eighteenth century all philosophers believed that ethical and aesthetic values were rooted in a transcendent principle such as the Good, the Beautiful, or God. Once the idea of God was challenged, philosophers looked around for other foundations or resigned themselves to living in a world without ethical and aesthetic norms. The first approach was typified by Kant, who argued for the existence of objective standards based on practical reason, the second by Friedrich Nietzsche, who called for a "revaluation of all values" based on life-affirmation rather than Christian or quasi-Christian life-denial.[33] Many of the most important writers, artists, musicians, and thinkers of the twentieth century were influenced by Nietzsche, among them James Joyce, Eugene O'Neill, Richard Strauss, Gustav Mahler, Paul Klee, Wassily Kandinsky, Sigmund Freud, Carl Jung, Michel Foucault, and Jacques Derrida. Yet others resisted Nietzsche's call, insisting that some sort of transcendence is needed for art to have any value and language to have any meaning. As critic George Steiner puts it in *Real Presences* (1986): "any coherent account of the capacity of human speech to communicate meaning and feeling is, in the final analysis, underwritten by the assumption of God's presence."[34]

Steiner's special target is deconstruction, a critical theory that claims that signs refer only to other signs and there is no presence (no "transcendental signified" in Derrida's jargon) outside the network of signs to provide a stable basis for meaning. Against this, Steiner maintains that the creation and appreciation of aesthetic value and the comprehension of verbal meaning presume a "presentness prior to consciousness and to rationality as we know them." Without this, "certain dimensions of thought and creativity are no longer attainable." The presence Steiner proposes seems to have something to do with the God of Christianity though he does not endorse Christianity per se. At the same time he admits that "on its own terms and planes of argument" deconstruction appears to be "irrefutable." He thus falls between the stools of religion and critical theory without proposing a viable solution to the problems of meaning and value.[35]

Despite the efforts of scientists such as Sperry and philosophers such as Chalmers to widen the scope of their fields, the materialistic/naturalistic worldview remains the foundation of intellectual activity in research institutions throughout the world. Few people reflect on the problems of deconstruction (which in recent years has become *démodé*), but many important modern writers (Franz Kafka, Samuel Beckett, Jean-Paul Sartre, Albert Camus, and their intellectual descendants) have showed that the assumption that art and life are inherently meaningful cannot be taken for granted. (Certainly there are enough Kafkaesque environments in the modern world—high-security prisons, ISIS brothels, gulags, cities under constant siege—to make people wonder whether the world does in fact make sense.) Faced by such challenges, many turn to the security of ancient religions, often in their fundamentalist forms. Hardline Muslims, Christians, and Hindus try to turn back the clock to the glorious days when Muhammad or Christ or Rama walked upon the earth. Signs of the conflict between scientific modernity and religious reaction are all around us. One possible solution is to find a way to combine a rejection of the supernatural with an openness to spiritual values. In the next section I look at the work of some recent thinkers who have tried to do this.

Spirituality without God

Born in Vermont in 1859, John Dewey received a strict Protestant upbringing. He was active in church during his early years as a professor, but by 1894 his views had changed so much that he did not bother to join a congregation when he accepted a position at the University of Chicago. In the years that followed, as he became one of America's leading public intellectuals, he avoided the topic of religion altogether. In 1933 he was one of thirty academics who signed the Humanist Manifesto, which declared that human values must not be based on superhuman claims. "Religious Humanism considers the complete realization of human personality to be the end of man's life and seeks its development and fulfillment in the here and now," the scholars wrote. The same year Dewey began a series of lectures he later published as *A Common Faith*. His aim was to show that "religious values are not a monopoly of any one class or sect" but were available even to people who had abandoned organized religion. He distinguished "the religious," an aspect or quality of experience, from "religions," specific creeds and sects that stood in the way "of the realization of distinctively religious values inherent in natural experience." Religious believers clung to a "particular Being" that they called God. Dewey did not reject this term but defined it, provisionally, as "the ideal ends that at a given time and place one acknowledges as having authority over his volition and emotion." The ideals that made a difference to human life were "unified by the action that gives them coherence and solidity." To live a religious life, Dewey concluded, was to associate oneself actively with the fulfillment of such ideals.[36]

By endorsing "the religious" while rejecting religions, Dewey took a step in the direction of what I call spirituality without God. In the first half of the twentieth century, this phrase would have seemed almost meaningless. Now it has a familiar ring. Here is a list of terms that have come into currency over the last sixty years: atheistic religion, religion of no religion, religion without God; secular Buddhism, Buddhist atheism; secular Christianity, Christian atheism; Death of God spirituality, secular spirituality, humanistic spirituality, atheistic spirituality.

All share a common theme: here is no need to believe in God to lead a religious or spiritual life.

In fact it is only in the modern West that the idea of godless religion is new. Jainism, some forms of Buddhism, and the Vedic schools of Samkhya and Mimamsa are atheistic. Classical Confucianism and philosophical Daoism had little interest in the gods. Epicureanism gave them such a minor role that it was atheistic in all but name. During the Renaissance, European humanists rediscovered the Epicureans, Stoics, and Skeptics and appropriated some of their ideas. Enlightenment philosophers such as René Descartes and Baruch Spinoza developed ideas of God that clashed with Christian and Jewish orthodoxy. For a while "Spinozism" was a synonym of atheism, but this did not prevent writers of the Romantic movement from praising Spinoza's mystical temperament.

The German theologian Schleiermacher, an admirer of Spinoza and a friend of Romantic writers, made the first explicit reference in modern European literature to the possibility of godless religion in 1799: "I do not accept the position, 'No God, no religion,'" he wrote. "To have religion is to have an intuition of the Universe, and while this idea of God suits every intuition, a religion without God might still be better than another with God."[37] It is clear from the context that while he considered religion without God to be a logical possibility, he ranked it low as a stage of religious development. Protestant Christianity remained the summit. Still, his concession was radical for his time and he was obliged to delete this passage from the second edition of his book.

Schleiermacher's idea that God is best known through feeling and intuition helped elevate inner experience to its current status as the hallmark of the spiritual life. James made religious experience the basis of his defense of the God-idea. There were, he said, worlds of consciousness beyond the normal reach of mind—subliminal but not supernatural—that were known to the mystics and accessible in principle by all human beings. Another name for such phenomena was "God" and God was real because it produced real effects.[38] He thought this concession would absolve him from the charge of atheism, but few conventional theists took much comfort in his ideas.

Thirty years after the *Varieties* appeared, Dewey proposed a version of religious humanism that excluded the supernatural in all its forms. This made him, as he acknowledged, an atheist in "the etymological significance of the word"—one who rejected theism—but not in the extended sense of one who denied "all ideal values as having the right to control material ones." The bottom line, he wrote in *A Common Faith*, was that "religious qualities and values if they are real at all are not bound up with any single item of intellectual assent, not even that of the existence of the God of theism."[39] In brief, there could be a religion without God.

In the half-century after Dewey wrote, a number of philosophers and theologians speculated on the form a godless religion might take. I speak of some of these thinkers in Chapter 7. But it was not until the beginning of the twenty-first century that systems of spiritual thought and practice that were explicitly nontheistic began to gain general acceptance. In what follows I look briefly at five contemporary thinkers who have approached this theme in different ways. Three are philosophers who reject the idea of God but recognize the importance of religion or spirituality for the grounding of human values. Two began their careers as ordained members of religious organizations but left conventional beliefs behind while remaining committed to spiritual practice. Only one or two would endorse the label "spirituality without God," but all agree that belief in God is not necessary for leading a spiritual life.

French philosopher André Comte-Sponville lost faith in God when he was 18, but he never thought of abandoning his spiritual pursuits. For some time he viewed spirituality in terms of the Western philosophical tradition, writing several books on the great themes of that tradition: virtue, truth, happiness. His prophets were Epicurus, Lucretius, Marcus Aurelius, Montaigne, and Spinoza, along with some thinkers of India and China. Yet he could not deny that he was deeply marked by the values of the Judeo-Christian tradition. The Gospels, he thought, contained much of lasting value, and some of the greatest philosophers of the West—Augustine, Descartes, Pascal, Leibniz, Kierkegaard—were devout Christians. For centuries the Christian religion was the only gate open to the spiritual life in Europe. This led people to conclude that spirituality and religion were synonymous. Comte-Sponville thought that this was an error: "Spirituality is the life of the spirit. Religion is just one of its forms." He was troubled when he saw that leaders of various religions—some of them dangerous fanatics—claimed to be the sole custodians of the spiritual life. This drove him to speak out. "Spirituality is far too important a matter to be left to the fundamentalists," he writes in *L'esprit de l'athéisme* (2009). Atheists need to invent a spirituality that goes along with their secularism: "Atheists have as much spirit as everyone else; why would they be less interested in spiritual life?"[40]

If we look back in time to the Greco-Roman philosophers or to non-Western traditions such as Buddhism and Daoism, it is clear that "there have always existed, and still do exist, forms of spirituality that were or are not religious—at least not in the Western sense of the word." Drawing on these models and on their own inner resources, people with no interest in God can lead spiritual lives. The goal is not to be an atheist—there are plenty of brainless atheists around—"but to be free, lucid, serene, and happy," in short to live a life of wisdom. Summing up what he means by that overused word in a 2013 article, he says that wisdom has three main ingredients—serenity, liberty, and unity with the cosmos—along with "a certain tendency to happiness."[41]

Thomas Nagel, like Comte-Sponville, was trained in the Western philosophical tradition and considers himself an atheist. Unlike the French thinker, he does not distinguish spirituality from religion, but he believes that the "religious temperament"—that is, the aspiration "to live not merely the life of the creature one is, but in some sense to participate through it in the life of the universe as a whole"—can play a role even in the lives of nonbelievers. For Nagel the basic problem of life is to determine the right relation between the human individual and the cosmic whole. Theistic people view this relation in terms of God. Nagel thinks we can reject the God-idea and still acknowledge our relationship with something larger than ourselves. We all are in the same position, he writes in *Secular Philosophy and the Religious Temperament* (2010): "Having, amazingly, burst into existence, one is a representative of existence itself—of the whole of it—not just because one is part of it but because it is present to one's consciousness."[42] We therefore have the right, indeed the obligation, to find out how we fit into the larger scheme of things.

Nagel explores a number of approaches to the problem of existence. First is theism, which demands that we subordinate ourselves to a supernatural power. For many in the modern world, this is not an option. The opposite of theism is "hardheaded atheism": denying there is anything more to life than the material and social worlds. Many of those who take this route believe that questions about the nature of existence are meaningless. Another approach is to regard our lives as "products of biological and cultural evolution" and surrender ourselves to this greater flow. Finally there is humanism, "the view that we ourselves, as a species or community, give sense to the world as a whole." Humanism comes in many forms. Nagel is drawn to the absurdist version of French philosopher Albert Camus: "making a virtue of the will to go on in spite of the complete indifference of the cosmos," finding meaning in the struggle against meaninglessness. This is the downbeat conclusion of his essay on the religious temperament. Elsewhere he finds a sort of deliverance in the fact of conscious experience: "Life is worth living even when the bad elements of experience are plentiful, and the good ones too meager to outweigh the bad ones on their own," he writes. "The additional positive weight is supplied by experience itself, rather than any of its contents."[43]

Ronald Dworkin was (until his death in 2013) as eminent in his areas of philosophy as Nagel is in his. Best known for his contributions to philosophy of law, Dworkin engaged with larger issues in his last two books: the nature of truth, the limitations of science, the foundations of value. In *Religion without God* (2013) he defends what he calls "religious atheism" and explains why this is important in an increasingly secular world. "Religion is deeper than God," he begins. Religion is a worldview that holds "that inherent, objective value permeates everything, that the universe and its creatures are awe-inspiring, that human life has purpose and the universe order." Most modern religions are theistic and they are all beset by problems, most notoriously their tendency to foster violence. Would it not be better to drop the word "religion" and use another—"spirituality" perhaps? Dworkin prefers enlarging the reach of the word religion rather than surrendering it to theists. Truly religious people accept that they have "an innate and inescapable responsibility" to live well, honoring one's personal ethical commitments and one's moral responsibilities toward others. They also affirm that what we call nature is "not just a matter of fact but is itself sublime: something of intrinsic value and wonder." It is not necessary to believe in God to accept this affirmation.[44]

Theists insist that God is needed to underwrite value judgments. Dworkin points out that such a belief "supposes a prior commitment to the independent reality of that value." In other words, our ideas of the good exist independently of God. This is the point Plato made in the *Euthyphro*, which Dworkin discusses at some length. He also proposes an aesthetic criterion of value: "a felt conviction that the universe really does embody a sublime beauty." Religious believers connect this sublimity with God, but atheistic poets and scientists (not to mention garden-variety unbelievers) are justified in saying that the source of beauty and truth is the universe itself. The "instinct of value" that they share with theists is the basis of their practice of the good life. The crucial point is this: "What matters most fundamentally to the drive to live well is the conviction that there is, independently and objectively, a right way to live." And this conviction is available equally to theists and nontheists.[45] Dworkin's attempts to find common ground have come in for criticism from two directions. Hardcore theists consider his aesthetic criterion insufficiently solid to support ethical claims. Hardcore atheists consider it too much of a concession to supernatural religiosity.

Scottish-born Stephen Batchelor became a novice monk in the Gelug tradition of Tibetan Buddhism at the age of 21. After years of study and practice in India and Europe he went to Korea, where he trained under a Seon (Zen) master. Subsequently he disrobed and became a lay practitioner and teacher and the author of well-regarded books on Buddhism. In *Confession of a Buddhist Atheist* (2010) he makes the case for a secular Buddhism that dispenses with religious dogmas and pieties. In Batchelor's reading, the Buddha was an "ironic atheist" who poked gentle fun at the gods of the Indian tradition. He was neither a theist nor an antitheist: God was "simply not part of his vocabulary." Batchelor arrived at a similar position after years of dutifully practicing the rituals of his sect. Now when he is asked whether or not he believes in God, he replies that he cannot understand what the question means. Likewise, when atheists deny God's existence, he wonders: "What is it they so emphatically do not believe in?"[46]

An erudite but independent reader of Buddhist scriptures, Batchelor takes issue with a number of established beliefs, in particular the doctrine of rebirth. In Buddhism (which does not admit the soul) rebirth implies that something in the aggregate that constitutes the apparent individual leaves the body at death and, under the impulsion of karma, is carried over into another aggregate. Batchelor found he could not accept this but, after a sleepless night, realized that "even if there was no life after death" and "no moral law of karma governing my fate, this would have no effect whatsoever on my commitment to the practice of the

Dharma." This sounded insane to his teacher and heretical to many readers of his books. He also ruffled feathers by challenging the notion that the enlightenment experience is a blissed-out superconscious state. The Buddha, he writes, "rejected the idea that freedom or salvation lay in gaining privileged access to an eternal, non-contingent source or ground." The freedom that the Buddha offered was "freedom from greed, from hatred, and from confusion." At a 2013 conference, Batchelor outlined his nonsectarian, nonmystical approach to Buddhism: "Rather than attaining nirvana, I see the aim of Buddhist practice to be the moment-to-moment flourishing of human life within the ethical framework of the eightfold path [of the Buddha] here on earth."[47]

Tenzin Gyatso, the 14th Dalai Lama, began his monastic education at the age of six. In 1959, when he was 23, he passed his final examinations and was awarded the Tibetan equivalent of a doctorate in Buddhist philosophy. The same year, in response to Chinese aggression, he escaped from Tibet and took refuge in northern India. Looking back on his early life in a *New York Times* piece, he wrote that when he was young he "felt that my own Buddhist religion must be the best—and that other faiths were somehow inferior." As he matured, he realized how naïve this was and recognized the possibility, indeed the necessity, of coexistence based on interfaith harmony. In 2011, in *Beyond Religion*, he went a step further: The best solution to the conflict between religions is to move beyond them all. Religions have helped millions in the past and will continue to do so in the future, but "in today's secular world religion alone is no longer adequate as a basis for ethics." Therefore, he concludes, "the time has come to find a way of thinking about spirituality and ethics that is beyond religion." Spirituality has two dimensions: an acquired form "tied to particular beliefs and practices" and an "underlying human disposition toward love, kindness, and affection." This "basic human spirituality" is "more fundamental than religion" and accessible even to those who are agnostic or atheistic.[48]

In the second part of his book, the Dalai Lama proposes methods of spiritual development that can be practiced by people of any religion or no religion. The first is heedfulness: being attentive to what is going on within and without. The second, mindfulness, is "the ability to gather oneself mentally and thereby recall one's core values and motivations." The third, introspective awareness, involves "observing our behavior as it is going on, and thereby bringing it under control." He goes on to describe some specific techniques, devoting a whole chapter to ways of dealing with destructive emotions. He recommends a two-pronged approach: reducing "the impact of the destructive potentials that are inherent within us" and enhancing "the positive qualities that also naturally exist within us." Such exercises can be practiced by religious people with the support of their mythologies and beliefs, but also by skeptics and agnostics as a form of autotherapy. Religious and ethical systems differ but "inner values like compassion and patience" are "an integral part of our basic outlook on life," and the cultivation of these and other spiritual values will have far-reaching effects on individuals and societies.[49]

None of the thinkers discussed above believes in the God of any organized religion. All of them distinguish between religion as commerce with supernatural beings and religion as ethical and spiritual endeavor undertaken by individual human beings. All of them say it is possible to live an ethical and productive life engaged with the lives of others without swallowing religious dogmas or practicing religious rituals. They therefore are representatives of what I call spirituality without God.

* * *

Most religions are theistic but since ancient times there have been systems of belief and practice that gave little importance to the role of supernatural beings. Some recent systems of thought and practice reject the supernatural altogether.

Religions differ greatly from one another, but most of them require their followers to accept certain teachings, perform certain rituals, and follow certain rules of conduct. A few religions give special importance to self-examination, personal autonomy, and individual effort. Over time these characteristics detached themselves from the religions in which they rose. The result was what we now call spirituality.

In the chapters that follow I sketch the development of nontheistic religions and spiritualities over the last 3,000 years in South Asia, East Asia, and the West. Among the highlights are Indian approaches stressing the need of liberation from the compulsions of desire, Chinese approaches emphasizing self-cultivation and social integration, Greek approaches focusing on freedom from the perturbations of passion, and modern Western ideas stressing individual self-expression.

Every religious and spiritual belief and practice is embedded in a cultural and historical framework. In Chapters 2–7 I will speak not of religion and spirituality in the abstract but of particular traditions: the religions of 18th dynasty Egypt or Zhou dynasty China, the spiritualities of nineteenth-century Europe or contemporary America. As I trace the history of the traditions under study, I will give special attention to the rise of unbelief and the emergence of subjectivity, autonomy, and individual practice. When disbelief in God met subjective spirituality the outcome was spirituality without God.

2 THEISTIC AND NONTHEISTIC RELIGIONS IN THE ANCIENT WORLD

Godless spirituality is a modern development but it has ancient roots. Spirituality grew out of religion and religion dates back to the beginnings of human society. Up until around 3,000 years ago all religions gave most of their attention to supernatural beings and forces. But during the first millennium BCE, systems of religion and philosophy arose that subordinated superhuman entities to cosmic principles and laws. These systems mark the beginning of a current of nontheistic thought and practice that is becoming increasingly important as more and more people pursue their spiritual lives unburdened by the concept of God.

In Chapters 2 to 7 I follow the course of this current from the earliest systems of nontheistic religion to contemporary forms of godless spirituality. I deal primarily with three geographical and cultural regions: South Asia, including what is now India, Pakistan, Bangladesh, and Afghanistan, which I sometimes for convenience call "India"; East Asia, including China, Japan, and neighboring countries; and the ancient Greco-Roman and modern Euro-American worlds, which I often refer to as "the West." I also look, by way of contrast, at western Asia, which was the birthplace of the three main monotheistic religions.

The range of spirituality is vast, and no book can hope to deal with all its expressions in every culture of the world. By choosing to concentrate on four Eurasian regions, I have had to exclude the ideas and practices of Africa, Oceania, and native America. I also have had to leave out many Eurasian traditions that are worthy of study: Gnosticism, Shinto, Siberian shamanism, Paganism, and a host of others. These omissions are regrettable but, given the space at my disposal, unavoidable. I hope that other writers will examine the nontheistic aspects of these traditions.

Despite these lacunae, my temporal and spatial canvas is large and this gives rise to some problems I have to address before proceeding. In each of the chapters I discuss developments in South Asia, East Asia, and the West. Contemporary cultural historians insist that developments in different regions have to be studied on their own terms. At the same time they feel the need to get beyond the parochialism of narrow regional accounts. To harmonize these opposed tendencies, it is necessary to keep one eye on local details and the other on global trends. This is what I have tried to do in this book. Avoiding the allure of evolutionary grand narratives, I have, like Japanese historian Hajime Nakamura, looked for "parallel developments" in the histories of the cultures I study.[1]

I call this book a history of spirituality without God, but it would be more accurate to call it a web of histories leading up to the recent appearance of spirituality free from God. Among its constituent stories are the birth and growth of nontheistic religions and philosophies such as Jainism, Buddhism, Confucianism, Daoism, Epicureanism, and Skepticism; the spread of unbelief, atheism, and agnosticism; the turn toward secularism and humanism; and the emergence of spirituality as distinct from religion. I give special attention to the components of spirituality I spoke of in Chapter 1—subjectivity, autonomy, and individual effort—showing how they arose in different places, assumed various forms, and gradually came together, making something that was latent a reality. At the end of each chapter I give a summary that highlights that growth of disbelief and the development of the components of spirituality during the period under study.

Although my canvas is large, the trends I am interested in form a small part of the overall history of world religions. This makes it possible to sketch the growth of godless spirituality in South Asia, East Asia, and the West in a single volume. It goes without saying that any attempt to squeeze 3,000 years of history into 300 pages cannot be comprehensive. I had to select movements and individuals that seemed especially significant, leaving out many others that deserved attention. Again, I hope other historians will look more deeply into the global history of nontheistic religions and spiritualities.

In this chapter I deal with the theistic and nontheistic religions and philosophies of the ancient world. First I look briefly at a very long period: hundreds of millennia during which the main form of commerce between humans and the superhuman was magic. I then turn to the religions of sacrifice that arose across Eurasia during the Bronze Age (third and second millennia BCE). This was the period when the great cosmic gods were born.

Between 1200 and 600 BCE, a technological revolution opened the way for radical cultural changes. During this period iron and steel replaced copper and bronze as the materials of choice for weapons and tools. Early adapters of this (literally) cutting-edge technology outstripped their neighbors in fighting ability and agricultural production. New cities rose, fostering new forms of political organization and cultural expression and generating novel ideas about the place of human beings in the universe. Remarkably, these ideas were formulated more or less independently in widely spaced regions within a few hundred years of one another, roughly between 800 and 200 BCE. Radical thinkers—in India, the Upanishadic sages, Mahavira and Buddha; in China, Confucius and Zhuang Zhou; in Greece, the philosophers from Thales to Chrysippus—challenged time-honored ideas about the relationship of humans with the gods and with one another. At around the same time Zoroaster in Iran and the later prophets of Israel laid the groundwork for monotheism in West Asia. Struck by these near-contemporaneous developments from one end of Eurasia to the other, twentieth-century German philosopher Karl Jaspers dubbed the six hundred years centering on 500 BCE the "axial age." It was, he said, the pivotal epoch when the history of humanity as we now know it commenced.[2] Many scholars have taken up Jasper's idea, others have criticized it as being unduly speculative. Whether or not the axial age was the historical reality Jaspers thought it was, the period certainly witnessed many extraordinary developments, and this makes it a useful starting point for this historical survey of godless religions and spiritualities.

Supernatural foundations

"At the very beginning, Plow married Earth / And they decided to establish a family and dominion." So begins the *Theogony of Dunnu*, a Babylonian creation myth dating back to the beginning of the second millennium BCE. Plow broke the virgin soil, creating the Sea, and the furrows of their own accord begat the Cattle God. Plow and Earth built the city of Dunnu and Plow established dominion over it. Then "Earth raised her face to the Cattle God" and said to him "Come and let me love you!" Thus tempted, "Cattle God married Earth, his mother, / And killed Plow his father, / And laid him to rest in Dunnu." Things went on like this for several generations: Cattle God married Sea, his older sister, with whom he had a son, Flocks God, who later killed his father and married his mother Sea. (Students of comparative mythology will recall that incest followed by parricide was not just a Babylonian problem: the theme is found in the myths of many cultures.) Much later Hayyashum, after marrying his sister, took over his father's dominion "But did not kill him, and seized him alive" and imprisoned him—a marginal improvement in moral standards. We never find out what happened in the end, because the clay tablet on which the myth was written is broken. But enough is clear to permit a couple of observations: The discovery of agriculture and animal husbandry leads to the foundation of cities. (In Akkadian, the word *dunnu* means "fortified farmstead.") This is in line with what anthropologists tell us about the societies of hunter-gatherers and of settled farmers. Hunter-gatherers had no great cities and no great gods. The rise of agriculture provided the conditions needed for the birth of the cosmic gods.[3]

It is something of an anthropological cliché to say that every human culture has left evidence of activities we now connect with religion. Some of it is spectacular, such as the stunningly beautiful paintings found in caves in France and Spain that date back more than 30,000 years. Some of it is touching, such as the flower-lined graves from a 13,000-year-old site in the Levant. But all of it is ambiguous, giving rise to multiple interpretations of almost every site. What is the meaning of the animal figures in cave paintings? Were they related to animal worship cults? Or magic rites? Or initiation rituals? There is no way of saying for sure, though it seems clear that the figures had something to do with hunting, a crucial activity for Paleolithic humans. The freestanding structures erected by many ancient peoples—Stonehenge is the most famous example—have also given rise to dozens of explanatory theories. It is impossible to say which of them is right, but it seems likely that many such sites were connected with seasonal rituals.

Before human beings learned to domesticate plants and animals they subsisted by hunting and gathering. Most anthropologists believe that the religious or prereligious life of hunter-gatherers centered around activities we now call magic. There are many theories about what magic meant to those who practiced it. Intellectualist anthropologists thought it was a flawed attempt to arrive at an understanding of the world: a sort of primitive science. Functionalist anthropologists viewed it as a means of navigating the hazards of life—a way "to bridge over the dangerous gaps in every important pursuit or critical situation," as Bronisław Malinowski put it.[4] In practical rather than theoretical terms, magic has to do with using spells and other techniques to gain control over spirits and invisible forces to remove obstacles, destroy enemies, cure or prevent illness, and otherwise make for a successful passage through life.

Millennia passed between the earliest attempts to tame local spirits and the appearance of complex religions featuring cosmic gods. It is hard to trace the intermediate developments because the archeological evidence is spotty and ambiguous. Written records began to appear around 3100 BCE and by that time the worship of great cosmic gods was an established part of the cultures of Mesopotamia and Egypt. Where did these gods come from?

There are three possible answers to this question: (1) The gods were always there and at some point specially endowed humans (shamans, priests, what have you) became aware of them and learned how to establish relations with them. (2) Humans invented the gods to satisfy psychological or social needs, or both, and integrated them into their social and personal lives. (3) The gods correspond to some sort of neurological formation that is hardwired into human brains. In Chapter 1 I looked briefly at options (2) and (3). What about option (1)? Have the gods or, if you prefer, has God always existed? That, as I have tried to show, is a question that cannot be answered with any certainty. What can be said for sure is that the evidence suggests that from the beginnings of literate culture until the middle of the first millennium BCE everyone took it for granted that the gods existed. Therefore they did exist—as social if not substantial realities. Everyone believed in them, as had everyone's parents and ancestors. The fact that the world went about its business in an orderly fashion—day followed night, spring followed winter, crops grew and were harvested—was sufficient proof, if proof was needed, that the gods and other superhuman beings were at work.

The structure of the societies of the ancient Near East was laid on supernatural foundations. The king was the son of the supreme local god, and as such could petition him for aid. During the Battle of Kadesh (c. 1275 BCE) the Egyptian pharaoh Rameses II cried out: "What is the matter with thee, my father Amon? Has a father ever forgotten his son? Have I ever done anything apart from thee?" Kings were born to tend the gods' estates but the labor was done by commoners. The Babylonian god Marduk told the lesser gods that he created man to be "burdened with the toil of the gods, that they [the gods] may freely breathe."[5]

In ancient Mesopotamia and other Bronze Age societies the main means of interaction between humans and gods was sacrifice. The sacrificial victim was "made sacred"—that is the meaning of the Latin *sacrificium*—by being offered to the gods before being killed and consumed. The ritual served a dual purpose. Humans fulfilled their duty of providing the gods with sustenance and at the same time sacralized the slaughtered animal for their own enjoyment. In time, the purifying power of sacrifice migrated to other situations. People learned they could atone for all sorts of sins and obtain all sorts of benefits by giving a steer or lamb to be slaughtered by professional priests.

East of Mesopotamia, sacrifice took on an especially exalted function. The earliest scriptures of India and Iran, the *Vedas* and the *Avesta* (datable roughly to 1500–600 BCE), are sacrificial hymnals and manuals. They affirm that the primary purpose of sacrifice (Vedic Sanskrit: *yajna*, Avestan: *yasna*) is to preserve the cosmic order. The task of priests is to make the offerings that are necessary to keep the universe running as it should. The *Shatapatha Brahmana*, a Vedic text, explains that if a priest makes a certain offering in the morning, he *creates* the sun that rises up resplendent, "but, assuredly, it would not rise, were he not to make that offering."[6]

Such was the cosmic purpose of sacrifice. From a more mundane point of view, the aim of sacrifice was to establish reciprocal relations between gods and human beings. *Dehi me dadami te*, runs a Vedic verse: "Give me, I give you." (This is echoed in the later Latin formula *do ut des*, "I give so that you will give.") Wherever the rites of sacrifice prevail, those who offer to the gods expect something in return: cattle, wealth, wives, or, in modern times, a well-paying job or admission to an Ivy League university.

The verses of the Vedic hymns were not just words but mantras with effectuating power. Preexisting the creation, they were revealed to ancient seers "as a loving wife, beautifully dressed, reveals her body to her husband."[7] Each syllable of every verse had to be pronounced in just the right way. Hence the importance of learning the fine points of Sanskrit, which only men of the priestly class could study. There were sacrifices for every sort of human–divine interaction, some to insure the growth and prosperity of the kingdom, others to accompany domestic ceremonies, still others to obtain specific objects of desire. Recipients of the offerings ranged from the great cosmic gods to deified ancestors to local spirits.

In early days, both Indians and Iranians sacrificed animals. This later became impossible in Iran and less common in India, where libations of milk and ghee gradually replaced blood sacrifices. In both India and Iran, priests prepared the juice of an unidentified plant (Sanskrit: *soma*, Avestan: *haoma*), which was connected with the attainment of immortality. "We have drunk the Soma; we have become immortal," runs a verse of the *Rig Veda*, "we have gone to the light; we have found the gods."[8]

We know less about the sacrifices of the people of Bronze Age China because the texts they used in their rituals have not come down to us. What we do have is an abundance of "oracle bones"—shoulder blades of oxen or bottom shells of turtles that were used for divination. Priests inscribed questions on the bones, burned them, and interpreted the cracks that appeared. This was one of the ways that people of the Shang dynasty (c. 1600–c. 1050 BCE) communicated with the gods and ancestral spirits. The supreme god was Shangdi, who ruled over Heaven. Shangdi's court was the celestial archetype of the emperor's court on earth. One of the emperor's primary functions was to preserve the harmony of earth and Heaven by means of sacrifice. He alone could make offerings to Shangdi; the common people approached lesser gods. But all, from the emperor down to the humblest peasant, made offerings to their ancestors. Imperial and family sacrifices were interlinked. It is written in an early ritual text: "The ceremonies of sacrifices to Heaven and Earth are meant for the service of the Lord on High [Shangdi], and the ceremonies performed in the ancestral temple are meant for the service of ancestors. If one understands the ceremonies of the sacrifices to Heaven and Earth and the meaning of the grand sacrifice and the autumn sacrifice to ancestors, it would be as easy to govern a kingdom as to look at one's palm."[9]

The Bronze Age culture of ancient Greece suffered a setback around 1100 BCE, when the Mycenaean civilization collapsed. It was not until around 800 BCE that people living on the shores of the Aegean Sea again built massive structures. The intervening centuries were the period of Greek history that forms the backdrop of the Homeric epics. The gods that the heroes of the *Iliad* and *Odyssey* worshipped were akin to the gods of India to the east and Italy to the west. Zeus Pater (cf. Sanskrit: *Dyaus Pita*, Latin: *Jupiter*) was the great Sky-father. Ouranos (cf. Sanskrit: *Varuna*, Latin: *Uranus*) was the original Lord of the Heavens. But the gods of the Greeks were not as remote as those of India and China. They dwelt on an earthly mountain and behaved a lot like ordinary folk. Still, the Greeks solicited their favor by means of sacrifice. One sort of ritual involved the slaughter and partial burning of an animal, which was offered to the gods and then eaten by the gods and men in what seems to have been a rather jolly gathering. Another consisted of the complete burning or burying of the victim in order to propitiate the gods of the underworld. Certain rituals were connected with the mystery religions and therefore reserved for initiates. Others were public offerings at temples and roadside shrines for supplication or thanksgiving. But in Greece, as in China and India, the coming of the axial age brought far-reaching changes. Thinkers of a new sort emerged who looked at the gods, the universe, and human beings in original ways.

The search for liberation in India

When Svetaketu Aruneya was twelve years old, his father Uddalaka Aruni summoned him and said: I want you to go and live with Vedic teachers and learn all they have to teach. So Swetaketu went forth and studied with learned Brahmins for twelve years. When he returned, his father looked at him and said: I see you are proud of your learning; but do you know the symbolic statement "by which the unheard becomes heard, the unthought thought, and the unknown known?" Swetaketu was flummoxed. None of his teachers had told him anything like that, so he asked his father to do so. Uddalaka then began the secret teaching: "In the beginning, good lad, this was being, one alone without a second." In its solitude, the one being thought: "Let me become many; let me be born," and it created heat and the waters and food, that is, the physical universe. This was the first of many symbolic statements that Uddalaka taught. His twelfth lesson began with an experiment. "Put this salt in water, and come to me in the morning," he said. Svetaketu did as he was told. The next day his father said: "Now bring me the salt that you put in water last night." Svetaketu could not find it. Uddalaka asked him to sip from all parts of the water. Svetaketu sipped from the top, the middle and the bottom. Each time Uddalaka asked, "What is it like?" Each time Svetaketu answered: "Salty." Uddalaka explained that it was the same with being: "You do not see *being* here, but it is here. This subtle part is what all this has as self. It is truth: it is the self. *You* are that, Svetaketu." This formula is one of the most famous phrases in the Upanishads.[10]

The early Upanishads, such as the *Chhandogya Upanishad* (which contains the story of Uddalaka and Svetaketu) were composed almost a millennium after the earliest hymns of the *Rig Veda*, that is, around 700 BCE. Much happened during the intervening centuries. The center of Vedic culture shifted from the upper Indus valley to the plains of the Ganges. Pastoral life gave way to settled agriculture. Members of the priestly caste preserved the Vedic texts and presided over sacrifices as they always had done, but toward the end of the Vedic period some priests began to wonder about the meaning of the sacrifice and the ultimate nature of the gods. In a hymn from the last book of the *Rig Veda*, the poet asks repeatedly: "Who is the god whom we should worship with the oblation?" Another late hymn takes a skeptical look at the creation of the cosmos: "Whence is this creation? The gods came afterwards, with the creation of this universe. Who then knows whence it has arisen?" Perhaps, the poet muses, the universe "formed itself," but then again "perhaps it did not." He ends in complete agnosticism: "The one who looks down on it, in the highest heaven, only he knows—or perhaps he does not know."[11]

Sometime around 900–700 BCE, priests began to compile prose commentaries known as Brahmanas that explained the nature and meaning of the sacrificial rites. Some of them appear to undermine the institution of sacrifice itself. A passage of the *Shatapatha Brahmana* acknowledges that people can gain "all objects of desire" by means of sacrifice but adds that it is better to reach the state "where desires have vanished." This desireless state cannot be achieved "by sacrificial gifts or by devout practices," but only through knowledge of reality. Some Brahmanas mention a being called *brahman* who is greater than the manifested universe. It is *brahman* who "created the gods" and "made them ascend these worlds" of earth and air and sky.[12]

The word *brahman* originally meant the power of the Vedic word, but in the Brahmanas and Upanishads it came to signify the one Spirit that is the source of the multiplicity of the universe. Another word, *atman*, which originally meant breath, came to signify the inner self or soul, which, as Uddalaka explained to Svetaketu, is identical with *brahman*. These two terms became reference points in the cosmological and psychological speculations of the Upanishads and later Indian philosophy. Equally important was another set of terms: *karma* (action), *samsara* (the cycle of birth-and-death), and *moksha* (liberation). In the Vedas, *karma* is the performance of ritual actions. In the Upanishads it came to mean all the acts of life with their inevitable effects on the condition of the doer in this and future lives. Existence was a cycle of birth, death, and rebirth from which the wise longed to be liberated.

We have come a long way from the *Rig Veda*. Rather than sacrificing to the gods in order to attain earthly goods and heavenly rewards, the sages of the Upanishads recommended meditation and self-discipline to escape from earthly and heavenly constraints. They did not deny the truth of the Vedas but greatly enlarged the meaning and application of the hymns. In the Vedas, human beings are parts of a rigid social order, subordinate to the gods with whom they are linked by sacrifice. In the Upanishads the essence of each human being is the self (*atman*), which is identical with *brahman*, an infinite being that is superior to the gods. The eponymous sage of the *Maitri Upanishad* explained that the one who attains *brahman* by means of knowledge, asceticism, and contemplation rises beyond the creator god "and reaches godhead over the gods. He attains indestructible, measureless, flawless bliss."[13]

The Upanishads are not a single, systematic body of doctrine. They offer a variety of viewpoints expressed by sages of different schools. Some passages are strongly theistic, others almost atheistic. In his lessons to Svetaketu, Uddalaka Aruneya hardly mentions the gods. He takes his metaphors from the natural world, as when he asks Swetaketu to pulverize the seed of a banyan fruit and tell him what he sees. "Nothing," Swetaketu replies. Uddalaka explains: "on this subtle part—the part you cannot see—rests the great banyan-tree." So it is with everything: "This subtle part is what all this has as self. It is truth; it is the self. *You* are that, Swetaketu."[14]

Whatever their character, the Upanishads all insist that the realization of *atman/ brahman* is superior to the worship of the Vedic deities. The *Kena Upanishad* tells a story to illustrate this: "*Brahman* won a victory for the gods, and the gods were triumphing in the victory of *brahman*." But *brahman* knew what they were up to and appeared before them. They couldn't figure out what this wonderful being was, and sent two of their best, Agni and Vayu, to investigate. *Brahman* placed a blade of grass before them, but they couldn't do anything with it and went back defeated. The gods then sent Indra, the Lord of Heaven. He went up to *brahman*, who disappeared, leaving the Great Goddess in his place. Indra asked her what that wonderful being was. "*Brahman*," she said, "you were triumphing in the victory of *brahman*."[15] What exactly *brahman* is remains a mystery, but there is no doubt that it is greater than the gods.

Why did Indians in the first millennium BCE turn away from time-honored rituals and seek unity with *brahman* and liberation from the cycle of birth-and-death? Some historians have suggested that political and social changes created a general sense of unease that pushed people in that direction. As the Vedic people spread across northern India, members of the warrior caste established small kingdoms. Towns and cities grew, giving a lift to artisans and merchants. The priesthood, on the other hand, seems to have lost its luster. (A late Vedic hymn compares chanting priests to croaking frogs.) Finding themselves in a world of shifting norms, some people lost faith in the old certitudes and went looking for that "great all-pervading self" that is "stable among the unstable."[16]

Sociopolitical explanations like this are speculative, of course. What is sure is that around 550 BCE there was a ferment of spiritual seeking in the lands between the Himalayas and the Ganges. Some of the seekers are mentioned in the Upanishads, others were omitted because they rejected the authority of the Vedas. Fortunately, the ideas of a few of these non-Vedic seekers or "strivers" (Pali: *samanas*, Sanskrit: *sramanas*) were recorded in other texts.

The *Samannaphala Sutta*, an early Buddhist scripture, sketches the ideas of six important *samanas*. First was Purana Kassapa, who denied the connection between actions and moral outcomes. Ajita Kesakambali declared there was no soul: our bodies dissolve into the elements after death. Pakudha Kaccayana believed that the world consisted of seven eternal substances that did not interact in any way. (He memorably said: "even if one were to behead a person one is not depriving that person of his life, but is simply creating some space between the seven elements with a knife.") Then there was Sanjaya Belatthiputta, who suspended judgment on all subjects. These proto-agnostics and proto-skeptics did not found long-lived schools, but the *sutta* speaks also of two *samanas* who had a more lasting impact: Makkhali Gosala, the founder of the Ajivika sect, and Nigantha Nataputta, otherwise known as Mahavira, the best-known teacher of Jainism. The *sutta* also discusses, at greater length, the teachings of the *samana* named Siddhattha Gotama, better known as the Buddha.[17]

Jainism, Ajivism, and Buddhism are the earliest Indian religions we know of that did not give central importance to the gods. All of them rejected the religion of sacrifice, promoting instead individual practices that allowed men and women to attain freedom from the rounds of birth-and-death. They therefore are important landmarks in the development of godless spirituality.

Jain scriptures speak of Mahavira as the twenty-fourth and last Tirthankara or "Ford-Maker." His traditional date of birth is 599 BCE, but some modern scholars believe he was born a half-century or more later. The first twenty-two Tirthankaras belong to the legendary past. Jain history, properly speaking, begins with Parshvanatha, the twenty-third Tirthankara, who seems to have lived a few generations before Mahavira. Parshvanatha was a strict ascetic. His teachings were based on four "restraints": the avoidance of killing, stealing, lying, and ownership. Insistence on nonkilling meant rejection of animal sacrifice, the central rite of the Vedic religion.

Jain tradition speaks of Mahavira as the rediscoverer of the teachings of Parshvanatha and other Tirthankaras. He made one addition to Parshavanatha's restraints: absolute celibacy. Since then Jain monks have taken the fivefold vow of noninjury, nonstealing, truthfulness, nonpossession, and celibacy. Early Jain texts devote a great deal of space to Mahavira's incredible austerities. For twelve years he roamed about naked and homeless, exposed to heat and rain, attacked by unfriendly villagers, fasting for long periods, meditating on reality. Finally he attained *kevala jnana* or omniscience. From then on "he knew and saw all conditions of the world, of gods, men, and demons" and understood "what they thought, spoke, or did at any moment."[18]

Kevala jnana brings *moksha*, liberation from the workings of *karma* and release from the rounds of birth-and-death. In Jainism *karma* is viewed as a fine form of matter that pervades the universe. Living souls, in themselves pure and conscious, get covered with karmic dirt as a result of passion. (Killing and other violent deeds attract the most *karma*, hence the importance of nonviolence to Mahavira and all practicing Jains.) By overcoming passion, the Tirthankaras were able to free themselves from the influx of new *karma* and get rid of *karma* accumulated in the past, thus achieving liberation. In the end, they departed from the world of matter, becoming *siddhas* or perfected souls. As Ford-Makers they show human beings the way across the river of *samsara*, but each individual must make the effort to cross it alone. The Tirthankaras give no direct help. Jains do not worship them but hold them in mind as models of perfection. Neither do they worship the gods, who like human beings are caught in the cycle of birth-and-death.

According to Jain scriptures, souls can be born as gods, humans, demons, or animals and plants. Gods live tremendously long lives and enjoy unsullied happiness, but eventually they must die and be born again. Dozens of different sorts of gods and demons fill the various regions of the cosmos, which is immeasurably vast and passes through cycles of billions of years. The cosmos has no beginning and no end. No God brought it into existence, no God is required to explain its regularities. Karma is the sufficient explanation for the way things are. If theism is defined as the belief in a creator God, Jains are atheistic; but few modern Jains would be comfortable with this description. They prefer to think of "God" as the sum total of the Tirthankaras and siddhas.

For part of the time that Mahavira wandered through northern India, he was accompanied by a *samana* named Makkhali Gosala. According to the Jains, Mahavira and Gosala were companions on the road for around six years but in the end fell out so badly that Gosala tried to murder Mahavira. Buddhist texts also portray Gosala in a rather bad light, and since the texts of his own sect have been lost, we have to use a bit of imagination to piece his ideas together. Like most other Indian thinkers of his time, Gosala accepted the twin truths of karma and rebirth, but he did not believe that human beings could do anything to improve their lot. All was determined by Destiny. Therefore, the tremendous efforts recommended by the Tirthankaras were just a waste of time. Still, Gosala and his followers performed austerities themselves—because they were destined to do so! Like Mahavira, Gosala rejected the idea of a God who created the universe and could be approached through sacrifice or prayer. How could anyone petition a blind force like Destiny? He accepted the existence of supernatural beings but believed they were as much subject to Destiny as human beings. Gosala's followers became known as Ajivikas, and for a couple of hundred years they gave the Jains and Buddhists a run for their money. But from around 200 BCE the Ajivikas went into decline, and after 1300 CE the remnants of the sect were absorbed into South Indian Jainism.

The most influential of the *samanas* of the fifth century BCE was Siddhattha Gotama (or, in Sanskrit, Siddhartha Gautama), now known throughout the world as the Buddha. When writing about famous Indians, one always has to struggle to separate myth from history. Was the Buddha born in 624 BCE, as most Buddhists believe, or sometime around 563 BCE or even 483 BCE, as some modern scholars suggest? There is no way of knowing for sure, nor is it terribly important. He apparently was born a short while after Mahavira in the same general region of South Asia. The two teachers are said to have known of one another but never to have met.

The traditional story of the Buddha's early life can be reduced to a few sentences. Siddhattha Gotama was the son of the chieftain of a city-state in what is now southern Nepal. After leading a happy, protected childhood, getting married, and having a son, he left the comfort of his home and became a *samana*, spending years engaged in harsh austerities to achieve liberation from birth-and-death. Realizing that extreme fasting left him too weak to meditate, he adopted a more normal physical regime, a middle way between asceticism and indulgence. Redoubling his efforts, he succeeded in attaining *nibbana* (Sanskrit: *nirvana*), the extinction of the passions and removal of delusion, resulting in liberation from *samsara*. From this point on he was known as the Buddha or Enlightened One.

After his enlightenment, the Buddha began to teach what he had learned in his meditations. In his first sermon he sketched the basic problem of existence and the way of solving it. The problem is that life is inherently unsatisfactory; this is because people crave what they do not possess; the only way out is to renounce craving; this can be done by following the right way of life. These are the "four noble truths" that are the foundation of all forms of Buddhism. It is customary to compare these steps to a course of medical treatment. First comes diagnosis: After recording the patient's symptoms (discontentment, dissatisfaction, frustration, anxiety, and so forth), the physician concludes that the nature of existence is, in a word, suffering. Next comes etiology: suffering has a cause, which is craving or desire. The third step is prognosis: a cure is possible if craving is renounced. Finally comes the prescription: the noble eightfold path of right understanding, right thought, right speech, right action, right livelihood, right effort, right awareness, and right concentration. What exactly is meant by these eight steps has been discussed at length over hundreds of years by Buddhists of different schools. The details need not detain us. Briefly, followers of the Buddha should have a good idea of the doctrines, abstain from doing things that are harmful to themselves and others (lying, stealing, and so forth), and cultivate practices such as meditation and concentration.

When the Buddha began his practice, he learned a number of meditation methods from other ascetics. He found that these required a huge amount of energy and in the end were ineffective. Then, according to the *Mahasaccaka Sutta*, he remembered how once when he was a child he had a spontaneous experience of meditation "accompanied by applied and sustained thought, with rapture and pleasure born of seclusion." This, he realized, was the right path to enlightenment. In another *sutta* he spoke of a technique called mindfulness, in which the practitioner observes the body as body, the feelings as feelings, the mind as mind, the mind-objects as mind-objects, and eventually attains "final knowledge."[19] Such techniques, diligently practiced, lead to right concentration, which culminates in *nirvana*. These methods of inner concentration are still practiced by Buddhists today.

The doctrines of Buddhism are laid out in hundreds of texts and philosophical treatises written in more than a dozen languages. I will look here only at a few ideas that will help us understand the relationship between Buddhism and the gods. The key to the Buddhist theory of existence is the principle of *pratitya-samutpada*, generally translated as "dependent origination." Briefly it means that everything that comes into being is part of a huge network of interrelationships. Nothing is independent. A classic formulation of *pratitya-samutpada* found in many Buddhist texts states that ignorance gives rise to mental formations, which give rise to consciousness, which gives rise to mind and matter... and so forth, down to birth, old age, and death. This linear chain of cause-and-effect is a schematic representation of an infinitely complex web of "interbeing," as contemporary Vietnamese monk Thich Nhat Hanh calls it: each link "is both a cause and an effect" of "all the other links in the chain." It follows that there is no "first and only cause" that "does not itself need a cause."[20] This rules out a creator God. It also means that there is no permanent self or permanent anything. The three characteristics of existence are impermanence, suffering, and nonself. All things are transitory, all things are unsatisfactory, and things are without inherent identity.

The Buddha rarely spoke about self or God or other metaphysical subjects. Questions like "Is the world eternal" or "Is the self the same as the body" were of no practical value on the path to liberation. He once told the story of a man who had been hit by a poisoned arrow. When a surgeon arrived, the patient told him not to remove the arrow until he had found out the name, caste and appearance of the archer and the materials he used for his weapons. If the surgeon had agreed, the patient would have died before the recitation was over. In the same way, the Buddha explained, people who thought they could not begin to practice before they knew whether the world was eternal or noneternal, and so forth, would die before they had taken the first steps on the path.

In one of his sermons the Buddha looked at the questions of karma, Fate, and God from a practical point of view. Some people, he said, with reference to the Jains, believed that everything that happened was the automatic result of karma. But those who thought this had "no real valid ground for asserting that this or that ought to be done or ought not to be done." This meant moral paralysis. Other people, he said with the Ajivikas in mind, believed that everything that happened was "uncaused and unconditioned." They too had no reason to believe that one course of action was better than another. Then there were those who thought that everything that happened was the result of God's creative power. For these theists the upshot was the same: they had no reason to engage in moral striving. Therefore, for pragmatic rather than metaphysical reasons, people should reject Jainism, Ajivism, and theism and follow the eightfold path.[21]

Buddhism had no use for a creator God, but like all other religions of the era it took the existence of supernatural beings—gods, demons, ghosts, spirits, and so forth—for granted. Even the Buddha accepted their existence—or at least did not deny it. Asked by a student named Bharadvaja, "Are there gods?" he replied: "It is known to me to be the case, Bharadvaja, that there are gods." Pressed further, he clarified: "It is widely accepted in the world, Bharadvaja, that there are gods." He did not try to contradict conventional beliefs but gave them no importance. In some of his sermons he made it clear that the gods of popular belief were inferior to human beings. Caught in the rounds of *samsara*, they were unwilling to make the effort needed to achieve liberation. In the *Brahmajala Sutta* he explained that a certain class of gods spent "an excessive amount of time addicted to merriment, play and enjoyment, so that their mindfulness is dissipated." They will have to be reborn as humans before they can make any progress.[22]

All Indians of that period, whether they accepted the Vedic, Jain, Ajivika, or Buddhist traditions, believed in the existence of nonphysical beings. Especially popular were nature-spirits known as *yakshas*, who appear in Vedic, Jain, and Buddhist scriptures and are depicted in the art of all three traditions. The Buddha does not seem to have discouraged *yaksha*-worship, which was just part of everyday life. On the other hand, he never suggested that people should invoke spirits or sacrifice to the gods to obtain superhuman assistance. They should look for help only to him, his teaching, and the Buddhist community: *Buddha, dhamma, sangha*. But in the final analysis, it was up to the individual: "You yourself must make the effort," Buddha said in a famous verse. "The Tathagatas (Buddhas) can only point the way."[23]

Following the way in China

In 1046 BCE Wu of Zhou overthrew the last Shang ruler, becoming the first king of the Zhou dynasty. King Wu ruled fairly but the people were restive and unhappy. Wu's brother, the Duke of Zhou, addressed them: The Shang dynasty came to power centuries ago because it was the Decree of Heaven that it should rule. All the Shang kings except the last governed "with illustrious virtue, were careful in the use of punishments, and thus were able to exercise a stimulating influence over the people." But the last Shang king "was lazy and slothful, slighted the labors of government, and did not make pure sacrifices, so that Heaven sent down this ruin on him." Heaven sought among the Shang "for one who might be attentive to its commands," but found no one. Heaven turned to King Wu of Zhou because he "treated the multitudes well and was virtuous, and presided carefully over the sacrifices to the spirits and to Heaven." In this way the Mandate of Heaven passed from the Shang to the Zhou. From that point forward the doctrine of the Mandate of Heaven has stood at the heart of Chinese statecraft and culture. The Shang rulers had based their claim to authority on the fiat of the superhuman power Shangdi. The Duke of Zhou made it clear that the king's right to rule was contingent on his human qualities. The same principle held in the lives of ordinary men and women. The Duke of Zhou practiced what he preached and still is celebrated as a model of virtue, ranking second only to Confucius as a Chinese cultural hero. Confucius himself was among his admirers. A famous saying of his runs: "How I have gone downhill! It has been such a long time since I dreamt of the Duke of Zhou."[24]

The Indian mind has always taken pleasure in constructing vast systems of mythology, cosmology, and philosophy. The thirty-three Vedic divinities gave way to the 330 million gods of popular Hindu belief. The straightforward world-systems of early Hindus, Jains, and Buddhists expanded into universes with countless subdivisions and ever-repeating cycles of billions of years. In contrast, the thinkers of Zhou dynasty China steadily diminished the place of the supernatural in religious life. During the Shang dynasty the influence of gods and spirits was all-pervasive. The supreme god Shangdi sent blessings or disasters according to his whim. But during the Zhou dynasty, Shangdi was identified with Tian or Heaven, and Tian lost most of the trappings of an anthropomorphic god. Heaven was paired with Earth to make a neat two-tier cosmology. The minor Shang gods continued to exist but they lost most of their clout. People were more likely to make offerings to the ancestors, whose popularity in East Asia has always surpassed that of their spirit cousins in India and the western parts of Eurasia.

In Bronze Age (Vedic) India, priests sacrificed to the gods to gain heavenly and earthly rewards for themselves, the rulers, and the kingdom and to ensure the right working of the cosmos. In Bronze Age (Shang) China, the ruler sacrificed to the gods and the ancestors for the same reasons. In axial-age India, Upanishadic sages and *samana* teachers introduced the idea of life-renunciation to achieve freedom from the rounds of birth-and-death. Nothing like this happened in axial-age China. Religion became increasingly this-worldly and humanistic. The person who did most to bring this about was a scholarly master of ritual called Kong Fuzi, known in the West as Confucius.

Confucius was born in northern China in 551 BCE. He thus was around the same age as or a bit older than the Buddha (depending on whose estimate of the Buddha's birth-year you accept). Living during the chaotic Spring and Autumn Period, when feudal lords defied the authority of established kings, Confucius looked back to the good old days of the early Zhou dynasty, when (he believed) kings ruled wisely and social harmony prevailed. As a young man he served in the government of a local duke but resigned when his suggestions were ignored. He then spent years searching for a ruler who was open to his ideas. He did not succeed in finding one, but his followers treasured his words. After his death they put together a collection of his sayings, the *Lunyu* or *Analects*, which became the main source of Confucianism.

During the 2500 years of its history, Confucianism has had its ups and downs, sometimes patronized by emperors, sometimes banned, but always influential. Confucian philosophers emphasized different aspects of the master's teachings but they all remained true to his core beliefs: through self-cultivation human beings can develop goodness and eventually become sages; a vanguard of cultivated elites is needed to promote goodness among the people; the wise and virtuous ruler creates the right conditions for a harmonious society. The central importance of self-cultivation (*xiushen*) is proclaimed in the first chapter of *The Great Learning*, a text generally attributed to Confucius: "From the Son of Heaven [the emperor] on down to commoners, all without exception should regard self-cultivation as the root." Self-cultivation requires an inward turn but its results must be directed outward. When a person becomes cultivated, *The Great Learning* explains, "harmony is established in the household; household harmony established, the state becomes well governed; the state being well governed, the empire becomes tranquil." An essential part of self-cultivation is study or learning (*xue*), by which Confucius meant primarily the mastery of the classics. But learning is sterile unless it is put into practice: "Is it not a pleasure, having learned something, to try it out at due intervals?" urges the first line of the *Analects*.[25]

Through self-cultivation, people develop true goodness or *ren*, a key term that can also be translated as "benevolence," "human-heartedness," or "humaneness." Asked by a disciple about benevolence, Confucius replied: "If for a single day a man could return to the observance of the rites through overcoming himself, then the whole Empire would consider benevolence to be his. However, the practice of benevolence depends on oneself alone, and not on others."[26] The word translated here as "rites" is *li*, another important Confucian term. Originally it signified formal rituals, such as sacrifices. Confucius took such rites very seriously. But for him and his followers *li* came to mean the rules of proper conduct in general. By practicing right conduct by his own efforts, an individual develops benevolence, which he passes on to society as a whole.

A person who is humane and acts in accordance with the rules of propriety is the exemplary person or *junzi*: the Confucian gentleman. Originally *junzi* meant a nobleman's son, but for Confucius the true sign of nobility was character and not birth. The gentleman speaks and acts appropriately in every situation, never worrying, never being of two minds, never being afraid. It is an exacting ideal, but one that people could aspire to. Not so the ideal of the sage (*shengren*), which is beyond the reach of present-day humanity: "I have no hopes of meeting a sage," Confucius once said, "I would be content if I met someone who is a gentleman."[27]

Confucius' moral universe was fundamentally human. He sometimes spoke of Tian or Heaven, but for him Heaven was a great moral force that supported the strivings of virtuous human beings. He did not believe in a creator God, but like everyone else of his era he accepted the existence of minor gods and spirits. He gave them little importance. Asked by a student the right way to serve the spirits, Confucius replied: "You are not able even to serve man. How can you serve the spirits?" The wise man kept his distance from gods and spirits and worked "for the things the common people have a right to."[28]

Two of Confucius' most important followers lived within 250 years of his death, and they laid down the lines of divergent interpretations that have been debated ever since. Mengzi, known in English as Mencius, believed that human nature was inherently good and needed only to be properly cultivated. Xunzi held that people were inherently evil and had to be kept in line by strong social controls.

Confucius was reticent about human nature but he seems to have implied that it was good. Mencius (c. 372–c. 289 BCE) came right out and said: "Man's nature is naturally good just as water naturally flows downward." All people have within them the seeds of virtue. Anyone who sees a child about to fall into a well naturally feels concern. This feeling, if properly cultivated, becomes *ren* or benevolence. Like Confucius, Mencius believed that *ren* was accessible to all who made an effort. "When in one's conduct one vigorously exercises altruism, humanity [*ren*] is not far to seek, but right by him." People differed not in their essential nature but in their degree of self-cultivation. Mencius went so far as to say that "the sage and I are the same in kind." His meaning was not that the sage was just like everybody else, but rather that "the sage is the first to possess what is common in our minds."[29]

Xunzi (c. 310–c. 235) was a generation or two younger than Mencius and a world apart in his attitude toward human beings. "The nature of man is evil," begins his most famous chapter, "his goodness is the result of his activity." By activity he meant training in accordance with the requirements of society. If one follows one's nature the result will be "strife and rapacity," which inevitably will lead to violence. Therefore, "there must be the civilizing influence of teachers and laws and the guidance of propriety and righteousness."[30] Xunzi's target here was Mencius and his doctrine of inherent goodness. People could not just wait for the seeds of goodness to develop; they had to make strenuous efforts to overcome their selfishness. The chief aids in this were propriety (*li*) and music. By means of their transformative power, individuals could eventually become sages.

Xunzi also differed from Mencius in his attitude toward Heaven. For Mencius, Heaven was the source of moral behavior, not an anthropomorphic god but still a power with definite intentions. Thus he could say that "when Heaven is about to confer a great responsibility on any man" it will make him suffer in order to make him ready for his task.[31] Xunzi saw Heaven as a natural phenomenon that neither rewards the good nor punishes the evil. It was up to human beings to make the best of what nature offered: "Respond to it with peace and order, and good fortune will result. Respond to it with disorder, and disaster will follow." He condemned the superstitions of popular religion. The gods and spirits had no influence on human life. What happened just happened: "This cannot be blamed on heaven; this is how the Way works."[32]

The last quotation suggests that Xunzi was familiar with the idea of the Way or Dao as understood by the Daoists, a loose group of thinkers whose ideas were on the rise during the third century BCE. The word *dao* (also spelled *tao*) means "path" or "way." It is an important concept in all schools of classical Chinese philosophy. To Confucius, *dao* was the path that men should follow to find happiness on earth. The accent is on humanity: "It is Man who is capable of broadening the Way," he said, "It is not the Way that is capable of broadening Man."[33] To the Daoists the Way was the primary thing, human effort was an impediment:

> Only when Dao is lost does the doctrine of virtue [*de*] arise.
> When virtue is lost, only then does the doctrine of humanity [*ren*] arise.
> When humanity is lost, only then does the doctrine of righteousness [*yi*] arise.
> When righteousness is lost, only then does the doctrine of propriety [*li*] arise.[34]

Humanity, righteousness, and propriety are not virtues that have to be cultivated in order to find the Way but ethical stopgaps that come into play after the Way has been lost. But there is another sort of *de* or virtue, not conventional morality but inherent quality or power. When people are in harmony with their inherent *de*, they return to *dao*, the true Way.

The origins of Daoism are hard to trace. The most famous Daoist text, the *Daodejing* (also spelled *Tao Te Ching*) is sometimes dated to the sixth century BCE, but more likely was composed during the fifth and fourth. Its traditional author is Laozi, which simply means "Old Master." Most modern scholars believe that the *Daodejing* is an anthology of sayings composed over more than a century by different members of a philosophical lineage. Its earliest surviving version is from the beginning of the third century BCE. Another Daoist text, the *Zhuangzi* (also spelled *Chuang Tzu*), was probably written a bit later than this. Its traditional author is Zhuang Zhou, who may have been an actual person. These two works form the basis of what is called philosophical Daoism as distinguished from religious Daoism. The distinction is somewhat artificial. Plenty of Daoist religion was being practiced when the *Daodejing* and *Zhuangzi* were composed but we have little knowledge of its nature. I confine myself here to the spiritual philosophy of the two classic texts, postponing consideration of Daoist religion to Chapter 4.

The thinking of all Daoist writers is based on the idea of the Dao, but it is almost impossible to say just what the Dao is. The *Daodejing* famously begins: "The Dao (Way) that can be told of is not the eternal Dao." It goes on to hint at the nature of the Dao through metaphors and symbols. Dao is "the mother of the universe." It is "open and broad, like a valley." Because it is like a valley, it "is called the subtle and profound female," and

> He who knows the male and keeps to the female
> Becomes the ravine of the world.
> Being the ravine of the world,
> He will never depart from eternal virtue,
> But returns to the state of infancy.[35]

This state of infancy comes into being by the union of the active (male) and passive (female) forces. The infant "possesses virtue in abundance" and acts spontaneously, in accord with its self-nature. Such action is described by the *Daodejing* as so-of-its-own (*ziran*):

> Dao is esteemed and virtue is honored without anyone's order.
> They ["the ten thousand things"] always come spontaneously [*ziran*].[36]

To act spontaneously is, paradoxically, not to act, or rather to engage in action without action. This is *wu wei*, a characteristic of the Dao, which "invariably takes no action, and yet there is nothing left undone." *Wu wei* also is a characteristic of the *shengren* or sage:

> The sage manages affairs without action
> And spreads doctrines without words.
> All things arise, and he does not turn away from them.
> He produces them, but does not take possession of them.[37]

Writing during the Warring States period (475–221 BCE), the authors of the *Daodejing* wanted to show how to stop political turmoil. Thus they addressed themselves to the king and the nobility: "If kings and barons would hold on to it [the Dao], all things would submit to them spontaneously." But to be an effective ruler, the king had to place himself below his people:

> The great rivers and seas are kings of all mountain streams
> Because they skillfully stay below them.
>   That is why they can be their kings.

In the same way, the sage "places himself in the background, but finds himself in the foreground." Because he "has no personal interests" his "personal interests are fulfilled." Thus the sage is the model not only for the ruler, but also for the wise and effective human being:

> One may know the world without going out of doors.
> One may see the Way of Heaven without looking through the windows.
> The further one goes, the less one knows.
> Therefore the sage knows without going about,
> Understands without seeing,
> And accomplishes without any action.[38]

It is passages like this that have made the *Daodejing* a perennial influence on spiritual thinking from the axial age to the Beatles. And it is a spirituality without God. There is only one line in the text that mentions a theistic entity, and this "Lord" is inferior to the Dao:

> Deep and still, it [the Dao] appears to exist forever.
> I do not know whose son it is.
> It seems to have existed before the Lord.

This skeptical approach to the idea of God was amplified by the author of the *Zhuangzi*: "They [human feelings] are right near by. But we don't know who causes them. It seems there is a True Lord who does so, but there is no indication of his existence."[39] Whatever the meaning of this enigmatic passage might be, it is clear that its author did not believe in a god who created and governs the universe.

Zhuang Zhou, the traditional author of the *Zhuangzi*, is said to have lived from 369 to 286 BCE. This would make him a contemporary of Mencius—although it must be added that the historicity of Zhuang Zhou is in dispute, while that of Mencius is not. What is certain is that the book attributed to Zhuang Zhou was well known by the second century BCE. Around that time, Daoism became recognized as one of the six schools of Chinese philosophy and the *Zhuangzi* took its place beside the *Daodejing* as a classic Daoist text. Since Zhuang Zhou never mentioned the *Daodejing*, it seems likely that the two works emerged independently from a somewhat amorphous tradition that was, among other things, critical of Confucian orthodoxy. Where the Confucians all stressed the importance of culture and proper conduct, the Daoists insisted on the centrality of nature and nonaction (*wu wei*).

To the Confucians, Tian or Heaven is a great moral force. In the *Zhuangzi*, Tian is often a name for the Dao, which expresses itself spontaneously through nonaction: "Heaven and earth do nothing and there is nothing that is not done," reads one passage. "Among men, who can get hold of this inaction?"

One person who did was Cook Ding. While cutting up an ox, he "slithered the knife along with a zing, and all was in perfect rhythm." How do you manage it? asked Lord Wenhui. Ding replied: "What I care about is the Way, which goes beyond skill." When Ding was new to his profession, he tried too hard and his eyes were fixed on the ox. Now, after years of practice, "Perception and understanding have come to a stop and spirit moves where it wants." Even when the going is difficult, he moves the knife "with the greatest subtlety, until—flop! the whole thing comes apart like a clod of earth crumbling to the ground."[40] Through practice Ding's action became nonaction, and as a result his cutting was perfect.

The *Zhuangzi* is filled with memorable passages that illustrate the nature of the Dao in rather earthy terms:

> Master Dongguo asked Zhuangzi [i.e., the man Zhuang Zhou], "This thing called the Way—where does it exist?"
> Zhuangzi said, "There is no place it doesn't exist."
> "Come," said Master Dongguo, "you must be more specific!"
> "It is in the ant."
> "As low a thing as that?"
> "It is in the panic grass."
> "But that's lower still!"
> "It is in the tiles and shards."
> "How can it be so low?"
> "It is in the piss and shit."

As the *Zhuangzi* says elsewhere: "From the point of view of the Way, things have no nobility or meanness." This superiority to the dualities is a theme that Zhuang Zhou returns to again and again: The True Man or sage is able to recognize "a 'this,' but a 'this' which is also 'that,' a 'that' which is also 'this.'" He could "wander in the world without taking sides" and at the same time "follow along with men without losing himself."[41]

The *Zhuangzi*, like the *Daodejing*, presents its teachings through paradoxes and metaphors rather than by direct statements. Only occasionally are there hints of the techniques cultivated by Daoist practitioners. The breath of the True Man "came from deep within," one *Zhuangzi* passage says. "The True Man breathes with his heels; the mass of men breathe with their throats."[42] This calls to mind the breathing exercises that were part of the repertoire of Indian *samanas*. Scholars have pointed out a number of other similarities between the mystical teachings of axial-age India and China without being able to establish a direct link between the two. The same holds true of some equally striking parallels between the thought and practices of these two Asian cultures and certain lines of philosophy in ancient Greece.

Therapeutic wisdom in Greece

Xenophanes was born in the Ionian city of Colophon sometime around 570 BCE. (He thus was a young man when Confucius was born in China.) At the age of twenty-five he left his native city and wandered throughout the Greek world for sixty-seven years. Along the way he met a variety of people who had differing opinions about everything including the gods. He observed, ironically, that the gods of the Africans were dark and snub-nosed, while those of Thrace were blue-eyed redheads. Clearly people conceived of the gods in their own image. If cows and horses had hands, he wrote, "horses would draw pictures of gods like horses, and cows like cows." The poets Homer and Hesiod depicted the gods as outsized human beings, ascribing to them "everything that brings shame and reprobation among men—theft, and adultery, and mutual deception." This was absurd, since the gods were by definition perfect. Xenophanes did not deny that there was a divine principle, but he said it was beyond human conception: "There is one god, greatest among gods and men" who is "not at all like mortals in form or even thought." This god "remains in the same state, in no way changing," and "shakes everything" by "the power of his mind." For centuries commentators have puzzled over what this single unchanging god was. Christian theologians such as Clement of Alexandria suggested it was the bodiless unitary God of monotheism; a modern scholar suggests that it may have been the equivalent of our idea of Nature. (A student of Indian philosophy might be reminded of the *brahman* of the *Isha Upanishad*: "one, unmoving, swifter than mind.") Whatever else Xenophanes' god might have been, it was not a run-of-the-mill member of the Olympian pantheon.[43]

The Bronze Age cultures of the Near East, India, and China arose in broad alluvial plains that favored the formation of large monarchial states. The people who settled on the margins of the Aegean Sea built their cities on narrow coasts or in isolated valleys enclosed by rugged mountains. This limiting geography prevented them from forming a unitary state, but they all maintained the sense of being Hellenes or, as we say in English, Greeks.

Around the ninth century BCE, some of the settlements on the Greek mainland, the Aegean islands, and coastal Anatolia (now western Turkey) developed into city-states that became centers of trade, politics, and culture. A number of important city-states were located in the region of Ionia, on the Anatolian coast. It was here that the enquiry into the nature of things that the Greeks called "philosophy" (from *philosophia* or "love of wisdom") began.

According to tradition, the first Greek philosopher was Thales, who was born in the Ionian city of Miletus around 624 BCE. He and two younger thinkers of the same city, Anaximander and Anaximenes, sought answers to questions about the world by studying the world itself rather than relying on religious authorities. All of them tried to identify the single substance underlying the plurality of phenomena. Thales said it was water; Anaximander, an "unlimited" element; Anaximenes, air. Later Ionian thinkers continued this search for a fundamental principle. Heraclitus of Ephesus (a city not far from Miletus) wrote that the *kosmos* or world-order was not created by gods or men but was and always will be "an ever-living fire." This cosmos was dynamic, always changing, never the same: "Everything is an exchange for fire, and fire for everything." Cosmos was held in order by *Logos*, a mysterious utterance or law that was "both unwilling and willing to be called by the name of Zeus."[44] Was Logos a god? Heraclitus left the question open.

Aristotle, who lived two centuries after Heraclitus, spoke of the Ionian philosophers as *physiologoi*—those who spoke about nature (*physis*)—as opposed to the *theologoi*—those who spoke about the gods (*theoi*). The chief *theologoi* were the poets Homer and Hesiod. Their medium was mythology. The protagonists of their stories were the gods. The *physiologoi* or natural philosophers tried to explain things in terms of natural entities. Anaximander, for example, devised a mechanical model of heavenly motion that relied on hollow concentric wheels filled with fire. This rather clunky solar system replaced the myth of the sun-god Helios, described in the *Homeric Hymns* as driving the chariot of the sun across the sky, "his bright locks streaming from the temples of his head."[45] The scientific outlook often brings about a loss of poetic charm.

The move from *theologia* or theology to *physiologia* or natural philosophy was viewed by later philosophers as an advance from *mythos* to *logos*. *Mythos* of course meant story or myth, but also a mode of explanation based on authoritative statements that could not be challenged. *Logos*, which to Heraclitus was the ordering principle of the cosmos, was for later philosophers such as Parmenides the human power of reason. *Logos* in this sense is the source of the English word "logic."

Like the Ionian philosophers, Parmenides (born in Elea, in Magna Graecia or southern Italy, around 515 BCE) was interested in nature, but he did not believe that the truths of nature could be found by observation, because appearances often are misleading. Only reason could uncover truth, and the truth that reason revealed was that everything was one eternal Being. This meant, contrary to what Heraclitus had taught, that change was impossible. Parmenides' follower Zeno of Elea tried to prove this by means of paradoxes, for example, that Achilles could never catch a tortoise with a head start, since to do so he would first have to cover half the distance between them, then half of what remained, and so on forever.

Zeno's arguments were clever but they did not really solve the problem of being and change. More impressive was the solution proposed by Leucippus and his student Democritus: The universe consists of "atoms" (indivisible particles) and the void. Atoms never change but combine with other atoms to create compound objects. Our world comes into being not as a result of divine providence but through the chance interactions of atoms. The gods exist but they are just apparitions composed of atoms on which humans project godlike attributes.

Democritus did much of his work in Athens, which during the fifth century BCE became the center of the Greek world. It was a time of intellectual and artistic exploration, which sometimes tested the limits of orthodoxy. The Athenian state expected its citizens to believe in the gods of the city, but some Athenian writers dropped hints that they doubted the majority view. The dramatist Euripides put skeptical ideas in the mouths of some of his characters. In *The Trojan Women* (produced in 415 BCE) Hecuba addresses the king of the gods in these terms:

> you boundless mystery
> Called Zeus, whether you are the fixed law of Nature
> Or man's Mind—whoever you are, I invoke you,

which sounds more like the thoughts of an Athenian philosopher than the cry of a wronged queen. In another passage, Euripides has a character say:

> Is there anyone who thinks there are gods in heaven?
> There are not. There are not, for any man who wishes
> Not to be a fool and trust some ancient story.[46]

No wonder Euripides was condemned by some as impious or atheistic. These were dangerous labels. Two of his contemporaries, the naturalistic philosopher Anaxagoras and the poet Diagoras, known as "the Atheist," were obliged to leave Athens after being accused of impiety.

Another philosopher who pushed the envelope was the sophist Protagoras (c. 490–c. 420). He began his treatise *On the Gods* with the agnostic sentence: "Concerning the gods I am not able to know either that they exist or that they do not exist or what their nature is; for there are many things which prevent one from knowing, both the unclarity [of the subject] and the short span of human life." Unlike most other Greek philosophers, Protagoras viewed knowledge as relative to the observer. The first and only surviving sentence of a book of his called *Truth* is this: "Man is the measure of all things, of the things that are that they are and of the things that are not that they are not."[47] Lacking the rest of Protagoras' text, it is hard to say exactly what he meant, but it certainly was far from the pious idea that everything depends on the will of the gods or Parmenides' theory that all appearances are based on one Reality.

In the dialogue *Theaetetus*, Plato (428/427–348/347 BCE) has his teacher Socrates refute the relativism of Protagoras. If all things are relative, Socrates says, "you cannot rightly call anything by any name, such as great or small, heavy or light, for the great will be small and the heavy light," and so forth. Remembered as the thinker who humanized philosophy, Socrates was not interested in abstract questions. "He would argue that to trouble one's mind with such problems is sheer folly," his student Xenophon wrote. "Rather, his own conversation was always about human things."[48]

On account of his humanistic outlook, Socrates rarely spoke about the gods. When somebody asked him whether an old tale about a god and a mortal girl was true, he said he had no time for such questions: "I investigate myself rather than these things."[49] Compare this to what Confucius said a hundred years earlier: "You are not able even to serve man, how can you serve the spirits?" Confucius taught his students to cultivate virtue by following the rules of propriety. For Socrates, the right way to cultivate virtue was to examine oneself and others. "The unexamined life is not worth living," he said; therefore it was "the greatest good for a man to discuss virtue every day." People should not spend their time amassing wealth or caring for their bodies. What was important was to cultivate "the best possible state of your soul."[50]

Socrates' method of teaching was to ask those he spoke with to think very carefully about the things they took for granted. His relentless questioning caused them to realize that their pet ideas contradicted one another. Once they had seen this, they were ready to try something new. Nothing was too sacrosanct for Socrates to examine and this got him into trouble with the state. In 399 BCE he was accused of not recognizing the gods of Athens and corrupting the youth of the city. Brought to trial he admitted that he challenged his students to examine their ideas and those of the community. His role, he said, was that of a philosophical gadfly who had been sent "by the god" to stir up the city, which had become sluggish as it grew large and powerful. Unfortunately for Socrates, it was not the best time for this sort of thing. Defeated by its rival Sparta in 404 BCE, Athens passed through a period of tyrannical rule before democracy was restored. The powers that be were not in the mood to be stung by a philosophical gadfly, particularly one who claimed to have been sent by a god.

What precisely was the god Socrates spoke of? It was, he said, a *daimonion* or divine thing that spoke to him or gave him a sign when he was about to do something wrong. This admission gave little comfort to the city fathers. Not only did Socrates not honor the gods of Athens, he was introducing a new god in their place! Clearly his accusers missed the significance of his *daimonion*: it was not a god in the ordinary sense but what a modern thinker might call the power of intuition or a practical man a "gut instinct." Socrates' friends all swore he was a very pious person, diligent in public worship and a model of virtue in his personal life. None of this impressed the jury. They found him guilty and sentenced him to death. Socrates was unperturbed. Those who rightly lived the philosophical life were "in training for dying," he said; therefore "they fear death least of all men." When the executioner brought Socrates his cup of poison, he "drained it calmly and easily."[51]

Socrates, his student Plato, and Plato's student Aristotle presided over the classical period of Greek philosophy. I will give only a quick glance at Plato and

Aristotle, first because their thought is very well known, second because they are not especially important in the history of nontheistic spirituality.

Plato turned away from Socrates' concentration on human things, searching instead for abstract principles such as the Forms (the ideal prototypes of things). Plato's Form of the Good became the basis of the One of Plotinus (204–270 CE), which in turn served as a model for the Platonic-Christian God of Augustine of Hippo (354–430 CE). Aristotle rejected Plato's theory of Forms, fixing his sights on the physical and social worlds. For him, the primary work of the philosopher was the discovery of truth through observation and logical argumentation. Aristotle systematized the study of logic in the fourth century BCE, drawing on Heraclitus, Parmenides, and other philosophers. It was he who finalized the three-term syllogism in the form: All men are mortal, Socrates is a man, therefore Socrates is mortal. Turning his logic to the problem of God, Aristotle came up with the idea of the Unmoved Mover, which was given classic form 1600 years later in the Christian theology of Thomas Aquinas.

Aristotle's most famous student was Alexander III of Macedon, better known as Alexander the Great. After helping his father Philip II overcome the city-states of Greece, he went on to conquer all the lands between Macedon and northern India. After his death in Babylon in 323, his empire broke up into smaller kingdoms, where Greeks confronted the ancient civilizations of Egypt, Syria, Persia, and India. The result was a "Greek-like" or Hellenistic world where competing currents of thought, art, and religion came together to produce a hybrid culture. Athens and other Greek city-states remained prominent for many years but eventually were overshadowed by regional capitals such as Alexandria and Antioch, and later by Rome, the capital of the empire that absorbed the Hellenistic world.

The seventy-six years between the death of Socrates (399 BCE) and the death of Alexander (323 BCE) were a time of intense philosophical activity in Athens. Out of the churning arose the various schools of Hellenistic thought, notably Epicureanism, Stoicism, and Skepticism. This period was, according to British cultural historian Isaiah Berlin, one of the three great turning points in Western intellectual history. Before the Hellenistic era, Greek philosophers always viewed the individual within a social framework. Hence the well-known Aristotelian dictum: man is a political, that is, a social animal. For Aristotle happiness, the highest good, was the activity of the rational soul in accordance with virtue. Happiness could be complete only if it was expressed in the active life. But in the decades following Aristotle's death, Athenian philosophers began to speak of human beings "purely in terms of inner experience and individual salvation." The philosopher Epicurus summed up the new approach in two sentences: "Vain is the word of a philosopher, by which no mortal suffering is healed. Just as medicine confers no benefit if it does not drive away bodily disease, so is philosophy useless if it does not drive away the suffering of the mind." What brought about the change from socially framed to therapeutic philosophy? Did the absorption of the Greek states into the Macedonian empire produce a psychological crisis, a Hellenistic "age of anxiety?" Did people find it hard to assimilate the influences pouring in from Asia? Or were there other reasons? It is hard to say for sure. For Berlin, the change was as mysterious as it was swift.[52]

An early harbinger of Hellenistic philosophy was the Cynic approach of Antisthenes of Athens. (The Greek word *kynikos* meant "dog-like," apparently a reference to the Cynics' unconventional habits. It had nothing to do with the cold-hearted attitude we call "cynicism.") Antisthenes, like Plato, was a student of Socrates. The two men took away different lessons from their master. Plato built an elaborate metaphysics based on Socrates' "love of wisdom." Antisthenes was struck by Socrates' toughness and emotional control and made these the basis of the Cynic way of life. His central idea was that happiness depends on the inner state of virtue alone. Property and passion just get in the way. "As iron is eaten away by rust," he said, so "the envious are consumed by their own passion." His pupil Diogenes similarly observed: "bad men obey their lusts as servants obey their masters."[53]

Diogenes is remembered chiefly for the stunts and one-liners he used to make philosophical points. Carrying a lighted lamp in the daytime, he replied to those who asked what he was doing: "I am looking for a man." He believed in the importance of physical training and went to great lengths to inure himself to hardship, by living in a storage tub, for example. During the summer, he rolled in hot sand; during the winter, he embraced snow-covered statues. Showing his disdain for social conventions, he performed his bodily activities in the open. Rebuked for masturbating in public, he said he wished "it were as easy to banish hunger by rubbing an empty stomach." About the gods he had little to say. Asked by someone what things were like in heaven, he replied: "I have never been up there."[54]

Antisthenes was in the habit of saying "I'd rather be mad than feel pleasure." Aristippus, another student of Socrates, said just the opposite: Pleasure, especially bodily pleasure, was the highest good and ought to be seized at every opportunity. That the enjoyment of pleasure was the true end of life could be proved "by the fact that from our youth up we are instinctively attracted to it, and, when we obtain it, seek for nothing more, and shun nothing so much as its opposite, pain." But Aristippus also thought that the enjoyment of pleasure did not mean enslavement to passion. Asked about his relationship with the courtesan Laïs, he replied, "I have Laïs, not she me; and it is not abstinence from pleasures that is best, but mastery over them without ever being worsted." (One wonders what Laïs thought about this.) Aristippus' followers became known as Cyrenaics, after Cyrene in North Africa, where he was born. They included his grandson, Antisthenes the younger, and the latter's student Theodorus the Atheist, who got his appellation because, as an ancient biographer wrote, he "utterly rejected the current belief in the gods."[55]

A later writer named Euhemerus, who was associated with the Cyrenaics, came up with a naturalistic theory of the origin of the gods: the myths of Homer and Hesiod were based on actual events; the gods were extraordinary human beings who became deified over the course of time.

The Cyrenaic school eventually ceded place to Epicureanism, which was founded by Epicurus after his arrival in Athens in 306 BCE. He took from Aristippus the idea that pleasure is naturally desirable and the basis of happiness. But precisely because it is "the first good and natural to us," we have to treat it with respect. Excessive indulgence is ruinous to pleasure and can even lead to pain. Therefore we must learn prudence, which "teaches us how impossible it is to live pleasantly without living wisely, virtuously, and justly." Pleasure is a negative state: the absence of pain (*aponia*) and the freedom from disturbance (*ataraxia*). Once pain and disturbance are removed, we enjoy the natural delight of existence.[56] The main cause of mental disturbance is fear, and the most potent causes of fear are the gods and death. People who took their myths seriously believed that the gods went out of their way to produce disastrous events. As a result, they lived "expecting and fearing some everlasting pain." Or else they were fearful about "the loss of sensation itself that comes with death."[57] All this was irrational. The gods are uninterested in human beings and death is not to be feared because when it comes there is no one to experience it.

Epicurus studied with Nausiphanes, who was a student of Democritus. He accepted Democritus' idea that the universe consists of indestructible atoms moving in an infinite void. Atoms combine to form compounds, which display the properties we perceive with our senses. But Democritus had a problem with combination, since atoms move in straight lines that never intersect. Epicurus got around this by introducing a new idea: every now and then an atom swerves into the path of another. A collision takes place that makes it possible for the atoms to combine. The universe we see is the product of billions of such combinations. And, crucially, the process is random. No one causes the atoms to swerve or combine, or planets to form and move across the sky. Therefore, he insisted, "the divine should not be introduced in any way into these considerations."[58]

Like virtually everyone else in the ancient world, Epicurus believed that the gods existed: We have, he wrote, "distinct knowledge" of them—a reference, apparently, to the fact that we sometimes see them in dreams.[59] But the gods are not what people imagine. Composed of atoms like everything else, they live in the empty spaces between the worlds and take no interest in human life. Therefore it is irrational to fear them. Once we have abandoned superstitious beliefs, we can approach the gods in a dignified way by means of contemplation. Their infinite happiness can serve as a model of the happiness we too can enjoy if we practice the Epicurean philosophy.

According to Epicurus, happiness in the sense of *ataraxia* or freedom from disturbance is easy to obtain. Ordinary food gets rid of hunger just as well as fancy dishes. The greatest of all causes of happiness is simply "the possession of friendship."[60] Affective communities based on Epicurean principles, where men and women practiced together, were a feature of the Graeco-Roman world from the time of Epicurus until the communities were suppressed by the Christian Church many centuries later.

The great rival of Epicureanism in ancient Greece and Rome was Stoicism, which was founded by Zeno of Citium around 300 BCE. Seeking a mentor on the Socratic model, Zeno frequented various teachers in Athens, notably a Cynic named Crates. Eventually he became a teacher himself, giving lectures at a *stoa* or portico on the northern side of the marketplace. Hence his followers were called Stoics. His teachings, a combination of Cynic self-discipline and Socratic rationality, spread throughout the Hellenistic world, and became the philosophy of choice of the Roman elite after the formation of the Empire. It is mostly through the writings of Roman-era Stoics such as Seneca, Epictetus, and Marcus Aurelius that we know the outlines of what Zeno taught, since his own writings, along with those of his successors Cleanthes and Chrysippus, were lost except for scattered quotations in the works of other writers.

The Stoics developed a systematic philosophy consisting of a physics or theory of nature, an ethical teaching with methods of self-discipline, and a system of logic. Their physics and ethics differed markedly from those of the Epicureans. As we have seen, Epicurus believed the universe came into being through the random combination of atoms. The gods are detached from what happens in the universe and take no interest in humanity. To the Stoics the universe is the creation of an active principle that can be viewed as a providential God. By living in accord with this active principle, also known as nature, human beings can achieve happiness. Zeno summed up this ideal in a phrase that would not be out of place in a modern self-help book: Happiness is "a good flow of life."[61] Stated otherwise, happiness is *apatheia* or freedom from passion. This is similar to the Epicureans' *ataraxia* or freedom from disturbance, but the two schools differed in how they approached the goal. The Epicureans sought happiness through the measured satisfaction of pleasure, the Stoics by controlling the passions or rooting them out entirely.

The Stoics gave great importance to Fate. Since Reason directs everything that happens, it could not have happened otherwise. This is the same thing as saying that all that happens is fated. The Stoic sage accepts what was bound to happen anyway and lives in tranquility. But the Stoics' acceptance of Fate was not completely passive. God, the divine Reason, has given us the power of reason to help us distinguish what is and is not in our power to change. Health, wealth, and reputation are not under our control, so it is foolish to worry about them, but we *can* control our mental states by rejecting regret, sorrow, anger, and so forth. Reason can also help us distinguish what is good, bad, and indifferent. Most things are indifferent, although some indifferent things, such as health and wealth, are to be preferred over their opposites since they promote human flourishing. The only things that are always good are virtues such as prudence, wisdom, and justice. The Stoics agreed with the Cynics in saying that virtue was sufficient for happiness but they thought the right way to cultivate virtue was mental self-discipline, not physical asceticism. Their best-known exercise was the premeditation of evil: imagining that the things we fear the most have already happened. Thus prepared, we can bear what actually does happen with tranquil acceptance.

The Socratics, Epicureans, and Stoics had different ideas about the nature of truth and virtue and all of them believed that they were right. Toward the beginning of the third century BCE two schools arose that questioned this dogmatic certitude. Proponents of both were called Skeptics, taking the word *skeptikos* in its original sense of inquiring or investigating. One of these schools grew out of the teachings of Pyrrho, who lived from around 360 to 270 BCE. The other took shape from around 266 BCE in the Academy that had been founded by Plato 150 years earlier. The Academic Skeptics were, well, academic. Questioning everything, they arrived at the conclusion that nothing could be known, not even the fact that nothing could be known. (In this they outdid their inspiration, Socrates, who was sure that he knew nothing.) After a couple of hundred years Academic Skepticism lost its edge, and a philosopher named Aenesidemus returned to Pyrrho's teachings, which had largely been forgotten, and made them the basis of a new school of Skepticism that became known as Pyrrhonism. According to the Pyrrhonists, the way out of epistemological muddles was to suspend judgment about contending opinions and in this way achieve freedom from disturbance.

About Pyrrho himself we know very little. He was born around 360 BCE in Elis, western Greece. As a young man he accompanied the army of Alexander as far as India, where he may have met with "gymnosophists" or naked philosophers. Returning to Greece, he lived a solitary life but taught his ideas to a few. Only fragments of his teachings survive but they show well enough the basic tendency of his thought: "No single thing is in itself any more this than that," he said. "There is nothing really existent, but custom and convention govern human action."[62]

Pyrrhonic Skepticism was given classic formulation around 200 CE—that is, five centuries after Pyrrho's death—by the physician Sextus Empiricus. His *Outlines of Pyrrhonism* is the source of most of what we know about Pyrrho's teachings. Troubled by the multiplicity of beliefs, some people—Sextus calls them Dogmatists—try to achieve tranquility by adopting the one right view. They fail because no particular view is better than any other. The Skeptics too long for tranquility, but they seek it in a different way. Suspending their judgment they oppose "to every account an equal account" that appears just as convincing and so end up holding no beliefs at all. In this way they achieve tranquility. They do not say that tranquility (*ataraxia*) is *caused* by suspension of judgment (*epoché*) because they do not accept causality. Rather they say that *ataraxia* follows *epoché* "fortuitously, as a shadow follows a body." Sextus illustrated the process with a story about the painter Apelles. Frustrated by his inability to depict foam in the mouth of a horse, he picked up a sponge and threw it at the painting, and hey presto!—a perfect impression of foam.[63]

It will come as no surprise that the Skeptics did not promote any belief about the gods. Early cultural relativists, they noted that people in different parts of the world had contradictory notions about the nature of the gods and the correct way of worshipping them. Most people believed only in the gods of their own countries. A few philosophers, such as Diagoras and Theodorus, denied that the gods existed at all. People who accepted God's existence differed about his nature. Aristotle thought that God was "incorporeal and the limit of the heavens," the Stoics believed God was present even in "loathsome things."[64] Sextus observed that if the nature of the gods were certain then everyone would have reached identical conclusions about them. To prove the existence of something as uncertain as the gods, there would have to be something certain on which to base the argument, but then it would be necessary to prove the certainty of that something, and so on ad infinitum. Then there was the problem of evil. If the gods provide for everything, they are responsible for evil. If they provide for some things and not for others, they are malign. And if they do not provide for anything, they are powerless. Therefore, Sextus concluded (not without a touch of irony): "we deduce that those who firmly state that there are gods are no doubt bound to be impious," for only an impious person would say that the gods are the cause of evil or that they are malign or powerless.[65]

The monotheistic alternative

By the union of Tiamat, the goddess of salt water, and Apsu, the god of river water, Lahmu and Lahamu, silt and mud, were born. From them came forth a new race of gods, the greatest of whom was Ea. So begins the story of creation in the *Enuma Elish*, which was written in Mesopotamia—the land formed of silt and mud between the Tigris and Euphrates rivers—sometime around 1700 BCE. Ea killed his progenitor Apsu and built his house on Apsu's body. Here Damkina, Ea's lover, gave birth to Marduk. When Tiamat, the primordial goddess, prepared to attack the new gods, they selected Marduk as their champion. He agreed to fight on condition that they grant him full sovereignty. After an epic battle, Marduk slew Tiamat and "sliced her in half like a fish for drying." From the two halves of her body he created the heavens and the earth. After placing the moon, sun, and other heavenly bodies in their places, Marduk decided it was time to create human beings. Ea concurred and slit open the arteries of Qingu, the leader of the rebel gods. From Qingu's blood were born men and women. Their function was to do the gods' labor. In gratitude to Marduk, the gods built Babylon and placed Marduk's temple at its center. Here they confirmed his supremacy by chanting his fifty names. Marduk reigned supreme for centuries, absorbing the functions of rival gods. In the end he was dethroned by Ashur, but the memory of his greatness lingered on. The creation story in the *Enuma Elish* became one of the sources of the book of Genesis; the sovereignty of Marduk set a precedent for Yahweh, the national god of Israel, who became the one and only God of the three West Asian monotheisms.[66]

Polytheism, the belief in many gods, was ubiquitous in the ancient world and formed the religious background of the philosophical and spiritual movements of axial-age India, China, and Greece. It still prevails in traditional cultures in South and East Asia, Africa, and other places. Monotheism, the belief in a single god, first appeared in West Asia during the axial period. Over the last 2,500 years it has spread to every continent, accounting for billions of adherents. But where did the idea that there is just one god come from?

In many polytheistic systems, one deity is recognized as the king (more rarely, the queen) of the gods. In the Vedas, he is Indra, in Greek mythology, Zeus. The top god often ascended the throne after a dynastic struggle, as when Zeus overthrew his father Kronos, who earlier had castrated and deposed his father Ouranos. Subordinate gods were related to the king by birth, marriage, alliances, or opposition. The hierarchies thus created were reflections of the political systems that prevailed among the worshippers of the gods in question.

Within every religion, specific groups of people accepted certain gods and goddesses as tutelary deities of places, cults, or professions. In Greece, each city had its patron god or goddess (Athena for Athens, Poseidon for Corinth, and so forth), each mystery religion had its associated deities (Demeter and Persephone for the Eleusinian mysteries, Dionysus for the Dionysian). These examples show that it was sometimes appropriate for polytheistic worshippers to treat a particular god or goddess as supreme. Occasionally these local preferences transformed an entire religion.

In the eighteenth century BCE, Marduk, the patron deity of the city of Babylon, rose to be head of the local pantheon. When Babylon became the dominant city of the region, Marduk became the supreme Mesopotamian god. Something similar happened in Egypt in the fourteenth century BCE. The pharaoh Amenhotep IV, later known as Akhenaten, abandoned the worship of the sun god Amen-Ra and instituted the short-lived religion of Aten, the divinized disk of the sun, whom Akhenaten and his consort Nefertiti worshipped as the only god. Several centuries later, in northern Iran, the priest Zoroaster had a vision that revealed to him that Ahura Mazda, the Wise Lord, was the sole god worthy of worship. At that time the prevailing religion in Iran was a sacrificial cult closely related to the religion of the Vedas. Zoroaster reformed Iran's sacrificial system, treating the *daevas* (negative counterparts of the Vedic *devas* or gods) as malevolent spirits allied with Angra Mainyu, the Principle of Evil. Zoroaster put himself forward as the prophet of a new religion, showing human beings the path to righteousness. In an early prayer he declared: "I who have set my heart on watching over the soul ... will, while I have power and strength, teach men to seek after Right."[67] In Zoroaster's religion, humans must choose between right and wrong. Their destinies depend on their choices. Each individual will be judged after death, and the fate of creation will be decided at the end of time after an apocalyptic battle.

The three religions discussed above were neither fully polytheistic nor fully monotheistic. Scholars have coined a number of terms to describe such borderline cases. One is "henotheism," the belief in the supremacy of one god without denying the existence of others. Another is "monolatrism," the exclusive worship of one god while acknowledging that others exist. The cult of Marduk could be considered an example of henotheism, while early Zoroastrianism might be called a monolatrism tending toward dualism. The cult of Aten was a state-supported monolatrism that aspired to become monotheistic but was too ephemeral to catch on.

The first sure case of a successful monotheism was the religion of Yahweh, the national god of the kingdoms of Israel and Judah, as instituted by king Josiah of Judah toward the end of the seventh century BCE. Since then, believing Jews have looked on Yahweh as the one and only god but he began his career as one among many. Hebrew scripture makes this clear. The first of the commandments Yahweh gave to Moses was: "You shall have no other gods before me."[68] This presupposes the existence of other gods.

The history of West Asian monotheism is long, and can be told in different ways. Faithful Jews, Christians, and Muslims believe there was from the beginning a single creator God, transcendent of his creation, who was all-wise, all-good, and so forth. The story of God is the sacred narrative of his self-revelation in history, in which the words and deeds of his prophets are of decisive importance. Historians, on the other hand, have to stick to the archeological and documentary evidence, and this makes it clear that Yahweh was originally an Iron Age storm god worshipped by a tribe in the southern Levant. In time Yahweh became the god of the Kingdom of Israel (roughly, present-day northern Israel with parts of the West Bank) and the Kingdom of Judah (roughly, present-day central Israel including Jerusalem). The two kingdoms were overshadowed by the Assyrians, who fought under the banner of Ashur, their patron god. Under constant threat, the kings of Israel and Judah took refuge in *their* patron god, Yahweh. Some in Israel and Judah continued to worship lesser deities. Making the prophet Hosea his mouthpiece, Yahweh railed against them: "But I have been the LORD your God ever since you came out of Egypt [in the days of Moses]. You shall acknowledge no God but me, no Savior except me."[69]

Toward the end of the eighth century BCE, the Assyrians conquered and absorbed the Kingdom of Israel. The kings of Judah could remain on the throne only by paying tribute. In 701 BCE the Assyrian king Sennacherib besieged Jerusalem. The city withstood the attack, but Judah became a vassal state of Assyria and remained so until Josiah ascended the throne as a child in 640. By this time, the Assyrian empire was in decline, and when Josiah came of age he was able to rule without outside interference. This allowed him and the high priest Hilkiah to rid the temple of all vestiges of idolatry and institute the exclusive worship of Yahweh. "Hear, O Israel: The LORD our God, the LORD is one": so runs a famous verse from the Hebrew Bible that came into currency around this time.[70] Josiah's reforms began a theological revolution that would transform Judaism, but his motives were as much political as theological. A kingdom surrounded by hostile neighbors was better off with a single powerful god than a multitude of deities, some of them also worshipped by Assyrians.

The Kingdom of Judah could not long avoid involvement in the politicomilitary rivalries of the region. In 609 BCE an Egyptian army allied with the Assyrians defeated the army of Judah under the command of Josiah, who died in battle. The Egyptians later deposed Josiah's son and established a puppet state in Judah. Worse was to come. In 599 BCE the Babylonian king Nebuchadnezzar laid siege to Jerusalem, which fell two years later. The king pillaged the city and the temple of Yahweh and carried off the booty to Babylon. He then depopulated Judah and made the kingdom his tributary. A decade later, after an abortive Judahite revolt, Nebuchadnezzar returned to Jerusalem, destroyed the city and the temple, and snuffed out the kingdom of Judah. He deported the intellectual elite to Babylon, where they remained for generations. This period, the so-called Babylonian captivity, was one of the low points of Jewish history. It was also the time when the worship of Yahweh became unambiguously monotheistic.

The great prophet of the exile was the poet known as Second Isaiah.[71] Through him, Yahweh spoke to his people. He had cast them into "the furnace of affliction" in order to refine them in fire. They had fallen into sin by worshipping other gods. Their defeat and exile were God's punishment: "she [Jerusalem] has received from the LORD's hand double for all her sins." Now the time of deliverance was near, but the people of Judah had to understand that Yahweh and Yahweh alone was their god: "I am the LORD, and there is no other; apart from me there is no God." This is something radically new. Yahweh is not just the top god of the Levant: he is "the God of all the earth." And his teaching is not for the Jews alone. He will make his chosen ones "a light for the Gentiles [non-Jewish nations], that my salvation may reach to the ends of the earth."[72] This is the God that the Jews took back to Jerusalem when they were allowed to return after Cyrus of Persia defeated the Babylonians in 539 BCE. This is the God that Jesus of Nazareth spoke of five and a half centuries later and that the apostle Paul preached to the Gentiles. This also is the Allah of the Quran, *al-Ilah* or *Allah* being the Arabic word for God. Jews, Christians, and Muslims have different scriptures and different beliefs, but they all agree that the God of Abraham and the other patriarchs, the God of Moses and the other prophets, is the only God there is.

To believing Jews, Christians, and Muslims, this sociopolitical framing of the history of God in axial-age West Asia approaches the question from the wrong standpoint. God, these believers would say, is simply the one and only Lord. The story of the development of the God-idea in history, even if it accounts for some of the archeological and literary data, completely misses the point. God is one. He created the universe and rules over it. If it took some time for the Jews to understand this, that was their fault and not God's. Historians cannot reply to arguments like this because they fall outside the scope of historiography. Theologians are free to argue theological points—though history shows that they are not terribly good at arriving at conclusions that are pleasing to all concerned.

Proponents of monotheism have one good empirical card to play: the global success of the West Asian religions. How could the God of Abraham become the deity of four billion people (more than half the population of the world!) unless he was in fact the one and only Lord, who created the world and everything in it? It is impossible to believe that an Iron Age storm god became the God of such an enormous number of people just because he won the lottery, so to speak. The prophets of the Jews, Christians, and Muslims must really have been on to something. They recognized before the rest of the world that the God of Abraham was the one and only God, whom everyone on earth must worship. The subsequent history of the Abrahamic faiths shows that the West Asian monotheisms were destined to spread across the world. Yahweh may have had humble origins, but he was marked out for greatness from the start.

Few historians would accept this line of argument because it is based on assumptions that are more characteristic of theological than historical demonstration. Still, the success of the monotheistic faiths is striking and invites investigation. One obvious reason for the spread of Christianity and Islam is that, unlike ethnic religions such as Hinduism and Shinto, they are open to all human beings. A corollary of the openness of Christianity and Islam is their proselytism and drive for conversion, which they frequently carry out through coercion and violence. This goes a long way to explain their diffusion, but it does not explain conversion as a result of free choice. Was there something about Judaism, Christianity, and Islam that made them certain to succeed, or was it just good luck? Probably a bit of both. A parallel case is the rise of English from a dialect spoken by a few illiterate West Germanic tribes to the third most commonly spoken language in the world and the de facto international language of science, technology, education, business, and other fields. Few would suggest that the expansion of English was divinely ordained. It has a few features that helped it gain speakers, such as a stripped-down grammar, but its success was due mainly to the imperial expansion of England between the seventeenth and nineteenth centuries. Monotheism similarly has a number of characteristics that make it attractive to converts, but it got where it did with the help of politicomilitary regimes, such as imperial Rome and the Umayyad Caliphate.

The Jews remained true to their covenant with God after their return to Jerusalem, but their faith was repeatedly tried by misfortune, and traces of doubt found their way into the "wisdom literature" of the Bible. In the Book of Job (c. 6th century BCE), God allows the devil to test Job's faith by making him suffer incredible loss and misfortune. In his misery, Job reflects on the prevalence of evil:

> Yet man is born to trouble as surely as sparks fly upward

and cries out against the world's injustice:

> Why do the wicked live on, growing old and increasing in power?...
> They spend their years in prosperity and go down to the grave in peace.

He seeks understanding but the poet declares that the way to wisdom is not through the intellect:

> They search the sources of the rivers and bring hidden things to light.
> But where can wisdom be found? Where does understanding dwell?

The poet's final word is to abandon everything except worship and obedience: "The fear of the Lord—that is wisdom, and to shun evil is understanding."[73]

There seems to be a conflict here between the spirit of inquiry of the axial-age philosophies and the ethical monotheism of the Jews. This comes out more clearly in the Book of Ecclesiastes, written probably toward the end of the third century BCE. Parts of it sound like Epicureanism: "So I commend the enjoyment of life, because there is nothing better for a person under the sun than to eat and drink and be glad." (The King James Bible's translation of this verse is the source of the modern catchphrase for the Epicurean style of life: "eat, drink and be merry.") There also are echoes of the Epicurean attitude toward death:

> For the living know that they will die, but the dead know nothing; they have no further reward, and even their name is forgotten.

But in the end, Ecclesiastes reverts to pure West Asian monotheism:

> Now all has been heard; here is the conclusion of the matter: Fear God and keep his commandments, for this is the duty of all mankind.[74]

Hellenistic *philosophia*—love of wisdom—is banished. There are only two ways of coming close to God: worship and obedience.

* * *

A brief summary will show how the nontheistic religions of the axial age helped prepare the way for godless spirituality. Magic and theistic religions dominated the ancient world, but between 800 and 200 BCE philosophies and religions arose in India, China, and Greece that downplayed the importance of spirits and gods and introduced methods of personal development that are still being practiced by spiritual aspirants today.

None of the axial-age systems were nontheistic in the strict sense of the term. Most of them took the existence of gods and spirits for granted. Some however gave more importance to cosmic principles and laws than to supernatural beings and forces. The sages of the Upanishads viewed *brahman*, the ultimate reality, as greater than the gods. Jains and Buddhists considered *karma*, the impersonal law of action, to be the self-sufficient explanation of the universe. This ruled out a creator God. In China, Confucians and philosophical Daoists turned away from the worship of spirits and gods, trying to align themselves with a greater Way. In Greece, some philosophers theorized that a single substance underlay all the phenomena of the world. Others thought that the universe consisted of uncreated atoms and the void. The gods lived in the spaces between the worlds and took no interest in human life. A few Greek writers suggested that the gods did not exist; others thought that no purpose would be served by speculating about such things.

The three characteristics of modern spirituality—subjectivity or innerness, autonomy, and individual effort—all have roots in the axial age. The sages of the Upanishads visualized the self as an inner being and urged seekers to look within to find the hidden truth. Buddhists rejected the idea of self but carefully examined the components of their apparent subjective being. Classical Greek thinkers developed the idea of the *psyche* or soul, which became the basis of the Western conception of selfhood.

Rejecting or reinterpreting the rituals of established religions, axial-age teachers developed a variety of techniques of self-cultivation. In India, the methods included physical asceticism, breath control, intellectual discrimination, and meditation. Through personal effort, students of the Upanishads and of the Jain and Buddhist sutras tried to achieve liberation from the cycle of birth-and-death. To Confucians, self-cultivation meant study and action aimed at the improvement of society. To Daoists, right action was, paradoxically, nonaction: attuning oneself with the Dao. In Greece, practicing philosophy was a way to achieve virtue and well-being. The classical schools emphasized rational discourse, while the Hellenistic schools developed psychological methods for achieving freedom from pain and from mental and emotional disturbance.

Toward the end of the axial period, the monotheistic religion of the Jews established itself in the Levant. Judaism provided the template for two later monotheisms, Christianity and Islam, that eventually spread throughout the world. For a while, these religions existed alongside earlier religions and philosophies. But by 800 CE, Christianity and Islam had suppressed or destroyed most of their nontheistic rivals.

3 DEFENDING AND DEBATING TRADITION

No matter how often it is pointed out, it remains an astounding fact: most of the religions that fill the world today got their start during a relatively short period some twenty-five or thirty centuries ago. Hinduism, Buddhism and Jainism, Confucianism and Daoism, Zoroastrianism and Judaism—all trace their origins to the first millennium BCE. Since then there have been new revelations—Christianity, Islam, Sikhism, Baha'ism, and many others—but most of them look back to one or more of the earlier teachings. Of course there are small religions untouched by the major faiths, but their influence has rarely extended beyond the tribal or ethnic groups among which they rose. Today the big four—Christianity, Islam, Hinduism, and Buddhism—account for around three-quarters of the world's 7.6 billion people. The only group that is making any headway against the established religions is "the nones"—atheists, agnostics, and undecided—who now make up at least 16 percent of the world's population.

In this chapter I look at the religions of South Asia, East Asia, and the West during the 1,000 years that followed the axial era, that is, from around 200 BCE to 800 CE. (For convenience I call this the late classical period, even though historians of India, China, and the West use this phrase in different ways.) Looking back from the present, the history of the late classical period seems to be characterized by the growth and final triumph of theism. But if we situate ourselves somewhere around 300 CE, we get a different perspective: nontheistic religions and philosophies were still going strong in all three regions. I deal with these nontheistic systems here, taking up the theistic religions of the era in Chapter 4.

During the late classical period, philosophers defended the foundational texts of their schools and engaged in debate with rival thinkers. Most of them viewed themselves as expositors of established truths. Originality was not a selling point. Philosophers of the Vedic schools wrote epigrammatic digests and commentaries on the classic texts. Confucian and Daoist scholars did the same. Buddhist innovators presented their works as teachings of the Buddha that had dropped out of sight for a few hundred years, hidden perhaps in underwater caves till the world was ready for them. Roman philosophers never failed to evoke the memory of their Greek predecessors.

During this era, India, China, and the Greco-Roman world were composed of kingdoms and empires with shifting borders. After 232 BCE the Maurya Empire, which had extended over most of South Asia, was replaced by regional dominions, some small, some practically imperial in extent. In 221 BCE the first Qin emperor united the Chinese heartland. For the next millennium long-lived dynasties such as the Han and Tang were offset by periods when regional factions contended for the imperial throne. After defeating Carthage and Greece in 146 BCE, Republican Rome became the dominant power in the Mediterranean. A century later the Republic gave way to the Empire, which eventually stretched from Spain to Mesopotamia.

These comparatively stable political units favored the continuance of established religions. Indian rulers supported Brahmanism, Buddhism, or Jainism but did not as a rule oppress the members of other faiths. In China, the emperor sometimes patronized and sometimes persecuted a given religion or philosophy. During the Republic and the first four centuries of the Empire, paganism was the state religion of Rome, but between the first century BCE and the second century CE members of the urban elite were attracted to Greek therapeutic philosophies, particularly Stoicism and Epicureanism. From the first century CE, exotic cults from western Asia, such as Mithraism and Christianity, took hold among the Roman populace. Eventually Christianity replaced paganism as the state religion, and Christian emperors expunged the last traces of nontheistic philosophy from the Empire.

Nontheistic philosophies in India

It is written in the *Samkhya Karika* that the ancient sage Kapila transmitted his teachings to Asuri, who transmitted them to Panchashikha, who systematized them. Afterwards they passed in an unbroken line to Ishwara Krishna, who wrote them down in the *Karika*. Ishwara Krishna was active in the fourth or fifth century CE. A couple of centuries later the scholar Gaudapada wrote the most important commentary on the *Karika*. He began by saying that Kapila felt compassion for men and women caught in the web of birth-and-death. He therefore taught Asuri the knowledge of twenty-five principles, which is the means of the removal of suffering. What are these principles? On the one side there is *purusha*, conscious soul, on the other is *prakriti*, unconscious nature. *Prakriti* emanates intelligence, ego-sense, mind, the five organs of knowledge, the five organs of action, the five subtle elements and finally the five gross elements that make up the material world. Count them (the word *samkhya* means counting): it comes to twenty-five. When you know these principles, you know existence. The universe is born when conscious *purusha* becomes associated with unconscious *prakriti*. That's when suffering starts. It ends when *prakriti* withdraws and *purusha* recovers its pure existence. In Sanskrit *purusha* is a masculine noun that means, among other things, "person." *Prakriti* is feminine and implies activity. This opens the way for a beautiful metaphor in the *Karika*: "As a dancer ceases from the dance after having been seen by the audience; so also *prakriti* ceases after having manifested herself to the *purusha*." When *prakriti* stops dancing, *purusha* regains his composure. But actually he never lost it, because he is eternally "free from error, pure and solitary."[1]

The Upanishads and the early Jain and Buddhist sutras contain a lot of philosophical thought but they are not works of philosophy. The systematization of Vedic, Jain, and Buddhist doctrines was the labor of generations of philosophers working between the third century BCE and the ninth century CE. That's 1,200 years of philosophy and hundreds of philosophers. I cannot do justice to the richness of these traditions here. In what follows I will look at the ways that Vedic, Jain, and Buddhist philosophers dealt with the question of God and at the practices they developed for escaping from the cycle of birth-and-death.

To philosophers of the Vedic tradition "orthodoxy" does not mean holding correct views but accepting the authority of the Vedas. According to a relatively recent tradition there are six orthodox Indian schools—Samkhya, Yoga, Vaisheshika, Nyaya, Mimamsa, and Vedanta—and three unorthodox schools—Jainism, Buddhism, and Charvaka (materialism). Historically the situation was not so neat. Many Indian schools that acknowledged the authority of the Vedas didn't make the orthodox list, while Jainism and Buddhism each consist of different schools that are as distinct from one another as Vedanta is from Samkhya. Still, the six plus three classification is useful and I retain it here.

Among the orthodox schools there were varying degrees of orthodoxy. To Mimamsa and Vedanta, the Vedas were inerrant revelation. Vaisheshika and Nyaya were more interested in rational argument than scriptural authority, while Samkhya and Yoga showed their respect for the Vedas by never mentioning them. None of these schools, in their original forms, accepted a creative deity on the West Asian model, although most of them eventually made room for God. The nonorthodox schools, on the other hand, denied the existence of a creator God, though Jainism and Buddhism admitted the existence of supernatural beings. Only Charvaka or materialism was unreservedly atheistic.

The teachings of the schools were formalized in collections of *sutras* or aphorisms that were composed between approximately 400 BCE and 400 CE. (The dating of ancient Indian texts is terribly imprecise and efforts to narrow down the range lead to interminable and pointless debates.) Aphorisms facilitated oral transmission: it's easier to memorize four than four hundred words. But the concision of the sutras meant that commentaries and commentaries on commentaries had to be written to make the meaning clear. This left a lot of room for interpretation, leading to the formation of subschools and sub-subschools, all of which claimed to possess the truth.

Each school states a problem and proposes a solution. The problem is always more or less the same: imperfection and suffering. The solution is release from suffering by liberation. The *Samkhya Karika* states the problem and solution in very few words: "Because of the torment of the threefold suffering" (personal, external, and cosmic) there arises the desire "to know the means of counteracting it." Knowledge comes to a *purusha* through analysis of the twenty-five principles. In the end the *purusha* looks on *prakriti* like a passive spectator watching a performance. The activity of *prakriti* ceases and, when the body falls away, the *purusha* "attains isolation (*kaivalya*) which is both certain and final."[2] This final liberation brings release from suffering.

There are several subschools of Samkhya, some of which gave a place to Ishwara, the Lord or God.[3] I concentrate here on the atheistic form of Samkhya as presented by the authors of the *Samkhya Karika* and *Samkhya Sutra*. Atheistic Samkhya has no need of God because the principles of nature are uncreated. *Purusha*, conscious soul, is not God. There are an infinite number of *purushas*: you, me, everybody else. All of us are involved with *prakriti* or unconscious nature. This means that we are, strictly speaking, not conscious. What we take to be consciousness is ego-sense, the second of the principles of nature. When we know the principles we return to pure consciousness. Each of us will be *kevala*, alone and free.

The author of *Samkhya Sutra*, responding to theistic philosophers, wrote that the existence of Ishwara or God is "not proved." The passages in Vedic scripture that speak about Ishwara are just "glorifications of the liberated soul"—that is, descriptions of *purushas* that have attained liberation—or else "homages to the recognized"—that is, respectful evocations of the gods that almost everyone believed in. God is not needed to get karma or action going, because karma is self-existent. He is not needed to distribute karmic rewards and punishments, because the process works automatically. If God was going to create, he would have to desire something, in which case he would not be divine. Or else he would be perverse, causing people to suffer gratuitously. In the end, there is no reason to believe in God's existence "because there is no evidence of it." The manifest world is the product of *prakriti* or nature, not Ishwara or God.[4]

The philosophy of Yoga accepts the twenty-five principles of Samkhya but does not have much to say about them. It gives special attention to *citta* or thought, which is a combination of the three mental principles of intellect, ego-sense, and mind. *Citta* is unconscious and its incessant turnings are a cause of suffering. According to the *Yoga Sutra* of Patanjali, Yoga is "the cessation of the turning of thought." Once thought has been stilled, "the spirit stands in its true identity as the observer of the world."⁵ The *Sutra* sketches an eightfold path leading from bondage to freedom. First, it proposes five moral principles and five helpful observances. Then it recommends two physical aids: good posture and breath control. Finally it speaks of four sorts of mental control: withdrawal of the senses from their objects, concentration, meditation, and pure contemplation. These eight limbs of yoga are now familiar to millions who practice physical yoga, though only two, posture and breath control, have much to do with what goes on in the studio after the students roll out their mats. Historically, the eight limbs go back to the axial period, when teachers of various traditions were learning from one another. The five moral principles of Yoga—nonviolence, truthfulness, nonstealing, celibacy, and the conquest of greed—are identical to the fivefold vow of the Jains and very close to the five moral precepts of Buddhism.

One of the *Yoga Sutra*'s helpful observances is "dedication to the Lord of Yoga." The *Sutra* explains that this practice helps bring about cessation of thought, and continues: "The Lord of Yoga is a distinct form of spirit [*purusha*] unaffected by the forces of corruption." In other words the Lord is a *purusha* who has never been bound by *prakriti* and who therefore can serve as a model to other *purushas*, like you and me, who pass our lives caught in the coils of physical and mental nature. But this Lord is not a God who creates and directs the universe. The author of the *Sutra* was uninterested in speculations about God, creation, and so forth. His aim was to help humans achieve freedom, which is a reversal of the movement of *prakriti*, allowing consciousness to rest in "a state of true identity."⁶

Samkhya and Yoga are sister systems, Samkhya providing the theory and Yoga the practical methods. Vaisheshika and Nyaya have a similar relationship: Vaisheshika presents a theory of being, Nyaya a method of knowledge. The universe of Vaisheshika is naturalistic. There are nine different substances: earth, water, fire, and air (these are the four types of atoms) along with ether, time, space, self, and mind. All the objects in the world are compounds of these nine substances. The process of combination is largely mechanical. There is no need for God, who is never mentioned in the *Vaisheshika Sutra*, but Destiny has a role to play.⁷ Nyaya is notable for its system of formal logic. It makes use of a syllogism similar to the one developed by Aristotle except that the Nyaya syllogism has five instead of three members.

Nyaya and Vaisheshika eventually merged into a single school that was openly theistic. One fourth-century Vaisheshika text says that the Supreme Lord is behind the combination of atoms. A medieval commentator went further: "scriptural authority and inferential reasoning" prove the existence of God. The inferential reasoning goes like this: "The four great elementary substances are preceded by someone having a knowledge of them, because they are effects,—anything that is an effect is preceded by one having a cognition of it, as, for instance, the jar (which is always preceded by the potter)."⁸ This of course is a version of the argument from design, although it only affirms the existence of a divine assembler, not a divine creator. Nyaya–Vaisheshika became the theistic school *par excellence* and therefore the target of nontheistic thinkers of the Jain, Buddhist, Mimamsa, and Charvaka schools.

One of the main differences between the various Indian philosophies is the number of "valid means of knowledge" (*pramanas*) that they accept. Classical Vaisheshika accepts only two: perception and inference. Nyaya adds two more, comparison and scriptural authority. The last two schools—Mimamsa and Vedanta—also rely on authority but only one of them uses scripture to prove the existence of God. Mimamsa gives so much weight to the words of the Vedas that God becomes superfluous.

Exponents of Mimamsa take seriously the dogma that the Vedas have no author. Both the words of the Vedas and the world to which they refer have always existed. Since nobody was there before the Vedas and the world, it cannot be said that God composed the Vedas or created the universe. The gods mentioned in the Vedas—Indra, Agni, and so forth—are real only because the words that name them are real. What is important is not the gods but the Vedic rituals, which have to be performed in just the right way if the world is to continue to exist.

Early Mimamsa philosophers had little interest in the question of God. Later thinkers, who had to debate with Nyaya and Vedanta rivals, developed various arguments to disprove God's existence. According to Kumarila Bhatta, if you believe that the world was created by God, you have to assume that God desired to create. But if, like most people, you believe that God is "without a material body," how can you imagine that he has "any desire towards creation?" If, on the other hand, you assume that God has a body, "assuredly this body could not have been created by Himself." If it was, you would have to "postulate another creator" for that body, and so forth *ad infinitum*.[9] These are the sort of arguments modern atheists put forward to disprove the existence of God, though they hardly would be happy to find themselves slotted with a thinker who believed that the Vedas were eternal and without author.

Vedanta, like Mimamsa, attaches great importance to scripture, but the texts it favors are not the Vedas but the Upanishads, which teach the knowledge of *brahman*. Unlike Mimamsa, Vedanta makes room for Ishwara as the creator and governor of the universe, but the various subschools of Vedanta differ over Ishwara's nature. The *dvaita* or dualistic subschool is just as theistic as Christianity. The *advaita* or nondualistic subschool sees Ishwara as the creator of an illusory universe and itself perhaps unreal. According to the eighth-century Advaita teacher Shankara, Ishwara is *brahman* seen through the lens of *maya* or cosmic illusion. *Brahman* itself is featureless or, to use the technical term, *nirguna* ("without qualities"). It becomes *saguna*, possessing qualities such as form and color, when acted upon by *maya*, the power of illusion. This explains why certain passages of the Upanishads speak of Brahman as possessing some pretty strange features, such as a golden beard! According to Shankara, such qualities are useful to people who seek *brahman* through *upasana* or worship, although in fact *brahman* is featureless.[10]

In Advaita the right way of finding *brahman* is by means of knowledge of the self. The student begins by hearing, thinking about, and meditating on the central utterances of Upanishads, such as "You are That, Svetaketu." The teacher then guides him (not her, women could not become students) into the deeper meaning of the texts. Well, who *are* you, the teacher might ask. If the student replies "I am a brahman's son belonging to such and such a family," and so forth, the teacher points out his error: "you have identified the *atman*, which is free from caste, family and purifying ceremonies, with the body." Answering the student's questions, quoting copiously from the Upanishads, the teacher gradually leads him to the truth: "you, *atman*, are the highest *atman* [which is the same as the universal *brahman*] and free from all the attributes of transmigratory existence [that is, the rounds of birth-and-death]."[11] In the end, fully absorbed in *atman/brahman*, the student becomes a *jivan-mukta*, one who is liberated while still alive.

During the late classical period defenders of the Jain tradition developed antitheistic arguments to refute the theism of Nyaya and Vedanta. Some Vedanta thinkers said that creation is the motiveless "sport" of the Lord. The Jains did not buy this. "If you say that he created to no purpose, because it was his nature to do so, then God is pointless," the ninth-century philosopher Jinasena wrote. "If he created in some kind of sport, it was the sport of a foolish child, leading to trouble." If God created the world out of something, who made that something? And if the something arose by itself, then the universe could just as well have created itself. Then there is the problem of evil: "God commits great sin in slaying the children whom he himself created." And if he kills in order "to destroy evil beings, why did he create such beings in the first place?" Overall, Jinasena concluded, "The doctrine that the world was created by God makes no sense at all."[12]

One of the most remarkable features of Jain philosophy is its "doctrine of perspectives," which maintains that anything can be understood from different points of view, none of which is final. As the fifth-century thinker Siddhasena Divakara explained: "every *naya* [perspective] in its own sphere is right, but if all of them arrogate to themselves the whole truth and disregard the views of rival *nayas* then they do not attain the status of a right view."[13] A famous illustration of this is the story of the blind men and the elephant. One of the men, touching the animal's legs, declared that the elephant was like a pillar. Another, holding onto the tail, said it was like a rope. A third, stroking an ear, insisted it was like a fan. All of them were right but none was completely right. Jain logicians formalized a "doctrine of maybe," according to which every philosophical proposition must be stated conditionally: In a certain way, a thing is; in a certain way, the same thing is not; in a certain way, it both is and is not; and so forth.

To the Jains, reality is irreducibly complex. Everything in the world has an infinite number of aspects. Any judgment we make about any subject deals only with a certain aspect from a certain point of view. This approach helped Jain thinkers sidestep some of the acerbity of theological disputation. But they kept a wildcard for themselves: The statements of Mahavira and other liberated beings were uttered from the state of omniscience, and were therefore not subject to limitation. It is as if a sighted person came upon the quarreling blind men and told them exactly what was there. Despite this dogmatism, Jain dialectical texts are comparatively balanced and nonaggressive.

Jainism prescribes physical austerities such as fasting and methods of meditation that are broadly similar to those cultivated by followers of Vedanta, Yoga, and Buddhism. "After renouncing all attachments and aversions, and adopting a sense of equanimity in all objects," a medieval Jain manual declares, "one should practice, many times, periodic concentration (*samayika*), the principal means to realize the true nature of the Self."[14] The same manual recommends worship of the Tirthankaras as models of perfection, but Jain philosophers never abandoned the belief that the universe is eternal and uncreated and that therefore there is no creative deity.

The late classical period saw an enormous development of Buddhist philosophy. Schools of different traditions offered a wide array of interpretations of the Buddha's teachings. The scriptures written to present these interpretations were ascribed to the Buddha or to semi-divine beings known as *bodhisattvas*. Some of them became the basis of a new approach to Buddhism that its proponents called Mahayana or the Great Vehicle.

Mahayana texts cover a huge amount of ground and take radically different approaches to the question of God and other supernatural beings. Some Mahayana thinkers argued against the God-idea, others composed works in which the Buddha and bodhisattvas were looked upon as deities. One of the most popular of all Buddhist texts is the *Buddhacharita* or *Acts of the Buddha*, which was written by the Indian poet-philosopher Ashvaghosa shortly after 100 CE, which is around the time that Mahayana was taking form. The *Buddhacharita* is an important source of legends about the Buddha's life, but it also contains discussions about "the many kinds of contradiction that arise from the conception of Isvara [the Lord] as the Creator." Some of its arguments were based on the doctrine of karma, for instance: "If a Creator produced the world, there would be no ordered process of activity [karma] in it, and men would not revolve in the cycle of existence" but remain forever in whatever state they were born to. For Indians of the period, the doctrine of karma was so fundamental that anything that seemed to contradict it was necessarily false. Other arguments picked holes in the concept of creation, for example: "If the Creator has no dominion over himself, what power can he have to create the world?" And "if his creation is not actuated by any intention, his actions are causeless like a child's."[15] These arguments are similar to those put forward by contemporary Jain and Mimamsa thinkers, suggesting that they were drawn from a common fund of examples. More original is the treatment of the question of God by the philosopher Nagarjuna, who was born in southern India around the time that Ashvaghosa was active in the north.

Nagarjuna was drawn to some comparatively recent Sanskrit texts known as the Perfection of Wisdom sutras, which are noted especially for developing the idea of Emptiness. A classic statement of this doctrine is found in the *Sutra on the Heart of the Perfection of Wisdom*. In this text the bodhisattva Avalokita is depicted as looking down on the five constituents of existence and seeing that they all are empty. He then declares: "form [i.e., all that is] is emptiness and the very emptiness is form; emptiness does not differ from form, nor does form differ from emptiness."[16] Modern readers, unused to Buddhist modes of expression, are likely to find such statements unspeakably profound or else meaningless gibberish. The Dalai Lama, in a passage intended to clear up the muddle, explains that to understand why things are "empty of inherent existence because dependently arisen," it is necessary to understand the process of cause and effect, the relationship of all things to their parts, and the conceptual and linguistic bases of the phenomenal world. He then goes on to relate all this to the idea of God: "When the Buddha says, 'Due to the existence of this, that arises,' he indicates that the phenomena of cyclic existence arise not through the force of supervision by a permanent deity but due to specific conditions." In other words, specific karmic causes give rise to specific karmic effects. God has nothing to do with it.[17]

The Dalai Lama is the head of a Tibetan Buddhist school that is linked philosophically with the Middle Way tradition of Mahayana, which was set in motion by Nagarjuna. Toward the end of his masterwork, *The Fundamental Wisdom of the Middle Way*, Nagarjuna affirms that dependent arising and emptiness are equivalent. He adds that the term "emptiness," which is a "dependent designation," "is itself the middle way."[18] He did not, in this text, examine the idea of God, but in another work attributed to him, *The Twelve Gate Treatise*, the author showed how the Middle Way approach made the God-idea untenable. A crucial passage affirms that it is impossible to justify "that suffering is made by itself" or "by another, by both or from no cause at all." Such "four-sided" arguments are characteristic of Middle Way thinking, but they have to be fleshed out. Taking up the four sides one by one, the author affirmed that if suffering was caused by itself, there could be no liberation, which is unthinkable. If it was caused by another, namely Ishwara or God, all sorts of illogicalities would follow: "If God is self-existent, He should need nothing" and creation would be pointless. If God created everything, then "who created Him?" If God determined everything, why are all things changing in obedience to *karma*? This leads to the problem of evil: "if God is the maker [of all things], there should be no sinfulness and blessedness"—but in fact there is. This shows that "all things are not made by God." But the knockdown argument (from the Indian point of view) is this: "if God were the maker, good, evil, suffering and happiness would come without being made [by men]." This would undo the principle that humans are rewarded for their good and punished for their evil deeds, which is inconceivable. Therefore, suffering is not caused by God, just as it is not caused by itself. Obviously, therefore, it cannot be caused by both. Finally, it is evident that "nothing is produced from no cause." All this goes to show that suffering is, fundamentally, empty.[19]

Some Buddhist philosophers felt that the Middle Way idea of Emptiness left a number of questions unanswered. If the objects of experience are empty of self-nature, what are these things we touch and see? And if conscious mind is empty of essence, who or what is it that seeks liberation? There was much debate over such questions between the second and fourth centuries, leading to the development of a new school of Mahayana Buddhism called Yogachara ("practice of yoga"), which is concerned primarily with the relationships between consciousness, the objects of experience, and ultimate reality. Briefly, Yogachara holds that the objects of the world do not exist in themselves but are just representations of consciousness. What does exist is consciousness itself and the ineffable "suchness" of reality, which sometimes is visualized as the "dharma-body" of the Buddha. Eventually the dharma-body became part of a Buddhist trinity: the created-body of the historical Buddha, the enjoyment-body that one sees in vision, and the transcendental dharma-body. These ideas became very important in subsequent Buddhist philosophy, especially in East Asia. They also were taken up by the devotional cults I discuss in the next chapter. But as originally formulated by Yogachara thinkers, the ideas of the dharma-body and the three bodies of the Buddha were not expressly theistic.

The leading philosophers of Yogachara were the half-brothers Vasubandhu and Asanga, who were born in what is now northern Pakistan during the fourth century. In his *Treasury of Abhidharma*, Vasubandhu examined the problem of God. The world is born from actions (karma), not God, he insisted. Responding to theists who said that God created the universe, he showed the logical inconsistencies in the ideas of creation and causality and pointed out the moral repulsiveness of a God who creates "for his own satisfaction" creatures who "are victims of all the sufferings of existence, including the torments of hell."[20] In the *Thirty Verses*, a later work, Vasubandhu did not speak explicitly of God, but he brought out the idea of the dharma-body in the context of yoga practice: "When cognition no longer apprehends an object," he wrote, "it stands firmly in consciousness-only." There can be no grasping when "there is nothing to grasp." When consciousness is freed from the tendency "to treat object and subject as distinct and real entities" it becomes identical with "the blissful body of emancipation, the Dharma body of the great Sage [the Buddha]."[21]

A central element of Yogachara thought and practice is the theory of the eight consciousnesses. Earlier Buddhist philosophy accepted six consciousnesses—the five sorts of sense-awareness and the mind. Yogachara added two more—deluded awareness and storehouse consciousness. The latter is—to put it in modern terms—a sort of unconscious mind. Its purpose is to explain the apparent stability of the material world and human personality in the face of Buddha's insistence that all things are impermanent and without self. Why does the physical world look pretty much the same when we return from the world of dreams? Why, after waking, do we think and feel pretty much the same as we did the night before? Theistic systems have no trouble with such questions: God creates and directs the world, and that's that. Yogachara's storehouse consciousness was a nontheistic way of dealing with them: the impressions of past experiences, good and bad, remain in an individual's storehouse consciousness in the form of seeds that are carried from birth to birth. And the storehouse consciousnesses of people in general give rise to a receptacle world—roughly, the physical universe—with its stable objects. To the philosophers of Yogachara all this was important not as a philosophical doctrine but as a basis for yogic practice. When the "seeds of defilement" in the storehouse consciousness are destroyed by means of Yogachara, the practitioner achieves nirvana.[22]

The Middle Way and Yogachara schools have remained at the forefront of Mahayana thought for the last 1,500 years, first in India and later in China, Tibet, Japan, and other places. Philosophers of both schools included arguments against God in their works. The Middle Way thinker Shantideva, who was born in western India during the eighth century, discussed the absurdities of Nyaya's creator God in his celebrated *Way of the Bodhisattva*. "If you argue that the cause has no beginning," Shantideva wrote, "how could there be a beginning to its effect?" Further, if God creates "out of the desire to create," then he is "subject to desire," and therefore undivine; yet if he "creates without desiring to create," he is "subject to something other than himself." Such a secondary creator would not be God.[23]

Shantideva's younger contemporary Shantarakshita, who was influenced by the Middle Way, Yogachara, and Logic schools, devoted a full chapter of his *Compendium on Reality* to a refutation of the Nyaya position. Most of his arguments are highly technical, but some rely on simple common sense, for example: "God cannot be the cause of born things, because he is himself devoid of birth, like the [imaginary] sky-lotus." If unborn things could create born things, then "all things would come into existence simultaneously," which is absurd.[24]

The aim of Buddhist practice is to free oneself from suffering by escaping from the rounds of birth-and-death. Buddhist teachers called this liberation *nirvana*, which they defined in different ways. Over the centuries, various schools developed different methods to achieve nirvana and to attain intermediate states, such as mental tranquility, that make it possible. Some of these methods make use of psychophysical means, such as observing the breath and controlling the mind. Others rely on active meditation: reflecting on points of doctrine or visualizing the forms of bodhisattvas. To accommodate these and other methods, Mahayana thinkers formulated the doctrine of "skillful means," which states that any technique is acceptable as long as it helps us free ourselves from suffering and eventually achieve nirvana.

The nontheistic philosophies I discussed above differ from modern European atheism in that they all accept the existence of supernatural beings and powers. Samkhya, in common with the other Vedic schools, took the existence of minor gods for granted. Yoga accepted Ishwara as a special *purusha* or soul, and made room for supernatural powers or *siddhis* that any comic-book superhero would envy. Mimamsa, which rejected Ishwara, insisted that the Vedas were eternal and unauthored. Jain thinkers rejected the creator God but affirmed the existence of superhuman Tirthankaras and Siddhas. Mahayana thinkers used the ideas of Emptiness or Consciousness-Only to undermine the reality of self and God but also took refuge in celestial buddhas and bodhisattvas, who in a way replaced the gods of the Vedic tradition. The only Indian school that was fully naturalistic was Charvaka, which anticipated many of the features of European atheism a millennium before Denis Diderot and Arthur Schopenhauer were born.

The beliefs of the Charvakas were set forth in the *Barhaspatya Sutras*, which were composed just before or just after the start of the common era. Suffering a fate common to works declared heretical, the *Barhaspatya Sutras* disappeared centuries ago and are known to us only in the form of quotations and summaries in later works. From these we learn that the Charvakas believed that there are no gods, no soul, no fate, no law of karma, no punishment or reward for bad or good actions, no rebirth, and no liberation from rebirth. The only reality is the physical universe inclusive of physical bodies. Consciousness arises from the body. The purpose of life is enjoyment. Heaven is physical delight and hell is physical pain. The Vedas are fraudulent. Sacrificial rituals are just a way to provide indolent priests with a livelihood. With assertions like these, Charvaka philosophers stepped on the toes of the proponents of every other Indian system.

Charvaka is unique among Indian philosophies for accepting only one valid means of knowledge: sense perception. It rejected even inference based on perception on the grounds that things perceived are always particulars, while inference treats them as universals. (If I see smoke and infer that there is fire, I am assuming that the smoke I see is like previous instances of smoke caused by fire, but this assumption is not valid.) A philosopher named Jayarasi, who was active toward the beginning of the ninth century, denied even the possibility of reliable perception. In his *Lion of the Dissolution of All Categories*, he attacked the very idea of "valid means of knowledge." Human knowledge, he argued, depends on categories that we ourselves create. If we try to establish the truth of our categories, we have to create a further set of categories, and so on *ad infinitum*. There is thus no absolute knowledge. Jayarasi did not call himself a follower of Charvaka but he shared many of the beliefs of those who did, rejecting the idea of karmic rewards and punishments, the afterlife, the supernatural, and so forth. But he was not so much a materialist as a skeptic, like Sextus Empiricus in the ancient world and Jacques Derrida in the modern.

Indian philosophy reached a pinnacle of brilliance between the sixth and ninth centuries, with philosophers of the Vedic, Jain, Buddhist, and Charvaka systems perfecting their ideas and criticizing those of others. Among the Vedic schools, only Nyaya and Vedanta fully backed the idea of a creator-God (Ishwara), and the dominant subschool of Vedanta looked on Ishwara merely as a prop for devotional practices. Many of the greatest thinkers of the era—Kumarila, Jinasena, Shantideva, Shantarakshita, and others that I had no space for—refuted the God-idea. Their arguments constitute the largest corpus of antitheistic reasoning in any philosophical culture before the European Enlightenment.

The three teachings in China

The Warring States period ended in 221 BCE when the King of Qin conquered the last of his six rivals. For the first time in its history, all China was united. At his court the new emperor was surrounded by flatterers, who assured him that his dynasty would last 10,000 generations. One day in 213 BCE the Confucian scholar Chunyu Yue stood before the emperor and spoke: "Your servant has heard that the fact that the Yin and Zhou reigned for more than 1,000 years was because they enfeoffed their sons and younger brothers and successful officials to provide branches and supports for themselves." Despite this precedent, the emperor refused to delegate responsibility. If disaster befell, "your subjects will have no means of support." The emperor passed Chunyu Yue's comments on to his chief minister Li Si, who answered caustically: "An achievement which will last for 10,000 generations is not something which a foolish Confucian would understand." The Qin emperor had "unified and taken possession of all under Heaven." Peace and order prevailed. Yet Confucians dared question his orders in accordance with their readings of the classics! This put the empire in danger. Li Si therefore recommended that all copies of the classics should be burned. People who continued to cite them should "be wiped out together with their clans." The emperor approved Li Si's proposals and had them carried out. Modern scholars debate what exactly took place during the subsequent "burning of books and burying of scholars." There is no doubt however that the emperor restricted access to ancient poetry and annals, together with the classics of the "hundred schools," which included Confucianism and Daoism. The Qin emperor died three years later while searching for the elixir of immortality. His son was too weak to stand up to rebel warlords, who battled for control of the empire. The winner, Lui Bang, established the Han dynasty in 206 BCE.[25]

At the beginning of the Han dynasty Confucianism was just one among many schools of thought, but around 140 BCE a scholar named Dong Zhongshu prevailed upon Emperor Wu of Han to make it the state religion. This was a remarkable turnabout after the traumatic events of 213 BCE. By this time Confucianism had absorbed many elements of magic and folk religion. Rationalist philosophers such as Yang Xiong (53 BCE–18 CE) and Wang Chong (27 CE–c. 100 CE) set themselves against this growth of supernaturalism. Asked "If there are no immortals in the world, why do people talk about them?" Yang Xiong replied: "Isn't all this talk hubbub? Because it is hubbub, it can make what is nonexistent seem to exist." Wang Chong criticized belief in the paranormal in the manner of a modern skeptical inquirer. Against the idea that people become *guei* (mischievous ghosts or demons) after they die, he wrote: "Man can live because of his vital forces. At death his vital forces are extinct" and the "body decays and becomes ashes and dust. What is there to become a spiritual being?"[26]

Daoism too came under the spell of the supernatural around this time. The Huang-Lao cult, a combination of philosophical Daoism and Yellow Emperor worship, rose to prominence during the second century BCE. One of the few significant Daoist works produced during this period was *The Masters of Huainan*, an anthology of writings by different scholars. Parts of it are mystical, parts rationalistic. One writer, after explaining that "heaven, earth, infinite space and infinite time are the body of one person," continues: "he who understands his nature will not be threatened by Heaven and Earth, and he who comprehends evidences will not be fooled by strange phenomena."[27]

Philosophical Daoism reemerged in the third century CE in the form of the Xuanxue or Neo-Daoist school. The most important commentaries on the *Daodejing* and *Zhuangzi* were written at this time. In his commentary on the *Zhuangzi*, the philosopher Guo Xiang linked the Daoist concept of the sage with the idea of having no mind of one's own: "'This' and 'that' oppose each other but the sage is in accord with both of them. Therefore he who has no deliberate mind of his own is silently harmonized with things and is never opposed to the world." As a result the sage "is contented wherever he goes" and "at ease wherever he may be. Even life and death cannot affect him. How much less can flood or fire?"[28] These lines are astonishingly similar to a well-known passage in the Samkhya-yoga chapter of the *Bhagavad Gita*.

Buddhism came to China during the first century CE but it did not become prominent for a century or more. Around 200 a scholar known as Mouzi wrote that the Indian religion was not well regarded at that time. Most Chinese people believed that rebirth was improbable and complained that Buddhist monastic practices stood in the way of the fulfillment of family duties. In spite of this, Mouzi became a convert and used the Daoist terminology he was familiar with to explain Buddhist ideas (he called Buddha dharma *Fo Dao* or Buddha Way, and compared Nirvana to *wu wei*). Translators of Buddhist sutras followed the same practice.

This made it easier for the Chinese people to adopt Buddhist ideas but it gave Chinese Buddhism a Daoist coloration. Buddhists made room for Daoist deities in their temples. Daoists did the same for bodhisattvas like Avalokiteshvara who, under the name Guanyin (and after gender reassignment), became a popular deity throughout East Asia. At the same time, Buddhists and Neo-Daoists learned to accept the obligations of Confucianism. As a result of these adjustments the followers of the *san jiao* or "three teachings" were able to live together in comparative harmony.

The teachings of Nagarjuna and other Middle Way philosophers reached China at the end of the fourth century through the efforts of the monk Kumarajiva. Leaving his native Kucha (in what is now Xinjiang, western China), Kumarajiva traveled to Kashmir, his father's homeland, where he mastered the scriptures of different schools. Before his death in 414, he translated dozens of Sanskrit texts into Chinese, the most notable being the *Diamond Sutra* and *Lotus Sutra* and Nagarjuna's *Fundamental Wisdom* and *Twelve Gate Treatise*. Kumarajiva's Chinese disciple Sengzhao was influenced by Daoism and used the *Daodejing*'s idea of nonbeing (*wu*) when explaining the Emptiness of Middle Way Buddhism: "The Supreme Vacuity which neither comes into [nor goes out of] existence is probably the subtle principle in the reflection of the mysterious mirror of *prajña* (wisdom) and the source of all existence." This led him to the *Zhuangzi*'s idea of the sage, who is able to "harmonize his spirit with the realm of neither existence nor nonexistence" and penetrate "the infinite with his wonderful mind." Sengzhao went on to relate this to the Confucian idea of *li* or principle: "Therefore the sage exercises his true mind and is in accord with principle (*li*), and there is no obstruction which he cannot pass through."[29] One could hardly ask for a better example of the harmony of the three teachings.

By 618, when the Tang dynasty began, there was a whole cornucopia of Buddhist schools in China. Satisfied with none of them, the young scholar Xuanzang decided to go back to the source. In 629 he departed for India and seventeen years later returned to China with a cartload of sutras, most of them of the Yogachara or Consciousness-Only school. Xuanzang set up a translation bureau, and he and his colleagues rendered hundreds of Sanskrit texts into Chinese. Many of the originals have since turned to dust while the translations survived. Partial to the writings of Vasubandhu, Xuanzang wrote a commentary on the Indian philosopher's *Thirty Verses* in which he defended the Consciousness-Only doctrine. Minutely analyzing the eight consciousnesses but denying the reality of the self, Xuanzang declared (in excruciatingly metaphysical language) that all things are nothing but consciousness and that this knowledge is the key to liberation. Xuanzang's work helped establish Yogachara as one of the leading Buddhist schools in China between the seventh and ninth centuries. Later it declined, but during the nineteenth and twentieth centuries, Chinese scholars used Xuanzang's version of Yogachara as a model for an indigenous form of philosophical idealism.

The Middle Way and Yogachara schools never lost their Indian branding during the millennium and more of their presence in China. But during the sixth and seventh centuries three Buddhist schools arose that had a distinctively Chinese stamp. Two of them, Tiantai and Huayan, synthesized the Buddhist teachings then current, giving special importance to the *Lotus Sutra* and *Flower Garland Sutra* respectively. The third put less stress on written scriptures and more on individual effort. This was Chan (better known by its Japanese pronunciation: Zen), one of the most practice-oriented and least theistic of all Buddhist schools.

The word *chan* comes from the Sanskrit *dhyana*, which means meditation or meditative state. According to tradition, the sage Bodhidharma brought the techniques of *dhyana* from India or Central Asia during the fifth or sixth century. More a figure of legend than of history, Bodhidharma is depicted as an irascible sage who used extraordinary methods to discover and transmit the truths of Buddhism. It is said that after reaching northern China, he sat in a cave for nine long years silently staring at a wall. Drawn by his intensity, a young monk stood in the snow hoping Bodhidharma would instruct him. Bodhidharma told him he was wasting his time. The monk then cut off his own left arm and placed it respectfully before the master. Touched by this demonstration of eagerness and sincerity, Bodhidharma took the monk as his disciple, giving him the name Huike.

A chronicle relates that after meeting Huike, Bodhidharma took the "four-roll *Lanka Sutra*," handed it to the young man, and said: "When I examine the land of China, it is clear that there is only this sutra." This stresses the textual foundations of Chan. Another story has it that the essence of the Buddha's dharma came to Bodhidharma through "a special transmission outside the teachings."[30] Each of these accounts may contain a bit of truth. The *Lankavatara Sutra*, a fourth-century Indian text, presents many of the ideas that became central to Chan. On the other hand, the school's greatest masters were celebrated more for nonverbal abilities than scriptural prowess.

An early Chan manual, The *Treatise on the Two Entrances and Four Practices*, says that an aspirant who wishes to become "enlightened to the Truth on the basis of the teaching" must understand that all sentient beings possess "one and the same True Nature." Unenlightened people fail to see this because their True Nature has been "covered up and made imperceptible by false sense impressions." Once they learn to abide in silent contemplation, identified with the True Nature within them, they will achieve a state that is "without discrimination, serene and inactive."[31]

The "True Nature" or "Buddha-nature" (Chinese: *Foxing*, Sanskrit: *Buddhadhatu*) is the inherent potentiality of all sentient beings to achieve Buddhahood. This idea became important in many East Asian Buddhist schools, notably Chan. Philosophically, it is related to the storehouse consciousness of the Yogacharas and to the "Buddha-in-embryo" of the *Lankavatara Sutra*.[32] These concepts are ways of accounting for the apparent individual who undergoes birth-and-death without bringing in the unBuddhist idea of a permanent self. In practical terms, the idea of Buddha-nature made it possible for Chan masters to insist that the goal of Buddhist practice was not the attainment of an impossibly remote superhuman state but the realization of what we already are.

Bodhidharma and Huike are regarded as the first two patriarchs of the Chan tradition, but it is not till we get to the fifth patriarch, Hongren (601–674), that we are firmly in the realm of documented history. Hongren established a training center on a mountain near Huangmei, where he gave instructions in meditation. Decades after his death, his followers compiled a treatise that set out his methods. One was to observe and neutralize the random thoughts that keep us from perceiving our true nature. "Make your body and mind pure and peaceful, without any discriminative thinking at all," one passage begins. "Sit properly with the body erect. Regulate the breath and concentrate the mind so it is not within you, not outside of you, and not in any intermediate location. Do this carefully and naturally." Once the mind becomes tranquil, "you can see how it is always moving, like flowing water or a glittering mirage." Eventually, all mental fluctuation will "dissolve into peaceful stability."[33] This method is remarkably similar to some of the techniques of the *Yoga Sutra*, which Hongren presumably had no direct knowledge of.

Hongren had many students, the most prominent of whom were Shenxiu and Huineng. These two came to be looked upon as the founders of two different schools of Chan: "Gradualist" and "Sudden." Shenxiu taught that aspirants should practice contemplation at every moment and while engaged in every action, while Huineng insisted that enlightenment comes suddenly when one realizes that one is not different from the Buddha-nature. Huineng's teaching of sudden enlightenment is memorably expressed in the *Platform Sutra*, a text complied by his followers. "Good friends!" Huineng cried out during a sermon:

> You already possess the prajna wisdom of enlightenment! But because your minds are deluded, you can't understand by yourselves. You need to find a truly good friend to show you the way to see your nature. Good friends, buddha nature isn't different for the ignorant and the wise. It's just that people are deluded or awake.

Linking this to his personal experience, Huineng explained that when he was with Hongren, "as soon as I heard his words, I experienced a great realization, and I saw the original nature of reality directly. Therefore, I am passing on this teaching to later generations so that those who study the Way will realize enlightenment directly and so that those who contemplate the mind will realize their original nature directly."[34] The sudden school came to dominate Chan teaching, and it was Huineng and not Shenxiu who was recognized by most as the sixth and last patriarch of Chan.

Chan achieved wide acceptance during the eighth and ninth centuries. The masters of this period developed a style of teaching that owed much to classical Daoism in thought as well as practice. This passage from the Chan classic *The Record of Linji*, which contains the words and acts of the ninth-century master Linji Yixuan, might almost have come from the *Daodejing*: "Motion and motionlessness both are without self-nature. If you try to seize it within motion, it takes a position within motionlessness. If you try to seize it within motionlessness, it takes a position within motion." Another exchange from the *Record* recalls the dialogical style of the *Zhuangzi*:

> A lecture master asked, "The Three Vehicles' twelve divisions of teachings make the buddha-nature quite clear, do they not?"
> "This weed patch has never been spaded," said Linji.
> "Surely the Buddha would not have deceived people!" said the lecture master.
> "Where is the Buddha?" asked Linji.
> The lecture master had no reply.

Exchanges like this were later collected in books of "cases" (Chinese: *gongan*, Japanese: *koan*) that were given by masters to their students to help them break through their thought-formations and have immediate perception of Buddha-nature.[35]

None of the literature of Chan, from lengthy discourses to lapidary *gongan*, has much to say about God or gods or even about buddhas and bodhisattvas. Linji insisted that "the true student of the Way has nothing to do with buddhas and nothing to do with bodhisattvas or arhats [enlightened sages]." He went so far as to say: "On meeting a buddha slay the buddha, on meeting a patriarch slay the patriarch, on meeting an arhat slay the arhat, on meeting your parents slay your parents, on meeting your kinsman slay your kinsman, and you attain emancipation. By not cleaving to things, you freely pass through."[36] For all his apparent iconoclasm, however, Linji, together with other Chan masters, belonged to the late classical Chinese world, which took for granted the existence of local spirits as well as the six states of incarnate existence—gods, humans, demons, animals, ghosts, and hell-dwellers. Most masters, Linji included, lived in temples surrounded by images of buddhas and bodhisattvas, which were worshipped by monks and visitors. The masters paid conventional respect to the images, but they were able to see through the conventions. People who performed worship or practiced asceticism, Linji said, were just creating karma for themselves. So were those who gave away all they possessed to others. It would be better for them to "do nothing and take it easy," as he himself did:

> When hunger comes I eat my rice;
> When sleep comes I close my eyes.

Fools laugh at me, but
The wise man understands.

This was the easy way to achieve Buddha-nature—but of course it was not that simple. First students had to "bring to rest the thoughts of the ceaselessly seeking mind." Only then could they realize that their own true nature was identical with Buddha-nature.[37] Far different was the self-described "easy path" of Pure Land Buddhism, the most popular of the Chinese schools. Based on the worship of Amitabha, the Buddha of Infinite Splendor, it promised rebirth in the Western Paradise to those who prostrated before his image, repeated his name, visualized his form, and prayed to him to remove their sins. Chan masters like Linji and Huineng dismissed such practices. "Deluded people chant the Buddha's name in order to be reborn there [in the Western Paradise]," Huineng said, "while those who are aware purify their own minds." Had not the Buddha himself said: "As their minds are purified, their buddhalands are purified?" The bottom line was self-discipline: "Each of you must practice yourselves." The Buddha and the dharma "won't do it for you."[38]

During the 840s, the emperor Wuzong of Tang unleashed a widespread persecution of Buddhism. There were political reasons for this—the empire was bankrupt after a war with the Uyghurs and the emperor coveted the wealth of Buddhist temples—but there were religious reasons as well. A convert to a fanatical form of Daoism, the emperor regarded Buddhism as a foreign religion with doctrines deleterious to Chinese society, such as renunciation and the search for nirvana. At first he just made life difficult for Buddhists, but in 845 he forced thousands of monks and nuns to reenter the worldly life and destroyed hundreds of temples and monasteries, confiscating their treasure along the way. The next year he died, but the damage had been done. Buddhist institutions resumed their activities but they never again had the influence they enjoyed before 845.

Between the second century BCE and the fifth century CE Confucianism was effectively the state religion of China and spread to Korea, Japan, and Vietnam. It declined during the heyday of Chinese Buddhism but began to make a comeback toward the beginning of the ninth century. Two Confucian scholars, Han Yu (768–824) and Li Ao (c. 772–836), mounted a vigorous critique of Buddhism and Daoism. As often happens in religious disputation, the critics absorbed many of the ideas of those they criticized. In an influential essay on human nature, Li Ao combined Mencius's idea of the inherent goodness of humanity with the mental discipline demanded by Chan masters: "If the mind is in the state of absolute quiet and inactivity, depraved thoughts will cease of themselves. If human nature shines clearly, how can depravity arise?"[39] Han Yu and Li Ao are regarded as forerunners of Neo-Confucianism, which became the dominant philosophy in China during the Northern Song dynasty (960–1127). I discuss Neo-Confucianism in the next chapter.

Therapeutic philosophy in Rome

One day in 78 or 77 BCE, five young Romans who were studying philosophy in Athens decided to pass the afternoon at the Academy, the school that Plato had founded three hundred years earlier. They found the place deserted. No wonder: the Roman general Sulla had devastated the Academy when he laid siege to Athens in 86 BCE. Now weeds grew in the pathways where Plato and his successors once walked, though their memory was still alive. Piso was thrilled to be within a few steps of the seat where Polemon used to sit. For Quintus the emotional trigger was the suburb of Colonus, the birthplace of Sophocles. Pomponius said he was practically overcome when they walked past the site of the Garden, where Epicurus had taught. Lucius almost blushed when he confessed: "I have actually made a pilgrimage down to the Bay of Phalerum, where they say Demosthenes used to practise declaiming on the beach." The last of the students, Marcus Tullius Cicero, spoke for all of them when he said: "It is a common experience that places do strongly stimulate the imagination and vivify our ideas of famous men." Just now, he continued, "it is that alcove over there which appeals to me, for not long ago it belonged to Carneades." The Academic Skeptic Carneades was famous for his ability to argue both sides of a question with equal success. This interested Cicero, who was a highly respected lawyer even before coming to Athens. Returning to Rome he went into politics, rising to prominence in 63 BCE, when he exposed the Catiline conspiracy. He remained at the center of Roman affairs until 43 BCE, when he was executed on the orders of Mark Antony. During the same twenty years he wrote a series of works that introduced Greek philosophy to Roman intellectuals.[40]

One of Cicero's best-known works is *On the Nature of the Gods*. It begins: "There are many questions in philosophy to which no satisfactory answer has yet been given. But the question of the nature of the gods is the darkest and most difficult of all." Finding an answer to this age-old question would not only enrich our religious life but also shed light "on the nature of our own minds." (This suggests that he thought that the gods were, at least in part, creations of our minds.) Most philosophers believed in the existence of the gods, though Diagoras and Theodorus were supposed to have been atheists and Protagoras "professed himself in doubt about the matter." But the views of the theists were so diverse that Cicero felt "it would be tedious to list them all."[41]

Most of the questions people asked about the gods—what did they look like, what sort of houses did they live in, and so forth—were philosophically trivial. But one question could not be brushed aside: Were the gods "detached from all concern with the care and government of the world" or were they active creators and rulers of the universe? A great deal hung on the answer. If the gods were indifferent to human life, worshipping them was pointless. But if they determined everything, it made perfect sense to ask the local astrologer what would happen the next day. The first was the approach of the Epicureans, which in practical terms was close to atheism. The second was the approach of the Stoics, which tended toward superstition. Was it possible to steer a rational course between the two extremes?[42]

To find out, Cicero imagines a conversation in the country house of a Skeptic named Cotta. Two of Cotta's friends, the Epicurean Velleius and the Stoic Balbus, present their points of view. After each man has his say, Cotta picks holes in his arguments. In the end, Cicero remarks that as far as he could tell the Stoic's opinions were closer to the truth than the Epicurean's. He had good reasons to end like this. Stoicism supported Roman religion. In the Republic, and later in the Empire, religion and the government were closely intertwined. Priests—pontiffs, augers, and the rest—were state officials who exercised great power. Religion was the basis of civic order and the cornerstone of law. The prosperity of the Republic and the success of its armies depended on the performance of public sacrifices. As a champion of Republican virtue in a time of political turmoil, Cicero was not about to suggest that the gods had no power over human affairs.

Cicero may not have been a full-blown Stoic but his descriptions of the Stoic sage or wise man (*sapiens*) are among the most detailed that have come down to us from the ancient world: "It is the peculiar characteristic of the wise man," Cicero wrote, "that he does nothing which he could regret, nothing against his will, but does everything honorably, consistently, seriously, and rightly, that he anticipates nothing as if it were bound to happen, is shocked by nothing when it does happen under the impression that its happening is unexpected and strange, refers everything to his own judgment, stands by his own decisions." In brief, the wise man knows that the "final good" is living in accordance with nature. "It necessarily follows that the happy life is in the power of the man who has the final good in his power. So the wise man's life is always happy." But it was not easy to achieve this psychological poise. The sage, Cicero had to admit, "is as rare as the phoenix."[43]

In Republican Rome as in Hellenistic Greece the great rival of Stoicism was Epicureanism. Around the time Cicero published *On the Nature of the Gods*, the poet Lucretius wrote the ablest defense of the thought of Epicurus since the latter's death two centuries earlier. Lucretius' *On the Nature of Things* was, by common consent, a masterpiece of poetry, but many in Rome, Cicero included, were shocked by its treatment of religion. Lucretius wrote that religion alone had the power to drive humans to "the heights of wickedness." He therefore took it upon himself to help people cut the knots of superstition and enjoy as much pleasure as they could before death put an end to them. In this he claimed no originality: he was just following in the footsteps of the "illustrious discoverer of the truth," Epicurus himself, who had lifted up his voice "to proclaim the nature of the universe" and reveal "the hidden blessings of life."[44]

Having paid his respects to his predecessor, Lucretius got down to business. To understand the nature of life we have to understand the nature of matter. Epicurus had shown that everything that exists, mental as well as physical, is composed of indestructible atoms that come together randomly to compose impermanent forms. Everything is the work of Nature, a force that acts "without the aid of gods." The idea that the gods created the world was "sheer nonsense." The gods certainly exist—people see them in dreams—but like everything else they are composed of atoms and space, and because their atoms are especially fine they are too insubstantial to produce any effect on the denser sorts of atoms that make up the human world. Besides, the gods have no interest in us and our doings. Praying to them is just a waste of time. Yet ignorant people hand their lives over to the gods, "making everything dependent on their whim" and saddling themselves "with cruel masters whom they believe to be all powerful."[45]

The Stoics were glad to honor the gods because they believed in providence. Everything that happens is fated to happen, and fate is just another name for the divine power or Logos that governs the world. It is impossible to escape one's fate but one can learn to accept it calmly and so achieve tranquility. The Epicureans, in contrast, stressed the importance of free will. There has to be something that can "snap the bonds of fate," allowing us to follow the path of pleasure "at the bidding of our own hearts." Since everything in the world is composed of atoms, freedom must originate at the atomic level. At unpredictable moments, atoms swerve as they move through space, striking and combining with other atoms, thereby creating the physical and mental worlds. When a sufficient number of atoms cluster in the heart, an impulse is created that is "transmitted throughout the body and the limbs."[46] This is what drives us to reach out for pleasure, especially the pleasures of food and sex. Unfortunately, such pleasures are followed by pain and renewed longing for pleasure. Therefore, for the Epicureans no less than the Stoics, the highest and most lasting form of pleasure is mental tranquility. But the Epicureans achieved it through measured satisfaction and not submission to fate.

The writings of Lucretius struck a chord with the intelligentsia of the late Republic and early Empire. The poet Horace alluded often to *On the Nature of Things* in his *Satires*. His famous admonition *carpe diem* ("seize the day") is in effect a two-word summary of the Epicurean approach to life. Catullus, the other great lyrist of the day, probably had Lucretius in mind when he told his girlfriend Lesbia that they ought to enjoy the pleasures of love before they slipped into the "perpetual night" of death. The younger poet Ovid was even more dismissive of the pieties of popular faith: "It is convenient that gods should exist," he wrote, "and as it is convenient, let us believe that they do."[47] This line is just a quip in a poem about courtship, but it shows that writers of the late Republic and early Empire had become rather insouciant about their gods. Meanwhile philosophers found nothing to prevent them from subjecting the gods to rational scrutiny. There was no point, wrote Pliny the Elder, to concern oneself with "the shape and form of God. Whoever God is—provided there is a God—and in whatever region he is, he consists wholly of sense, sight and hearing, wholly of soul, wholly of mind, wholly of himself." The hordes of gods in the various countries of the world clearly were human inventions. Pliny refrained from denying their existence, but he felt, like Lucretius, that it was absurd to imagine that the gods were interested in our lives. At the same time he was comfortable with the Stoic idea that God was identical with Nature.[48]

After a century of unrest, civil war, and dictatorship, the Republic was extinguished in 27 BCE when the Senate gave supreme power and the title Augustus to Julius Caesar's adopted son Octavian. This was the start of an empire that would last 500 years. During the first two centuries of the imperial era, Stoicism was the philosophy of choice of the Roman elite. Its most prominent defender during the reigns of Claudius and Nero was the philosopher and statesman Seneca the Younger (4–65 CE).

Like other Roman Stoics, Seneca used the word *Deus* or God as a synonym for the Logos that governs the world, but he was ready to discard the word if it opened the door to the "idiotic heresy" of superstition. "What difference does it make whether you deny the gods or bring them into disrepute?" he asked. What really is important is the search for wisdom, and for this the gods' help is not required. "There is no need to raise our hands to heaven," Seneca insisted: "God is near you, is with you, is inside you." This inner divine spirit watches over our deeds, and "prompts us to noble and exalted endeavours."[49]

The divine being—"whether all-powerful god, or incorporeal reason creating mighty works, or divine spirit penetrating all things"—has arranged things in such a way "that only the most worthless of our possessions would come into the power of another." Among such possessions are reputation and wealth, neither of which is in our power to control. It is a principle of Stoic psychology that things we cannot control are not worth worrying about. What we *can* control is our reactions to outer events, such as the gaining or losing of wealth. By controlling our reactions we can enjoy a tranquil life whatever the circumstances. "Great equipment"—today we might say "a whole lot of stuff"—is not necessary. "External goods are of trivial importance and without much influence in either direction: prosperity does not elevate the sage and adversity does not depress him." In a comment on Roman consumer culture that has an amazingly modern ring, Seneca admonished a friend: "Look at the number of things we buy because others have bought them or because they're in most people's houses." True prosperity is to be content with little, to be able to cry out "we have water, we have barley: we may vie with Jupiter himself in happiness."[50]

The key to happiness is detachment: to bear everything that happens with composure. For this we have to cultivate tranquility, a state in which the mind follows "a smooth and steady course, well disposed to itself, happily regarding its own condition and with no interruption to its pleasure, but remaining in a state of peace with no ups and downs." One way to attain this state was to practice *premeditatio malorum* or premeditation of evils. "If you want to be rid of all anxiety," Seneca wrote to a friend who was worried about a lawsuit, "suppose that anything you are afraid of happening is going to happen in any case, then mentally calculate all the evil involved in it and appraise your own fear: you will undoubtedly come to realize that what you fear is either not great or not long-lasting." Exile? Imprisonment? Burning? Death? Imagine that they have come and then think of the sages who rose above them. Above all, "banish life's turbulence" and look deeply into "the essence of everything. You then will realize that there is nothing fearful there except fear itself."[51] One would like to think that Seneca faced his death—a suicide ordered by Nero—with the composure he described in this passage. There is reason to doubt that he did. According to classicist Mary Beard, he tried to stage his death as a reenactment of Socrates' execution but fell far below that standard. Whatever the value of Seneca's philosophy, there was, Beard observes, "something elusive, even a whiff of 'spin,'" about his life.[52]

The same cannot be said about the philosopher Gaius Musonius Rufus, whose conduct during the reign of Nero was stoic in the best sense of the term. Banished unjustly after the conspiracy that led to Seneca's death, he lived quietly on a desolate island until summoned back to Rome by Nero's successor Galba. According to Musonius the philosopher is like a doctor: he must "not only learn the principles of his own skill but be trained to act according to those principles." Indeed, all of us have to "live like doctors and be continually treating ourselves with reason." Musonius' surviving teachings consist mainly of practical advice about everything from marriage and sex to diet and personal grooming. Often platitudinous, they still contain much of interest. The body as well as the mind should be trained, Musonius said, because the virtue within us has to use the body to express itself. One way to train the body is to "accustom ourselves to cold, heat, thirst, hunger, scarcity of good, hardness of bed, abstaining from pleasures, and enduring pains." Endurance is necessary, because "the person who is himself unwilling to endure pain all but condemns himself to being worthy of nothing good."[53] This is classic Stoic doctrine, found also in the works of Seneca, but carrying more conviction in Musonius' plain phrasing than in Seneca's elegant rhetoric.

Musonius's ideas about God followed the Stoic line. God knows all without the need of reason but he has given reason to us so that we, acting rationally, can achieve a life of virtue. God has put some things in our control, among which "the most beautiful and important thing, the thing because of which even the god himself is happy" is the power to confront life experiences without labeling them good or bad and reacting to them as such. The things themselves are not under our control so we have to entrust them to the gods, which is the same thing as entrusting them to the universal Logos or Reason.[54]

These ideas were developed by Musonius' most famous student, Epictetus (55–135). His background was quite different from his teacher's. Musonius was born into the Roman aristocracy of central Italy; Epictetus came to Rome from far-away Phrygia as the slave of a man who became Nero's secretary. He obtained his freedom while still an adolescent, then devoted himself to the study of philosophy. Eventually he began to give lectures on his own. These *Discourses*, recorded by one of his students, are the source of much of what we know about Stoic philosophy.

According to Epictetus, "the first thing to learn is that God exists, that he governs the world" and that he knows everything we do. But we have to understand that God and the world are not distinct: he is within the world and within humanity as well. God has put "divine sparks of his being" into our souls, and by means of these portions of himself he knows what we are thinking and doing. Epictetus clearly is a theist, but there is an enormous difference between his philosophical theism and the monotheism of the West Asian religions. Epictetus' God is the creator of the universe but not different from what he creates. From a certain point of view, he *is* the universe and the universe is him. Similarly, God is the creator of humankind but at the same time the "individual guardian deity" within us all.[55]

Epictetus believed in Fate but he was not a fatalist. Human beings have the power to reflect, choose, and act. He called this "making good use of impressions." (In Stoic psychology, the world presents itself to our mind in the form of *phantasiae* or impressions.) We have no power over the impressions themselves but do have the power to give or withhold our assent to them. This faculty of moral choice is what makes us human. It comes to us from God and if we use it well we can become almost godlike—or at any rate can lead a calm and rational life.[56]

For students of godless spirituality, what is interesting about Epictetus' philosophy is not its theological foundations but its therapeutic applications. He wrote that he viewed his school as a hospital: "When you leave, you should have suffered, not enjoyed yourself." He asked his students to practice mental exercises with as much application as the exercises they practiced in the gym. "As soon as you leave in the morning," he wrote, "subject whatever you see or hear to close study. …Today what did you see—some beautiful woman or handsome man? Test them by your rule—does their beauty have any bearing on your character? If not, forget them." As they went about their daily activities, students should try to understand that all the things around them—dishes, clothing, livestock, family members, their own bodies—will sooner or later be gone. To be prepared for this, they should "mentally discard them" beforehand. Finally, before going to bed, they should review what happened during the day, recognize their mistakes, and resolve to avoid making them again.[57]

Epictetus was banished from Rome around 93 along with many other philosophers. He settled in Nicopolis, western Greece, where he founded a new school. His fame was such that the emperor Hadrian is said to have visited him. His *Discourses* were widely read. One of its admirers was Marcus Aurelius, who became emperor of Rome in 161. Trained by teachers from different traditions, Marcus was drawn to Stoicism but he kept his mind open about other teachings. Sometimes he set the views of the Epicureans and Stoics against one another without coming to a final decision: "One way or another: atoms or unity. If it's God, all is well. If it's arbitrary, don't imitate it." The gods (if they exist) have placed at our disposal "everything a person needs to avoid real harm." But the effort must be ours. What was important was not to get caught by appearances: "Death and life, success and failure, pain and pleasure, wealth and poverty, all these happen to good and bad alike, and they are neither noble nor shameful—and hence neither good nor bad."[58]

Marcus wrote his aphorisms—published posthumously as *Meditations*—for his own use while going about his business as a political and military leader. In 172 or 173, while in a fortress on the Danube, he wrote this reminder to himself: "Keep hold of this alone and remember it: Each of us lives only now, this brief instant." The first step toward achieving a state of tranquility was "to define whatever it is we perceive—to trace its outline—so we can see what it really is, its substance." For "nothing is so conducive to spiritual growth as this capacity for logical and accurate analysis of everything that happens to us."[59]

Uninterested in the technical details of Stoicism, Marcus was able to get to the core of Epictetus' thought with a minimum of philosophical jargon: "The fact that my son is sick—that I can see. But 'that he may die of it,' no. Stick with first impressions. Don't extrapolate. And nothing can happen to you." What is this well-garnished meal before you? "A dead fish. A dead bird. A dead pig." What was that lovemaking you enjoyed last night? "Something rubbing against your penis, a brief seizure and a little cloudy liquid." The purpose of such exercises was not to become insensitive but to learn to see things without superfluous descriptions (*great* food, *fantastic* sex) that open the way to attachment and disappointment. One had to be able "to welcome with affection what is sent by fate. Not to strain or disturb the spirit within [one] with a mess of false beliefs" but to approach the end "in purity, in serenity, in acceptance, in peaceful unity with what must be." As all the Stoics starting with Zeno had said: the sage must live in accordance with nature. And death was just a process of nature that only children could be afraid of.[60]

Marcus' ambivalence about the Gods may have been, in part, a reflection of the skepticism that prevailed among educated Romans during the second century. One finds a striking instance of this in the works of the satirist Lucian (c. 125–c. 185). In *Dialogues of the Gods* he mocks the absurdities of Greek mythology, while in *Hermotimus* he skewers the pretentions of philosophers of every school. In one scene Lycinus, Lucian's mouthpiece, asks Hermotimus, an eager Stoic, if he could name a single student who had tried out all the paths and found the only one that "leads straight to happiness." Hermotimus has to admit that he cannot. Perhaps then, Lycinus observes, "The best and safest course is for everyone to start by making his own way through every philosophical system and to study critically what each says." In the end he convinces Hermotimus that even his beloved Stoicism is not as advertised, and Hermotimus resolves to shave off his beard, stop trying to look tranquil, and go about his life like a normal human being.[61]

It was around this time that the philosopher Sextus Empiricus wrote his *Outlines of Pyrrhonism*. I discussed this work in Chapter 2 because it is the only complete source we have of Pyrrhonian Skepticism, which was conceived in Greece five centuries before Sextus was born. (Most scholars place his birth around 160 though it might have been fifty years earlier or later.) Pyrrhonism is, according to Sextus, the therapeutic philosophy *par excellence*. The Pyrrhonists desire only "to cure by argument, as far as they can, the conceit and rashness of the Dogmatists." Like skillful doctors, they choose remedies—that is, arguments—that are appropriate for the illnesses of the patients. But, one might ask, aren't their arguments just as dogmatic as those of the Dogmatists? No, because they are intended only to show that the Dogmatists' views are invalid, not that the Pyrrhonists' are valid. "We do not affirm definitely" that our arguments are true, Sextus wrote; rather "we say that they can be destroyed by themselves, being cancelled along with what they are applied to, just as purgative drugs do not merely drain the [disease-causing] humours from the body but drive themselves out too along with the humours."[62]

The Pyrrhonists sought freedom from disturbance by suspending judgment on matters that were not self-evident. I showed in Chapter 2 how they applied their methods to the question of the existence or nonexistence of God. But the Pyrrhonists distinguished matters of belief from matters of behavior. In regard to the former they had, or claimed to have, no preferences; in regard to the latter they lived "in accordance with everyday observances"—that is, the customs of the lands they lived in. Sextus therefore began his discussion of the gods with the following preface: Taking into consideration that almost everyone believes in and worships the gods, the Pyrrhonists say "that there are gods and we are pious towards the gods and say that they are provident."[63] It is hard not to see this as a cop-out. Sextus certainly wanted the inner tranquility that came from suspension of judgment but also, one imagines, the outer tranquility of not having to deal with censors and magistrates. Roman polytheism was still the state religion and dissenting philosophers always ran the risk of deportation or worse.

During the third century a new school of philosophy appeared in Rome that gradually eclipsed Stoicism, Epicureanism, and Skepticism. This was what we now call Neo-Platonism, although its originator, Plotinus (204–270), saw it simply as the correct interpretation of Plato. I avoid discussing Plotinus here for the same reason I avoided a full discussion of Plato in Chapter 2: his work is more theistic than not, and its afterlife belongs more to the history of Christian, Jewish, and Muslim theology than to the history of nontheistic spirituality.

The school of Plotinus, along with those of the Epicureans, Stoics, and Skeptics, hung on in Rome even after the religion of Christ became the dominant creed of the empire. Persecuted during the first three centuries of its history, Christianity became a persecutor after gaining the favor of the emperor Constantine in 312. The situation remained fluid during the turbulent fourth century, when much Christian blood was shed by Christians. There was a brief restoration of philosophical paganism under the emperor Julian, who ruled between 361 and 363; but in 380 Theodosius I made Nicene Christianity the state religion of the Empire. For a century or more the state tolerated non-Christian teachings, but in 529 the Eastern Roman emperor Justinian closed the Neo-Platonic Academy in Athens, effectively ending the Greco-Roman philosophical tradition, which had endured for more than a millennium. Now, with the victory of militant theism, there would be a thousand years of mandatory monotheism in most parts of Europe.

* * *

During the late classical period, proponents of philosophies and religions that had been founded in the axial age defended their systems and debated with one another. Many of the debates were about the idea of God. Some of the schools of the Vedic tradition were atheistic or agnostic; others turned to forms of God as aids to meditative practice; only one school, Nyaya, was unambiguously theistic. Jain and Buddhist philosophers rejected the idea of a creative Lord and formulated arguments against the theism of Nyaya and Vedanta. Popular Jainism and Buddhism made room for the worship of superhuman beings, but many worshippers realized that personal effort was needed to achieve liberation. Meanwhile, members of the Charvaka school denied the existence of superhuman beings and rubbished all religions. In China Confucianism remained true to its nontheistic roots, though it, like Daoism, absorbed elements of Chinese folk religion. Roman polytheism enjoyed the patronage of the state until the fourth century, but philosophers offered therapeutic teachings in which the gods played minor roles. The Epicurean Lucretius, who opposed all religions, said that the gods were beyond the reach of prayer. Roman Stoics accepted the established gods but still laid great stress on human effort; Roman Skeptics neither affirmed nor denied the idea of God.

The nontheistic philosophies of the late classical age encouraged subjective enquiry and some of them developed systems of psychology. The Vedic schools of Samkhya, Yoga, and Vedanta viewed consciousness as a person or self, and treated the movements of the mind as unconscious or semi-conscious activities that had to be stilled if the person or self was to be freed from the cycle of birth-and-death. Buddhists denied the existence of the self but analyzed the movements of consciousness with as much attention as their Vedic counterparts. Some thinkers developed the concept of an inner Buddha-nature that is the true nature of sentient beings. Confucians avoided elaborate metaphysics but developed practical theories of human nature. In Rome philosophers of the therapeutic schools recommended self-study and encouraged self-reliance. Some viewed reason or *logos* as an inner divine principle.

These psychological theories were grounded in self-observation that was carried out with the assistance of psychophysical techniques. Vedic, Jain, and Buddhist teachers developed a large number of such methods during the late classical period. Some relied on physical control: fasting, holding postures, observing and regulating the breath. Others used meditation and concentration to still the movements of mind. Most Indian schools developed systems of dialectics that were meant to clear away erroneous patterns of thought, allowing the higher truth to shine through. Buddhist missionaries took Indian philosophy and methods to China, where under the influence of Daoism they became the basis of the Chan school. Some Chan teachers recommended silent meditation; others, reflection on paradoxical statements. The goal of both approaches was identity with the inner Buddha-nature. In Rome, dialectical philosophy was the primary method of the therapeutic schools, but some relied also on psychological exercises to free the mind and emotions from attachment. Philosophers had to apply themselves what truly mattered: the mastery of self: "As wood is the material of the carpenter, and marble that of the sculptor," Epictetus said, "so the subject matter of the art of life is the life of the self."[64]

4 THE TRIUMPH OF THEISM

In the Neolithic Age, when most humans were hunter-gatherers, the main supernatural agents were spirits, demons, and local gods and the main religious technology was magic. The Bronze Age saw the rise of agricultural kingdoms, great gods (Marduk, Indra, Shangdi), and rituals associated with sacrifice. During the Iron Age, when small kingdoms and republics prevailed in India, China, and Greece, some thinkers conceived of abstract cosmic principles (Brahman, the Dao, the Logos) and developed psychophysical techniques such as asceticism and meditation. Meanwhile in West Asia, pastoral societies ruled by powerful kings came up with the idea of a single supreme deity (Ahura Mazda, Yahweh) who demanded exclusive homage. These concepts and technologies were cumulative. Spirits and magic were carried over into the regime of great gods and sacrifice, which were carried over into the regimes of abstract principles and of monotheistic gods. By the end of the axial age, the religions of India, China, Greece, and West Asia resembled dense geological formations, with spirits, great gods, abstract principles, and single divinities extending in distinct strata or intruding into one another.

During the four hundred years between 200 BCE and 200 CE a new sort of agent with a technology to match was added to the mix: personal deities that could be approached through worship. The new gods on the block were not unrelated to the old. Shiva was a form of the Vedic god Rudra. Huangdi (the Daoists' Yellow Emperor) derived from the great god Shangdi. Dionysus was the son of Zeus and Semele, a mortal woman. Jesus, the son of God, was born to the mortal virgin Mary. Worship, the new technology, was a variant of the old technology of sacrifice but with important differences. The gods of sacrifice were remote and responded to humans only when placated by offerings; the gods of worship were approachable and responded to love with love.

Both sacrifice and worship begin with the acknowledgment of the greatness of a divine being or beings. Both express themselves through offerings and supplications, but the framework of the acts differ. Sacrifice, which is modeled on tribute paid to kings, is a *quid pro quo* exchange. If the sacrificial animal is properly killed and the prayer is properly recited, it doesn't really matter what the sacrificant is thinking or feeling. Worship is modeled on intimate personal relationships: parent and child, lover and beloved. The physical offering, if any, is symbolic; what matters is the mental and emotional state of the worshipper.

So much for the sociological framework of worship. What about its psychological sources? Why do some people feel the need to give homage to invisible beings and forces that are in some respects similar to them? Let's assume that most of us have the sense that there is something infinitely greater than ourselves—Life, Existence, the Universe, God. This sense may be accompanied by a feeling of astonishment and gratitude, an instinctive acknowledgement that our own existence is in some way linked to the existence of that greater something. So far so good. But why worship? For the devout, the question is meaningless: They adore because they adore. The nondevout tend to look on worship as an expression of human psychic needs. As English poet Percy Bysshe Shelley put it: "There is a tendency to devotion, a thirst for reliance on supernatural aid inherent in the human mind."[1] To say that something is inherent is to leave it unexplained, and it may be that worship is unexplainable. It is enough for worshippers to feel devotion welling up from within along with the certainty that God will respond.

The strong emotions involved in devotion give religions of worship an intensity that normally is lacking in religions of sacrifice. Some worshippers are happy to give their lives for the sake of the god they adore. Others are delighted to persecute, exile, and execute those who they believe pose a danger to the beloved deity.

An adequate account of the growth of devotional religions would require hundreds of pages and be out of place in this history of nontheistic spirituality. But it is important to have a general idea of the theisms that rose to prominence in India, China, the Greco-Roman world, and especially West Asia between 200 BCE, when they competed on equal terms with sacrificial religions and therapeutic philosophies, and 800 CE, when they dominated the planet. When I discussed this period in the last chapter, theism was the elephant in the room. In the present chapter I track the animal in its own habitat. To understand nontheistic religions and spiritualities, we have to have some idea of how theism was born, how it grew, and how it reproduces.

The ideal political environment for the propagation of theism is empire. Christianity spread slowly across the Roman Empire between the first and third centuries and rose to power after it was legalized in 313 and made the official state religion in 380. After the Western Empire collapsed during the fifth century, the Eastern (Byzantine) Empire became the stronghold of orthodox Christianity. A millennium later, Catholicism and Protestantism followed the flags of the European imperial powers to Asia, Africa, and the Americas. Islam spread rapidly through West Asia and Northern Africa under the Abbasid Caliphate (750–1258) and Fatimid Caliphate (909–1171). Theistic Hinduism achieved notable success during the Gupta Empire (320 to 550) and Vijayanagara Empire (1336–1646). Theistic forms of Buddhism and Daoism received imperial favor at different times during the middle empires of China (c. 600–1300).

As theism rose to greatness, nontheistic religions and philosophies lost ground, in part because people turned from them to the comforting arms of deities, in part because theistic religions—particularly the West Asian monotheisms—suppressed their nontheistic rivals. Nevertheless nontheistic beliefs and practices survived in parts of Asia: Neo-Confucianism and Chan in China, Zen in Japan, the *nirgun bhakti* of the sants and Sikhs in India, Sufism in the Islamic world. In Europe, during the fourteenth and fifteenth centuries, unorthodoxy and anticlericalism challenged the monopoly of the Catholic Church. The sixteenth-century Protestant Reformation opened the way to a new approach that would give a lift to subjective spirituality.

Personal gods

The *Bhagavad Gita* is set on a battlefield. Arjuna and his brothers have been defrauded of their kingdom by their cousins. After many eventful years, the two branches of the family meet at the field of Kurukshetra to fight it out. As the poem opens, Arjuna asks Krishna, his friend and charioteer, to drive between the two armies. Looking at his opponents, Arjuna loses heart. What good is victory if he has to kill his guru, his grandsire and other relatives to obtain it? Krishna insists that it is his duty to fight, and explains why in a series of religio-philosophical lessons. After learning about Vedanta, Samkhya, Yoga and *bhakti* or devotion, Arjuna asks Krishna to reveal his "supreme form, greatest of persons." He soon regrets his impulsiveness. Krishna appears before him in his universal form, with "many mouths and eyes, innumerable wonderful aspects," and "countless divine weapons at the ready." Terrified, Arjuna cries out: "Seeing you touching the sky, shining, rainbow-hued, cavern-mouthed, with luminous distended eyes, I am shaken to the core." Krishna explains that he is Time, the destroyer of the universe, and demands that Arjuna perform his martial duty. Arjuna declares his devotion to Krishna and begs his forgiveness for having treated him as an equal while Krishna was in his human form. Then, somewhat inconsistently, he asks the cosmic Krishna to reassume that very human form. Krishna complies, and closes with an endorsement of the religion of *bhakti*: "Neither through the Vedas, nor through asceticism, neither by alms-giving, nor by sacrifice is it possible to see me in the way you have seen me," but only through "exclusive devotion."[2]

The worship of personal gods was a relatively late development in the history of religions but there were hints of it during the age of sacrifice. The *Rig Veda* contains a number of passages in which humans address gods as friends and brothers. The earliest Chinese inscriptions mentioning the Yellow Emperor are from the early Warring States period, which began in 475 BCE. The cult of Dionysus was a force to be reckoned with by 405 BCE, when Euripides' *Bacchae* was first performed. But the period from 200 BCE to 200 CE provided especially fertile ground for the seeds of devotion to germinate. The *Bhagavad Gita* cannot be precisely dated but it was composed sometime between 300 BCE and 300 CE. The *Lotus Sutra* (the most important text of devotional Buddhism) was composed in India between 100 BCE and 100 CE and translated into Chinese a century or two later. The Huang-Lao sect, which combined elements of classical Daoism and the cult of the Yellow Emperor, became influential during the second century BCE. The mysteries of Bacchus became popular in Rome around 200 BCE, and the earliest accounts of the life of Jesus were written toward the end of the first century CE. There is much to distinguish these religions from one another, but they all have one thing in common: a belief in the divinity of a humanlike being who can be approached by means of worship and who responds to prayer.

The *Shwetashwatara Upanishad* and the *Bhagavad Gita* are the earliest Indian texts to deal at length with worship. Both combine ascetic and devotional methods, suggesting that a movement from one to the other was underway around the time they were written.[3] Both speak of the *nirguna/saguna* distinction I mentioned in Chapter 3. This is crucial for understanding worship. *Nirguna* means without features or qualities: plain vanilla. *Saguna* means possessed of qualities: butterscotch or strawberry or whatever. Features are necessary for worship and the *Shwetashwatara* and *Gita* serve them up. Rudra, says the sage Shwetashwatara, has "eyes on every side and faces on every side," but he also has a *shiva* or auspicious form, "not terrifying nor evil-appearing." Krishna in the *Gita* is "infinite in form" and also the "form of everything."[4]

Nirguna and *saguna* coexist in the *Shwetashwatara* and the *Gita*: some passages praise asceticism and meditation, others worship and adoration, and a few a combination of both, as when Shwetashwatara says that he found *brahman* by the power of asceticism *and* by God's grace. But both texts give the last word to theism: devotion to the god in question is the *only* way. "There is no other path by which to go," says Shwetashwatara (twice). "My final word," says Krishna, is this: "vow yourself to me alone."[5] Exclusivism, the bane of devotional religion, was present at its birth.

The most exclusive forms of devotional religion are those directed toward God in human form: the avatar or incarnation. The worship of Krishna as an avatar of Vishnu grew out of earlier cults of Vasudeva and Narayana. The former was well established by around 100 BCE, when an ambassador from an Indo-Greek kingdom erected a column honoring Vasudeva, the god of gods, in central India. The Vasudeva and Narayana cults eventually merged to form the Bhagavata religion, which in turn absorbed the sects of various local deities, some of whom eventually found a place in lists of Vishnu's avatars. During Jesus' lifetime most of his disciples believed he was the messiah, the anointed king whose coming is foretold in the Hebrew Bible. After Jesus' death, this belief was transformed into the dogma that he was God incarnate. Around 100 CE the author of the Gospel of John wrote: "The Word [Logos] became flesh and made his dwelling among us." This beautiful image is followed by an assertion of Christian exclusiveness: "We have seen his glory, the glory of the one and only Son."[6] This exclusivity mirrors that of the authors of the *Shwetashwatara* and *Gita*.

The idea that gods have human forms found expression in material forms of gods. The earliest sculptural images of Indian deities date from the mid-second century BCE. The first anthropomorphic images of the Buddha appeared a century or so later. Earlier Buddhist art represented the teacher symbolically—an empty throne, a pair of feet, the wheel of dharma—and early Buddhist texts gave little importance to the physical Buddha. "Why do you want to see this foul body," the Buddha tells an elder who had gone to some trouble to meet him. "One who sees the Dhamma sees me; one who sees me sees the Dhamma."[7] Yet people began to worship the Buddha even during his lifetime and fought over his relics after his death. With the rise of Mahayana during the first century BCE, two new teachings—the ideal of the bodhisattva and the dharma-body of the Buddha—gave followers of the dharma models of perfection that in time became foci of worship.

The author of the *Lotus Sutra* has the Buddha declare he is an eternal being who attained *nirvana* ages ago and since then has never been out of touch with living beings. He formulated various doctrines appropriate to the needs of different people to help them "quickly acquire the body of the Buddha." For people of every order he "manifests himself in various different forms, depending on what is appropriate to salvation." Sometimes he acts through the intermediary of bodhisattvas such as Avalokiteshwara, who is able to "to wipe out the pains of existence" and "offer aid and support" in every circumstance.[8]

To the author of the *Lotus Sutra*, earlier Buddhist scriptures were useful in their day but now are obsolete. The supreme and final teaching is the *Lotus Sutra* itself. To underline its potency, the author has the Buddha observe that if anyone should slander it or those who adore it, that person "will enter the Avichi hell"—the hottest of the eight hot hells—and remain there without any chance of escape for uncountable ages. Those who take refuge in the *Lotus Sutra* are guaranteed liberation. After he heard it, one of the Buddha's disciples was able to enter the stream (take the first step toward *nirvana*) "through faith alone."[9]

Faith was an element of Buddhist practice from the time of the Buddha, but in earlier scriptures it played a subordinate role. The Buddha of the *Samyutta Nikaya* speaks of five faculties needed by the aspirant: faith, energy, mindfulness, concentration and wisdom. All five lead to enlightenment, but among them wisdom is chief, as the lion is chief among animals. Faith is unnecessary once wisdom has been achieved. The philosopher Nagarjuna spoke in similar terms a few centuries later:

> Due to having faith one relies on the practices,
> Due to having wisdom one truly knows.
> Of these two wisdom is the chief,
> Faith is its prerequisite.[10]

Devotional scriptures such as the *Lotus Sutra* and *Infinite Life Sutra* reversed the ranking. Faith was not just the chief but, for some, the only faculty that was needed.

So great is the appeal of devotion that even Jainism found a way to accommodate it. Jains do not recognize a creator god and admit that Mahavira and the other Tirtankaras have no interest in human existence. Yet Jainism has produced an abundant devotional literature. A mid-second-century BCE inscription by a Jain king of eastern India begins with a salutation to the Jain *arihants* (Tirthankaras and other victorious souls) and *siddhas* (perfected ones). This same salutation forms part of a prayer that is recited by pious Jains today.[11] Jain shrines and temples contain images of Tirthankaras that are artistically and functionally similar to images in Hindu temples. There are of course important differences between Jain and Hindu worship—Jains do not, as a rule, ask for divine intervention—but the psychological motives behind them are the same. People need someone greater than themselves to turn to, and worship is one form this dependence takes.

During the fifteen centuries following the germination period of devotional religion, that is, from around 200 to 1700 CE, several streams of belief and practice came together to constitute what we now call Hinduism. The age-old river of Vedic ritualism was refreshed and transformed by two young tributaries: *bhakti* and *tantra*. Bhakti means the love of and devotion to personal gods, expressed through worship and prayer. Tantra is the use of specialized techniques to contact and control divine beings and energies. Both systems have produced enormous literatures and influenced every aspect of Indian cultural life: art, architecture, poetry, philosophy, even social organization and politics. They touched non-Vedic as well as Vedic religions, and eventually colored the West Asian faiths that came to the subcontinent.

The myths collected in the *Puranas*, which were written between 300 and 1000 CE, provide many of the themes of the songs of the *bhaktas* or devotees, who took *bhakti* to the masses between 700 and 1700. By the beginning of this period the practice of worshipping images in temples was well established in southern India and had begun to spread to the north. Unlike Vedic worship, which was always the preserve of male members of the priestly class, image worship was open to all Hindus. Some of the most famous *bhaktas* were women, a few were from the lower strata of society. This inclusiveness was one of the positive contributions of the bhakti movement. Among its negative outcomes was the growth of sectarianism leading to intolerance and, occasionally, violence.

The use of spells to produce specific effects—curing diseases, captivating lovers, killing enemies—goes back at least as far as the *Atharva Veda* and may derive from pre-Vedic magic. By around 500 CE, specialists in this occult lore, Buddhist, Hindu, and Jain, began writing down their techniques in texts called *tantras*. These how-to guides differ greatly from one another but they share a few common themes. By means of special rituals and incantations, practitioners invoke personified supernatural powers—gods, goddesses, buddhas, demons, and so forth—to obtain spiritual or material favors. Hindu tantrism became widespread between the seventh and thirteenth centuries and had a major influence on more orthodox forms of Hindu practice. Manuals of temple-building and image-worship, for instance, are tantric in inspiration.

Scholars of Chinese religion distinguish between philosophical Daoism (*daojia*) and religious Daoism (*daojiao*). Philosophical Daoism, which is based largely on the teachings of Laozi and Zhuang Zhou, took form around 300–200 BCE. Religious Daoism consists of practices that were formalized toward the end of the Han Era, that is, around 100–200 CE. Eventually the Daoist pantheon encompassed hundreds of deities, some descended from historical or legendary figures, others borrowed from popular religion. Among the historical-legendary figures, the most important were Taishang Laojun, the deified form of Laozi, and Huangdi, the Yellow Emperor. Mythological figures included the Jade Emperor, ruler of the gods of heaven, and the Queen Mother of the West, a bountiful goddess first worshipped in the second millennium BCE. There were in addition innumerable nature gods appropriated from pre-Daoist cults. This host of supernatural beings was arranged in a complex hierarchy: Taishang Laojun is one of the Three Pure Ones, who are direct emanations of the Dao. The Jade Emperor is the head of the heavenly court, which was modeled on the bureaucratic government of the imperial dynasties.

Toward the middle of the second century, a Daoist recluse named Zhang Daoling started a movement called the Way of the Celestial Masters, which briefly ran a theocratic state in central China. Zhang, who identified himself as the first of the Celestial Masters, was an expert in longevity, the primary goal of religious Daoism from its beginnings right down to the present. The Peaches of Immortality became a fixture in Chinese literature, the more prosaic pills of immortality were compounded by alchemists who were patronized by emperors and anyone else with the necessary cash.

Daoist priests were experts in drawing up prayers that were offered to the gods like petitions presented to magistrates. Priests also carried out ritual and magical services, communing with the gods and ancestors. They were not above borrowing from Confucian and Buddhist sources and even devised a story to explain the relationship between Laozi and the Buddha. The fourth-century *Classic of the Conversion of the Barbarians* relates that Laozi traveled to India, where he became the Buddha in order to convert the "barbarians" who lived there. Afterward he sent missionaries to take the Indian version of Daoism—that is to say, Buddhism—back to China!

Most of the schools of Chinese Buddhism are based on teachings that originated in India but took original forms in their new home. The Pure Land Sutras are the textual basis of the Jingtuzong or Pure Land school, which promotes the worship of the celestial Buddha Amitabha. His devotees will be reborn in the Pure Land or Western Paradise, where eventually they will understand the Buddha's teachings and achieve nirvana. To reach the Pure Land they must repeat the name of Amitabha and try to visualize him, his qualities, his attendants, and the Pure Land itself. These devotional practices are based on the assumption that in the present age it is impossible for people to achieve nirvana on their own. The path of self-discipline was only effectual when the Buddha and his disciples were on earth. For people like us, the religion of Amitabha is the only option.

The Pure Land sect took root in southeast China in the beginning of the fifth century and has remained a major strand in East Asian Buddhism ever since. Other schools, such as Tiantai ("Platform of the Sky"), took form around the same time. Zhiyi, the formulator of Tiantai, synthesized all the Buddhist teachings he was aware of, from the most philosophical to the most devotional. Each doctrine and practice had its place in the hierarchy, but the *Lotus Sutra* was supreme. (Tiantai masters hold, anachronistically, that the *Lotus Sutra* was spoken by the Buddha just before he achieved final nirvana and was therefore his ultimate word.) The Tiantai synthesis is all-inclusive and of universal application. Through it, all beings can achieve Buddhahood.

In the eighth century Chinese monks took the Tiantai school to Japan, where it became known as Tendai. By the beginning of the ninth century, it won imperial patronage, becoming the dominant school of Japanese Buddhism. During the late Heian and Kamakura periods (eleventh to thirteenth centuries) there was an explosion of Japanese Buddhist subschools. Here I will examine the two main devotional paths: Jodo (Japanese Pure Land Buddhism) and the school of Nichiren. Honen (1133–1212), the founder of the Jodo school, trained as a Tendai monk from an early age but became dissatisfied with its complex philosophy and practices. Discovering the Chinese Pure Land teachings, he formulated a practice based on *nembutsu*, the repetition of the name of Amitabha Buddha (in Japanese: Amida Butsu). This was all that was needed for anyone—priest, monk, or layman—to achieve full buddhahood. Indeed, in the current age of *mappo*, the degenerate age, this is the only practice that is effective.

Unlike most other Buddhist innovators, Nichiren (1222–1282) came from the working class. Ordained a monk at the age of 16, he studied the Pure Land, Zen,

Tendai, and esoteric Shingon teachings, but eventually became convinced that the *Lotus Sutra* alone contained the Buddha's true teaching. So convinced was he of the power of this scripture that he insisted that the chanting of its title in Sino-Japanese, *Namu Myoho Renge Kyo*, and the veneration of a scroll that features these words was the only way to achieve salvation. In 1253 he began to proselytize, condemning all other schools and remonstrating with VIPs to suppress them. This won him few friends and he was exiled twice. Each time he returned to the metropolitan region, he began to proselytize, condemn, and remonstrate again. This set the tone for the subsequent history of Nichiren Buddhism, which has aggressively promoted its doctrines for more than 700 years.

The gods of Greece and Rome were personal in form but as a rule not objects of personal devotion. That said, there is evidence of intimate relations between humans and Greco-Roman gods from an early period. Greeks and Romans made votive offerings to particular gods, praying for assistance or giving thanks for deliverance from danger. (This practice gave the Cynic philosopher Diogenes the chance to observe that there would have been more votive offerings at a certain sacred place if those who had *not* been saved had been able to place them there.) There was no lack of shrines outside Athens in the fourth century BCE, but Plato considered them contrary to the spirit of Greek religion. In the *Laws* he wrote that anyone who wanted to make an offering to the gods should do so in the presence of the state priest.

The most personal expressions of Greek and Roman religion were the *mysteria* or mystery cults. Some went back to the fifth or sixth century BCE, but they became especially popular during the Hellenistic period. This was right around the time that devotional religions were taking shape in India and China. These developments were not unrelated: Hellenistic religion left its mark on devotional Buddhism in the Greco-Bactrian kingdoms of what is now Afghanistan and Pakistan; Greek soldiers and travelers took Asian ideas back to the Mediterranean.

Each of the mystery religions was tied to its locality and involved specific gods, making it difficult to speak of "the mysteries" in general terms. But most of them had to do with death—which is, after all, the ultimate mystery—and the hope of a better life hereafter. The Orphic, Eleusinian, and Dionysian mysteries all featured a god who descends into the underworld and returns. The main themes of the Greek mysteries—sex, fertility, death, and renewal—were also central to the non-Greek cults of Cybele, Isis, and Mithras, which merchants and soldiers encountered on their travels and brought back to their home countries. The *mystai* or initiates of all the mysteries reenacted the sufferings and deliverance of the cults' central figures, thus making themselves apt for salvation. This sort of personal involvement was lacking in the Greco-Roman civic religion. Another important difference between the mysteries and the state religion was their openness. Anyone—citizens, foreigners, slaves, even women—could be initiated and have a shot at salvation.

Christianity began as a messianic movement within Judaism, the archetypal West Asian monotheism. Jesus saw himself as a reformer of Judaism and directed his message to other Jews. Central to his gospel was a belief in the imminent arrival of the Kingdom of Heaven. In contrast to the Hebrew prophets, who demanded obedience to a stern, remote God, Jesus laid stress on love. Asked by a legal expert what was "the greatest commandment in the Law," he replied: "Love the Lord your God with all your heart and with all your soul and with all your mind." Second in importance was "Love your neighbor as yourself."[12] His unconventional statements and acts got him in trouble with conservative Jews and the Roman rulers of Palestine, who tried and executed him. His crucifixion was interpreted by his disciples as an act of self-sacrifice that rendered formal sacrifice and professional priests unnecessary.

Christianity as we know it owes more to the apostle Paul than to Jesus. One of Paul's innovations was to open the movement to Gentiles or non-Jews. The story of Jesus' life and death was, Paul wrote, "the power of God that brings salvation to everyone who believes: first to the Jew, then to the Gentile." But what were Christians supposed to believe in? There were differences about this even during Paul's lifetime, and two millennia of pronouncements, councils, schisms, heresies, and persecutions haven't really cleared things up. But one point Paul stressed has always remained central to Christian dogma: If you declare "Jesus is Lord" and believe "that God raised him from the dead, you will be saved."[13]

Paul and his successors used terms and ideas from Greco-Roman philosophy to explain their doctrines to prospective converts. Hebraic monotheism became colored by pagan wisdom. The classic example of this is found in the Gospel of John, which opens: "In the beginning was the Word [*Logos*], and the Word was with God, and the Word was God."[14] By *Logos* the author was referring to Jesus, but an educated reader of the original Greek would have heard echoes of other senses of the term going back as far as Heraclitus. The bulk of John consists of anecdotes illustrating the divinity of Jesus and explaining the necessity of belief. In the last verse the writer says that the book was written "that you may believe that Jesus is the Messiah, the Son of God, and that by believing you may have life in his name."[15]

In principle, Christian worship is directed exclusively to God the Father, God the Son, and God the Holy Spirit: three persons who are one. But from an early period Christians began to worship Mary the mother of Jesus as well as other saints. Theologians eventually distinguished the "adoration" of God from the "veneration" of Mary and the saints, but few worshippers bothered with this distinction. What they longed for was a caring intermediary between themselves and the unnamable Absolute. All devotional religions recognize a class of such beings: Mary and the saints, the chosen deities (*ishta devatas*) of Hindu devotees, the celestial buddhas and bodhisattvas of devotional Buddhism, and so forth.

Christianity flew under the radar of the Empire for the first 150 years of its existence. After the Great Fire of Rome (64 CE) Nero made scapegoats of some

Roman Christians but for the most part the authorities just ignored them. One of the few classical authors to mention them was the second-century satirist Lucian, who wrote in his *Death of Peregrinus* that after the worshippers of the "crucified sophist" (i.e., Jesus) had repudiated the Greco-Roman gods, they came to despise "all things equally and regard them as common property, accepting such teaching without any sort of clear proof."[16] The refusal of Christians to acknowledge the gods of the state or participate in public sacrifices caused people to regard them as anti-Roman atheists. This opened the door to sporadic persecutions between the first and third centuries. The Edict of Milan, issued by the emperor Constantine in 313, promised official toleration. Sixty-seven years later, in a stunning reversal of fortune, Christianity was proclaimed the state religion of the Empire.

The subsequent history of Christianity is too long and complex to summarize here. I pass on to Islam, the third of the major West Asian monotheisms, and the least interesting from the point of view of godless spirituality. Islam is based on the teachings of Muhammad, who lived in Arabia from around 570 to 632. According to Islamic tradition, he received a series of revelations from the angel Gabriel, which were meant to restore the original monotheism of Abraham, Moses, Jesus, and the other prophets. Muhammad is the final prophet and there will be no further revelations.

The five pillars of Islamic religious practice are testimony, prayer, alms-giving, fasting during the month of Ramadan, and the pilgrimage to Mecca. Testimony is the recitation of the *shahada* or declaration of faith: "There is no god but God. Muhammad is the messenger of God." Prayer, the mainstay of Muslim worship, must be performed in the prescribed manner five times a day. The use of images of any sort is forbidden, and there is nothing corresponding to the personal gods of Hinduism or the helpful bodhisattvas of Mahayana Buddhism. Congregational worship is performed in *masjids* or mosques. Shrines surmounting the graves of saints are found in many parts of the Islamic world and these sometimes become centers of popular devotion, but such practices are frowned upon by the orthodox, who quote a *hadith* or saying of Muhammad: "May Allah curse the Jews and Christians who took the graves of their prophets as Masjids."[17] In Islam all worship must be directed to Allah alone.

Theism and violence

Pope Innocent III had many reasons to want to eliminate the Cathars. First, their doctrines were unorthodox. They believed for example that Jesus had never been incarnate. Human souls were trapped in unclean bodies and the only way for them to achieve salvation was to reject the world completely. This meant there was no need for churches, sacraments or priests. Second, the Cathars refused to accept the authority of the Church. When a legate sent by Innocent was murdered, supposedly by Cathar sympathizers, Innocent pronounced the sect heretical and launched a crusade against them. The King of France had his own reasons for wanting to suppress of the nobles of Languedoc, the region of southern France where the Cathars were concentrated, and was glad to supply troops for the campaign. In the summer of 1209, ten thousand crusaders assembled near Lyon and began to march toward Languedoc. The first Cathar stronghold they encountered was Béziers, to which they laid siege on July 23. Irregular soldiers entered the gates. Knights, eager for plunder, followed. Unable to tell the Cathars from the Catholics, the knights rushed to their abbot and asked him what to do. He replied: "Kill [all of] them! Truly, God will know his own!" This famous command was first recorded a decade later, and some historians doubt its authenticity. But the abbot's own account is no less bloodcurdling. He wrote to the pope that his soldiers "spared no order of persons (whatever their rank, sex, or age) and put to the sword almost twenty thousand people. After this great slaughter the whole city was despoiled and burnt, as divine vengeance raged marvellously." The crusade went on for two decades, until Catharism was all but extinguished in France with the loss of hundreds of thousands of lives. It was, some scholars maintain, the first ideological genocide, and it was done in the name of the Church.[18]

"What is it about religion that can turn nice people into murderers?" asked social psychologist Ara Norenzayan in a 2008 interview. His tone was blunt but personal experience gave him the right to speak bluntly. Growing up in Beirut during the Lebanese Civil War, he saw first-hand how religious passions fueled the violence that tore his country apart. Afterward he went to North America, earned a doctorate in psychology, and is now a leading researcher in the field of psychology of religion. Reflecting as an adult on what he had witnessed as an adolescent, Norenzayan concluded that those involved in the violence were "not psychopaths. They were nice people doing terrible things out of ideology."[19] Which raises the further question: Why do people, nice or not, allow ideologies, specifically religious ideologies, drive them to do terrible things? This problem has been studied by researchers in various disciplines—ethology, anthropology, sociology, psychology—and their findings are too important to be ignored. I therefore feel it necessary, before proceeding with this historical study, to review what researchers in these fields have said about religion and violence.

Religion is a complex phenomenon. So is violence. It follows that any attempt to find a simple solution to the problem of religious violence is doomed to failure. But simple or even simplistic solutions are what most people offer. "As I write," proclaimed essayist Christopher Hitchens, "people of faith are in their different ways planning your and my destruction… *Religion poisons everything.*" Biologist Richard Dawkins concurred: "Only religious faith is a strong enough force to motivate such utter madness [terrorist bombings] in otherwise sane and decent people."[20] Looking at the same phenomena from the opposite point of view, theology professor William Cavanaugh wrote that "religious violence" was just a myth created to legitimize the liberal nation-state. Popular writer Karen Armstrong agreed, going to great lengths to show that religious violence is a fiction invented by seventeenth-century thinkers, and that there is always a political explanation for violence done in the name of religion.[21] I will try to steer clear of such one-sided viewpoints. There is, to be sure, no *necessary* connection between religion and violence, and much of the violence that defiled the last century had no direct link with religious ideologies. But it certainly is true that many religions, especially theistic ones, create psychological attitudes and social configurations that encourage the commission of violent acts.

Violence is part of our evolutionary heritage. Early humans lived among powerful animals who treated them as prey. To survive, they used their mental and social abilities to kill creatures that were larger and stronger than they were. They also attacked fellow humans while competing for territory, resources, and mates. We still do the same today, although we have moved from the savanna to the city and have developed social rules that allow most of us to live most of our lives in peace. Still, as Freud famously observed, we retain an inborn "tendency to aggression" that we struggle to keep out of sight. This fundamental hostility toward other human beings simmers just below the surface and as a result "civilized society is constantly threatened with disintegration."[22]

Instinctive aggression forms the background of animal as well as human violence, but violence related to religious beliefs is a social and cultural phenomenon that is unique to *Homo sapiens*. Anthropologists, sociologists, and social psychologists have different ways of accounting for this characteristically human pattern of behavior. They have reached no consensus within their disciplines, much less across them, but they have made some interesting observations and developed a number of useful theories that I will touch on here.

Social theorists have long been fascinated by the way that religious rituals express or transform our tendencies to violence. Sociologist Émile Durkheim thought that the excitement generated by tribal rituals produces moments of transfiguring exaltation that bind the group together. This was, he thought, the underlying truth of religion. More recently, anthropologists Candace Alcorta and Richard Sosis found that painful and violent rituals have measurable effects on the autonomic nervous system. This invests "symbols, beliefs, and other social abstractions with emotional significance" that strengthens social cohesion. Sacrifice is the central ritual of many religions, and sacrifice is at root an act of killing. Philosophical anthropologist René Girard believed that sacrifice was a way for human beings to expiate the guilt of an "original act of violence," projecting it onto a scapegoat that could be killed or driven away. In a similar vein, classical scholar Walter Burkert wrote: "Sacrificial killing is the basic experience of the 'sacred.'"[23] The common factor in all these theories is the role played by violence in creating social order.

Social theorists provide insights into the underlying causes of religious violence, but they have little to say about why particular individuals do violent things in the name of their religions. And it is concrete individuals, not society in the abstract, who perform religious acts, such as visiting holy sites (to give a positive example) or destroying sites linked to an enemy (to give a negative one). Both pilgrimages and terrorist attacks are socially defined activities, but some people prefer the former and some the latter. To understand why we have to examine the intersection between social conditioning and individual choice. This is what social psychologists do. Among their central interests are the dynamics of authority and obedience and the formation of in-groups and out-groups.

History provides abundant evidence that people do terrible things in obedience to the orders of a leader. The Milgram experiment of 1961—in which subjects were told by an authoritative figure to give painful shocks to others and carried out the orders about 60 percent of the time—showed how easy it is to turn ordinary people into agents of violence. In the experiment no actual shock was delivered. In the historical event the experiment was meant to mirror—the participation of ordinary people in the Holocaust of the Jews—the effects were real and horrific.

After World War II, intellectuals asked how the barbarism of the Nazis was possible. Philosopher Hannah Arendt proposed that the perpetrators did not really reflect on their actions; they were just going about their ordinary business. The only thing driving Adolf Eichmann, the officer in charge of the Holocaust, was "an extraordinary diligence in looking out for his personal advancement."[24] Arendt's conclusion has been challenged by recent social scientists, among them Stephen Reicher, Alexander Haslam, and Rakshi Rath, who argue that people who participate in mass violence do so willingly. Killing becomes acceptable, indeed virtuous, "when it can be celebrated as the *right thing to do*." This happens when one group succeeds in portraying another group as a threat to its existence. A common way of doing this is dehumanization: the use of animal or demonic imagery to show that the enemy is less than human and therefore unworthy of moral consideration. When Jews are equated with rats and Tutsis with cockroaches, their extermination is not just permissible but praiseworthy.[25]

Social scientists who study outbreaks of religious violence have tried to identify its characteristics. Their lists are not definitive—both religion and violence are too complex to permit that—but some of them are useful. Almost every list includes one feature: absolute, inflexible beliefs. People who participate in religious violence are inclined to think: There is only one truth. All other beliefs are false. There is no room for negotiation or compromise. Negotiation is impossible, writes social psychologist R.M. Williams, because religious values are "final and irrevocable" and therefore "*by definition* not subject to compromise or resolution."[26]

Another feature of religious violence is the instrumental role of symbolism. All religions rely on symbolic representations of the more-than-physical reality that is the focus of their interest: sacred images, sites, buildings, and so forth. These symbols often become flashpoints in conflicts, as in the Temple Mount/Haram al-Sharif problem in Jerusalem and the Babri Masjid/Ram Janmabhumi conflict in India. Religious scholar Mark Juergensmeyer claimed that "religious terrorism ... is almost exclusively symbolic."[27] This goes a bit too far. Religious violence has material as well as symbolic dimensions. The Islamic State of Iraq and Syria (ISIS) wants to do more than attack symbolic targets: it wants to control Iraq and Syria. But symbolism certainly is important, and when it is combined with absolute beliefs, the result is often what Juergensmeyer calls a "cosmic war." Perpetrators of religious violence view their struggle as "a defense not only of lives but of entire cultures." Even if the outcome seems "hopeless in human terms," the cosmic warrior can transport it to "a sacred plane, where the possibilities of victory are in God's hands."[28] And with God's help anything is possible.

All religions tend toward absolutism. All religions make use of symbolism. Most religions have been involved in wars. Yet some religions have been more inclined to violence than others. If we look back on the traditions I have spoken of in this book, it is clear that the nontheistic ones have had little to do with organized violence. Jains have never engaged in wars of religious conquest. Neither have Confucians, philosophical Daoists, or nontheistic Buddhists or Hindus. This is not to say that Jain, Confucian, Daoist, Buddhist, and Hindu rulers were never involved in wars or that they had no interest in cultural, including religious, expansion. But they never declared war for no other reason than to force their beliefs on others. Theistic religions, on the other hand, have always been prone to righteous battle. This is especially true of the two West Asian monotheisms that regard conversion as a religious duty. To Christians and Muslims, salvation is reserved for people who accept the one and only God. Because salvation is the ultimate goal of life, those who are not born Christian or Muslim must be persuaded or compelled to embrace the one true faith. It is therefore not surprising that these two faiths have been responsible for most of the religious violence that has troubled the world over the last two millennia. Still, other forms of theism have added to the toll. Before examining the special problems of monotheism, I will look at a few examples of religious violence committed by theistic Buddhists and Hindus.

Nonviolence or *ahimsa* is one of the key precepts of Buddhism, but the Buddhist *sangha* or community has been involved willy-nilly in politics and social conflict since the days of the Buddha. Buddhist rulers have sometimes taken up arms to defend their faith against perceived aggressors, and members of Buddhist sects have often behaved aggressively toward other sects. The Kamakura period in Japan (1192–1333) was an especially fruitful time for factional struggles, with members of the Pure Land, Zen, and other schools engaging in mutual denigration. Among the contenders, the monk Nichiren was probably the most belligerent. "I attacked the Zen sect as the work of devils, and Shingon as a heresy that will ruin the nation and insisted that the temples of the Nembutsu [Pure Land] priests, the Zen sect, and the Ritsu priests be burned down, and the priests of the Nembutsu beheaded," he wrote in a letter of 1276.[29] For centuries, Nichiren's words and deeds have been an inspiration to Japanese religious extremists, for instance Nissho Inoue, who organized the League of Blood, an extremist group, in 1932. In February and March of that year, members of the League plotted a series of political killings, two of which were successful. Inoue was arrested and put in jail, but the remnants of his group helped organize the assassination of the prime minister of Japan that May. This was an important milestone in the rise of Japanese militarism, which led the country into World War II. Members of other Buddhist sects also supported Japanese militarism before and during the war. A 1939 statement by Zen teacher Harada Daiun Sogaku has become emblematic of the use of Buddhist ideas to support institutionalized violence: "The unity of Zen and war of which I speak comes to the farthest reaches of the holy war."[30]

Most violence committed by Buddhists in recent years has been connected with ethnicity and politics. The exploits of medieval kings of Sri Lanka who resisted invaders from India were invoked by modern Buddhist monks to fuel recent clashes between Sinhalas and Tamils, which cost perhaps 100,000 lives. Sri Lankan Buddhists also use religious rhetoric to justify attacks against Sri Lankan Muslims. Similar appeals to religious and ethnic identity have contributed to the rise of anti-Muslim violence in Myanmar. "They would like to occupy our country, but I won't let them. We must keep Myanmar Buddhist," declared a popular monk after a series of deadly riots in 2013.[31]

Hinduism has often endorsed nonviolence but it also proclaimed the necessity of righteous battle. When Krishna in the *Bhagavad Gita* urges Arjuna to return to the battlefield, one of his first arguments is that Arjuna must follow the *dharma* of his caste, for there is "nothing better for a warrior than a duty-bound war."[32] Arjuna accepts Krishna's advice and rejoins his brothers and their allies on the battlefield. Eighteen days later virtually everybody on both sides is dead. In the *Ramayana*, the avatar Rama defends the *dharma* by fighting demons but also by killing humans who unsettle the fixed order of things. When he learns that Shambuka, a member of the laboring caste, is practicing austerities (something only members of the higher castes should do) he cuts off Shambuka's head. This anecdote is a literary prototype of the countless instances of violence against the lower castes that have been carried out in India from the earliest times to the present.

The most successful revolt against the rigidity of caste came from the bhakti movement. Starting from the seventh century, devotees worshipped the deity of their choice without the intervention of priests and without regard to their position in the caste hierarchy. But devotion to a single god often gives rise to "hideous fanaticism," as nineteenth-century reformer Swami Vivekananda observed.[33] Two of the greatest medieval devotees of Shiva, Tirunavukkarasar and Sambandar, were hostile to Jains and denigrated them in their hymns. Once (the story is told) Sambandar was summoned to a town where Shaivites and Jains were holding a contest to determine whose scriptures were best. The winners would have the right to slaughter the losers. The Shaivites, led by Sambandar, came out on top, so 8,000 Jains were impaled on stakes and left to die. This anecdote was included in the *Periya Purana*, a twelfth-century Tamil scripture, and the impalement of the Jains was often depicted by Shaivite artists. (The scene is rather grisly: birds peck out the eyes of dying Jains and dogs lick up their blood.) The story may well be legendary but it accurately evokes the hostile Shaivite attitude toward Jains, who around that time were driven from southeast India never to return.

The bhakti poets of southwest India also were inclined to aggression. "One should not commit violence against any living being, but yet the sinners who abuse Siva must be killed without hesitation," wrote the medieval poet Panditaradhya.[34] The *Basava Purana* is filled with descriptions of violent acts performed in Shiva's name. Nonplussed by all the gore, scholars of Shaivite literature have theorized that the glorification of violence was "a way of exhibiting one's faith in Siva" as well as "an attempt to organize a closed cult." But it had real-world results. Shaivites destroyed or repurposed Jain and Buddhist temples and sometimes committed deadly acts of violence.[35]

In northern India during the same period, Hindus suffered greatly at the hands of Muslim marauders. This was part of the enormous wave of violence that accompanied the spread of Islam through Central and South Asia. But by the eighteenth century, Indian Muslims and Hindus had learned to live together in comparative harmony. The balance was upset during the colonial period, when the British rulers of the country learned to play the two communities off against one another. Hindu–Muslim violence during the independence movement led to the partition of the British India along religious lines. In the resulting chaos a million people died. Today Hindu minorities in Pakistan and Bangladesh live in subjugation and fear. The Muslim minority in India is better off but still vulnerable. In areas of mixed population, writes political scientist Paul Brass, interreligious rioting is an organized technique for consolidating political power. Those who participate are willing to loot and kill because they accept the image of the dehumanized religious "other" that is purveyed by local leaders.[36] Muslims are routinely depicted by Hindus as aliens who have to be driven from the holy land: "The time has come for us to take back what's ours, to claim Hindustan [i.e., India] for Hindus," proclaims the spokesman of a Hindu group which encourages the use of violence against people (mostly Muslims) suspected of killing cows.[37]

In *The Natural History of Religion* (1757) David Hume wrote that polytheism had one great advantage over monotheism: "By limiting the powers and functions of its deities, it naturally admits the Gods of other sects and nations to a share of divinity, and renders all the various deities, as well as rites, ceremonies, or traditions, compatible with each other." On the other hand, "almost all religions which have maintained the unity of God" were intolerant. Hume mentioned in particular "the implacable narrow spirit of the Jews" and the "still more bloody principles" of Muslims. If Christians had become tolerant in recent times it was because of "the steady resolution of the civil magistrate, in opposition to the continued efforts of priests and bigots."[38]

Since the publication of Hume's *Natural History* 260 years ago, many other scholars have examined the nexus between monotheism and violence. An important recent contribution is Jan Assmann's *The Price of Monotheism*, which argues that the inflexible "Mosaic distinction" between true and false religion is the theological basis of exclusivism and violence among followers of the monotheistic faiths.[39] The Jews themselves became victims of such violence after their expulsion from the Holy Land. Anti-Jewish pograms in Europe, recurrent since the Middle Ages, became severe in Russia and Poland during the nineteenth century. A movement to resettle European Jews in Palestine began around 1897 and picked up momentum after World War I. This brought Jewish settlers in conflict with the Arab world. One result was Jewish terrorism. Avraham Stern, founder of the paramilitary group Lehi, which carried out a number of terrorist acts between 1944 and 1948, cited the Bible and God's covenant with Israel as grounds for the "renewal of Hebrew sovereignty" over Palestine and the expulsion of the "alien" population (i.e., the Arabs who lived there). Recent terrorist acts, such as the assassination of Prime Minister Yitzhak Rabin in 1995, were the work of men convinced they were acting in accordance with the teachings of Judaism. After shooting the prime minister, who had recently signed the Oslo peace accords, his assailant declared: "I acted alone on God's orders and I have no regrets."[40]

The New Testament presents Jesus as a prophet of peace, who preached against hatred and retaliation. "I tell you, do not resist an evil person," he says in the Sermon on the Mount. "If anyone slaps you on the right cheek, turn to them the other cheek also."[41] During the early years of Christianity, many believers emulated Jesus in this respect. Few served in the Roman imperial army. This was one of the reasons they were persecuted by the Roman state. The situation changed radically during the fourth century, when Christianity was legalized and then became the state religion. But just as Christians began to taste the fruits of power, their religion was shaken by internal turmoil. A group called the Donatists thought that the settlement with Rome was a betrayal. They made such a nuisance of themselves that Constantine sent troops to quiet them down. The result was a massacre of Donatists. Something similar happened in 356 when Constantine's son Constantinus, who favored the Arians, sent troops to depose an Athanasian bishop in Egypt. Again the result was slaughter.

It was not just rulers and soldiers who supported violence. Fourth-century archbishop—later saint—John Chrysostom recommended that Christians who encountered a blasphemer should "smite him on the face; strike his mouth; sanctify thy hand with the blow."[42] This is a far cry from turning the other cheek. John also is notorious for his anti-Jewish sermons. After blaming all Jews for the death of Jesus he slandered them in vulgar terms. To those who said that Jews worshipped the same God as Christians, he replied: "No Jew adores God!" and continued with his vilification.[43] No wonder the Nazis found it convenient to reprint John's sermons when they were gearing up for the Final Solution.

One of John's contemporaries, the bishop and future saint Augustine, was as harsh toward followers of Roman polytheism as John was toward the Jews. In his *City of God* he wrote in glowing terms of Roman officers who "overthrew the temples and broke the images of the false gods." Since that happened, he added, "who does not see how much the worship of the name of Christ has increased?"[44] A few years later, the Egyptian abbot Shenoute, who was on the warpath against a local pagan, led a group of rioters who ransacked the man's house and smashed his idols. Summoned by a magistrate and charged with banditry, Shenoute cried out: "There is no crime for those who have Christ."[45]

Rome was sacked in 410 and by the end of the century the Western Roman Empire ceased to be. The Eastern Roman Empire survived and Eastern Christianity took its own course, separating from the Church of Rome in 1054. Forty-one years later the head of Eastern Empire sent a message to Pope Urban II asking for help against the Muslims who held Jerusalem and threatened Byzantium. The result was the First Crusade. Religious leaders used inflammatory rhetoric to persuade soldiers and civilians to join this campaign to recover the Church of the Holy Sepulchre, which was being "polluted by the filthiness of an unclean nation." On the way to the Holy Land, crusaders robbed and massacred thousands of German Jews and laid waste vast stretches of Europe and Asia. Eventually they captured Jerusalem, killing tens of thousands of its Muslim and Jewish inhabitants. "In the temple and portico of Solomon," wrote a chaplain who witnessed the sack of the city, "men rode in blood up to their knees and the bridle reins. Indeed it was a just and splendid judgment of God, that this place should be filled with the blood of the unbelievers, when it had suffered so long from their blasphemies."[46] The crusaders decided to keep Jerusalem for themselves rather than restore it to Byzantium, opening the way to centuries of chaos in the region.

Religious fanaticism has also incited Christians to wreak violence on other Christians. In the twelfth century the Church inaugurated the Inquisition to investigate and punish heretics. Over the next 800 years, countless thousands were executed in France, Spain, Portugal, Italy, the Americas, Asia, and Africa for holding unorthodox opinions, belonging to the wrong community, or being accused of witchcraft. Sometimes the number of heretics was so great that military action was required, as during the Albigensian Crusade, which brought about the death of hundreds of thousands of Cathars.

Body counts tell us little about the horror of religious wars as experienced by the people who lived through them, but they help put things in perspective. At least ten million people died during the Wars of Religion that followed the Protestant Reformation. This series of conflicts involving more than a dozen belligerents and stretching over 130 years had many causes, but most people at the time connected the bloodshed with religion. The writer Michel de Montaigne was well acquainted with the atrocities committed during the French Wars of Religion. (At least two million people died, including twenty or thirty thousand during the St. Bartholomew's Day Massacre of August 1572, an event that was joyously celebrated by Pope Gregory XIII.) Montaigne wrote in this connection: "Our [religious] zeal does wonders when it is seconding our leaning toward hatred, cruelty, ambition, avarice, detraction, rebellion." The worst of all conditions, he noted in another essay, was where "wickedness comes to be legitimate and … assumes the cloak of virtue." Turning as he often did to the classics of Latin literature, he concluded with a quote from the Roman historian Livy: "Nothing is more deceptive in appearance than a depraved religion, in which the will of the gods is offered as a pretext for crimes."[47] Four hundred years later, American historian Natalie Zemon Davis made an exhaustive study of the riots that took place during the French religious wars. She found a mixture of religious, political, and socioeconomic motives but concluded that the riots were "essentially religious." And because the conflict was connected with the community's fundamental values, the violence carried out by the rioters was unusually brutal.[48]

The end of the European Wars of Religion overlapped with the beginning of the Age of Enlightenment. The great thinkers of that period—Thomas Hobbes, Baruch Spinoza, John Locke—never doubted that the carnage of the previous century was due mainly to religious differences. Locke's solution was the separation of politics and religion. This idea caught on, first in the United States and France, then other countries of Europe and America. As a result the Christian world has seen few wars of religion since the beginning of the eighteenth century. This does not mean that religiously sanctioned violence ceased to be. The slave trade, which was defended from many pulpits, continued for two centuries. The political domination and economic exploitation of the Americas, Australia, Africa, and much of Asia were justified by the need to impose the so-called benefits of Christianity on "natives" who were happy with their own religions, which were older, richer, and often less violent than Christianity. The conflicts that arose in the wake of decolonization, such as the Troubles in Northern Ireland (1968–1998) and the Sudanese Civil Wars (1955–2005) were primarily ethnic and economic but had a strong religious coloration. Protestant preachers in Belfast and Muslim preachers in Khartoum stoked the fires of sectarian hatred that made the violence last as long as it did. In the United States, Christian terrorists have bombed abortion clinics and gay and lesbian bars and murdered abortion providers. Michael Bray, an Army of God ideologue who was convicted for his role in some of these bombings, defended the use of violence against "the new pagan 'order' of godless democracy and sexual libertinism" in his book *A Time to Kill*.[49]

Islam has been the dominant religion of West Asia and North Africa for more than a millennium. It exists in dozens of different forms—from the hyperconservative Wahhabism of Saudi Arabia to the mystical Sufism found in scattered communities from Morocco to Indonesia. It therefore is difficult to speak of the relationship between Islam as a whole and violence. But all interpretations of Islam are based on the Quran and Hadith (the recorded words and acts of Muhammad) and passages of these texts lay great stress on the performance of violent deeds. There were historical reasons for this. When Muhammad received the verses of Quran, he and his followers were engaged in a struggle with the polytheists of Mecca. Different verses of the Quran suggest different ways of dealing with this situation. Sometimes the advice is to avoid confrontation, for example: "Then declare what you are commanded and turn away from the polytheists." At other times, the need is defensive warfare: "Permission [to fight] has been given to those who are being fought, because they were wronged." Some verses stress the need of acting lawfully if violence is required, for example, by avoiding bloodshed during the month of Ramadan. Still, those who prevent Muslims from worshiping must be killed, for such oppression is more sinful than killing. Finally, in some circumstances the faithful are urged to engage in unrestricted warfare: "When the sacred months have passed, then kill the polytheists wherever you find them and capture them and besiege them and sit in wait for them at every place of ambush."[50]

During the last ten years of his life, Muhammad took part in twenty-seven raids or battles and ordered his followers to launch seventy-three more. The aim of these expeditions varied, from gathering booty (a traditional form of economic activity in the region) to regaining Mecca and establishing monotheism throughout Arabia. Whenever Muhammad appointed a leader he told him: "Fight in the name of Allah and in the way of Allah. Fight against those who disbelieve in Allah. Make a holy war [*jihad*]."[51] The word *jihad* has many meanings. The basic sense is "striving" and this has no necessary connection with holy war. But there is no getting around the fact that Muhammad often promoted *jihad* in the sense of fighting. When a man asked him what was the best sort of action, he replied, first, "Faith in Allah and His Messenger," and second, "Jihad (holy fighting) in the Cause of Allah."[52] Some medieval Muslim scholars distinguished "greater" jihad (the struggle against one's baser self) from "lesser" jihad (fighting against the enemies of Islam) but there is little support for this distinction in the Quran and authoritative hadiths.[53]

After Muhammad's death, his followers stabilized his gains and then embarked on a series of campaigns that in little more than a century brought a huge swath of territory, from the Atlantic to Afghanistan, under Muslim control. How was this astonishing conquest possible? The lust for booty certainly was a factor (an entire chapter of the Quran is devoted to the division of the spoils of war). The weakness of the Byzantine and Persian empires made it easy for the Arabs to begin their advance, but the ideal of jihad helped them follow through. "The concept of holy war quickly became a powerful motivator," as one historian dryly puts it.[54]

As Islam was spreading across three continents, its heartland lurched into civil war. The second and third caliphs or successors of Muhammad were assassinated. So was the fourth, Muhammad's cousin and son-in-law Ali. From this point on the Muslim world has been divided into two main sects, the Sunnis (who regard themselves as the orthodox group) and the Shias (the followers of Ali). Their mutual hostility over the last 1,300 years has provoked hundreds of major conflicts and numberless small acts of violence. There is no way of knowing how many thousands of people have died as a result.

Islamic civilization reached a dazzling peak between the ninth and seventeenth centuries. Since then it has been overshadowed by the West. After World War I, the Ottoman Caliphate was abolished and colonial leaders carved out the mandates of Syria and Lebanon, Palestine and Transjordan, and Mesopotamia (Iraq). The Middle East has been unstable ever since. Dictatorships thrived, civil wars broke out, and terrorism found a place to grow.

Statistics support the popular notion that Islam is associated with much contemporary violence. It "has been centrally or peripherally involved in more than 80 percent of civil wars since 1940," wrote political scientist Monica Duffy Toft in 2013. There were, she acknowledged, political and economic reasons for this phenomenon; but there also was a significant link "between violent conflict and faith as embodied in the concepts of jihad." Factions that succeeded in putting their agenda forward gained "increased access to arms, cash, and fighters." Conscripts traveled to conflict zones and supported "whichever leader has done the best job of establishing his religious credentials." The rise of the ISIS in 2014 substantiated Toff's analysis.[55]

Between 1980 and 2017, hundreds of Islamist terrorist attacks took place throughout the world, resulting in many thousands of deaths and billions of dollars in damage. Reports of such attacks appear frequently in the media, creating an atmosphere of fear and confusion that makes it hard to get at the root of the problem. Scholars have published hundreds of books and articles highlighting the many factors—religious, political, economic, sociological, cultural, psychological, criminal—that push certain people in the direction of Islamist terrorism. Social scientists who study the problem make it clear that there is no single "root cause" of Islamist radicalization. Rather, writes social psychologist Nafees Hamid, "Multiple factors interact in complex ways that cause radicalization to emerge in individual people and groups."[56]

Here we are concerned with one specific question: is there a direct connection between Islamic religious beliefs and terrorist violence? People with different backgrounds offer different answers. Many devout Muslims insist that terrorism "has nothing to do with Islam." (I heard this more than once in Morocco after the November 13, 2015, attacks in Paris that resulted in 137 deaths.) This does not explain the current escalation of the problem. On the other hand, many non-Muslims believe that Islam is inherently prone to violence. There is no reason to think that this is any more true than equivalent statements about other religions would be. It is however true that followers of Islam have a large body of scriptural statements to draw on to rationalize violent deeds. Members of the ISIS, from the highest leaders to the newest recruits, cite the Quran and other Islamic texts to justify suicide bombings, the beheading of captives, and the systematic rape of sex slaves.[57] Other Islamist groups are equally clear about their religious motives. After 148 people, most of them students, were killed at a Kenyan university in April 2015, the Somali terrorist group Al-Shabaab explained that it allowed Muslims to escape before the others were massacred because "Muslim blood is inviolable whereas the blood of a Kafir [disbeliever] has no protection."[58]

It would be foolish to say that all religions or certain religions are intrinsically prone to violence; it would be just as foolish to say that there is no connection at all between the teachings of many religions and the performance of violent acts. The scriptures of the three West Asian monotheisms prescribe the use of violence in certain circumstances, and followers of these religions quote these prescriptions when they kill or maim other people. Followers of Hinduism appeal to mythological texts when they engage in violence against non-Hindus. Followers of the Buddha cry "Buddhism in danger" when they draw swords against non-Buddhists. And so on. There is therefore good reason for critics of religion to bring up the question of violence when they argue that religious fanaticism is a serious threat to civilization.

Doubt, dissent, and reform

Born in northern Syria in 973, Abul 'Ala al-Ma'arri lost his eyesight to smallpox when he was a child but this did not prevent him from mastering Arabic literature and becoming one of the greatest poets of his age. After the appearance of his first collection he was fêted in Baghdad's literary salons, but he refused to write panegyrics for pay and eventually returned to his hometown of Ma'arrat al-Nu'man, where he lived the rest of his life. A strand of pessimism runs through his poetry, along with a contempt for hypocrisy. Human beings, he wrote in a sardonic couplet, fell into "two great schools / Enlightened knaves or else religious fools." He thought it idiotic that believers never reflected on what they were taught: "Monks in their cloisters and devotees in the mosques accept their creed just as a story is handed down from him who tells it, without distinguishing between a true interpreter and a false." Without true understanding, even the pilgrimage to Mecca was just "a heathen's journey." When he wanted to say things that were even more shocking, al-Ma'arri attributed his thoughts to unnamed others: "In the opinion of some whom I do not mention," he once wrote, "the Black Stone is only a remnant of idols and (sacrificial) altar-stones." He then threw his critics off the scent by continuing with verses of conventional piety. For the most part the dissimulation worked, though sometimes people murmured that the blind poet of Syria had gone too far. Somehow he managed to avoid prosecution and died old and honored in his hometown in 1057. But his heterodoxy was not forgotten. In 2013 a bust of him in Ma'arrat al-Nu'man was decapitated by members of an al-Qaeda affiliate.[59]

By the end of the eighth century the great theistic religions extended across Eurasia, from Ireland to Armenia, from Spain to Iran, from Kashmir to Sri Lanka, and from Tibet to Japan. Each existed in different forms (Roman/Nestorian, Sunni/Shia, Shaiva/Vaishnava, Pure Land/Tiantai, and so forth) but was focused on a single deity (God, Allah, Parameshwara, Buddha) who was regarded as omnipotent and omniscient. The nontheistic traditions that had flourished in classical India and Europe were now defunct (Epicureanism, Skepticism) or in decline (Samkhya, Yoga) or increasingly amalgamated with devotional theism (Vedanta). Nontheistic philosophies and practices survived among Neo-Confucians and Zen Buddhists, and influenced the thought and practices of sufis, *sants*, and Sikhs. In Europe unbelief was almost unheard of but protests against the Roman Church swelled from the fifteenth century. By fostering subjectivity and individual practice, Protestants unwittingly opened the way for modern nontheistic spirituality.

In 750 al-Mansur, the second caliph of the Abbasid dynasty, established Baghdad as his capital. It soon became the most cosmopolitan city in the world, attracting writers, artists, and philosophers from every direction. Scholars collected stories from West Asia and India and immortalized them in the *Book of One Thousand and One Nights*; mathematicians drew on Indian number theory to develop algebra; architects borrowed from Persian and Central Asian motifs while creating the Abbasid style; philosophers read and translated Plato and Aristotle, helping to preserve these almost forgotten writers for future generations.

Most Abbasid thinkers remained safely within the bounds of Islamic orthodoxy, but some dared examine the basic assumptions of their religion. Ibn al-Rawandi (827–911) began his career as a rationalist theologian but ended up a skeptic who doubted the miracles of the prophets and questioned the revelations of the Quran. His younger contemporary Abu Bakr al-Razi (c. 854–c. 925), a respected physician and alchemist, wrote a work on religion that was branded as heretical and survives only in passages quoted by detractors. Razi did not deny the idea of God but argued that God, being all good, should not give special knowledge to some and deny it to others. The result of such an unequal distribution would be disaster, for "each group would decree the veracity of its own *imam* [religious leader] and the falsehood of [all] others, and they would draw swords against each other." Indeed, he added in the indicative mood, "many people have perished in this way, as we can see." The problem with revealed religion was that people blindly followed their leaders, rejecting "rational speculation and inquiry about the fundamental doctrines." This led to closed-mindedness which sometimes led to violence: "If the people of this religion are asked about the proof for the soundness of their religion, they flare up, get angry and spill the blood of whoever confronts them with this question. They forbid rational speculation and strive to kill their adversaries. This is why truth became thoroughly silenced and concealed." Razi's work, in the opinion of two modern scholars, constitutes "the most violent polemic against religion in the course of the middle ages."[60] It's no surprise his books were not preserved.

In the middle of the eleventh century the Seljuk Turks swept down from Central Asia, taking control of northern Iran and occupying Baghdad. The Seljuk ruler declared himself the protector of the caliph; the caliph reciprocated by granting him the title of sultan or king. This division of labor between spiritual and temporal authorities made it hard for the forces of orthodoxy to mandate a single approach to Islam. Three approaches vied for supremacy: scholastic theology, rationalistic philosophy, and Sufi mysticism. This tripartite struggle was summed up in the life of the Persian theologian al-Ghazali (1058–1111). In his autobiography he relates how, after a period of agonizing doubt, he was able to "recover the truth from amidst the confusion of sects" and raise himself up "from the abyss of blind belief in authority to the height of discernment." After a period of intense Quranic study he took refuge in the beliefs and practices of the sufis.[61]

Sufism is so different from orthodox Islam that some scholars have speculated that its origins must lie outside, in Neoplatonism or Gnosticism or Hindu asceticism. Muslims who support Sufism reject such ideas, insisting that it is based on the Quran, while fundamentalists declare that Sufism has nothing at all to do with Islam. Sufis have always acknowledged their submission to Allah but like mystics of other religious traditions they have yearned for the unitive experience that dissolves the distinction between the divine and the human:

> Make me one with the One, thou unique One,
> in a true act of confession that God is one,
> to which no path serves as Way! As I am potential Truth
> and actual truth is my own potential, may our separateness cease to be![62]

So wrote the Persian sufi Mansur al-Hallaj (858–922), who is notorious for saying "I am the Truth," a blasphemous utterance since Truth (*al-Haqq*) is one of the names of God. For this heresy he was arrested, imprisoned, and tortured to death.

Al-Hallaj was the most famous of the "intoxicated" sufis, those who lose themselves so utterly in the experience of union that they tend to make extravagant claims. Less disruptive to society are the "sober" sufis, whose feet are firmly grounded in Islamic theology. But even the soberest sufis have a conception of God that is wider and more flexible than orthodox theology allows. Ibn 'Arabi (1165–1240), perhaps the greatest sufi philosopher, wrote daringly of the interrelationship between God and the human being:

> How can He be independent when I help and aid Him?
> For that cause God brought me into existence,
> And I know Him and bring Him into existence.

God and the universe are not distinct. Between them stands the Perfect Human, who is "the image of God and the archetype of the universe." God "reveals Himself in every form and belief in a degree proportionate to the pre-determined capacity of the believer."[63]

Born in Spain, Ibn 'Arabi lived his last days in Damascus, where he completed his major works and taught his philosophy to the students who had gathered around him. Some of them were also in contact with the younger sufi Jalal ad-Din Rumi (1207–1273). It is possible that the two men met in Damascus, but if they did it was not a memorable event for either. Their styles of Sufism were worlds apart. Ibn 'Arabi's approach was mostly through the mind, Rumi's predominantly through the heart.

The decisive event in Rumi's life was his meeting with the wandering dervish Shams al-Din, who became his friend and guide. Much of Rumi's poetic output is focused on his love for Shams, who was for him the image of the divine beloved. When his students asked him to speak about his master, all Rumi could say was, "Don't bother me, for I am annihilated! My thoughts are wiped out." To the sufi, annihilation or *fana* is the extinction of self in the bliss of union. Some of Rumi's verses hint at the love that opens the doors to unitive experience:

> Listen, if you can stand to.
> Union with the Friend means not being who you've been,
> being instead silence: A place: A view
> where language is inside seeing.[64]

After his death, Rumi's followers founded the Mevlevi order of Sufism to perpetuate his teachings and the practices associated with them, such as the *sama* or whirling dance for which the order is famous. Around the same time, other Sufi orders were founded in Turkey, Iraq, and India. Originally loose groups of seekers, they eventually became formal organizations, often well endowed and sometimes allied with the powers that be. Their sheikhs or leaders transmitted the teachings by oral initiation or through esoteric texts, usually written in Arabic and Persian. But there also were dervishes who lived in isolation or wandered from place to place. Admired for their austerity, speaking the local languages, they helped spread Islam from Spain to Southeast Asia.

In 1258, fourteen years after Rumi's meeting with Shams al-Din, a Mongol army under Hulagu Khan plundered Baghdad and executed the caliph, bringing the Abbasid dynasty to an inglorious close. Meanwhile other descendants of Genghis Khan were extending the boundaries of the Mongol Empire from Korea to Ukraine. Wherever they went, the Mongols wreaked destruction and slaughtered all who opposed them. Traditionally followers of shamanism, they found it expedient to tolerate, patronize, and eventually adopt the religions of those they conquered. The descendants of Hulagu became converts to Islam, while Hulugu's brother Kublai Khan favored Tibetan Buddhism. In 1271, after a series of military victories, Kublai proclaimed himself emperor of China. Eight years later he finished off the Song dynasty, which had ruled most of the country for more than 300 years.

Like the Abbasid caliphate, the Song dynasty (960–1279) was a period of great cultural efflorescence. In philosophy it was the golden age of Neo-Confucianism, which laid down patterns of thought and practice that would shape East Asian society for almost a millennium. Roughly speaking, Neo-Confucianism is a blend of Confucian ideas with philosophical concepts and practices adapted from Buddhism and Daoism. Classical Confucianism had no metaphysics and little cosmology. Buddhism had plenty of both but was viewed by many Chinese as a foreign import. When Neo-Confucian thinkers constructed Buddhist-influenced systems, they made use of traditional Chinese concepts, in particular *li* or principle and *qi* or psychophysical substance. *Li* is perfect and identical in all. The *qi* allotted to each individual is different and malleable. By learning to refine their *qi*, people can improve themselves.

Neo-Confucianism was formalized by Zhu Xi (1130–1200), often considered the greatest Chinese philosopher after Confucius. His rationalistic school won out over the idealism of the younger thinker Lu Jiuyuan (1139–1192). Philosophically, the two teachers differed in the way they looked at principle and substance. For Lu Jiuyuan, the two were identical, because a single mind upheld them both. Zhu Xi considered them separate and distinguished between the human mind, which is liable to error, and the moral mind which is in harmony with the Way. But when the two men spoke of practice or investigation their ideas converged. Lu Jiuyuan wrote that if a man "plumbs, investigates into, sharpens, and refines himself, a morning will come when he will gain self enlightenment." Zhu Xi wrote similarly: "When one has worked at this for a long time, a day will dawn when suddenly everything will become clear ... and the mind and its operations will be completely enlightened."[65] For both men the Confucian idea of self-cultivation (*xiushen*) was colored by the Buddhist idea of enlightenment (*bodhi*). But they differed over the means of investigation. Lu Jiuyuan recommended "quiet sitting" (*jing zuo*), which was similar to Buddhist meditation. Zhu Xi laid stress on "the investigation of things" (*gewu*) which included study of the classics and observation of the natural world.

The debate between rationalistic and idealistic Neo-Confucianism dominated Chinese philosophy for more than four centuries. At first Zhu Xi's rationalistic school prevailed, but during the Ming dynasty, Wang Yangming (1472–1529) revitalized the idealistic approach and the practice of quiet sitting. Since *li* (principle) was present in everything, Wang said, the best way of approaching it was to investigate oneself. He told his disciples: "Everyone says that in investigating things one should use the method of Zhu Xi, but how can it actually be done?" When he and a friend tried to investigate a bamboo by studying it for days on end, they became exhausted and fell ill. The right way to proceed, Wang concluded, was to examine one's body and mind. Once, after a day of tending the sick, he suddenly realized the meaning of the expression, "investigate things so that knowledge may be extended to the utmost." Leaping out of bed, he told his astonished disciples: "Now for the first time I understand the teachings of the sage. My nature is in itself sufficient."[66] The terminology is Confucian, but the parallels with Buddhism are evident. Wang admired some aspects of Buddhist thought, but he could not condone the way the Buddhists he observed withdrew from active life. They "neglect everything," he scoffed, "and therefore are incapable of governing the world." The ideal Confucian sage, on the other hand, saw no difference between thought and action, and it became possible for him "to assist in and complete the universal process of production and reproduction and apply it to the benefit of the people."[67]

Zhu Xi's most enduring achievement was to synthesize the teachings of Confucius, Mencius, and other classic writers and establish the Confucian canon. Other Song-era thinkers produced canonical collections of poetry, historical narratives, and so forth. This habit of compiling "best-of" albums was also taken up by Chan Buddhist masters, who during the twelfth and thirteenth centuries put together the three main collections of *gongan*, the most famous of which is the *Gateless Gate* of Wumen Huikai (1183–1260). Wumen's sixth *gongan* begins with the story of the silent transmission of the *dharma*: Once, before his assembled disciples, the Buddha held up a flower. The disciples remained silent, but one of them, Mahakashyapa, broke into a smile. The Buddha entrusted him with "the eye treasury of the true Dharma," which was, he said, "specially transmitted outside all teachings." Wumen's commentary on this story begins with a jolt: "The golden-faced Gautama insolently suppressed noble people and made them lowly. He sells dog's flesh under the label of sheep's head." Wumen's meaning, according to a twentieth-century teacher, was that phrases like "eye treasury of the Dharma," which seem very lofty, are really "nothing but another name for your own self, something very common. And what is more common than dog's flesh?" His aim was to get people to stop thinking that Buddha-nature was beyond them. It is both "the essential nature of our own self" and at the same time "the essential substance of the whole universe."[68]

Wumen was one of the greatest masters of the Linji school of Chan. In contrast with the teachers of the Caodong school, who stressed the importance of "simply sitting" to achieve silent illumination, Linji masters prescribed reflection on the critical phrase of the *gongan* to achieve a sudden breakthrough. The quintessential critical phrase is the single word "Wu" that comes at the end of the following encounter: A monk asked the master Zhaozhou Congshen: "Does a dog have a Buddha nature or not." Zhaozhou replied "Wu!" Wu means no. The doctrinally correct answer is yes: dogs do have Buddha nature. What was Zhaoshou trying to get at? According to Wumen, the problem cannot be resolved mentally. The student has to "extinguish all thoughts of the ordinary mind," concentrating exclusively on Wu, turning one's body into "a solid lump of doubt," until at length there is release into sudden enlightenment. Penetrating the secrets of Chan "involves no particular cleverness," Wumen said. "It's just a matter of rousing the mass of doubt throughout your body, day and night, never letting up. After a long time it becomes pure and ripe, and inside and outside become one."[69] The antiauthoritarianism and subjective approach of Chan (known in Japan as Zen) have made it a touchstone for modern people interested in the possibilities of nontheistic spirituality.

During the Kamakura Period (1185–1333) the people of Japan enjoyed freedom from external aggression but suffered from domestic insecurity. The government passed from the emperor to the *shogun* or military leader, but rival families engaged in civil war. In the midst of all this, Mongol forces invaded the country in 1274 and 1281. Both times they were repulsed by Japanese defenders with the help of fortuitous typhoons. (This was the birth of the legend of *kamikaze* or "divine wind.") Despite or perhaps because of the political instability there was a blossoming of Buddhism during this period. The theistic Pure Land sect was by far the most popular, but nontheistic Zen caught on after pioneers like Myoan Eisai and Eihei Dogen took its teachings and practices from China to Japan. Eisai did most of his training under a Linji master and is regarded as the founder of Japan's Rinzai school. (Rinzai is simply the Japanese pronunciation of Linji.) Dogen studied mainly under a Caodong master, and after returning from China founded the Japanese branch of the school, called Soto. Both the Rinzai and Soto schools are still active today.

Dogen sometimes used *gongan*—pronounced *koan* in Japanese—but he put most of his emphasis on seated meditation: simply sitting with a quiet mind. "Even if you obtain some ideas by studying koans and words," he wrote, "it may cause you to go further away from the Buddha ancestors' path. Instead, dedicate your time to sitting upright, not seeking achievement, and not seeking enlightenment." Enlightenment was not something to be sought because we all already possess it: "Between aspiration, practice, enlightenment, and nirvana there is not a moment's gap." Yet, paradoxically, we have to exert ourselves, for "enlightenment and clarity of the mind occur only in response to the sustained effort of study and practice." And this effort cannot be half-hearted. Everyone is getting older;

everyone is going to die; therefore, Dogen told his students, "Mindful of the passing of time, engage yourself in zazen [sitting meditation] as though saving your head from fire." Spiritual perfection comes about through the power of miracles, but miracles happened "three thousand times in the morning and eight hundred times in the evening." Quoting an old Chinese poem, Dogen concluded: "Miracles are nothing other than fetching water and carrying firewood."[70]

Rinzai Zen had its ups and downs after Eisai got it going in the twelfth century. During the early part of the Muromachi period it prospered under the patronage of the shoguns and the direction of masters such as Bassui Tokusho (1327–1387). Like his Chinese predecessor Wumen, Bassui encouraged his pupils to direct their enquiry within, grappling with existential doubt rather than scriptural teachings or conventional religious practices. "As you pursue this inquiry more deeply," he told a student, "your piercing doubt will penetrate to the depths, ripping through to the bottom, and you will no longer question the fact that your mind is Buddha." The scriptures were important but they were just "fingers pointing at the moon," not the moon itself. Bowing before Buddhas and bodhisattvas was a way of "throwing down the ego-banner." This act of surrender helped practitioners realize their own inner natures. Buddhas and bodhisattvas were worthy of reverence, but their names—Amida, Kannon, Jizo—were "just different names for the nature of mind." The historical Buddha "defined things using certain names, and with these names he pointed to the truth." Unfortunately religious people became "attached to the names" and sought "the Buddha and Dharma outside their minds." This was, Bassui said, "like cooking sand in the hope of producing rice."[71]

Japan was safeguarded from Mongol invasion by the sea and its navy. India was protected by the Himalayas and the army of the Delhi Sultanate. Parts of western and northern India had been under Muslim rule since the end of the seventh century but the heads of those kingdoms took their cues from Baghdad or Ghazni. The Turkic rulers of the Delhi Sultanate (1206–1526) settled down in the country and established efficient governments. Some of them looted or destroyed Hindu temples but for the most part they let people worship as they liked as long as they paid their taxes. With the revenues, the rulers built palaces and mosques, and patronized poets, musicians, and historians. One of the beneficiaries was Amir Khusrau (1253–1325), who was a poet, a sufi, and one of the fathers of Hindustani music, credited with inventing the *tabla*.

Buddhism had by this time all but disappeared from the subcontinent, but Jainism was strong in certain regions, and some Jain teachers tried to preserve the nontheistic and nondevotional strands of the religion. The fourteenth-century philosopher Gunaratna argued effectively against the theism of the Nyaya school of Vedic philosophy. During the fifteenth century a layman named Lonka Shaha started a movement against image worship. His efforts were not appreciated by the priests of his day, but his sect took root and its offshoots still survive.

Some scholars speculate that Lonka was influenced by Muslim attitudes. (Islam forbids the creation of images.)[72] So, perhaps, were the devotees of the *nirgun* or formless Divine, who were especially active in northern India during the fifteenth and sixteenth centuries. The *nirgun* devotees, also known as *sants*, sang the praises of an impersonal god, a god without qualities. The object of their devotion resembled the formless Brahman of *advaita*, but their inspiration was not Vedanta (which was closely guarded by the priestly caste) but Vaishnava bhakti, Sufi devotionism, and Tantra. Like the theistic *bhaktas*, the *sants* gave voice to their love for the divine, but they did not invoke avatars or worship in temples (another priestly monopoly). Like the sufis they longed for union with the One, but they were as little attached to the Quran as they were to the Vedas. Like the tantrics they practiced mantras and meditation but avoided mechanical techniques. Outward observances were not the way to achieve union, because the formless one dwelt within:

> Him whom I went out to seek,
> > I found just where I was:
> He now has become myself
> > whom before I called "Another"!

This quatrain is by Kabir, the greatest of the *sants*, who was born to a family of Muslim weavers in Varanasi, a city sacred to Hindus, around the beginning of the fifteenth century. Claimed by adherents of both religions, Kabir saw no difference between the two: "For the Hindu and for the Turk there is but one Way," he wrote. So "what matter if one calls 'Ram' or 'Khuda.'" *Khuda* is a Muslim word for God, *Ram* is the name of a Hindu avatar, but by the fifteenth century *Ram* was a generic term for the Divine, and when Kabir used it he meant not a particular deity but the formless inner godhead, with whom he found identity:

> My mind thinks only of Ram, my mind is Ram alone;
> Now that I have become Ram, to whom will I bow my head?[73]

One reason that the *sants* rejected orthodox Hinduism was because it was inseparable from the caste system, which excluded millions from the consolations of religion. Many who were barred from temples knocked at the doors of mosques. Kabir, born a Muslim, avoided mosques as well as temples, searching instead "in the heart, in the heart alone."[74] Another *sant* who looked within was Raidas, who lived a little after Kabir. "Within your heart, without tongue give praise," Raidas sang,

> In the temple of the mind
> > Let incense be burnt,
> Offer up to Ram,
> > The garland of love and affection.

Raidas was born into an untouchable caste, the bottom rung of the Hindu social ladder. He must have experienced countless acts of contempt during his lifetime, but he came to see that the true measure of a man was his inner status, not his outer rank. It made no difference whether one's family is "caste or outcaste, destitute or noble." Despite his references to Ram, Krishna, and Bhagavan (God), Raidas believed the divine being to be unique, ineffable, formless, and immanent in the universe. Those who heeded Vedic scholars or worshipped idols in temples would never be liberated from the rounds of birth-and-death. True liberation was the state of *sahaj*, spontaneous inner experience:

> There is no heaven, no mountain, no earth,
>   no body filled with breath, no moon
> no Ram, no Krishna, no *guns* [qualities], brother,
>   when spontaneity speaks.

For all the *sants*, the name of God was the purest revelation of its being—not a particular name like Ram or Krishna, but Name itself, the liberating power of the divine. "Believing in Your Name I abandoned 'self' and 'other,'" Raidas sang. In the present Dark Age, "the Name is the only support."[75]

The *sant* who placed the greatest stress on the liberating power of the Name was Guru Nanak (1469–1539), whose path became a separate religion, Sikhism. God, Nanak sang, "has neither form, colour, nor material sign, but He is revealed through the true Word." One, eternal, formless, and ineffable, God is beyond human understanding but "is known by means of the Word."[76] Born in Punjab during the closing years of the Delhi Sultanate, Nanak wandered through northern India and, according to some, voyaged as far as Baghdad and Mecca. He learned the songs of sants, sufis, and bhaktas, some of which were later included in the Sikhs' holy book, the *Adi Granth* ("Primordial Scripture"). But most of the songs in the *Adi Granth* were composed by Nanak and five other Sikh gurus. All of them sang of a single all-pervading spirit that transcends yet is immanent in the universe. Through individual effort and the grace of the gurus, human beings can achieve union with this One. Grace comes mainly in the form of the Name. As Guru Tegh Bahadur sang:

> Let us enshrine the Name in our hearts,
>   for none is its equal.
> The Name dispels our suffering;
>   the name brings us to the sight of You.[77]

Tegh Bahadur was executed by Aurangzeb, the sixth emperor of the Mughal dynasty, in 1675. Guru Gobind Singh, Tegh Bahadur's son and successor, formalized the Sikh *khalsa* or community in 1699. At the time of his death nine years later he named as his successor the *Adi Granth* itself, which became known as the *Guru Granth Sahib*: the guru in the form of an inerrant holy book.

Around the time Guru Nanak began to preach, a Portuguese vessel landed in Calicut, in the southwest corner of India. Two centuries later, when Guru Gobind Singh died, there were twenty-two European settlements dotting the Indian coastline. Compared to the vast body of the Mughal Empire, these trading posts were like a mild case of hives. But after the death of Aurangzeb, the empire began to fragment, and this gave the foreign settlers the chance to intervene. By the end of the eighteenth century the British East India Company had made itself the dominant power in the subcontinent.

Between the end of the fifth century, when the Western Roman Empire collapsed, and the beginning of the ninth century, when the Holy Roman Empire was established, Europe passed through that period of economic and cultural impoverishment known as the Dark Ages. During the so-called Carolingian Renaissance of the ninth and tenth centuries, there was a brief revival of classical learning, art, and literature. At that time and for many years thereafter, the most culturally advanced areas of Europe were the Muslim caliphates of Spain. For centuries Arab scholars had been studying the Greek philosophers. Now they gave them back to the West. Ibn Rushd's translations of and commentaries on Aristotle revolutionized European thought. Works of Islamic medicine and mathematics, for instance the treatises of Abu Bakr al-Razi (mentioned earlier for his skepticism), had a similar effect on European science.

In 1241, while a Mongol army was battling the Delhi Sultanate in Punjab, another Mongol force was ravaging the plains of Hungary. There was no significant opposition. It seemed likely that central Europe might soon go the way of Russia and Ukraine, which the Mongols had devastated between 1237 and 1240. Then, for reasons that are not completely clear, the Mongol army withdrew. To Europeans it seemed as if God had intervened to preserve Western Christianity. Be that as it may, the political, economic, and cultural developments that were underway—the so-called Renaissance of the high Middle Ages—were able to continue. Europe, which had been playing catch-up with Asia for 800 years, began to attain a level of culture that was comparable in some respects to that of the Song dynasty or Abbasid Caliphate.

In the early twelfth century, a growing population brought dynamism back to European cities. Merchants built cathedrals and later established universities. Scholars applied Aristotle to the study of scripture, but there were vehement debates about how far the new approach should go. During the thirteenth century the faculty of the University of Paris issued lists of condemned philosophical propositions. In an early instance of the Streisand effect, the lists publicized the propositions, facilitating rather than stifling debate. But orthodoxy still came out on top. Thomas Aquinas (1225–1274) appropriated Aristotelian rationalism and used it to support Church doctrine. His synthesis put a bridle on academic skepticism but did not break it. William of Ockham (c.1285–c.1347) was a master of scholastic philosophy as well as a pioneer in science (the name "Ockham's razor" is still applied to the principle of scientific parsimony), but he believed that neither philosophy nor science could help in understanding God. Only faith and revealed scripture could do that. This kept intact the supremacy of dogma but acknowledged a sphere of rational inquiry outside the purview of religion. In 1324 Ockham was summoned to Avignon, then the papal seat, to answer charges that some of his views were heretical. Four years later he turned the tables on Pope John XXII by writing that some of John's views were heretical and that he no longer was pope! Shortly afterward, Ockham fled Avignon, taking refuge with a friendly German ruler.

The tentative reawakening of Europe ended abruptly in the fourteenth century. The Great Famine of 1315–1317, and smaller famines that continued till the end of the century, killed millions of people and left a trail of poverty and crime. Around the same time Europe was struck by a series of epidemics—typhoid, anthrax, and finally the Black Death—which reduced the population by something like 40 percent. Trade collapsed and most forms of cultural activity ceased. In times of stress, people turn to religion, but in fourteenth-century Europe, the reputation of the church was at an all-time low. The relocation of the papacy to Avignon (1309–1377) was followed by a 39-year schism during which two or more would-be popes laid claim to the Throne of Saint Peter. These controversies exacerbated the sense of distrust that many people felt for organized religion. Giovanni Boccaccio's *Decameron* (1348), set in Italy during the Black Death, is bitingly critical of the clergy. In one tale a man who was trying to convert a Jew is afraid that if the prospect should go to Rome and see "what foul and wicked lives the clergy lead, not only will he not become a Christian, but, if he had already turned Christian, he would become a Jew again without fail."[78]

There were, of course, sincere members of the clergy but many were just as unhappy about the state of Catholicism as the laity. Rebel priests such as John Wycliffe (c.1331–1384) and Jan Hus (c.1369–1415) attacked the beliefs and practices of the Church. It would be better, Wycliffe thought, to put one's trust in the Bible, so he and his colleagues translated it into English, an innovation the clergy opposed because it challenged their monopoly on truth. In May 1415, thirty years after Wycliffe's death, a church council condemned him as a heretic and ruled that his works and his exhumed bones should be burned. Two months later the still living Hus was tried, convicted of heresy, and burned at the stake.

There can be no doubt that Wycliffe and Hus and virtually everyone else in Europe were believing Christians. Atheism as we now understand it did not exist. Many parishioners must have had doubts about specific points of doctrine. (Is Christ *really* physically present in the host?) And who has ever been completely sure about the existence of God? But there was no well-considered atheism in fourteenth-century Europe—certainly nothing comparable to contemporary Jainism or Samkhya in India. Nor was there anything in Christian monastic practice to compare with the "piercing doubt" that Bassui asked his students to grapple with. Radical doubt did not come to Europe until the Renaissance and Reformation of the fourteenth and fifteenth centuries.

This is not the place to retell the history of the Renaissance and Reformation. An adequate account would require hundreds of pages covering 300 eventful years of literature, art, architecture, music, science, philosophy, and religion, not to mention politics and commerce. In this book devoted to godless spirituality, we are interested primarily in philosophy and religion, but even in these fields too much happened to allow a detailed treatment here. It will be enough to point out a few major trends that prepared the way for the skepticism of the seventeenth century and the atheism of the eighteenth.

There is general agreement the Renaissance began with the rediscovery of Greek and Latin literature. Up to the mid-fourteenth century a small number of scholars had studied translations of a good deal of Aristotle, some fragments of Plato, and a few works of Cicero and Seneca, but they had never seen a manuscript of Euripides or Epicurus. During the late fourteenth century, humanistic scholars ransacked the monastic libraries of Europe and found copies of Cicero's letters, Lucretius' *On the Nature of Things*, and other works of secular Latin literature. After the fall of Constantinople in 1453, Byzantine scholars fled to Western universities carrying manuscripts of Greek literature and philosophy, which they taught their new colleagues to read.

By 1570 humanists throughout Europe were studying works by Greek and Roman Stoics, Epicureans, and Skeptics. The impact of their thought on Aristotelian–Aquinian orthodoxy would shape Western philosophy and theology for the next 200 years. Christians found Stoicism relatively easy to assimilate because the Stoics accepted the idea of a providential God. In 1584 the humanist Justus Lipsius devised a synthesis of Stoicism and Christianity that he hoped would help people free themselves from the passions and find contentment through submission to the will of God. Epicureanism was harder for Christians to digest because it had no room for a beneficent Creator. Lucretius was labeled an atheist but this did not prevent *On the Nature of Things* from circulating throughout Europe and influencing the natural philosophers (the word "scientist" had not yet been coined) who would revolutionize the thought of Europe during the seventeenth century.

Of more immediate interest to Renaissance humanists was the Pyrrhonian Skepticism of Sextus Empiricus. Montaigne helped introduce it to Europe. In *Apology for Raymond Sebond*, the longest and most important of his *Essays* (1580), he wrote that the Skeptics, unlike the Aristotelians, Epicureans, and Stoics, learned to avoid dogma by suspending their judgments. This led them to *ataraxia*, "a peaceful and sedate condition of life, exempt from the agitations we receive through the impression of the opinion and knowledge we think we have of things."[79] Montaigne stopped short of openly endorsing Skepticism—his stance was that of a Catholic trying to overcome doubt by faith—but he polished up a philosophical tool that less cautious skeptics would put to different use in the next century.

One of the advantages of Skepticism, Montaigne wrote, was that it kept people from getting caught up in "seditious and quarrelsome divisions."[80] He was alluding to the sectarianism and violence of the Wars of Religion, which he witnessed at close hand. At the time he wrote the *Essays*, Europe had been convulsed by almost continuous war for more than fifty years. The first conflict broke out in 1524, seven years after Martin Luther nailed his *Ninety-Five Theses* to the door of a church in Wittenberg, Germany. Luther opposed the idea that Christians could gain remission of sin through letters of indulgence sold by priests. His attack undermined the status of the clergy and challenged a ready source of income. More important in the long run, Luther shifted the locus of the struggle for salvation from the outer to the inward sphere. Salvation was the concern of ordinary believers and not just anointed priests. "Through baptism all of us are consecrated to the priesthood," Luther wrote in a letter to the German nobility. And since "we are all priests … why should we not also have the power to test and judge what is correct or incorrect in matters of faith?"[81] It is hard, 500 years later, to see how revolutionary this was. For the first time since the closing of the Greco-Roman philosophical schools, subjectivity and individual effort became the focus of the religious life.

Luther was as good a Greek and Latin scholar as most of the humanists of his time, but he opposed a central humanist idea: that philosophical skepticism was a useful way of dealing with contending dogmas. Yet skepticism was part of the fabric of the times, and Luther owed more to it than he was ready to admit. Sixteenth-century skeptics grappled with a fundamental problem: What is the criterion of truth? If dogmatic assertions cannot be proved, how do we know what is right? According to humanistic theologian Desiderius Erasmus, we should follow the Bible and, if the Bible is unclear, fall back on the teachings of the Church. For Luther this was unacceptable. The truth of the Bible is clear to those who seek it, and in full agreement with the inner certitude given by the Holy Spirit. But what happened when people found themselves convinced about different things? Luther's rival John Calvin, faced with the same problem, wrote confidently of "a conviction that requires no reasons" and "a feeling that can be born only of heavenly revelation," which is "nothing other than what each believer experiences within himself."[82] But Calvin had his own ideas about which beliefs were acceptable and which were not. When as facto ruler of Geneva he learned that the radical theologian Michael Servetus was in his bailiwick, he had him arrested, tried for heresy, and burned alive.

Servetus was one of many martyrs of conscience in late-sixteenth-century Europe. In the 1580s an Italian miller known as Menocchio told his parish priest some of his unorthodox ideas about God and the universe, for example, "God is nothing but a little breath" and "Everything we see is God, and we are gods."[83] The priest reported him to the authorities, who brought Menocchio to trial for heresy. He abjured his statements but still was put in prison. After his release, being a loquacious sort, he again began to broadcast his ideas. Arrested and tried a second time, he was condemned as a heretic and burned at the stake. At the opposite end of the intellectual spectrum was Menocchio's contemporary Giordano Bruno. After early education in Naples, Bruno entered holy orders and eventually became an internationally known philosopher and scientist. His ideas were much more sophisticated than Menocchio's—he speculated for instance that the universe was infinite and that the stars were suns with their own planets—but they went against the doctrines of the Church, and the results were just as deadly. Brought before the Inquisition, he was convicted of heresy and executed by fire in 1600.

* * *

Between around 200 BCE and 200 CE, religions that were focused on the worship of personal gods arose across Eurasia. These theistic religions gradually replaced the Bronze Age religions of sacrifice and the nontheistic philosophies of the axial age. Worshippers of gods such as Shiva and Huangdi and incarnations such as Krishna and Christ formed personal relationships with the deity of their choice, harnessing the power of human emotions to the religious life. Most followers of such religions claimed that theirs was the best if not the only path to the divine. This exclusivity fostered intolerance, which often gave rein to violence.

During the heyday of theism, some nontheistic religions and philosophies—Confucianism, Daoism, Buddhism, Jainism, Samkhya, and others—held on in East and South Asia. The teachers of these traditions encouraged subjective investigation and some sort of individual practice. Similar techniques found their way into certain forms of West Asian monotheism, such as Christian monasticism and Muslim Sufism.

Anticlericalism was a recurrent theme throughout the age of theism but it first had a major impact on political and social life in sixteenth-century Europe. The rise of critical modernity marked the beginning of the end of triumphant theism.

5 THE COMING OF MODERNITY AND THE DECLINE OF GOD

In Europe the age of theism reached its zenith toward the end of the sixteenth century. The Reformation and the savage wars that followed critically weakened institutional Christianity. Europe and America remained predominantly Christian for another 300 years but many began to question the assumptions on which the theistic worldview was based. First scientists and philosophers, then other educated people, challenged the authority of scriptural and classical texts. For centuries people had turned to the Bible and the works of Aristotle and other ancient authors for knowledge of the supernatural and natural worlds. Now they began to put their faith in empirical evidence and rational reflection. As a consequence, writes historian David Wootton, between 1600 and 1733 or so "the intellectual world of the educated elite [in Europe] changed more rapidly than at any time in previous history."[1]

The momentum of change had begun to build up during the preceding century. The discovery of lands across the Atlantic in 1492 and the realization a decade later that they were not "the Indies" but continents unknown to ancient authorities greatly enlarged the extent of the known world. Aristotle had been sure that the equatorial regions were too hot for human habitation. Now any uneducated Portuguese sailor knew that this was nonsense. In 1543 Polish mathematician Nicolaus Copernicus published his heliocentric theory of the universe. This eventually caused the collapse of the geocentric theory of Ptolomy, which had prevailed since antiquity. The same year Belgian anatomist Andreas Vesalius showed that another Greek authority, Galen, was wrong about the structure of the human body. Danish polymath Tycho Brahe's *De nova stella* (1573) made it clear that the time-honored belief in an unchanging celestial sphere was unfounded. In 1608 Dutch lens-makers invented the telescope. Galileo Galilei improved its design, turned it on the night sky, and saw things no human eyes had ever seen and grasped their implications: Jupiter had moons, proving that heavenly bodies could revolve around something other than the earth. Venus had phases, proving that it orbited between earth and the sun. Now the only way for people to believe that the sun moved around the earth was to refuse to examine the evidence. This is just what many people did. When Galileo invited critics to look through his telescope, they simply turned away. When he tried to explain his findings to officers of the Inquisition, they recited the church-approved teachings of the Bible and Aristotle. When he refused to cooperate, they accused him of heresy and demanded that he recant. He found it prudent to do so—Bruno had been executed just thirty-three years earlier—and he spent the rest of his life under house arrest. It took the Church 359 years to admit that he was right.[2]

From this time forward, religious thinkers ceased to command respect in the world of knowledge. Of course they continued to write books and deliver sermons but few important scientists and philosophers paid them any attention.

In the first section of this chapter I give an overview of the work of the leading European scientists and philosophers of the seventeenth century. Most of them—Galileo, Descartes, Newton, Locke—were pious Christians who never imagined that their discoveries might undermine belief. But by showing that God was constrained by physical laws, they took away much of his majesty. More radical thinkers, such as Hobbes and Spinoza, had views about God that some considered impious if not atheistic. Neither accepted the label "atheist"—it would have been foolhardy to do so—but their work prepared the way for the all-but-open atheism of the eighteenth century.

The main scientific discoveries of this era were the work of European thinkers, and European traders and rulers were the first to benefit from them. Asia was slow to adapt to the new dispensation. Culturally and economically dominant for centuries, India, China, and the Islamic world had begun to move slowly toward their own versions of modernity as early as the fifteenth century, but by 1700 they found themselves outflanked by newly minted European states. How did this come about? There were a multitude of reasons but two stand out: the discovery and exploitation of uncharted countries by European explorers and traders and the description and harnessing of the forces of material nature by European scientists and inventors. The people of Asia, formerly leaders in these fields, now looked on from the sidelines.

During the seventeenth and eighteenth centuries the religious life of China and Japan continued on its way in well-worn grooves, protected from the pressures of colonialism by political isolation. India succumbed to European imperialism, but its religious and philosophical thinkers took little note of the changes in the political order. Theism reigned supreme throughout the subcontinent but there were scattered voices of nonconformity, notably among the *sant*s and sufis.

In Europe orthodox religion maintained its sway during the first half of the seventeenth century. But as the influence of science and philosophy grew, some believers looked for ways to escape the domination of reason. Leaders of movements such as pietism, quietism, and evangelicalism urged their followers to base their faith on feeling and intuition rather than scripture and tradition. By making inner experience the basis of religion, they helped prepare the way for subjective spirituality. Meanwhile the examples of Epicureanism and Skepticism and the continuing success of science made philosophical disbelief possible for the first time since the Roman imperial era. Spirituality and godlessness, divorced for centuries, began to come together.

Science, skepticism, rationality

Sometime around 1585, Michel de Montaigne paid a visit to a prince he knew and the two got to talking about witchcraft. Finding that his guest had some doubts about the subject, the prince took Montaigne to his prison to show him some women who were known for sure to be witches. Montaigne reviewed the evidence and heard the confessions, but he still thought it might be better to treat them as madwomen rather than tools of the devil. He did not for a moment doubt that there was such a thing as witchcraft: the Bible, he reminded his readers, "offers us of such things, very certain and irrefragable examples." But he felt that where absolute proof was lacking it would be best to suspend one's judgment. "After all," he observed, "it is putting a very high price on one's conjectures to have a man [or woman] roasted alive because of them." Montaigne was writing in the middle of the witch-hunting craze of the sixteenth and seventeenth centuries, when tens of thousands of women and men were convicted of witchcraft and put to death. In countries where Catholicism prevailed, sorcery was viewed as a special case of heresy and dealt with efficiently by the Inquisition. But in Germany, Scandinavia, Scotland, England, and New England, whole communities got caught up in riotous dramas of accusation and counter-accusation, generally leading to executions. Then, after a run of a hundred fifty years, the show trials became rare and finally stopped. Not everyone was pleased with this. In 1768 John Wesley, the founder of Methodism, expressed disappointment that "most of the men of learning in Europe, have given up all accounts of witchcraft and apparitions, as mere old wives' fables." This was a perilous error, he thought: "The giving up witchcraft is, in effect, giving up the Bible."[3]

Belief in spirits, demons, and witches had been standard fare in all the world's cultures since the start of recorded history. It still prevails in many parts of the world, but since the seventeenth century witchcraft has been excluded from the generally accepted body of human knowledge. This was one result of a wide-ranging reconception of what "knowledge" is. Up to the end of the sixteenth century, knowledge consisted primarily of beliefs supported by scriptural and classical authorities. It was the job of modern scholars to recover what the ancients had known. After the start of the scientific revolution, knowledge was something that had to be *discovered*. Its fullness would come in the future.

The empirical approach to knowledge acquisition was of course nothing new. Farmers, sailors, doctors, and other curious people had been making discoveries about the physical world for centuries. But it was not until Galileo, Francis Bacon, and others developed what we now call the scientific method that the acquisition of knowledge became methodical and replicable. Galileo may or may not have dropped two spheres of unequal weight from the Leaning Tower of Pisa to show that they would, contra Aristotle, hit the ground at the same time, but he certainly designed experiments that demonstrated that balls rolling down inclined planes exhibited constant acceleration regardless of mass. Just as important, he presented his conclusions in mathematical formulas. It now was clear to anyone who did the math that the distance covered by bodies in naturally accelerated motion is proportional to the square of the elapsed time. But to understand the formula—and nature itself—you had to know geometry. Galileo made this clear in a letter to a colleague: "Philosophy is written in this grand book, the universe, which stands continually open to our gaze. But the book cannot be understood unless one first learns to comprehend the language and read the letters in which it is composed. It is written in the language of mathematics, and its characters are triangles, circles, and other geometric figures without which it is humanly impossible to understand a single word of it; without these, one wanders about in a dark labyrinth."[4]

No one in the seventeenth century understood the language of mathematics better than Isaac Newton and he, like Galileo, had no time for the purely verbal reasoning of scholastic philosophers. He called his 1687 masterwork *Mathematical Principles of Natural Philosophy*, with the accent on "mathematical." By showing that a theorized force of gravity could explain the movements of heavenly bodies and also falling bodies on earth, he annulled the immemorial distinction between the earthly and heavenly spheres. Nevertheless he held on to a watered-down concept of God: "This most beautiful system of the sun, planets and comets," he wrote in the *Principles*, "could only proceed from the counsel and dominion of an intelligent and powerful being," namely the God of the Christian Bible. In a later work he noted that the "wonderful uniformity" of the solar system as well as the "uniformity in the bodies of animals" proved that "the wisdom and skill of a powerful ever-living Agent" was at work. God let gravitation and other "active principles" do most of the work but he sometimes intervened, as a sort of cosmic repairman, to correct irregularities that "may have risen from the mutual actions of comets and planets upon one another."[5]

Newton was far from being an atheist but his mechanistic God was closer to the remote heavenly beings of Lucretius than the omnipotent creator of the Book of Genesis. He in fact drew on Lucretian atomic theory without uttering the name of the notorious Roman thinker: "God in the beginning formed matter in solid, massy, hard, impenetrable, moveable particles, of such sizes and figures ... as was most conducive to the end for which he formed them," he wrote in his 1704 study *Opticks*.[6] A fervent if unorthodox Christian, he would have been appalled to think that mathematical philosophy might lead to a weakening of religion, but this is just what happened. The inactive God of deism replaced his "ever-living Agent." Genetics and natural selection explained the "uniformity in the bodies of animals." Convinced that God was still at work, he and other seventeenth-century scientists and philosophers developed tools that later thinkers would use to show that God did not exist.

The problem of skepticism that troubled Montaigne and other humanists during the sixteenth century grew even more acute during the seventeenth. Borrowing a metaphor from Zen, it became like a red-hot ball of doubt that the greatest thinkers of the day could neither swallow nor spit out. Ancient and modern skeptics showed that theological and scholastic dogmas no longer could be taken for granted. Pious Christians put their trust in scripture and Church tradition, but for many this was not enough. Among those looking for a different approach was a young French soldier and mathematician named René Descartes. While studying in a Catholic school he read everything he could get his hands on—literature, rhetoric, philosophy, theology—but found nothing that gave him the certitude he was looking for. The various systems of moral philosophy seemed like palaces built on sand, while metaphysics turned round and round in endless circles: "There is not a single matter within its sphere which is not still in dispute, and nothing, therefore which is above doubt," he wrote in *Discourse on the Method* (1637). Geometry and algebra were more interesting "on account of the certitude and evidence of their reasonings," but they only seemed useful when applied to technical matters.[7]

Descartes stopped studying the masterworks of the past and spent nine years wandering about Europe, talking to all sorts of people. None of them was able to show him a way to reliable knowledge. In the end he decided the best way to proceed was to start by studying himself. In this he followed three rules of thumb: first, to hold on provisionally to the customs of his country and to the tenets of the faith he was brought up in (this is the only allusion he made to Catholicism in the story of his intellectual development); second, to follow his reasoning resolutely wherever it led him; and finally "to endeavour always to conquer myself rather than fortune," accepting that "there is nothing absolutely in our power" except "our own thoughts." The third rule is a paraphrase of the main principle of Stoicism, which Descartes knew from his reading of Epictetus. But he resolved to accept as final neither the teachings of the ancient philosophers nor the doctrines of the church but only "what was presented to my mind so clearly and distinctly as to exclude all ground of doubt."[8]

But what was beyond all possibility of doubt? The skeptics had shown that sense-evidence was unreliable and reason prone to error. But there was something no skeptic could make him doubt: his own existence, as demonstrated by the fact that he was thinking. Descartes summed this up in his famous formula, "I think, therefore I am," and made it the first principle of his philosophy. He then used the clear and distinct idea of his own being as the basis of two lines of argument which led him to two problematic conclusions.[9]

First, Descartes deduced that his mental existence was completely independent of his body. Mind is a substance that is characterized by thought, body a separate substance characterized by extension in space. It seemed to him self-evident that mind or soul—the French word he used, *âme*, could mean both—continues to exist after the body ceases to be. Descartes's mind–body dualism created a problem that has stymied all subsequent philosophers: How can the mind have anything to do with the body? How, for instance, can the mind cause the arm to move? He eventually worked out a solution involving the pineal gland, but this satisfied no one, and the mind–body problem remains unsolved to this day.

Descartes' second problematic line of reasoning was part of his attempt to prove that God exists. His began with a variant of the ontological argument: Because he was able to doubt, he knew he was imperfect. Evidently this awareness of his own imperfection was "placed in me by a nature which was in reality more perfect than mine," a nature which possessed all possible perfections, which was, in a word, God. Descartes found this demonstration at least as certain "as any demonstration of geometry can be" but it failed to convince anyone who didn't already believe in God. Descartes picked up his theology from the priests of his Catholic school and he was never able to get rid of the dogmas he thought he had jettisoned.[10]

What truly was remarkable about Descartes' approach was his methodology and not his conclusions. He did not (overtly at least) base himself on scriptural or classical authorities. Neither did he rely on the dubious perceptions of the senses. For him the basis of knowledge was the clear and distinct perceptions of his reason. On this foundation he built a system that confirmed the existence of God and the soul; but his methodology could be put to different use. As twentieth-century philosopher Bernard Williams observed, "the [philosophical] construction he produced is one that made it easier for God to disappear from the world and from people's understanding of the world."[11]

English philosopher Thomas Hobbes was an early reader of Descartes and in 1641 he wrote a series of objections to the younger man's philosophy. Descartes asserted that the mind has an innate idea of God. This was a part of his proof that God exists. Hobbes denied that the mind has innate ideas of God or of anything else. All ideas derive, directly or indirectly, from experience. We know that God exists by deduction from sensory evidence: All objects have a cause, each of which has a cause. This obliges us to conclude that there must be an eternal cause that has no prior cause. We give the name "God" to this eternal cause but we can form no idea of what it is. This is the old idea of the Prime Mover updated for the seventeenth century.

Basing himself on the work of Galileo and other scientists, Hobbes insisted that "the whole mass of all things that are"—God included—is "corporeal, that is to say body."[12] His insistence that "body" (we would now say "matter") is the only substance made him one of the first proponents of philosophical materialism (a term that would not be coined until the middle of the next century). For him, as for Galileo, everything that exists can be explained in terms of bodies and motion (in modern terms, matter and energy). It therefore made no sense to speak of incorporeal beings. The Christian idea that God is bodiless, Descartes's idea that mind is distinct from body, the popular belief in spirit-beings such as angels and demons were all flat wrong.

Hobbes' unorthodox idea about God caused some to accuse him of atheism. He vehemently denied the charge: "He that holds there is a God, and that God is really somewhat (for *body* is doubtlessly a *real substance*), is as far from being an atheist, as it is possible to be," he wrote. "But he who says that God is an *incorporeal substance*, no man can be sure whether he be an atheist or not."[13] This cannot have satisfied many Christians, for whom God is, precisely, incorporeal. Hobbes was a careful reader of the Bible but he insisted that religious conceptions were human ideas. "Seeing that there are no signs, nor fruit of religion, but in in man only," he wrote in *Leviathan* (1651), "there is no cause to doubt but that the seed of religion, is also only in man."[14] This was the first clear declaration of the human origin of religion since Lucretius.

Leviathan is primarily a work of political philosophy. Hobbes wrote it while in exile during the English Civil War, which lasted eleven years and was responsible for around 200,000 deaths. He held that the primary cause of the conflict was differences over religious beliefs, so when he wrote about religion his aim was, briefly, to find a way to keep people from killing one another. His political theory is based on the idea of the social contract: rational beings in society surrender some of their freedoms to a sovereign who is obliged to protect them. For this arrangement to be effective, there must be no division between civil and ecclesiastical authority. Just as the sovereign is supreme in matters of state, so too he has to be absolute in matters of religion—with one qualification. The sovereign can exercise his religious authority only in things that have to do with actions and words, for in matters of conscience there is "no judge at all, but God."[15] This is one of the earliest philosophical articulations of the distinction between the inner and outer spheres of religion, which would become an essential element of modern spirituality.

On July 27, 1656, the leaders of a synagogue in Amsterdam issued a writ of excommunication against one of its members on account of his "evil opinions," "abominable heresies," and "monstrous deeds." The charges were vague but the sentence was clear: "We excommunicate, expel, curse, and damn Baruch de Espinoza," wrote the rabbis, execrating him with all the curses that are written in the Bible and forbidding anyone in the congregation, his family members included, from communicating with him in any way. What had Baruch de Espinoza (better known as Baruch Spinoza) done to warrant such a sentence? His crimes were not specified and we have no account of his beliefs at the time, but we can get an idea of what bothered the rabbis from statements in his later works: the Jews are not God's chosen people, the Bible is not the word of God but just an inspired work of literature, and—worst of all—God is not the creator of the universe but in some sense identical with it. When he learned he had been expelled from his community, Spinoza is supposed to have replied: "All the better; they do not force me to do anything that I would not have done of my own accord if I did not dread scandal."[16] Now he was free to pursue his studies and writing without hindrance.

For the past few years, Spinoza had been reading the works of Descartes and other contemporary philosophers. He also was familiar with the Stoics, either directly through the works of Seneca and Cicero, or indirectly through the Neostoicism of Justus Lipsius. The Stoic touch is clear in his earliest surviving writing, *Treatise on the Emendation of the Intellect*. After realizing that "all the things which were the source and object of my anxiety held nothing of good or evil in themselves save insofar as the mind was influenced by them," he began, "I resolved at length to enquire whether there existed a true good," whose "discovery and acquisition would afford me a continuous and supreme joy to all eternity." The first step was to find a way to purify the intellect "so that it may succeed in understanding things without error and as well as possible."[17] Like Descartes, Spinoza made the intellect or reason the basis of his approach. He also, more explicitly than Descartes, made reason the basis of a way of life that would lead to unblemished happiness. This marked a return to the classical ideal of therapeutic philosophy that had been dormant in the West for more than a thousand years.

Spinoza's first published work was *Principles of Cartesian Philosophy* (1663), an outline of two parts of Descartes' *Principles of Philosophy*. In this Spinoza developed the "geometrical" form of presentation he would bring to perfection in his masterwork, the *Ethics*, which he began to work on around this time. In 1665 he set the *Ethics* aside to write a treatise on politics and theology that was inspired by the banning of a book by one of his friends. Spinoza's *Theological-Political Treatise* is now considered one of the most important defenses of freedom of expression ever written. Most early readers saw it in a different light. One critic declared that the book was "full of studious abominations and an accumulation of opinions which have been forged in hell."[18] Although he was one of the most rational of philosophers, Spinoza failed to see that many apparently reasonable people would not be able to understand him.

In the *Treatise* Spinoza argues that the greatest enemy of peace was religious conflict. The way to avoid conflict was to let the sovereign regulate "the practice of religion and the exercises of piety." In writing this he was following Hobbes, but he added more clearly than Hobbes ever did that by "practice of religion" he meant only its "outward forms," not "piety itself and the inward worship of God." Summing up in terms that today would seem routine but in seventeenth-century Europe were revolutionary, he said that "everyone should be allowed freedom of judgment and the right to interpret the basic tenets of his faith as he thinks fit."[19]

The idea that inner conviction was the touchstone of religion had been put forward by Luther and Calvin a century earlier, but both of them insisted that everyone's convictions had to accord with the Bible as they understood it. Anyone who went beyond established doctrine had to be punished. To Spinoza the basic doctrines of Christianity were clear: "love, joy, peace, temperance and honest dealing with all men." Why then did Christians "quarrel so fiercely and display the bitterest hatred towards one another?" The problem was not religion itself but the spurious religion he called "superstition," which is engendered and preserved by fear. Superstition is kept alive by ambitious priests, who go to great lengths to "invest religion, true or false, with such pomp and ceremony that it can sustain any shock." True religion, Spinoza insisted, has "no need of the trappings of superstition. On the contrary, its glory is diminished when it is embellished with such fancies."[20]

To Spinoza, the Bible was a treasury of great and simple truths that virtually no one abided by. Rather than follow its ethical doctrines, people used the Bible to breed "bitter hatred and faction which readily turn men to sedition." In order to recover the Bible's true meaning, Spinoza went back to the original text. His guiding principle was that "the method of interpreting Scripture is no different from the method of interpreting Nature, and is in fact in complete accord with it." This would be an innocuous statement today except in fundamentalist circles, but in the seventeenth century it was a denial of the foundations of the Judeo-Christian tradition. If there was one thing Jews and Christians agreed on, it was that the Bible was literally the word of God. Spinoza was the first European philosopher to argue that scripture is a form of human literature. (Hobbes was moving in this direction but never came right out and said it.) Spinoza went so far as to say that all books "that teach and tell of the highest things are equally sacred, in whatever language and by whatever nation they were written." The eternal Word of God, the "true religion," was written not in Hebrew or Greek or Chinese but "divinely inscribed in men's hearts." And what was the true religion? "To love God above all, and one's neighbour as oneself." This was the essence of scripture and at the same time "the universal divine law."[21]

After completing the *Treatise*, Spinoza returned to the *Ethics*, which he finished by 1675. Apprehensive that publication would expose him to imprisonment or worse, his friends persuaded him to wait. In 1677 he died of a lung disease, precipitated probably by the glass-dust he inhaled while grinding lenses. Later the same year his friends published the *Ethics*, which promptly was condemned by Dutch religious and civil authorities, and later placed on the Catholics' *Index of Prohibited Books*.

What was it about this Latin tome with the not-so-snappy title *Ethics, Demonstrated in Geometrical Order* that made it so contentious? Briefly, Spinoza formulated an idea of God that omitted virtually everything that characterized the God of monotheism: transcendence, creation *ex nihilo*, distinctness from the created world, personality, providential care, the habit of working miracles. What then was God? Spinoza's answer is straightforward if highly abstract: "By God I mean an absolutely infinite being, that is, substance consisting of infinite attributes, each of which expresses eternal and infinite essence." To understand this definition fully it would be necessary to grasp what Spinoza meant by "substance," "attribute," and "essence," each of which he defined in equally abstract terms. Generations of philosophers have written thousands of pages trying to clarify his meaning. For our present purposes it will be enough to remark that for Spinoza there is only one substance and that substance is what he called *Deus* or God. In this he differed from Descartes, who proposed two substances, mind (or spirit) and body, and from Hobbes, who proposed that the only substance was body. And because Spinoza said that God was the only substance it followed that Nature was the same as God. This was such an astonishing identification that Spinoza did not state it outright but snuck it in briefly in the course of another argument: "we have demonstrated ... that Nature does not act with an end in view; that the eternal and infinite being, whom we call God, or Nature, acts by the same necessity whereby it exists."[22] With the phase "God, or Nature" (*Deus, sive Natura*) Spinoza struck down a cardinal assumption of West Asian monotheism: that nature is God's creation and therefore different from and inferior to him.

The idea that God or Nature acts by its own inherent necessity and not "with an end in view" is central to Spinoza's philosophy. God is not a humanlike person moved by needs or desires. God is simply that which is, and what happens in the world is the inevitable result of God's being. Nothing is accidental. All actions, including the actions of human beings, are bound to take place exactly as they do. This would seem to suggest that human beings are unable to do anything to improve themselves, but this was not Spinoza's intent. The essence of all things in nature, humans included, is a striving to persevere in being. In the body–mind complex this striving takes the form of desires and passions (what we now call emotions). Humans can, Spinoza insists, learn to control their desires and emotions and so move closer to perfection.

Spinoza devoted much of the third book of the *Ethics* to developing a theory of the emotions. He proceeded using "the same method as I have used in treating of God and the mind," that is, the geometrical method. In other words, he investigated "human actions and appetites just as if it were an investigation into lines, planes, or bodies [geometrical solids]."[23] (This makes Spinoza seem like the ultimate seventeenth-century nerd. In fact, those who knew him found him rather good company, enjoying conversation, food, and the occasional pint of beer.) The details of his theory of the emotions need not detain us. His main point was that those who aspired to perfection had to free themselves from bondage to negative thoughts and feelings. The method was to avoid dwelling on the causes of troublesome thoughts and emotions, replacing agitation with detachment. When this was done, "love or hatred toward the external cause, and also vacillations, that arise from these emotions will be destroyed."[24] This approach is reminiscent of the methods that the Stoics used to destroy passion. The difference is that Spinoza felt that the emotions were essential parts of nature that could never be destroyed. The best one could hope for was a relative freedom from disturbance.

Once their emotions had been mastered, human beings could concentrate on perfecting their intellects, for in this perfection lay "the highest happiness or blessedness." Blessedness, which Spinoza also called freedom or salvation, consisted of a "constant and eternal love toward God," which was identical with "God's love toward men." It was, as he wrote in a very difficult sentence, "the love of God wherewith God loves himself not insofar as he is infinite, but insofar as he can be explicated through the essence of the human mind considered under a form of eternity."[25] This intellectual love had had nothing to do with the blind adoration of the personal God of the theistic religions.

I have devoted so much space to Spinoza because I believe his philosophy can be looked on as a Western prototype of modern godless spirituality. All the characteristics of spirituality I identified in Chapter 1—innerness, distrust of religious organizations, individual effort, cross-cultural similarities, scientific methodologies, the importance of the body—are present to some degree in his thought. Even the modern distinction between "religion" and "spirituality" has a precedent in his contrast between "superstition" and "true religion." To be sure, Spinoza's philosophy could hardly be called "godless." The *Ethics* is saturated with God from the first page to the last, but the God of Spinoza had little to do with the transcendent creator of the Judeo-Christian tradition.

Twenty years after Spinoza's death, the English mathematician Joseph Raphson coined the neo-Greek term *pantheismus* to mean belief in "a certain universal substance, material as well as intelligent, that fashions all things that exist out of its own essence."[26] Later writers brought *pantheismus* into modern European languages—"pantheism" appeared in English in 1732—and used it when referring to Spinoza's philosophy. The fit was not perfect—Spinoza would never have used "fashion" (in the sense of "create") to describe the origin of the universe—but the description caught on and to this day Spinoza is often called a pantheist, that is, one who believes that God and nature are one. Other writers feel that his "intellectual love of God" makes him more a closet theist than a pantheist (German writer Johann Wolfgang von Goethe called him *theissimus* or supremely theistic). Still others, such as Spinoza's biographer Steven Nadler, think he was more an atheist than anything else. However he might be labeled, Spinoza put together a system of philosophy that is compatible with godless spirituality as I understand it.

Atheism in the sense of disbelief in God, all but inconceivable during the sixteenth century, became during the seventeenth an actual problem that church and state had to deal with. A handful of thinkers published heterodox ideas despite the risks made evident by the martyrdom of Bruno in 1600. The eccentric Italian thinker Lucilio Vanini was put on trial for atheism by the *parlement* of Toulouse and executed in 1619. A half-century later, the Polish nobleman Kazimierz Łyszczyński wrote a manuscript entitled *On the Non-Existence of God* that fell into the hands of the clergy. Convicted of atheism in Warsaw in 1689, he was given the same treatment as Vanini (both men had their tongues pulled out before they were executed and burned). The English deist Charles Blount avoided a similar fate by publishing his works anonymously or pseudonymously. His *Oracles of Reason* (1693), in which he denied the possibility of revelation and miracles, was described by a contemporary English clergyman as "the first Book I ever saw which did openly avow Infidelity."[27]

The religious life of England at the end of the seventeenth century was a confused welter of beliefs and practices endorsed by different denominations that were supported by rival political factions. The government of Charles II (reigned 1660–1685) upheld the established Church of England but tolerated Nonconformists, who had been on top during the Commonwealth (1653–1659). Charles' brother James II, who eventually succeeded him, was Roman Catholic. This led to his deposition and replacement by the Protestant co-regents William and Mary in 1689. These religiopolitical developments mattered to the people of England because they took their religion very seriously. Sectarian questions such as what prayer book should be used were decided by act of Parliament and if necessary enforced by the army.

In this charged atmosphere the philosopher John Locke published his influential *Letter Concerning Toleration* in 1689. Locke argued, contra Hobbes, that any attempt by the government to regulate religious practices would exacerbate rather than reduce conflict. The purpose of religion was to help individuals achieve salvation "according to the rules of virtue and piety." But each individual had to find his or her own way. "To take up the outward show of another man's profession" would be deceitful: "Faith only and inward sincerity are the things that procure acceptance with God."[28]

Locke's stress on the individual made it impossible for him to accept that the sovereign should hold sway in religious matters. Hobbes and Spinoza believed that a single authority was needed to keep people from fighting over points of public worship, and that this authority should be the state and not the church. To Locke, the problem was not differences of opinion—they were inevitable in questions of religion—but the state's unwillingness to tolerate diversity. The state was constituted by consenting individuals "for the procuring, preserving, and advancing their own civil interests." In the same way, when individuals wanted to regulate their collective religious lives, they constituted themselves into voluntary assemblies called churches. "The business of these assemblies," Locke wrote, "is nothing but what is lawful for every man in particular to take care of—I mean the salvation of their souls." He therefore thought that the state should tolerate all forms of religious expression that did not contravene civil law. The main exceptions were people who delivered themselves up "to the protection and service of another prince" (i.e., Catholics, who owed allegiance to the pope) and atheists (not because of their philosophical ideas but because they could not swear oaths and covenants, which are necessary for the existence of civil society).[29]

Early reactions to Locke's *Letter* were not uniformly positive. Some clergymen thought it was part of a Catholic plot to overthrow the government. Other critics feared that Locke's defence of individual conscience and acceptance of religious diversity would open the doors to unorthodoxy or even atheism. They may not have been wrong in this. By making belief and practice a matter of individual choice, Locke helped make possible the critique of religion that shook Christianity to its foundations during the eighteenth and nineteenth centuries.

Tradition and decline in Asia

The fiercest debate in the literary salons of Paris and London at the end of the seventeenth century pitted those who looked to Greece and Rome for models of perfection against those who believed that modern writers were in some ways superior to the ancients. The so-called Quarrel Between the Ancients and the Moderns lasted more than twenty years and like most quarrels soon became complicated. But the basic issue was clear. As French philosopher Voltaire put it: "Was antiquity more fertile in great monuments of genius of every kind, down to the time of Plutarch, than modern ages have been?" The answer, according to the Moderns, was No. Contemporary Europe was in some ways superior to ancient Greece and Rome. This was shown not only by literary works but also technological innovations, in particular the Three Greatest Inventions: the printing press, firearms, and the nautical compass. The irony here was that all these inventions were Chinese. Woodblock printing was common during the Tang dynasty; moveable type was introduced in the eleventh century. The invention of gunpowder also dates from the Tang; four centuries later the Mongols carried it to the Muslim world and Europe. Cannons, developed by the Chinese during the thirteenth century, reached the West by the same route. Both Greeks and Chinese were familiar with magnetism, but it was the Chinese who developed the nautical compass, which later made its way westward. But there was a second irony. After using its technology to make massive advances in communications, warfare, exploration and trade, the Chinese drew back and let the people of Europe make use of their inventions as they explored, colonized and dominated the world.[30]

Why did China, India, and the Islamic world fall behind the West during the sixteenth and seventeenth centuries? This is one of the big questions in the study of early modern history, and there is no easy answer. What is certain is that during this period the economic output of Europe and America soared while the production of most parts of Asia stalled. Along with this downturn there was a marked diminution of technological, literary, artistic, and religious innovation. Which came first, the economic chicken or the cultural egg? Looking back it is clear that the cultural contraction was both an effect and a cause of the economic decline.

A few examples from maritime history will give a glimpse of some of the factors involved. Up to the thirteenth century, merchant and naval vessels from northern and southern India sailed west to Arabia and east to Indochina, where Hinduism and Buddhism became the dominant religions. Later such voyages became rare: crossing the "black waters" of the ocean was a religious offence. Between 1405 and 1433 the Chinese admiral Zheng He commanded a series of "treasure voyages" in the South China Sea and Indian Ocean, going as far as the eastern coast of Africa. A generation later the Neo-Confucian bureaucracy discouraged and finally prohibited such expeditions. After the Ottoman Empire conquered Constantinople in 1453, its navy engaged in war and trade throughout the Mediterranean and even along the Atlantic coast. But as the Empire declined during the seventeenth century, its navy withdrew to the eastern Mediterranean and eventually was outclassed by the Russians.

There is much more to civilization than maritime expansion, but these examples make it clear that at the very moment when the navies of Spain, Portugal, England, France, and the Dutch Republic were planting their flags in far-flung regions and bringing back goods and treasure, the empires of Asia were turning their backs on the political and economic challenges of modernity. During the same period the religious teachers of China, Japan, India, and the Islamic world became fixated on the greatness of earlier ages, adding little to the richness of their traditions. The Asian equivalent of the quarrel between the ancients and the moderns would not take place until the nineteenth century, and then only in response to Western pressure.

Up to the beginning of the seventeenth century, Ming dynasty China enjoyed political stability and economic prosperity and this encouraged a great flourishing of literature and art. The Zhu Xi brand of Neo-Confucianism remained the official philosophy, though the idealistic version of Wang Yangming caught on briefly during the early seventeenth century. According to Wang's followers, the extension of knowledge was available to all, peasants and scholars alike. This blurring of social boundaries produced a conservative backlash and a revival of orthodox Neo-Confucianism.

From around 1600 Ming rulers had to deal with the Manchus, an aggressive people of northeastern Asia, who eventually defeated the Mings and established the Qing dynasty (1644–1911). The Qing emperors used the structures of classical Confucianism to bolster their alien regime. As a result Chinese thinkers produced little original philosophy between the seventeenth and twentieth centuries. The main exception to this rule, the materialistic Neo-Confucianism of Wang Fuzhi (1619–1692), did not become influential until the rise of Communism two centuries after his death. Wang Fuzhi had no time for the debate between rationalists and idealists over the nature of principle or li. What really mattered, he said, was material force or qi. "Principle," he wrote, "depends on material force. When material force is strong, principle prevails. When Heaven accumulates strong and powerful material force, there will be order, and transformations will be refined and daily renewed." Reversing the traditional Chinese outlook, Wang wrote that "the world consists only of concrete things," and that the Way (Dao) itself is "the Way of concrete things." If concrete things are present, "there need be no worry about there not being its Way."[31]

Wang's materialism is similar in some respects to that of his English contemporary Hobbes, although there was no direct or even indirect contact between the two. Confucian thought reached Europe during the late seventeenth century in the form of translations of the works of Confucius and other writers by Jesuit missionaries. The Jesuits were impressed by Confucian ethical teachings but were troubled by the absence of God. This was a problem for European philosophers as well. Voltaire, a deist, insisted that European scholars had refuted the charge that the Chinese were godless heathens. This was only partly true. Scholars were divided over whether Shangdi was equivalent to the Judeo-Christian God.

No lover of popular religion, Voltaire averred that Chinese priests were no worse than those of Europe: both filled people's minds with "a thousand ridiculous prejudices." In science the Chinese were, he wrote, "just where we were two hundred years ago," and they were quickly closing the gap.[32] Confucian scholars in fact were happy to learn all the science the Jesuits brought them, but they showed little interest in European religion and remained convinced of the overall superiority of Chinese civilization.

Both Jesuits and traditional Confucians condemned Neo-Confucianism as too much influenced by Chan Buddhism, even though the Chan of that period was a shadow of what it had been during the golden age of the Tang and the silver age of the Song. The heads of the various schools looked back to legendary figures such as Huineng and Linji. Conformity with the teachings of the ancient masters was insured by the *gongan* system. Students who produced the correct answers were awarded certificates of proficiency. (In this respect *gongan* sessions were not that different from government examinations, which ensured that all bureaucrats knew the classic Confucian texts as interpreted by Zhu Xi.) Most Chan masters of the Ming and Qing periods incorporated some of the practices of the Pure Land school, and this gave their teachings a theistic patina similar to that of contemporary Daoism.

Rinzai Zen, the Japanese offshoot of the Linji school of Chan, fell into decline by the beginning of the Tokugawa era (1600–1868), when government-approved priests were more interested in flattering officials than in helping their students advance. But in the mid-eighteenth century Rinzai was invigorated by the maverick master Hakuin Ekaku (1686–1769). According to Hakuin, Zen practitioners of his day fell into three broad categories: those who chanted the *nembutsu* mantra, those who practiced silent meditation, and those who did nothing at all. Those in the first group were no better than Pure Land Buddhists who longed to be reborn in the Western Paradise. Those in the second group—the followers of Soto Zen— sat so long in silence that they turned their minds into "complete blanks, blissfully unaware that they are, in the process, doing and thinking a great deal." The third group, in which he included most Rinzai practitioners, were "incapable of devoting themselves single-mindedly to Zen practice," so they went around "telling others that Zen practice is useless." What was necessary for all who called themselves Buddhists was to get the intuitive insight of *kensho*, after which everything would change. Even if they were "constantly thinking and acting" they would be "totally free and unattached."[33]

To those who became his students, Hakuin suggested working on a *koan*, perhaps "Mu" (the Japanese form of "Wu" or "No!") or his own "The sound of one hand clapping." Dwelling on a *koan* was the key to success in Zen: "If you work at it relentlessly, with unflagging devotion," he wrote, "you will penetrate it whether you want it or not." Like his fourteenth-century predecessor Bassui, Hakuin encouraged his students to grapple with existential doubt. He quoted the thirteenth-century Chinese master Gaofeng Yuanmiao, who said there were three essentials for practicing Zen: "A great root of faith. A great ball of doubt. A great tenacity of purpose." The faith needed was the conviction that everyone has "an essential self-nature he can see into." The doubt became acute while the student was working on koans. This was something to be cherished for, as Gaofeng said, "At the bottom of great doubt lies great realization." One had to bore through doubt with the same one-pointedness as one would use when seeking "a lost article of incalculable worth." At the same time one had to be "as hostile toward the teachings left by the Buddha-patriarchs as you would be toward a person who had just slain both your parents."[34] How different from the theisms of East and West, which punish doubt and treat ancient texts as final, irrevocable revelations.

The response of the Tokugawa shogunate to the challenges posed by foreign exploration and trade was to seal off Japan from the rest of the world. Between

1636 and 1853 it was illegal for Japanese to leave the country or for foreigners to enter. The government permitted a limited amount of trade with China, Korea, and the Dutch Republic but prohibited missionary activity. In this way Japan protected itself from European colonialism, which destroyed the old order in the Philippines, Indonesia, Indochina, and India. At the same time it cut itself off from European science and technology, which left it at a disadvantage in the commercial and cultural competitions of the seventeenth to nineteenth centuries.

During the same period, China kept close watch over the traders it allowed to operate in a few coastal enclaves. Its humiliating defeat in the First Opium War (1840) and subsequent unequal treaties with European powers shattered its sense of cultural superiority. Fourteen years later the United States forced Japan to open itself to trade. By the middle of the nineteenth century, the civilizations of East Asia had been dragged unwillingly into the Europe-dominated modern world.

European traders set up shop in India at the beginning of the sixteenth century, but for many years they were minor players in the affairs of the subcontinent. The Mughal Empire, founded in 1526, grew in extent and power for almost 200 years. Muslim rulers established pragmatic partnerships with Hindu generals and administrators and for the most part let people practice the religions of their choice without undue interference. Akbar (1542–1605), the greatest Mughal emperor, encouraged dialogue between members of the religions that prevailed in his domains. The country was home to the indigenous sects that we now refer to by the collective name "Hinduism," along with Jainism, stray remnants of Buddhism, and innumerable local and tribal practices, not to mention Islam which, owing to the influence of the sufis, had taken a characteristically Indian turn.

Almost all of these Indian religions were theistic. Most Hindus regarded themselves as Vaishnavas (worshippers of Vishnu in one of his many forms), Shaivas (worshippers of Shiva), or Shaktas (worshippers of Shakti or the Mother Goddess). They performed rituals invoking their chosen deities in temples and in homes. Even nominally atheistic Jains made room for devotional practices inspired by the Hindu *bhakti* movement. Samkhya, the least theistic of the Vedic schools, ceased to be a living tradition after 1400. This left Advaita Vedanta as the sole important school that gave more importance to meditative than devotional practices.

Shankara's version of Advaita formed the philosophical basis of a number of scholarly works of the fourteenth to sixteenth centuries, such as Vidyaranya's *Fifteen Chapters*, Sadananda's *Essence of Vedanta*, and Appayya Dikshita's *Brief Compendium of Doctrines*. These digests provided concise explanations of the principal topics of Advaita without breaking much new ground. Often they gave an opening to theism. Vidyaranya wrote that those who were incapable of finding the self "by the help of supporting arguments" could worship "the Supreme Brahma in the invisible manner."[35] Dikshita created a system synthesizing Advaita and

South Indian Shaivism. These concessions to theism are not surprising in an age when the *bhatki* movement was sweeping all before it. Two important schools of Vedanta founded in the sixteenth century were based on the teachings of devotees of Krishna, Vallabhacharya (1479–1531) and Chaitanya (1485–1533).

Around this time the philosopher Vijnanabhikshu wrote commentaries on the primary texts of three different Vedic schools: Vedanta, Samkhya, and Yoga. Although a theist, he wanted to include nontheistic Samkhya in his synthesis. To do this he had to explain away passages of the *Samkhya Sutra* that denied the existence of God. His argument ran like this: If Kapila, the traditional author of the *Sutra*, had taught the truth that God exists then "the practice of discrimination [on which Samkhya is based] would be hindered by desire after seeing perfect lordliness." That is, serious aspirants might be distracted by desire for psychic powers. Or perhaps Kapila wanted "to impede the knowledge of the wicked" for fear they would acquire and misuse such powers. To prevent these outcomes, Kapila deliberately taught the false doctrine of God's nonexistence.[36] This clearly is a lame response to the unambiguous atheism of the *Sutra*.

Vijnanabhikshu lived at a time when the Mughal Empire was approaching its zenith, but he never mentioned Islam, the religion of the ruling class, much less tried to include it in his synthesis. Muslim scholars showed a similar lack of interest in Hindu polytheism. The tolerance that characterized Akbar's administration continued to some extent during the reign of his son and successor Jehangir, but the next Mughal emperor, Shah Jahan, was an orthodox Muslim who undid the liberal policies of his father and grandfather. Shah Jahan's first son, Dara Shikoh (1615–1659), was a sufi, a patron of the arts, and a scholar of religion who translated the Upanishads into Persian. He was less accomplished in diplomacy and warfare, and was defeated by his younger brother Aurangzeb, who deposed Shah Jahan and ruled as emperor from 1658 to 1707.

Aurangzeb forced unbelievers to pay a special tax, executed the Sikh guru Tegh Bahadur, and destroyed many Hindu temples, including the famous Kashi Vishwanath Temple of Varanasi. The Mughal Empire reached its greatest extent during his rule, but shortly after his death it began to fall apart, as would-be successors fought viciously with one another. Seizing the opportunity, the European trading companies, particularly those of France and England, selectively deployed their military forces, now propping up and now waging war against different successor states. Arms and diplomacy favored the English, and by 1818 the British East India Company had won control over most of the subcontinent.

The political instability of the eighteenth and early nineteenth centuries put a damper on the expression of spiritual ideas. Few important representatives of the *bhakti* and *sant* traditions emerged during this period, and those who did mostly followed in the footsteps of their predecessors. Notable among the *sants* was Paltu Sahib, who lived in Ayodhya, a pilgrimage center in northern India, during the eighteenth century. Like Kabir and Raidas, he railed against the pretentions of priests and the futility of religious observances:

> Vain is the counting of beads, worthless are visits to holy rivers;
> Empty and profitless is keeping vows, barren are practices of yoga.
> Indeed, all rituals, ceremonies and religious observances give not salvation.

The key to salvation was mental self-discipline: "Subdue or conquer the mind if you wish to pierce the veil [of illusion]." In some of his songs, Paltu alluded to the elevated state he achieved through spiritual practice:

> In the beginning was I, in the ages primeval I was,
> Even when the world comes to an end, I shall abide.
> In every particle I abide, mine is the flavor in all, there is none else.
> Brahma, Vishnu and Shiva, all are but forms in which appears my essence.[37]

Such claims, along with his condemnation of ritual, won Paltu no friends among the Brahmins of Ayodhya, who are said to have conspired to kill him by having him burned alive.

Paltu Sahib was against all forms of organized religion. Prannath, who lived in central India around the same time, tried to harmonize the teachings of four disparate religions: Hinduism, Islam, Judaism, and Christianity. One of Prannath's poems contains an account of the Day of Judgment, when "Christ, Muhammad, and the Imam [of Shia Islam]" will come and everyone will "bow before them." Budh Kalanki (apparently Vishnu's last avatar Kalki) also will appear: "he will make all alike; east and west will both be under him."[38] Prannath's syncretism was one response to the cacophony of religions that prevailed during the eighteenth and early nineteenth centuries. Another was the nihilism of an ascetic named Bakhtawar, who lived in Hathras, a town south of Delhi, a little after 1800. Parts of his principal work, the *Essence of Emptiness*, have echoes of Kabir: "Hindus and Musselmans are of the same nature, two leaves of one tree—these call their teachers Mullas, those term them Pundits… One cuts off the foreskin, the other puts on a sacrificial thread. Ask them the difference, enquire the importance of these distinctions, and they will quarrel with you: dispute not, but know them to be the same." Other passages follow the lead of Nagarjuna by undermining the foundations of knowledge: "All that is seen is nothing and is not really seen; lord or no lord it is all one. Maya is nothing; Brahm is nothing; all is false and delusive. The world is all emptiness," as are the sun, the moon, and the gods. Religious practices are futile: "nought is the worship of nought and nought the prayer addressed to nought." This "doctrine of Nihilism," the writer concludes, makes those who possess it "drunk with the wine of perfect knowledge."[39]

"In the tides of history," wrote scholar of Islam Annemarie Schimmel, "the eighteenth century is usually considered to be the time of lowest ebb for the Islamic peoples between the Balkans and Bengal." After reaching a pinnacle of power and influence at the end of the sixteenth century, the Ottoman Empire swiftly declined and by 1700 was no longer a major player on the world's stage. Around the same time, Persia surrendered chunks of its territory to Russia, while the British reduced the once-proud Mughal Empire to a tiny plot around Delhi. This loss of political clout was accompanied by a contraction of creative activity in art and religion. "The dusty veil of stagnation seemed to cover everything," Schimmel wrote, "not allowing of new enterprises for redirecting the spiritual energy of the Muslims."[40] This was true even of the sufis. Practitioners felt that they had arrived too late and were out of touch with the great ones of the past. Masters continued to guide and inspire but they increasingly put their teachings in written treatises rather than relying on oral transmission. The result was a stiffening of sufi doctrine.

This tendency was less marked among those who spread their teachings through vernacular poetry and songs. In the western part of the Indian subcontinent popular sufis disparaged book-learning and urged their listeners to look within: "There is no room for rationality where there is the glorious mystery of divine unity," wrote the Punjabi sufi Sultan Bahu (1630–1691):

> Here there are neither mullas, pandits, and astrologers, nor the outward meaning of the Qur'an.
> When Ahmad [Muhammad] appears as the One, all else is destroyed.
> Perfect knowledge is obtained, Bahu, by those who close the revealed scriptures.

South of Punjab, in the province of Sind, Sachal Sarmarst (1739–1826) sang of the unitary state in which the very idea of God is superfluous:

> In that state, there is neither affliction nor comfort;
> Neither this nor that, neither attributes nor arts;
> Neither prayer nor devotion, neither revelations nor miracles;
> Neither pain nor feeling, neither sorrow nor joy; ...
> Neither mystery nor modesty, all is wonderment:
> Sachu! It is pure Truth, it is all Tranquillity.[41]

Enthusiasm and enlightenment

Married in 1663 at the age of fifteen, Jeanne Guyon was widowed when she was twenty-eight. Now she was free to devote herself fully to the religious life. At that time a current of Catholic practice known as quietism was spreading through Spain, Italy and France. Its originator, the Spanish priest Miguel de Molinos, recommended silent, passive contemplation as a way to achieve union with God. By nature an introvert, Guyon was drawn to quietist circles. Leaving her children behind, she followed her spiritual guide, the friar François Lacombe, to Geneva, Turin and Grenoble. Lacombe encouraged her to write down her thoughts and experiences and in 1685 she published a book called *A Short and Very Easy Method of Prayer*. All the aspirant had to do, she wrote, was to turn within, stay focused on God, and let him do the rest. In one of her lessons, she used a metaphor from science: The soul has an inborn tendency to be united with its godly center, just as a stone "by its own weight falls to the earth as to its center." Guyon was writing a half-century after Galileo published his *Two New Sciences* and a few years before Newton published the *Principles*. Solid mechanics was all the rage. She and others of her generation stood at the cusp of two opposed tendencies that would dominate the eighteenth century: subjective spirituality and scientific materialism. Both were at odds with organized religion. In 1687 Pope Innocent XI condemned quietism as heretical. The next year Guyon was arrested and thrown in jail. She repented and was released but again was imprisoned between 1695 and 1703. From then till her death in 1717 she corresponded widely with Protestants as well as Catholics, spreading her ideas across Europe.[42]

The political situation in Europe stabilized after the Peace of Westphalia (1648), which ended the Wars of Religion. Now the Christians of Europe could go about their business without undue fear of violence. Catholicism, Eastern Orthodoxy, and the Protestant denominations had well-defined spheres of influence and, except in the colonies of America, Africa, and Asia, did not contend aggressively with one another. There was, however, considerable unrest within the Protestant and Catholic worlds. Many congregations and individual worshippers were unwilling to follow the dictates of ecclesiastical leaders. Preachers of pietism in Germany and Scandinavia, evangelicalism in Great Britain and North America, and quietism in Spain, France, and Italy encouraged their listeners to seek guidance within and to read and interpret the Bible on their own.

These changes in Christian thought and practice were paralleled by advances in science and philosophy that overshadowed and in the end transformed the religious life of Europe. For the first time since the second century, nontheistic philosophy played a major role in the cultural life of the continent. Religion remained powerful, of course, and religious professionals thought they could ignore the scientists and philosophers who stated or implied that religion was subordinate to reason. Such complaisance was impossible during the eighteenth century, when science+philosophy began to replace religion as the dominant cultural force. Later French historians dubbed this period *le siècle des Lumières*, the century of Lights. German and English historians followed suit with the equivalent terms *die Aufklärung* and the Enlightenment. It was a time when (in the view of its supporters) ignorance was replaced by knowledge and darkness was dispelled by light—and this light was not the radiance of God but the brilliance of human reason.

The pietist movement began in the late 1660s, when Lutheran clergyman Philipp Spener convened devotional gatherings called "schools of piety" in western Germany. In his sermons he stressed personal engagement with Christian teachings rather than the mechanical following of ritual. Laypeople, he said, should bypass the clergy, study scriptures on their own, and try to bring the truths of religion into their daily lives. Unsurprisingly most members of the Lutheran hierarchy resisted his ideas, but the movement flourished for more than a century and influenced many later developments.

Echoes of Protestant pietism are found in Catholic quietism, which was developed by Molinos during the mid-1670s. His works were first tolerated, then condemned as dangerous. In 1687 he was arrested, tried, and sentenced to life imprisonment. Guyon, a quietist in all but name, had many admirers among the French clergy, among them the powerful bishop François Fénelon; but even he was unable to shield her from the Catholic hierarchy, who feared that her example would undermine their authority. The only way to find God, Guyon insisted, was to look within: "Do not seek God outside of you, in Heaven or in images, or any other place, but seek it first within you where it truly resides," she wrote. Anyone who opened the inner door to God's presence, "will very soon become spiritual [*deviendra bientôt spirituel*]." She and Fénelon were among the first writers in Europe to use the word "spiritual" in something like its modern sense.[43]

English clergyman John Wesley considered Madame Guyon "a woman of very uncommon understanding, and of excellent piety" but rejected her quietism. Inspired by the zeal of the German Pietists and the related Moravian Brethren, he launched a movement of renewal within the Anglican Church, exhorting his listeners to be born again in Jesus. The secret of the new birth, he said in a 1743 sermon, could not be grasped intellectually even by the wisest of men. It was a change "wrought in the whole soul by the Almighty Spirit of God," raising it "from the death of sin, to the life of righteousness." The purpose of reason was to help people understand the teachings of Jesus, the apostles, and the prophets, but it was "utterly incapable of giving either faith, or hope, or love: and, consequently, of producing either real virtue, or substantial happiness."[44]

Wesley's exaltation of experience and downgrading of reason were central to the evangelical movement, which spread throughout Great Britain and New England by means of enormous revival meetings. Moved by fiery sermons delivered by ministers such as Jonathan Edwards, whole communities became possessed by religious "enthusiasm" that expressed itself in bizarre behavior: fainting, fits, vocalizations, and so forth. Conservative preachers condemned the revivalists for encouraging delusional feelings. Mistaking "the workings of his own passions for divine communications," the enthusiast "fancies himself immediately inspired by the SPIRIT of GOD, when all the while, he is under no other influence than that of an over-heated imagination," declared Boston minister Charles Chauncy in 1742. The passions had to be kept "in their proper place, under the government of a well inform'd understanding."[45] Wesley, Edwards, and other evangelicals took the opposite view: believers had to follow the promptings of faith, refusing to be led by "that blind leader of the blind, so idolized by the world, Natural Reason." Wesley therefore avoided "all perplexed and intricate reasonings" except when discussing the Bible, the literal truth of which he never doubted.[46]

Belief in the inerrancy of scripture was all but universal at that time. The Bible was simply the word of God, and everything that God said was true. The only serious challenge to this dogma came from Hobbes and Spinoza, who pointed out difficulties in the text of the Old Testament. One almost comical example: If Moses was the sole author of Deuteronomy how did he write the description of his death with which the book closes? By the middle of the eighteenth century, theologians who had trained as classical scholars saw that it was necessary to study Biblical texts with the same minute care as Greek manuscripts. This led to disturbing discoveries. Lutheran scholar Johann Semler (1725–1791) ended up doubting the authorship of several New Testament epistles. The fact that he was head of the faculty of theology at the University of Halle made it hard to brush his findings aside. Eventually he was forced to retract some of his statements, but his historical approach, which became known as "higher criticism," grew in influence during the eighteenth and nineteenth centuries.

One of Semler's students at Halle was Friedrich Schleiermacher, about whom I spoke in Chapter 1 in connection with spirituality, faith, and godless religion. In his 1799 book *On Religion: Speeches to its Cultured Despisers*, Schleiermacher wrote there was no conflict between reason and faith because they belonged to different spheres. True religion did not, like metaphysics, seek "to determine and explain the nature of the Universe, nor like morals to advance and perfect the Universe by the power of freedom and the divine will of man. It is neither thinking nor acting, but intuition and feeling."[47] Schleiermacher's intuitionalism opened the way to new approaches to Christian belief, but it also appealed to writers and thinkers who had left Christian doctrine behind.

During the eighteenth century the worst an unorthodox author might fear was academic exile and social ostracism. This was definitely an improvement over the situation two hundred years earlier, when heretical authors were burned at the stake. Still, outspokenness could be dangerous. It was to avoid the fate of Servetus, Bruno, Vanini, and Łyszczyński that French priest Jean Meslier (1664–1729) kept his unorthodox ideas to himself. His posthumously published *Memoirs* were unambiguously atheistic. Not only did he deny the existence of God, he also offered "clear and evident demonstrations of the vanity and falsity of all the divinities and all the religions of the world." All religions are false because they are human inventions. Faith, the foundation of religious belief, is a principle of error. Visions, revelations, and Biblical prophecies are illusions. The greater part of the teachings of the church are untrue. Religion survives because the rich and powerful use it to keep the poor in chains. Like Hobbes and Spinoza, Meslier threw doubt on the idea that the Bible was divinely inspired. A priest himself, he criticized the priesthood for enriching itself at the expense of the peasants and cooperating with the nobility in the abuses of the feudal system. (He excused his own forty years' work as a priest by saying he did his parishioners no harm and helped them whenever he could.) After presenting his arguments, he addressed his flock directly: "I am convinced that if you follow carefully the natural lights of your spirit, you will see at least as well and as certainly as I that all the religions of the world are nothing but human inventions, and that all your religion teaches you and compels you to accept as supernatural and divine is at root nothing but error, lies, illusion and imposture."[48]

Unable to publish his views, Meslier made several copies of his testament, which were discovered after his death, transcribed, and circulated. In 1735 one of Voltaire's friends told the philosopher about Meslier's writings. Twenty-seven years later, Voltaire published extracts, with alterations and additions, as *The Testament of J. Meslier*. The book caused an uproar in Paris literary circles, strongly influencing radical thinkers such as the Baron d'Holbach. In this way Meslier's ideas helped make possible the scarcely disguised atheism of the French Enlightenment.

Enlightenment philosophers had three main ways of approaching the problem of God: deism, atheism, and skepticism. At that time deism meant the belief that God could be understood rationally without the need of revelation, tradition, or faith. Voltaire gave classic expression to this view in his *Philosophical Dictionary*: "It is perfectly evident to my mind that there exists a necessary, eternal, supreme, and intelligent being. This is no matter of faith, but of reason."[49] Understood in this way, deism was more or less synonymous with "natural religion," the belief that God's existence could be demonstrated rationally by means of empirical evidence. To deists the Bible was a human document, in parts sublime, in parts ridiculous. Priests were people like the rest of us, some good, some bad, some outright criminals.

Like many other deists, Voltaire was strongly, even violently anticlerical. *Écrasez l'infâme*—"crush the infamous thing," that is, the church and priesthood—was his battle cry. In a letter to Frederick II of Prussia, he wrote that religion was "made only to deceive," and that Christianity was "indisputably the most ridiculous, the most absurd and the most sanguinary [religion] that has ever infected the earth." But he never abandoned his belief in God, writing to Frederick that it was not enough to say, as atheists did, that God did not exist: one had to *prove* God's nonexistence. But this could never be done, because all nature cries out that God exists, "that there is a supreme intelligence, an immense power, an admirable order" upon which humanity depends.[50] This is the old theological argument from design, but at the time Voltaire wrote, it had lost its ability to convince a new brand of thinker.

Historian Jonathan Israel draws a distinction between the "moderate" Enlightenment inspired by Newton and Locke and the "radical" Enlightenment set in motion by Spinoza. One of the main differences between the moderates and radicals was their approach to God. The moderates clung to the belief in a Creator, although they had no time for organized religion. If they accepted Christianity it was a stripped-down version without any supernatural clutter. (Thomas Jefferson, a moderate Enlightenment man, prepared a version of the Gospels from which he cut out—physically, with a razor—the miracles, the resurrection, and the claims that Jesus was divine.) The radicals on the other hand came close to rejecting God altogether. According to Israel, it was radicals such as Diderot and d'Holbach and not moderates such as Locke and Voltaire who were the real creators of the Enlightenment values of universality, equality, and democracy, which changed the history of Europe and eventually the world.[51]

Both radicals and moderates took part in the key project of the French Enlightenment: the *Encyclopédie*, a "Systematic Dictionary of the Sciences, Arts, and Crafts" published between 1751 and 1772. Its main editors were philosopher and critic Denis Diderot and mathematician Jean le Rond d'Alembert. Originally a deist on the model of Voltaire, Diderot came under the spell of French physician Julien Offray de la Mettrie, whose *Man a Machine* proposed a materialist theory of human nature that left no place for a soul. Matter was the source of sensation or consciousness; mind was the effect and not the cause of the body's movements. Diderot took up La Mettrie's idea of thinking matter in his *Letter on the Blind* (1749), in which he suggested that the universe generated itself and that its apparent order was the result of the chance interaction of atoms. Soon he found himself sitting in a solitary cell in a fortress outside Paris, where he resolved to be more careful in the future.

Protected by his wealth and social position, radical philosopher Paul-Henri Thiry, Baron d'Holbach, was even more outspoken than his friend Diderot. Gathering up the ideas of Lucretius, Hobbes, Spinoza, Meslier, La Mettrie, Diderot, and others, he put together a readable compendium of materialistic, antireligious views in his *System of Nature* (1770). The universe, he wrote, was just matter in motion, "an immense, an uninterrupted succession of causes and effects." There was therefore "no necessity to have recourse to supernatural powers, to account for the formation of things." Most people were ignorant of the system of nature and fearful of the forces it contained and therefore fell prey to comforting stories told by the masters of religion. The remedy was not to move from ignorance to greater ignorance, but "to study Nature, to scrutinize her laws, to search out her expedients, to discover her properties." By actively using reason instead of passively accepting authority, people could free themselves from fear and superstition and dispel the "fictitious powers" known as gods.[52]

Toward the end of the *System* d'Holbach took up the question of the relationship between religion and morality. Religious people believed it was impossible to lead a moral life without the aid of scripture. If religion should ever cease to be, society would plunge into chaos. D'Holbach thought the opposite: religion in general and Christianity in particular stood in the way of moral development. "To establish morality upon a steady foundation," people had to abandon "those chimerical systems upon which the ruinous edifice of supernatural morality has hitherto been constructed." The aim of morality was not to evade the punishments of hell or win the rewards of heaven but to achieve true happiness on earth. For this, it was necessary to cultivate virtue, which d'Holbach defined as gaining happiness for oneself by giving happiness to others. An atheist who reasoned well would arrive at "principles more determinate, more humane, than the superstitious" and would never believe, as religious fanatics did, "that violence, injustice, persecution, or assassination are either virtuous or legitimate actions."[53]

In 1772 d'Holbach published *Common Sense*, a brief popularization of the *System of Nature* that contains some of his wittiest takedowns of religion. Anyone with a bit of common sense, he began, will easily see "that all religion is a castle in the air; that Theology is just ignorance of natural causes reduced to a system, a long tissue of chimeras and contradictions." The name God, "which excites respect and fear in every heart, is just a vague word that people have constantly on their lips without being able to attach to it ideas or qualities that are not contradicted by facts."[54] D'Holbach's friends, who met at his mansion every week, must have found this *boutade* amusing. The d'Holbach coterie, as it was called, was made up of radical *Encyclopédie* writers, such as Diderot, d'Alembert, and the philosopher Claude Adrien Helvétius, along with more moderate thinkers, such as Jean-Jacques Rousseau, whose sympathy for religion often made him seem the odd man out. Occasionally a writer from abroad was invited. Among anglophone visitors were Edward Gibbon, Joseph Priestly, Benjamin Franklin, Adam Smith, and David Hume.

When Hume met d'Holbach and his circle around 1765, he was famous as the author *The History of England* and notorious as the writer of philosophical works that took skepticism to new heights. Was it possible to say that the self really existed, or cause and effect, or God? Few people understood his treatment of these questions, but university authorities in Edinburgh and Glasgow decided that his remarks on God unfitted him to be a professor. Perhaps, it was whispered, he was an atheist—a word that in eighteenth-century Britain meant something like "infidel" or even, loosely, "scoundrel." Things were different across the Channel. When Hume first visited d'Holbach's salon, he remarked to his host "that he did not believe in the existence of atheists, that he never had seen any." D'Holbach replied: "Monsieur, count how many of us there are here." Hume counted eighteen. D'Holbach continued: "I am lucky enough to be able to show you fifteen atheists at one glance. The other three have not yet made up their minds."[55]

When Hume wrote about religion he proceeded cautiously. In *The Natural History of Religion* he observed there were two main approaches to the subject: one "concerning its foundation in reason," the other "concerning its origin in human nature." The rational approach admitted "the most obvious, at least the clearest solution": no reasonable person could doubt that "the whole frame of nature bespeaks an intelligent author." No purpose would be served in discussing such "obvious" truths (which, as I show below, Hume did not wholeheartedly accept), so he confined himself in the *Natural History* with the human origins of religion.[56] As he imagined it, primitive humans found themselves surrounded by natural forces whose workings they could not understand. Some forces brought pain, and became objects of fear, others brought pleasure, and became objects of hope and longing. Unlike modern Europeans, prehistoric people did not conceive of these forces in abstract terms, but imagined them as living beings: demons, gods, and so forth. Each natural phenomenon—the sun, the rain, the wind—had a particular being attached to it. Therefore primitive religions were polytheistic. Over time, the followers of these cults began to favor one god over the others. This gave rise to what Hume called theism and what we today call monotheism.

To Hume the birth and development of the god-idea was a natural, not a supernatural phenomenon. Humans created the gods using their natural faculties, and it was the emotional rather than the intellectual faculties that played the leading role. The ruling motive was not "the pure love of truth," but "the anxious concern for happiness, the dread of future misery, the terror of death, the thirst of revenge, the appetite for food and other necessaries." Driven by hope and fear, humans invented modes of worship to keep the gods on their side. These practices were not necessarily a sign of elevated morals. History amply demonstrated that "the greatest crimes have been found, in many instances, compatible with a superstitious piety and devotion."[57]

Hume avoided taking up the question of God's existence in writings that appeared during his lifetime, but he spent more than twenty years developing his ideas in a manuscript that was published after his death. In the opening scene of *Dialogues Concerning Natural Religion*, he presents three characters who will be the spokesmen of the positions he wants to examine: Demea, a conventional theist; Cleanthes, a defender of natural religion; and Philo, a philosophical skeptic. Demea, as might be expected, takes the existence of God for granted: No man, he says, at least no man of common sense, "ever entertained a serious doubt with regard to a truth so certain and self-evident." The problem is not God's existence but his nature, which is "altogether incomprehensible and unknown to us" because of the limitations of human thought. Philo, the skeptic, agrees with Demea that human minds cannot fathom God's nature but adds that we have no reason to believe that God possesses human qualities such as goodness and concern.[58]

Cleanthes, the deist, is unwilling to accept that we can just assume that God exists. To understand anything we have to reason on the basis of experience. He offers a technological version of the argument from design: The world is "nothing but one great machine, subdivided into an infinite number of lesser machines," all of which "are adjusted to each other with an accuracy, which ravishes into admiration all men, who have ever contemplated them." Philo asks if it is legitimate to compare human constructions to the universe: houses have builders but the universe is not a house. He also points out (anticipating an important element of Darwinism) that many things that seem to be consciously designed are products of organic forces: "A tree bestows order and organization on that tree, which springs from it, without knowing the order: An animal, in the same manner, on its offspring."[59]

The rest of the chapters follow the same format: Demea and Cleanthes propose apparently solid arguments; Philo listens politely, then tears them apart. Finally, in the second-to-last dialogue, Philo brings up the problem that has bedeviled theists since antiquity: how can all the evil in the universe go along with the idea of a divine creator? He paints a dismal picture of the world of living things: "How hostile and destructive [they are] to each other! How insufficient all of them for their own happiness! How contemptible or odious to the spectator!" If God is the origin of everything, then God is responsible for this sorry state of affairs. At this point it looks as if Philo has undone both the revealed religion of Demea and the natural religion of Cheanthes. But in the last chapter he pulls a surprise. Turning to Cleanthes, he says that the argument by design is, after all, too strong to ignore: "A purpose, an intention, a design strikes everywhere the most careless, the most stupid thinker; and no man can be so hardened in absurd systems, as at all times to reject it." The real problem is not religion in its revealed or natural forms, but false religion, which comes in two shapes: superstition and enthusiasm. Superstition is the cause of factionalism, civil strife, intolerance, revolt, oppression, and slavery; enthusiasm opens the way to "superstitious terror and dejection." In the end, Philo announces that philosophical skepticism—his own position—is in fact "the first and most essential step towards being a sound, believing Christian."[60]

If we ignore Philo's nod to Christianity (which Hume presumably added to avoid problems when the book was published), his skepticism becomes more interesting. True skeptics cannot dogmatically deny the possibility of God's existence. If, like Hume, they incline toward disbelief, their position is what we now call agnosticism. If they incline toward belief, their position is fideism, the reliance on faith rather than reason to arrive at spiritual certainty.

Immanuel Kant began his career as a rationalist philosopher and a Christian (he was raised as a Pietist), but was shaken out of his "dogmatic slumber" by a careful reading of Hume. He was particularly struck by Hume's discussion of cause and effect. Everyone assumes that certain events (such as striking a match) are causes of other events (combustion). The connection seems so obvious we don't bother to think it through. Hume showed however "that it is wholly impossible for reason to think such a connection *a priori* and from concepts." All we can say for sure is that one event comes before the other: it is a matter of experience, not reason.[61]

Hume's demonstration troubled Kant. He felt he had to find a way to derive causation and other rational concepts without depending on experience. The only way to do this, as far as he could see, was to rethink reason from the bottom up, or rather from the outside in. We generally assume that thought or cognition has to "conform to the objects" of experience: things are the way they are and the intellect figures them out. Kant said it would be better to assume "that the objects must conform to our cognition": we see things the way we do because our minds have certain inbuilt categories such as cause and effect and space and time that structure our experience. These categories exist *a priori* or prior to experience. They cannot be logically proved, for they are the stuff of logic itself. One consequence is that there are a number of things that reason is incapable of knowing, "things-in-themselves" that lie beyond the phenomenal world. Among them are God, freedom, and immortality. Kant thought that any attempt to prove the existence of God by means of reason was a simple waste of time. Nevertheless he devoted pages of his *Critique of Pure Reason* (1781) to showing how the classic arguments for God are defective. (I discussed his counterarguments briefly in Chapter 1.) God can only be known by moral intuition; reason just gets in the way. Kant therefore had to deprive reason of its "pretension to extravagant insights." Put otherwise, he "had to deny *knowledge* in order to make room for *faith*."[62]

At the time Kant wrote, philosophy had become a specialized academic field in which diploma-holding experts communicated with one another in language that was all but impenetrable to ordinary readers. Kant thought this was a betrayal of philosophy's ancient purpose. "A concealed idea of philosophy had long been present among men," he remarked in one of his lectures. Yet "either they have not understood it or else they have considered it a contribution to scholarship." But "if we take the ancient Greek philosophers—such as Epicurus, Zeno, and Socrates—we discover that the principal object of their science had been the destiny of men, and the means to achieve it." He went on to tell a story about another Greek philosopher: "Plato asked an old man who had told him he was following his lectures on virtue: 'When are you finally going to start *living* virtuously?' The point is not only to speculate: ultimately we must think of actual practice. Nowadays, however, he who lives in a way which conforms with what he teaches is taken to be a dreamer."[63]

The late eighteenth century was not a time when philosophers could resuscitate the wisdom of the Stoics and Epicureans. The glamour of reason was still too great, the need to tame religion too urgent. Religious people, on the other hand, were too concerned with defending their dogmas to go deep into rational enquiry. Kant's aim was to find a "middle way" between the two, to build a bridge between "the dogmatism that Hume fought" and the philosophical skepticism that Hume introduced in its place.[64] Kant's bridge-building efforts were not successful. Dogmatists and skeptics went their separate ways, each thinking that the others' days were numbered.

* * *

In Europe during the early modern period it became possible, for the first time since the late classical age, for thinkers to doubt the existence of God. Few sixteenth- and seventeenth-century scientists and philosophers were openly atheistic but some reduced the role of the deity to that of a demiurge working through physical laws. Scientists redefined what was meant by knowledge, relying on observation and mathematics rather than the Bible and Aristotle. Some philosophers formulated theories of natural religion, using the facts of the natural world and the power of human reason to prove that God exists. From around the middle of the eighteenth century, natural religion began to give way to atheism.

From the late seventeenth century unorthodox Christian groups such as pietism, quietism, and evangelicalism encouraged believers to look within themselves for illumination and guidance. They also promoted methods of practice that emphasized individual effort: pietistic devotion, quietistic meditation, evangelical enthusiasm. These new approaches led to an upsurge of religious revivalism, which shook the foundations of the established churches. Locke condemned the revivalists' enthusiasm but like them stressed the importance of personal choice and voluntary association. His belief that the state had no business interfering in the religious lives of its subjects helped to encourage the development of multiple Christian denominations in Britain, America, and elsewhere.

Some intellectuals who rejected religion but longed for personal self-discipline turned to the practices of the Greek and Roman Stoics. As European philosophy became more and more academic, Kant looked back wistfully to the old Greek ideal of philosophy as a way of life. In the next century philosophers influenced by Kant such as Schopenhauer and Kierkegaard tried to recover this ideal.

Most Asian religious thinkers of the sixteenth to eighteenth centuries looked on their founding scriptures—the *Analects*, the Upanishads, the Buddhist and Jain sutras, the *Quran*—with unqualified respect. Such new thinking as there was took the form of commentaries and commentaries on commentaries. As the nations of the West took the lead in exploration and exploitation, China, Japan, India, and the Muslim world slipped into political isolation and economic stagnation. This led to a loss of creativity in religious and spiritual thought and practice. Even practitioners of meditative traditions such as Vedanta, Zen, and Sufism were content for the most part to blindly follow the lead of the masters of the past.

6 SECULARIZING THE SACRED

The nineteenth century was a time of political, economic, social, and cultural upheaval throughout the world. Empires rose and fell; nations gained freedom and lost it; revolts broke out, were suppressed, and broke out again. In the West, science and technology gave birth to the Industrial Revolution, which upended patterns of life that had lasted for centuries. Writers, artists, and critics tried to keep pace with the change but inevitably fell behind. Literary and artistic schools arose, reigned for a moment, and were replaced. There was a constant stream of economic and social gospels and competing cults of nationalism that drove the world into "a war to end all wars," which in the end cleared the way for a series of increasingly destructive conflicts.

Nowhere was the flux of the age more evident than in religion. Traditional faiths were challenged by new religions, imported religions, substitutes for religion, and irreligion. Believing or not believing became, for the first time in history, a matter of individual choice. During the eighteenth century only a few radical philosophers had the audacity to question the religious status quo. During the nineteenth century, many famous writers, among them Goethe, Wordsworth, Emerson, Stendhal, Eliot, and Dostoyevsky, expressed unorthodox views—pantheism, agnosticism, even outright atheism—in widely read poems, novels, and essays. Institutional religion remained influential but church attendance plummeted.

As religion lost its appeal, people searched for secular substitutes. Writers and artists of the Romantic movement held up Nature as an object of worship and source of redemption. Philosophers such as Schopenhauer and critics such as Arnold looked on music, poetry, and art as surrogate religions. Literary, artistic, and musical "geniuses" (a new catchword) were revered as latter-day prophets. Even after Realism elbowed out Romanticism as the dominant movement in the arts, writers and artists regarded themselves as vessels of a higher power.

The most influential book published during the century was not a novel or philosophical treatise but a work of natural history. Charles Darwin's *Origin of*

Species showed that biological species were not special creations of God but the results of natural processes. Anthropologists, sociologists, and historians theorized that religions were human creations that evolved over the course of time. People who felt the need of the supernatural clung to conventional religions or turned to esotericism.

During the seventeenth and eighteenth centuries, as European powers established control over vast stretches of Asia, the religions of India and the Far East dwelt on the achievements of the past. During the nineteenth century, the negative stimulus of missionary aggression and the positive stimulus of European scholarship pushed Hindu and Buddhist innovators to reconceive their traditions. Toward the end of the century, some people in the West became interested in Eastern teachings, which seemed to offer a framework of thought and practice free from the constraints of monotheism. To make themselves attractive to this new clientele, Vedanta and Buddhism repackaged themselves as universal religions based on personal experience. These hybrid religions eventually become components of modern spirituality.

Natural supernaturalism

On the morning of Sunday, November 10, 1793, a group of Parisian men and women passed through the doors of the Cathedral of Notre Dame to take part in a Festival of Reason. A day or two earlier, a band of revolutionaries had looted, smashed or covered up all religious icons and built a stage representing a mountain with a small Greek temple on top. The temple, labeled "TO PHILOSOPHY," was surrounded by busts of Voltaire, Rousseau, and others. Beneath it was an Altar of Reason, on which a Flame of Truth burned. On the day of the festival, two columns of young women wearing tricolor sashes and oak-leaf crowns stepped carefully down the mountain and bowed before the Flame. The Goddess of Reason—an actress from the Opéra—emerged from the temple clad in a long white robe and azure cloak. Seating herself on a plot of grass, she received the adulation of a chorus of Free Men, who sang a hymn of liberation. The goddess then rose and moved toward the temple. Just before entering, she turned to the audience, flashed a brilliant smile and made a theatrical gesture that brought the house down. The Festival of Reason was a relatively benign episode in the forced dechristianization of France at the time of the Revolution. During the Reign of Terror (1793–94) public worship was forbidden, churches were plundered and some, like Notre Dame, transformed into Temples of Reason. Maximilien Robespierre, head of the Committee of Public Safety (who in this capacity sent hundreds to the guillotine but still had a soft spot for religion) was not amused by the cult of Reason and transformed it into a cult of the Supreme Being. Inaugurated on June 8, 1794, this deistic faith did not outlive its founder. Indicted by his enemies on July 27, Robespierre was taken into custody and the next day executed without trial.[1]

The French Revolution shook the two main pillars of the European political and social order: monarchy and monotheism. Both recovered, but from this time forward monarchies had to concede more and more power to democratic institutions and theism became an option that many chose to reject. Catholicism made a comeback during the Bourbon Restoration (1814–1830), but in France, as in Germany, England, and the United States, secular activities such as literature and art began to replace religion as guides to life. The earliest priests of this humanistic faith were the poets, novelists, artists, and musicians of the Romantic movement.

Arguably the greatest revolution in styles and tastes in the history of European culture, Romanticism is too vast and complex a subject to be given full treatment here. Broadly speaking, it was a revolt against the intellectualism of the Enlightenment, although it remained deeply rooted in Enlightenment values. Most Romantic writers were hostile or indifferent to institutional Christianity, but they took up and transformed many features of eighteenth-century religion, such as inwardness and validation by experience. In effect, wrote critic M.H. Abrams, Romantic poets stripped away the "dogmatic understructure of Christianity" but saved what they could of "its experiential relevance and values." Their lasting contribution to cultural history was "to naturalize the supernatural and to humanize the divine."[2]

There were stirrings of the Romantic view of life as far back as the mid-eighteenth century, but it began to take its characteristic form during the German *Sturm und Drang* movement, notably in the work of Johann Wolfgang von Goethe. His wildly popular novel *The Sorrows of Young Werther*, published in 1774, became the handbook of wannabe tragic heroes throughout Europe. His poem "Prometheus," written around the same time, reveals his scorn for conventional religion. The titan Prometheus, enchained by the gods, taunts his tormentors:

> I know of no poorer thing
> Under the sun, than you gods!

Although a captive, he holds his head high, because he is able to create free beings modeled on his own image:

> A race that shall be like me,
> A race that shall suffer and weep,
> And know joy and delight too,
> And heed you no more
> Than I do!

Goethe was no atheist, but his concept of the divine exceeded all Christian formulas. In a scene from his masterwork *Faust*, Gretchen, Faust's beloved, begs him to tell her plainly whether or not he believes in God. He replies:

> Who dares name the nameless?
> Or who dares to confess:
> "I believe in him"?...
> Call it then what you wish,
> Joy! Heart! Love! God!
> I have no name
> For it! Feeling is all:
> Names are sound and smoke,
> Veiling Heaven's bright glow.

Gretchen replies, somewhat baffled, "The priest says much the same, / Only, in slightly different words." A similar bafflement was the lot of many Christians at the beginning of the nineteenth century.[3]

Like Schleiermacher (who adored his poetry), Goethe made inner feeling the touchstone of religion. His worship of a formless, impersonal deity has led many to call him a pantheist, and he certainly wrote things that are pantheistic in spirit, for example, this jotting from a diary: "To treat of God and nature separately is difficult and dangerous; for we know God only through nature."[4] But his view of the relationship between God and nature was too complex to be expressed by a one-word label. The same can be said of his younger contemporary William Wordsworth, who, along with his friend Samuel Taylor Coleridge, launched the Romantic movement in England.

It is conventional, indeed trite, to speak of Wordsworth as a poet of nature. It is often forgotten that the Romantic idea of nature—the universe regarded as a benign organic whole, as opposed to the artificial world of human society—was just catching on when Wordsworth took up his pen. In *Intimations of Immortality* (1804) he wrote that during his youth, nature

> To me was all in all.—I cannot paint
> What then I was. The sounding cataract
> Haunted me like a passion: the tall rock,
> The mountain, and the deep and gloomy wood,
> Their colours and their forms, were then to me
> An appetite; a feeling and a love,...

Later, as an adult, when he looked on nature he felt

> A presence that disturbs me with the joy
> Of elevated thoughts; a sense sublime
> Of something far more deeply interfused,
> Whose dwelling is the light of setting suns,
> And the round ocean and the living air,
> And the blue sky, and in the mind of man.

Ten trillion photographs of waterfalls and sunsets later, it is hard for us to realize how original this was when Wordsworth wrote his poem. People then were far more likely to look on mountains and woods as inconvenient barriers between cities than as sources of beauty and sublimity.

Unlike Diderot and d'Holbach, Wordsworth did not feel the need to repudiate the God of Christianity. He simply ignored him, transferring God's attributes to the impersonal force of Nature, which impels

> All thinking things, all objects of all thought,
> And rolls through all things.[5]

Although uninterested in Christian doctrine, Wordsworth took up many themes of Christian mythology—the Garden of Eden, the millennium, the Earthly Paradise—and made them parts of a secular mythos of earthly redemption. So did the younger and more openly rebellious Percy Bysshe Shelley. His *Queen Mab* (1813) is filled with biblical allusions, such as "A garden shall arise, in loveliness / Surpassing fabled Eden." But the poem also contains the blunt declaration "There is no God." In a note Shelley explained that the theory of God, like any other theory, had to be proved before it could be accepted. Neither the senses, nor reason, nor authority provided adequate proof; therefore "the mind CANNOT believe the existence of a creative God." He supported his argument with a long quotation in French from d'Holbach's *System of Nature* and passages in Latin from Pliny's *Natural History* and Newton's *Principles*. But he was careful to add that the statement "There is no God" had to be understood "solely to affect a creative Deity. The hypothesis of a pervading Spirit co-eternal with the universe remains unshaken." This is pantheism, not atheism, and it is not surprising that Shelley concluded his note with a quotation from Spinoza's *Tractate*.[6] The pantheistic thread is found throughout his poetry:

> The awful shadow of some unseen Power
>> Floats though unseen among us; visiting
>> This various world with as inconstant wing
> As summer winds that creep from flower to flower; ...
> Dear, and yet dearer for its mystery.

Humans give the names "Demon, Ghost, and Heaven" to this mysterious Power. Shelley calls it Beauty, and implores it to descend into his heart so that he can fight to free "this world from its dark slavery."[7]

Among the English Romantic poets, Coleridge was the most attached to Christian doctrine; but he also took up themes that became central to modern spirituality, such as subjectivity and inner experience. (It was he who popularized the Kantian terms "subjective" and "objective" in the senses still current in English.) In his theological treatise *Aids to Reflection* (1825), Coleridge wrote that to the Christian the ideas in the Bible are more convincing "*subjectively*, that is, in the economy of his own soul, than are all the inducements that can influence the Deist *objectively*, that is, in the [rational] interpretation of Nature." This was his answer to the natural religion of the Enlightenment: feeling and not reason was the bedrock of religion. The Scriptures convey "objective truth" to the "subjective experiences of the Believer," and these experiences give living affirmation to scriptural texts.[8] But what if they don't? It was left to Coleridge's admirers in the United States to explore this disturbing possibility.

The first American edition of *Aids to Reflection* was published in 1829 with a preliminary essay by clergyman and educationist James Marsh. Called by critic Louis Menand "one of the originary texts of American Transcendentalism," Marsh's edition introduced Coleridge's ideas to American thinkers, who took them up and gave them an original turn. In his essay, March wrote that Coleridge offered "philosophical grounds for the *possibility* of a truly spiritual religion," but added that "the *reality* of those experiences, or states of being, which constitute experimental or spiritual religion, rests on other [non-philosophical] grounds."[9] The bedrock of "spiritual religion" was "experiment"—a word that at the time was virtually a synonym of "experience." Marsh's linking of the spiritual life with personal experience was a step toward the emergence of spirituality in its modern form.

When the young Ralph Waldo Emerson read *Aids to Reflection*, he was struck by Coleridge's Latin maxim *quantum sumus, scimus*, "as much as we are, we know." Coleridge continued: "That which we find within ourselves, which is more than ourselves, and yet the ground of whatever is good and permanent therein, is the substance and life of all other knowledge." This chimed with Emerson's own ideas: "That man will always speak with authority who speaks his own convictions" and does not regurgitate "superstitions got in conversation, or errors or truths remembered from his reading." This applied even to passages from the Bible. Written revelation was important but not as important as personal insight: "My own mind is the direct revelation which I have from God."[10]

Emerson gave fuller expression to this idea in his 1841 essay *The Over-Soul*: "We distinguish the announcements of the soul, its manifestations of its own nature, by the term *Revelation*. These are always attended by the emotion of the sublime. For this communication is an influx of the Divine mind into our mind." This is far indeed from the accepted Christian view of revelation: the communication by God of higher truths by supernatural means to specially chosen vessels, in particular the prophets of the Old Testament and the apostles of the New Testament. Emerson was claiming that an ordinary human being, himself for instance, could receive "an influx of the Divine Mind." The only "prophet" that mattered was "that great nature in which we rest as the earth lies in the soft arms of the atmosphere; that Unity, that Over-Soul, within which every man's particular being is contained and made one with all other." Every human soul is capable of saying: "I am born into the great, the universal mind. I, the imperfect, adore my own Perfect. I am somehow receptive of the great soul."[11] In Emerson's essay, the God of the Christian Bible is replaced by an "Over-soul" that looks a lot like the Brahman of the Upanishads. Humans, far from being tainted by original sin, are capable of uniting themselves with this Over-soul.

Emerson sometimes used the word "experience" when writing about the juncture between the Over-soul and the individual soul. For people of his day this word evoked on the one hand the "experience-meetings" or revivals of the Wesleyans and on the other the empirical philosophy of Locke. Emerson appropriated Locke's idea that experience is the only source of knowledge and made it a benchmark of the spiritual life: "The definition of *spiritual* should be, *that which is its own evidence*," he wrote in the essay *Experience*. Spiritual truths became evident by means of personal practice. To Emerson this meant developing "the power of Thought and of Will" and other forms of "individual culture."[12]

In Emerson the three defining characteristics of modern spirituality—subjectivity, wariness of traditional religion, and stress on individual experience—came together in a robust combination. He could not be called an atheist—he often spoke of "God"—but his equation of God with the Over-Soul or Divine Mind placed him beyond the range of Christian theism. Viewed retrospectively, he was an important forerunner of what I call godless spirituality.

Emerson had considerable influence on two younger American writers—Henry David Thoreau and Walt Whitman—who matched him in the strength of their subjectivity, autonomy, and individualism, but emphasized a side of spirituality he overlooked: the importance of the body. Thoreau met Emerson in 1837 just after graduating from Harvard. Emerson took an interest in the young man and encouraged him to write. In 1841 he told Thoreau that his writing style was good but that he lacked original ideas. For all his cleverness he had "not yet told that which he was created to say."[13] Thoreau did not record what he thought of Emerson's patronizing remarks, but they may have helped him find his voice. At the time he was publishing formal essays and poems in the Transcendentalists' journal, *The Dial*. Meanwhile he was developing his signature style in his diary. Unlike his mentor, who tended to lapse into ponderous abstractions when writing about spiritual things, Thoreau kept close to the concrete details of the physical world. His aim as a writer was "to watch for, describe, all the divine features which I detect in Nature." In this the body had a role to play: "The mind may perchance be persuaded to act, to energize, by the action and energy of the body."[14]

This stress on the physical was a new departure in Western spirituality, an innovation readers of *Walden* often miss. In the chapter called "Higher Laws" Thoreau wrote that Hindu lawgivers taught people "how to eat, drink, cohabit, void excrement and urine, and the like" and did not consider such things trifles. He summed up: "Every man is the builder of a temple, called his body, to the god he worships, after a style purely his own.... We are all sculptors and painters, and our material is our own flesh and blood and bones."[15]

A strait-laced New Englander, Thoreau found it hard to embrace the corporality of the spiritual in full measure. After reading Whitman's *Leaves of Grass*, he wrote that the poems had done him a great deal of good, but that two or three were "disagreeable to say the least, simply sensual."[16] He must have been thinking of pieces like "Poem of the Body," which begins:

> The bodies of men and women engirth me, and I engirth them,
> They will not let me off, nor I them, till I go with them, respond to them, love them.

The poem continues:

> Be not ashamed, women! your privilege encloses the rest, it is the exit of the rest,
> You are the gates of the body and you are the gates of the soul!...
> The male is not less the soul, nor more—he too is in his place,
> He too is all qualities, he is action and power, the flush of the known universe is in him...
> If any thing is sacred the human body is sacred,
> And the glory and sweet of a man is the token of manhood untainted,
> And in man or women a clean, strong, firm-fibred body, is beautiful as the most beautiful face

Whitman's physicality infused his idea of God:

> I have said that the soul is not more than the body,
> And I have said that the body is not more than the soul,
> And nothing, not God, is greater to one than one's-self is.

He had no interest in Christian scriptures but was willing to honor the Christian myths so long as people understood that they were human creations:

> We consider bibles and religions divine—I do not say they are not divine,
> I say they have all grown out of you, and may grow out of you still,
> It is not they who give the life, it is you who give the life,
> Leaves are not more shed from the trees, or trees from the earth, than they are shed out of you.[17]

In a later poem, Whitman made his view of the relationship between the soul and God more explicit:

> What do you suppose will satisfy the Soul, except to walk free and own no superior?
> What do you suppose I have intimated to you in a hundred ways, but that man or woman is as good as God?
> And that there is no God any more divine than Yourself?[18]

Whitman did not practice a spiritual discipline but he celebrated all forms of physical labor and spent the Civil War years working as a hospital orderly. His primary rule of life—his spiritual practice if you will—was this: "Love the earth and sun and the animals, despise riches, give alms to every one that asks, stand up for the stupid and crazy, devote your income and labor to others, hate tyrants, argue not concerning God."[19]

Emerson, Thoreau, and Whitman propagated an American strain of spirituality that has spread throughout the world. But while it was germinating in Boston and New York, philosophers and novelists in Berlin, Copenhagen, and Paris were attacking the idealism that constituted the soil in which it grew. All forms of idealism in modern Europe are based on the philosophy of Kant. German idealists of the generation after Kant tried to "perfect" his work by discarding his distinction between the phenomenal world of appearances and the noumenal world of things-in-themselves. There was, they insisted, just one unconditioned, absolute principle underlying all experience. For Georg Wilhelm Friedrich Hegel this principle was *Geist* (Spirit or Mind). In Hegel's enormously elaborate system *Geist* occupies a position similar to that of the God of Christian theology. This infuriated the younger philosopher Arthur Schopenhauer, who wrote that Hegel's "pseudo-philosophy is but a monstrous amplification of the Ontological Proof" of God's existence, which Kant had effectively disproved.[20]

Schopenhauer went back to the Kantian distinction between the phenomenal world and things-in-themselves, but he reformulated it from the standpoint of the embodied human being. The world, Schopenhauer said, is Representation and Will. Every embodied human can say, as he himself said, "The world is my representation." By this he meant that the world around each human individual "exists only as representation, that is, exclusively in relation to something else, the representing being that he himself is." But what is the nature of this being? It is not some intangible thing-in-itself. No, it is Will, something "immediately familiar" to everyone who has a body. In fact, Schopenhauer insisted, will is *identical* with body. This, he proclaimed, is "*philosophical truth par excellence*"— a very different truth than those proposed by Plato, Shankara, Hegel, and other idealists.[21]

Philosophers of many cultures have tried to identify the stable reality that underlies the flux and change of the world. For most idealists this principle is mental: idea, mind, spirit, consciousness. For Schopenhauer the root-principle is utterly *non*mental, a blind, unconscious, irrational force that is the source of the drives and desires of embodied human beings. In each individual it takes the form of strivings after physical satisfactions. These strivings are opposed by the strivings of others. As a result each person experiences conflict, frustration, and suffering.[22] This sounds a lot like Buddhism, and Schopenhauer in fact was familiar with Buddhism, Samkhya, and Vedanta, although he seems to have arrived at his ideas on his own and later refined them with reference to these Indian traditions.

For Schopenhauer, as for the Buddha, the central problem of life is suffering. The solution, he wrote, is the "negation of the will to life." There are three ways of doing this: aesthetic experience, moral awareness, and asceticism. When we appreciate an artwork or the natural world, our consciousness "tears itself free from the service of the will"; we cease to be "merely individual," becoming "absorbed in a steady contemplation of the object presented." The second way is through the growth of the moral consciousness. By becoming aware of other people's sufferings and acting selflessly to alleviate them we eventually reach the negation of the will to life. Finally, he says, we can achieve freedom through asceticism, that is, by the "*deliberate* breaking of the will by forgoing what is pleasant and seeking out what is unpleasant, choosing a lifestyle of penitence and self-castigation for the constant mortification of the will."[23] Schopenhauer practiced only the first of these three methods: the disinterested contemplation of beauty. He was not particularly moral, leading a moderately sensuous life and finding sex both irresistible and intolerable. Noted for his anger, he threw a talkative old woman downstairs, causing her serious injury. Nevertheless he spoke in glowing terms of self-control, chastity, and benevolence. One could conclude from this he was a hypocrite, and this would not be wrong, but the disconnect between his ideas and his life illustrates a central point of his philosophy: the fundamental irrationality of will.

Schopenhauer sincerely admired the religious practices he praised, though he despised theistic religions in general and Christianity in particular: "Throughout the entire Christian era theism has lain like an incubus on all intellectual, especially philosophical endeavour and has prevented or stunted all progress," he wrote. "When anyone has possessed the rare elasticity of mind which alone can slip free of these fetters, his writings have been burned and sometimes their author with them, as happened to Bruno and Vanini." He felt more comfortable with nontheistic traditions such as Buddhism and Vedanta as he understood them (his knowledge was entirely textual and he knew nothing about Buddhist and Hindu religious practices). As for pantheism, he said that "to call the world God" explained nothing; it just made God a "superfluous synonym for the word world."[24] He himself was an unembarrassed atheist. His disbelief was so entrenched that he did not even think it necessary to argue against God's existence.

For Kant and Hegel (and other Western idealists as far back as Plato) the world is rational and can be known by reason. For Schopenhauer the world is irrational and the power of reason is limited. From his time forward, irrationalism became a recurrent theme in Western philosophy and social science, notably in the frankly atheistic thought of Nietzsche and Freud. But there is another sort of irrationalism that actually supports theism, namely that reliance on faith in preference to reason that since the end of the nineteenth century has been known as fideism. Many Protestant theologians—Luther, Wesley, Schleiermacher, Coleridge—exalted faith over reason but none of them went so far in this direction as Danish thinker Søren Kierkegaard. Like Schopenhauer, Kierkegaard rejected the abstractions of Hegel's philosophy and laid stress on the concreteness of life as actually lived. Unlike Schopenhauer he thought that the crucial question of life was the relationship of the individual to God. This was not something that could be grasped by the mind: "If I can grasp God objectively, then I do not have faith, but just because I cannot do this, I must have faith."[25] Faith is not rational, but the certitude it brings is more powerful than anything that comes as a result of rational thought.

Kierkegaard's theology belongs to the history of Christianity but his philosophical writings touch on many ideas that are important in the history of modern spirituality, in particular the central themes of subjectivity, anticlericalism, and individual practice. "True religiousness," he wrote, was "the hidden inwardness in one who is religious"—and being religious meant a great deal more than belonging to a given religion. He had nothing but scorn for the comfortable Christianity of the Danish elite. For him Christianity was hard. It meant taking a solitary decision without the help of reason or the support of the crowd. A person became Christian "not by the 'what' of Christianity" (doctrines and so forth) but by "the 'how' of the Christian" (actions). Personally, Kierkegaard found meaning in his Christian faith, yet he also felt it was "possible both to enjoy life and to give it meaning and substance outside Christianity, just as the most famous poets and artists, the most eminent of thinkers, even men of piety, have lived outside Christianity."[26] His stress on the individual and on the struggle to achieve meaning in the face of absurdity has made him a point of reference for many non-Christian writers, among them Jean-Paul Sartre, Simone de Beauvoir, and Albert Camus, the leading figures of atheistic existentialism.

For Kierkegaard, as for Schopenhauer, art was a way of expressing the inwardness of life. The artist was not just someone who made artworks but someone who "was himself an existing work of art."[27] The idea that the artist was an exemplary human being was relatively new at that time. Up until the seventeenth century, artists were looked upon as highly skilled craftsmen. Toward the end of the eighteenth, people began to distinguish the "artist" from the "artisan" and "genius" from humdrum "talent." Soon the possessor of genius was elevated to a semidivine level beyond the reach of ordinary mortals. "Beethoven's mighty genius intimidates the musical rabble," wrote German critic E.T.A. Hoffmann in 1810. His music "unveils before us the realm of the mighty and the immeasurable," annihilating us, his listeners, but "not the pain of infinite yearning," in which we "live on as ecstatic visionaries."[28] By using the terminology of sacred discourse, Hoffmann implied that art and literature performed a religious function. Later critics and poets went farther: art and literature *were* religions. In an 1828 essay, Scottish writer Thomas Carlyle suggested that poetry was "but another form of Wisdom, of Religion; is itself Wisdom and Religion." A few years later French poet Alfred de Vigny wrote: "Art is the modern religion, the modern spiritualism."[29]

This apotheosis of the arts was a natural continuation of the secularization of the sacred that had begun with the early Romantic poets. Toward the middle of the nineteenth century the same creed was taken up by a school of writers who viewed their craft in highly unromantic terms. Literary Realists such as Honoré de Balzac rejected their predecessors' idealism but appropriated their belief that the writer was a hierophant: "Today the writer has replaced the priest," Balzac wrote in a letter of 1844. "His voice does not fill only the nave of the cathedral. At times it resounds from one end of the world to the other." The writer owes nothing to kings, for "he has received his mission from God."[30] Balzac was not a religious man but he felt no qualms about borrowing the vocabulary of the belief-system he rejected.

Realism sought truth not by rising above the details of life but by observing them closely and recording them with scientific precision. This meant looking carefully at everything that happened without imposing moral judgments. "A novel," pioneer realist Stendhal explained, "is a mirror, taking a walk down a big road. Sometimes you'll see nothing but blue skies; sometimes you'll see the muck in the mud piles along the road." It would be pointless to blame the mirror for the muck: that's just the way life is. In their novels, Stendhal, Balzac, and other French Realists aimed to provide a faithful reflection of contemporary life, but they did so from an irreverent point of view. In their writings religious figures and institutions are usually depicted in negative terms. As for God, his "only excuse," Stendhal remarked, "is that he doesn't exist."[31] A hundred years after Meslier's death, European atheism was coming into its own.

Ways of worldly and otherworldly perfection

On September 6, 1851, Matthew Arnold, a recently-married writer and inspector of schools, spent the night at the Grande Chartreuse, a remote twelfth-century monastery in eastern France. Wordsworth, one of his literary heroes, had visited it during the Revolution and later wrote of the desolation he found in the wake of attacks by marauding soldiers. After the Restoration the monastery reopened and soon became a stop for cultured travelers doing the Grand Tour. Driving up from the valley through the fog and rain, Arnold and his wife reached the palatial but gloomy buildings just before nightfall. Entering alone—his wife had to remain in the lodge—he found himself in clammy halls where, "ghostlike in the deepening night," the hooded monks passed by. Arnold admired their asceticism but felt painfully out of place. Thinking about the "masters of the mind" who had guided his studies at Oxford, he asked himself what he was doing "in this living tomb." Christianity had nothing to offer but empty symbols and illusory certitudes. Yet, he reflected, the life of secular culture also was far from perfect. The "kings of modern thought" promised much but delivered little and he was left "Wandering between two worlds, one dead, / The other powerless to be born." All that he and his peers could do was hope for something better in the future. Arnold went on to become one of the leading English poets and critics of his generation. Many of his poems, such as "Dover Beach," exude a sense of pessimistic resignation, but his essays are filled with positive prescriptions for self-improvement. The goal of life, he wrote in *Culture and Anarchy*, was the "full, harmonious perfection" of the individual and society. This meant developing "*all* the voices of human experience": not only religion but also art, science, history, philosophy and poetry.[32]

Arnold was no admirer of institutional religion, but religion loomed so large in nineteenth-century discourse that he published four volumes on the subject between 1870 and 1877. In them he developed a secular idea of God that infuriated Christian writers. The word "God," he wrote, was an effort to suggest "a not fully grasped object of the speaker's consciousness." The Hebrew prophets were aware of a "*not ourselves* that makes for righteousness" and called it God. Modern scientists considering the same object of consciousness might be inclined to call it a "stream of tendency by which all things fulfil the law of their being," but they would have no objection to others calling it God so long as they discarded the usual theological baggage. Arnold's critics were not amused when he wrote in 1880 that "most of what now passes with us for religion and philosophy will be replaced by poetry."[33] He did not foresee that within a few decades the novel would supplant poetry as the dominant form of literature, but otherwise his prediction was spot on. From that time onward, people who struggled with personal problems were more likely to pick up a work of fiction than the Bible. Many of the classic novels of the period were concerned with the consequences of living in a godless world, among them George Eliot's *Silas Marner*, Jens Peter Jacobsen's *Niels Lyhne*, and Fyodor Dostoyevsky's *The Brothers Karamazov*.

Eliot was born Mary Ann Evans in 1819. Intensely religious as a child, she lost her faith as a young women and fell in with a group of liberal thinkers who encouraged her to study and write. Her first published works were translations of humanist classics: David Strauss's *The Life of Jesus Critically Examined*, Ludwig Feuerbach's *The Essence of Christianity*, and Spinoza's *Ethics*. In 1857 she launched her career as a writer with *Scenes of Clerical Life*, three stories recounting the misadventures of ineffectual provincial clergymen. She went on to write seven of the best-known works of mid-century English fiction. Following the example of the French Realists, she treated her novels as "a set of experiments in life," but unlike Stendhal and Balzac she tried to hold onto the "gains from past revelations and discipline" as she looked for themes that promised "a better after which we may strive."[34] To some, such as Nietzsche, this was backdoor Christianity. Others were struck by the absence of God in Eliot's moral universe. Her novels, a contemporary critic wrote, presented "a world of high endeavour, pure morality, and strong enthusiasm, existing and in full work, without any reference to, or help from, the thought of God." This seemed to mark a fundamental change in the tenor of European life: "The sun that we once all walked by has for many eyes become extinguished; and every energy has been bent upon supplying man with a substitute."[35]

The urge to find substitutes for God and religion was a primary, perhaps *the* primary motive of nineteenth-century intellectual and spiritual life. We spoke in the previous section of nineteenth-century religions of literature and art. In this section we examine two other sorts of surrogate religion that arose during the century: scientific (or quasi-scientific) gospels of social salvation and mystic (or pseudo-mystic) creeds of personal redemption.

French theorist Auguste Comte, often called the father of sociology, wrote in his *Course in Positive Philosophy* (1830–1842) that humanity passes through three historical stages—theological, metaphysical, and positive—in which things are explained with reference to supernatural beings, abstract concepts, and scientific facts. Now that the physical sciences were well established, it was time to move on to "social physics" or sociology. By understanding the structures that contribute to stability ("social statics") and the changes that result in progress ("social dynamics"), enlightened social philosophers or "sociologists" will be able to guide humanity to a happier state.

In his voluminous writings Comte gave classic form to two of the defining ideas of the nineteenth century: progress and evolution. Both were taken up and elaborated by English philosopher Herbert Spencer. The universal law of evolution, Spencer wrote, was "change from the homogeneous to the heterogeneous." He spelled out the meaning of this abstruse phrase in rather grandiose terms: "Whether it be in the development of the earth, in the development of Life upon its surface, in the development of Society, of Government, of Manufactures, of Commerce, of Language, Literature, Science, Art, this same advance from the simple to the complex, through successive differentiations, holds uniformly."[36] An enormous generalization but Spencer spent thirty-five years trying to fill in the details.

He received timely help from Charles Darwin, who published his theory of "descent with modification" in *On the Origin of Species* in 1859. Darwin used the verb "evolve" only once in the first edition of his book but the term was taken up and popularized by Spencer and others. Soon everyone in England was talking about evolution, though most of the talk was about the nonscientific implications of the theory. The science was relatively straightforward. Specific traits of organisms, such as form, color, and size, are passed from parent to offspring in accordance with the laws of heredity. Certain traits are advantageous in the struggle for resources and mates and organisms possessing them are more likely to survive and reproduce than those that lack them. (Darwin called this "natural selection." Spencer coined the catchphrase "survival of the fittest.") If a new variety arises that possesses advantageous traits, it will prosper and may in time may give rise to a new species. The implication, which Darwin did not spell out, was that plant and animal species are not special creations of God.

When Darwin shipped out for South America aboard H.M.S. *Beagle* in 1831, he harbored no doubts about the Biblical account of creation. This changed after he immersed himself in the study of biological species; but as late as 1858 he defined nature as "the laws ordained by God to govern the Universe." Even after publishing the *Origin of Species* he wrote to a colleague that he was inclined "to look at everything as resulting from designed laws"—that is, laws designed by an omniscient Creator—"with the details, whether good or bad, left to the working out of what we may call chance."[37] Later he drew back from this compromise, but he never believed that his theory was in conflict with religion. It was not he but some of his supporters who turned it into a battering ram to attack the fortress of Christianity.

Darwin took no part in the public debates that followed the book's publication, leaving the work of defense to scientific colleagues such as Thomas Henry Huxley. Trying to steer clear of religious controversies, Huxley coined the word "agnosticism" to signify the position that it is impossible to arrive at positive knowledge about things like God and immortality. The neologism caught on. By 1900 British essayist Leslie Stephen (father of the novelist Virginia Woolf) could write, with a touch of irony, that agnosticism was "the only reasonable faith for at least three-quarters of the [human] race."[38]

Darwin's theory fit in nicely with existing theories of social evolution, such as those of Comte and Spencer. Both these men were political conservatives who believed that evolution would gradually bring about an improvement of human life. Karl Marx disagreed. The grand lines of social development were evolutionary, he said, but social change could only come about by means of revolution. As a young man, he was influenced by German philosopher Ludwig Feuerbach, who declared in his *Essence of Christianity*: "The divine being is nothing else than the human being, or, rather the human nature purified, freed from the limits of the individual man" and "revered as another, a distinct being." Marx took this as the starting point for one of the most devastating put-downs of religion ever written. Religion was indeed, as Feuerbach had said, "the self-consciousness and self-esteem of man," but man was "no abstract being encamped outside the world." Man was "*the world of man*—the state, society." Religion, a product of society, was—in a metaphor that soon became famous—"the *opium* of the people," that is, "the *illusory* happiness of the people," which had to be abolished before people could acquire real happiness. For this to be possible, the socioeconomic conditions of society had to be transformed.[39]

Sociology has become a narrowly framed discipline focused on specific phenomena (structures, interactions, and so forth) and problems (suicide, mass incarceration, and so forth) that shies away from grand explanatory theories. The early-nineteenth-century originators of the field had larger ambitions. Each tried to diagnose the causes of society's ills and to offer prescriptions for their cure. Comte thought that the anarchy of the modern world was the result of individualism, which he called "the Western disease." The solution was a Religion of Humanity, the worship of humanity itself, which would add a healing touch of emotion to the scientific synthesis of Positivism.[40] According to Spencer, the miseries of society are "nonadaptations" to external conditions. These "pathological states" will disappear in the course of evolution.[41] To Marx, the chief sign of socioeconomic imbalance was alienation (the estrangement of workers from their work, its products, and themselves), which was caused by the exploitation intrinsic to capitalism. The solution was socialist revolution.

Comte, Spencer, and Marx all believed that their systems were based on science, but each of them borrowed from religion. Comte's Religion of Humanity became a full-blown belief-system, with doctrines, icons, ceremonies, holy days, and saints. (One of the saints was Comte's deceased beloved Clotilde de Vaux, who became the Virgin Mary of the new faith.) Spencer's conviction that the First Cause was unknowable did not prevent him from describing it as "an Infinite and Eternal Energy from which all things proceed" or explaining that it stood "towards our general conception of things, in substantially the same relation as does the Creative Power asserted by Theology."[42] Marx's atheism remained undiluted throughout his life, but the communist society he looked forward to had obvious similarities with the earthly paradise of Christianity. After his death in 1883,

Marx's "scientific socialism" became a secular religion that was just as dogmatic and prone to violence as medieval Catholicism.

During the half-century that followed the publication of Darwin's theory, scientists and scholars used the idea of evolution to revolutionize the study of every expression of the human mind, religion included. English anthropologists Edward Tylor and James Frazer published studies that proposed, on the model of Comte, that human cultures passed through three distinct stages, each characterized by a specific sort of religious or quasi-religious activity. According to Tylor humans traversed savagery and barbarism on their way to civilization. For Frazer, the developmental stages were characterized by magic, religion, and science. Around the same time, two European scholars helped create the academic field of religious studies. Dutch theologian Cornelis Teile's first book on the history of religion came out in 1872. The next year Max Müller inaugurated the comparative study of religions with his *Introduction to the Science of Religion*. All of these authors depicted Christianity as the pinnacle of religious evolution, but by showing that other religions were stages of that evolution, they granted them historical legitimacy. They also showed that all religious beliefs, including the belief in the God of monotheism, were culturally and historically determined.

During the same years that sociologists and scholars were applying reason to the study of religion, other European thinkers were trying to break free from the bonds of rationality. One expression of this was a revival of interest in secret teachings and invisible beings and forces. There is no space here for a detailed history of the nineteenth-century revival of Western esotericism. I will confine myself to a sketch of the work of a few important figures.

There were two main lines of Western esotericism, which I call "scientific" and "traditional," even though the scientific approaches was not reliably scientific and the traditional approaches frequently based on fictitious traditions. An important precursor of the scientific approach was Emmanuel Swedenborg (1688–1772), a Swedish polymath and inventor who began to see visions and commune with spirits when he was in his fifties. Resigning his professional post, he composed a number of visionary works in which he described his contacts with the spirit-world. After his death some of his followers established a Neo-Christian church based on his ideas and published his works in many languages. Among his readers were Kant, William Blake, and Emerson, all of whom eventually became disenchanted with the Swedish sage.

In 1774 Austrian physician Franz Mesmer discovered a force he called "animal magnetism" while treating a female patient. Later he learned how to direct this force to promote healing. His séances in Paris caused such a stir that the king appointed a scientific committee to find out what was going on. The committee declared that the force was not physical and that the therapeutic effects were due to the patients' imaginations. Mesmer was ruined but others carried on his work. One of them observed that animal-magnetism sessions frequently threw patients into a semiconscious state in which they were subject to automatic activities (labeled "somnambulism") and open to suggestions from the "mesmerist." This power of suggestion became a major ingredient in many late-nineteenth-century self-help practices, such as New Thought (a nontheistic school of positive thinking started by the American clockmaker Phinias Quimby around 1840) and Christian Science (a religious denomination focused on prayer-healing launched by Mary Baker Eddy around 1870). Meanwhile scientific mesmerism, rebranded "hypnotism," became part of the newly founded science of psychology.

The spiritualist movement began in 1848 in a town in upstate New York when two adolescent sisters, Margaret and Catherine Fox, convinced their elder sister that they were in touch with spirits who communicated with them by means of "rappings"—mysterious knocks on furniture or floors. Soon they were showing off their mediumistic skills to neighbors and later to dignitaries. Many people became convinced that the girls were in touch with the souls of the departed. In the decades that followed a mania of table-rapping spread across America and Europe. Hundreds of mediums plied their trade, and thousands of clients believed their departed loved ones had spoken to them. In 1888 the sisters confessed that they had produced the "rapping" sounds by cracking their joints, but by then spiritualism—the word was coined in 1853—had too much momentum to stop.

During the 1850s French educator Allan Kardec (born Hippolyte Léon Denizard Rivail in 1804) developed a doctrine he called Spiritism, which incorporated elements of spiritualism and mesmerism, along with a dash of Swedenborgism. His primary instrument was a "talking board," on which spirits spelled out messages with the aid of a moving planchette. (This was the origin of the trademarked "Ouija Board.") Kardec insisted that Spiritism was a science, not a religion; but as it spread through Europe and the Americas it took on many of the characteristics of traditional religions. Kardec's works were treated as a third revelation (after the Old and New Testaments), which Spiritists studied and discussed. They also undertook works of charity on the Christian model.

From the mid-nineteenth century some English intellectuals began to meet to discuss spirit phenomena. One group devoted to this study, the aptly named Ghost Club, was started informally at Trinity College, Cambridge, and launched officially in London in 1862. Among its early members were the novelist Charles Dickens, some noted academics, and at least two future Anglican bishops. The Club ceased to exist after 1870, but interest in what were now called "psychical phenomena" remained strong, and in 1882 the Society for Psychical Research was organized. Its mission was to examine "that large group of debatable phenomena designated by such terms as mesmeric, psychical and spiritualistic," proceeding "in the same spirit of exact and unimpassioned enquiry which has enabled Science to solve so many problems."[43] Its founders were Henry Sidgwick, Professor of Moral Philosophy at Cambridge, Frederic Myers, a classical scholar and poet, and Edmund Gurney, a researcher and writer. Early members included politician (and future prime minister) Alfred Balfour and scientist William Crookes, the inventor of the Crookes tube, which hastened the discovery of X-rays. The American Society for Psychical Research, founded in 1885, had an equally illustrious lineup: office-bearers included psychologist and philosopher William James and psychologist G. Stanley Hall. Early activities of the two groups included experimental investigations of mesmerism, clairvoyance, and telepathy (a term Myers coined in 1882).

From its onset psychical research was rocked by controversy. Accusations of fraud were common and some were substantiated. Crookes was taken in (and possibly seduced) by the young medium Florence Cook. Gurney died of an overdose of chloroform, possibly self-administered, after discovering that his research assistant, a former theatrical entertainer, had fabricated many of his results. On the positive side the societies for psychical research helped establish the methods and protocols of the still active but disputed science of parapsychology.

The traditionalist schools of esotericism took off around the same time as the scientific schools but had a different orientation. Instead of looking for empirical evidence of supraphysical beings and forces, traditionalists turned to antique teachings that they believed were remnants of the original Tradition that was the source of all the world's philosophies, religions, and occult practices. A classic presentation of this idea is found in Éliphas Lévi's *Dogme et rituel de la haute magie*, published in two volumes in 1854 and 1856: "Behind the veil of all the sacred and mystic allegories of the ancient dogmas", one could find "traces of a doctrine that was always the same but always carefully concealed," which had served as the "nurse or god-mother of all religions, the secret lever of all intellectual forces, the key of all divine mysteries."[44] In his effort to uncover this primordial tradition, Lévi invoked the mystic teachings of Assyria, Egypt, India, Persia, and other exotic lands, but his immediate inspirations were European magic, alchemy, Hermeticism, Rosecrucianism, and Kaballah, not to mention the Catholic Church. (Born Alphonse Louis Constant in 1810, Lévi had trained to be a priest but had been expelled from his seminary for getting a student pregnant.) His publications were a mishmash of snippets from multiple sources combined with fictional material—an "invented tradition" rather than one with a verifiable pedigree. Despite or perhaps because of this they helped spark the late-nineteenth-century revival of Western esotericism.

Between 1860 and the beginning of World War I, dozens of esoteric groups were founded in cities across Europe and America. By far the most successful was the Theosophical Society, founded in New York in 1875. Many of its members had spiritualistic backgrounds, combined often with a fascination with science. Their aim, they wrote in their founding document, was "to obtain knowledge of the nature and attributes of the Supreme Power, and of the higher spirits *by the aid of physical processes*." They hoped in this way to obtain "proof of the existence of an 'Unseen Universe'" and its inhabitants. Theosophy was not, they stressed, "a Spiritualistic schism" or "the foe or friend of any sectarian or philosophic body." Neither was it a religion: it had "no dogmas to enforce, no creed to disseminate."[45] Within two decades the Theosophical movement was riven by schisms, mired in sectarian controversies, and burdened by an extravagant creed complete with theological dogmas, ceremonial rituals, and an ecclesiastical hierarchy. Empirical experiments gave way to unverified descriptions of a subtle world pullulating with invisible beings and forces. The society's main guide to this world of wonders was Helena Petrovna Blavatsky.

Born into a wealthy Russian family in 1831, Blavatsky had the run of a library built up by her great-grandfather, a Rosicrucian and Freemason. Married at 18, she left her husband after just three months and took to the road. Between 1849 and 1873 she traveled almost constantly, with stops in Europe, North Africa, Asia, and America. She was in search of Masters, and she found a good number, some of them embodied human beings, others denizens of the subtle worlds. When she arrived in the United States in 1873 she was thrilled to find herself in the birthplace of modern spiritualism, but her enthusiasm was short lived. Many Yankee spiritualists, she found, were "cheating mediums" or pawns of "the undeveloped Spirits of the lower Sphere." She, on the other hand, was on the track of a system that would disclose the "'deepest depths' of the Divine nature."[46]

Soon she began to sketch the outlines of this system. The result was *Isis Unveiled: A Master-Key to the Mysteries of Ancient and Modern Science and Theology*, published in 1877. It consists of two volumes, each more than 600 pages long. The first deals with science—not the materialistic science of Darwin and Huxley but the ancient sciences now called magic, occultism, Kabbalah, and so forth. Volume two, which deals with theology, shows how Christianity is related to Gnosticism, Hinduism, Buddhism, Zoroastrianism, and so forth. Contemporary humanity had to recapture the secrets of ancient religions, because "the Hermetic philosophy, the anciently universal Wisdom-Religion" was "the only possible key to the Absolute in science and theology."[47]

Whatever else might be said about *Isis Unveiled*, it is a tour de force of speculative scholarship. Blavatsky cited passages from dozens of works from the Greek, Egyptian, Neoplatonist, Persian, Indian, Tibetan, and other traditions as well as dozens of modern writers from Giordano Bruno to Éliphas Lévi. And because, like Lévi, she was convinced that the wisdom-religion was the same in all ages and all countries, she was free to build arguments combining elements from disparate cultures that had no historical relationship. The result, according to magician and writer Henry R. Evans—a nineteenth-century Amazing Randi—was "a hodgepodge of absurdities, pseudo-science, mythology and folk-lore, arranged in helterskelter fashion, with an utter disregard of logical sequence." Evans also pointed out that scholars who examined *Isis Unveiled* found dozens of cases of unattributed borrowings or outright plagiarisms.[48] Many similar appraisals have been made in the 140 years since the book's publication, and today the scholarly consensus is that *Isis Unveiled* has little intrinsic value. But Blavatsky popularized a number of ideas that are important in the history of modern spirituality, such as the law of karma and spiritual evolution. Her spirit-haunted universe was a throwback to the worldview of the age before Confucius and Socrates, but her concept of God was surprisingly modern: a "boundless and endless Entity, possessor of that invisible Will which we for lack of a better term call GOD."[49] Blavatsky refined her ideas after she voyaged to Bombay in 1879. I touch on her Indian incarnation in the next section.

The flowering of spiritualism and esotericism was a sign of discontent with organized religion and discomfort with materialistic science that became widespread during the late nineteenth century. A romantic nostalgia for the good old days of dogma was combined with a craving for empirical confirmation of invisible forces. In the decades that followed the appearance of the *Origin of Species*, men and women were drawn to the supernormal as a way to reassert their human dignity. At the same time some Westerners turned to Eastern religions, which seemed to offer a meaningful view of life free from the limitations of Christianity.

Reinvented traditions in Asia

The organizers of the World's Columbian Exposition of 1893 wanted it to bring lasting fame to the city of Chicago. Along with halls exhibiting the marvels of science and industry there were spaces for recreation and venues for cultural uplift. Among the most popular attractions were the world's first Ferris wheel and life-sized reproductions of the *Niña*, the *Pinta* and the *Santa Maria*—the ships Columbus sailed across the Atlantic four hundred years earlier. For highbrow visitors there were musical performances, art exhibitions, and international conferences, the most famous of which was the World's Parliament of Religions, held over seventeen days in September. The majority of the participants were Christians, but there also were Jews, Hindus, Buddhists, and representatives of other Asian faiths. The aim of the organizers was to usher in "a new epoch of brotherhood and peace," but they discovered that many religious leaders were opposed to the whole idea. The Sultan of the Ottoman Empire, nominal head of the world's Muslims, flatly refused to cooperate, as did the Archbishop of Canterbury. "The fact [is] that the Christian religion is the one religion," this prelate wrote. "I do not understand how that religion can be regarded as a member of a Parliament of Religions without assuming the equality of the other intended members and the parity of their position and claims." The archbishop had political as well as theological reasons for his stance. Christians regarded their religion as the only path to salvation. This justified the missionary activities they carried out around the world, notably in the European colonial empires. As head of the established church of the kingdom that ruled the largest of these empires, the archbishop could hardly sit as an equal with members of "native" religions. Even the parliament's organizers, despite their interfaith pretentions, conceived of it mainly as a showcase of global Christianity. Ironically the Parliament is remembered today primarily as a landmark in the revival of Asian religions.[50]

The late nineteenth century marked the apogee of Western colonial expansion. Between the 1490s and 1890s Portugal, Spain, England, France, the Dutch Republic, and other European powers established direct and indirect rule over huge swathes of territory in Asia, Africa, the Americas, and Australasia. Sometimes the colonizers all but obliterated local populations. More commonly they established hegemonic relationships, draining the colonies' wealth and imposing their own social and cultural values on the colonized peoples. In this project they were aided by Christian missionaries, who regarded all "heathen" religions as inferior, even if they were older and less prone to violence than Christianity.

The Asian reaction to European cultural imperialism was complex. Attracted by aspects of Western life that seemed to be linked to political success, such as science, individualism, and social mobility, reformers in India, Ceylon, Japan, and, to a lesser degree, China, Turkey, and Iran tried to imitate Western behavior without abandoning their own values. Then the pupils became teachers. English-knowing evangelists such as Swami Vivekananda, Anagarika Dharmapala, and D.T. Suzuki went to the West and explained to rapt audiences that Hinduism and Buddhism were more scientific and more pragmatic than Christianity. One result of this counteroffensive was the development of hybrid religions and philosophies, such as neo-Vedanta, Buddhist modernism, Western Zen, and Christian yoga, that have played significant roles in the development of modern spirituality.

It was not until the late eighteenth century that European scholars made serious efforts to understand Hinduism, Buddhism, and other Asian religions. Early landmarks of this scholarship were Charles Wilkins's English translation of the *Bhagavad Gita* (1785) and William Jones' monograph on the relationship between Sanskrit, Greek, and Latin (1786). Both Wilkins and Jones were officers of the British East India Company, and it is certain that the Company viewed their work in terms of its imperial strategy. As Governor-General Warren Hastings wrote in his preface to Wilkins's translation, "Every accumulation of knowledge, and especially such as is obtained by social communication with people over whom we exercise a dominion founded on the right of conquest, is useful to the state."[51] This epitomizes the attitude modern historians call "Orientalism": scholarship at the service of political and cultural expansion. It applies to some instances of Western scholarship about Asia, but not all of them. Many of the most important European scholars of Sanskrit were Germans, and Germany had no colonies in India. Most colonial-era orientalists were in fact deeply interested in the texts they read and translated, and the products of their labor exerted a huge influence on European and American thought. Schopenhauer's idealism took a new turn after his exposure to Buddhism and Vedanta; Goethe's Romanticism was touched by the charm of the classical Indian dramatist Kalidasa; Emerson's poetry and Thoreau's reflective writings were enriched by the ideas of the *Gita*.

Soon the winds of cross-fertilization were blowing both ways. After South Asian intellectuals learned European languages, they absorbed the ideals of the Enlightenment, the French Revolution, and Romanticism. Returning to their own traditions, they reread them in this borrowed light. Between 1815 and 1820 Indian scholar and reformer Rammohan Roy published English translations of four Upanishads and two Vedantic texts along with a number of explanatory essays. In them he argued that the basis of Hinduism was the monism of the Upanishads and that the polytheistic practices of modern Hindus were corruptions of that ancient teaching. In 1828 he and his associates founded the Brahmo Sabha, later renamed the Brahmo Samaj (Assembly of Brahman). Its purpose was to encourage the worship of the "Eternal Unsearchable and Immutable Being, who is the Author and Preserver of the Universe." By using the language of British deism to describe the Vedantic idea of Brahman, Rammohan was trying to bridge the gap between Eastern and Western religions.[52]

After Rammohan's death in 1833, the Brahmo Samaj went through one reorganization and two schisms. The reorganization was the work of Devendranath Tagore, who merged his own group with the then inactive Samaj in 1843. Like Rammohan, Devendranath was an admirer of the Upanishads, but he rejected the Advaitic concept of liberation by means of renunciation. "By the grace of God the soul is infinitely progressive," he wrote in his autobiography. "Overcoming sin and sorrow this progressive soul must and will progress onwards and upwards."[53] This Spencerian take on Vedanta permitted him and his colleagues to remain active in the world. (He was a major landowner and the father of twelve children, one of whom was the Nobel-Prize-winning poet Rabindranath Tagore.)

In 1859 Devendranath met Keshab Chandra Sen, a dynamic young man who became his heir apparent. The two men broke in 1866, in part over Keshab's interest in Christianity and his defense of Christian missionary work—something Devendranath abhorred. Keshab founded a splinter group called the Brahmo Samaj of India with himself as secretary (the president was God). In 1870 he sailed for England, where he lectured widely and had an audience with Queen Victoria. Back in India he applied himself to social activism, championing such causes as marriage reform and female education. He lost his credibility when he married his underage daughter to a Maharaja's son. This was the cause of the second Brahmo schism, resulting in the creation of the Sadharan Brahmo Samaj, which concentrated on social reform.

In 1881 Keshab founded a yet another group, the Church of the New Dispensation. He called it "the science which binds and explains and harmonizes all religions."

All prophets and earlier dispensations were included, but special prominence was given to the revelations of India, for Indians were "specially endowed with, and distinguished for" the "power of spiritual communion and absorption." Keshab's religion was short-lived but influential. He was one of the first to claim, in the face of missionary censure, that Asian religions were superior to Christianity. He also was one of the first to say that individual spiritual experience—"the direct apprehension of God and Heaven in consciousness"—was the basis of religious life.[54]

Swami Vivekananda—born Narendranath Dutta in 1863—took part in the activities of the Sadharan Brahmo Samaj and had some contact (it is hard to say how much) with Keshab. He read widely though not deeply in Western philosophy and for a while was a member of the Freemasons. Then, in 1882, he met a Hindu holy man named Ramakrishna. This was the defining event in his life. When Ramakrishna died in 1886, Vivekananda stepped forward as the leader of his disciples. Two years later he began to travel around India as a *sannyasin* or religious mendicant. Learning about the 1893 Parliament of Religions, he voyaged to Chicago and after some trouble (he had not been invited) was named one of the delegates of Hinduism.

The Brahmo Samaj was one of many organizations that promoted religious and social reform in nineteenth-century India. Another was the Arya Samaj, founded by Swami Dayananda Saraswati in Bombay in 1875. Like Rammohan, Dayananda thought that contemporary Hinduism was a distortion of the pure, original faith, but he based his criticism of image-worship not on the Upanishads but on earlier Vedic texts, which (as he read them) celebrate a single formless *parameshwara* or Supreme Lord.

In 1877 one of Dayananda's followers put him in touch with Henry Steel Olcott, the American cofounder of the Theosophical Society, which was then in the second year of its existence and not doing very well. Olcott and Dayananda began to correspond with the help of Indian intermediaries. Olcott explained that Theosophists were seekers of the one impersonal God, "an Eternal and Omnipresent Principle which, under many different names, was the same in all religions." This seemed to make sense to Dayananda's followers, and there was talk of bringing the two groups together. With this in mind, Blavatsky and Olcott sailed to India in 1879. After their arrival they found they had little in common with Dayananda. Doctrinal disagreements soon gave way to vituperation. Dayananda was, Olcott concluded, "not an adept at all," but only a learned ascetic. The foreigners were, Dayananda declared, "dangerous atheists" and their claims to be in touch with disembodied masters mere "chicanery."[55]

Dayananda was distressed that Olcott and Blavatsky were interested in Buddhism, a heterodox religion that rejected the authority of the Vedas. Their interest took them to Ceylon (now Sri Lanka) in 1880. During their stay they recited the Buddhist profession of faith, becoming the first Westerners to be received into the religion in a public ceremony. To some this looked like an abandonment of the Theosophical principle of nonsectarianism. They justified it on the grounds that becoming a "regular Buddhist" had nothing to do with accepting the practices of the "debased modern sectarian." For Olcott to be a regular Buddhist meant following the teachings of "the Master-Adept Gautama Buddha," which were (in his Theosophical view) identical to "the Wisdom Religion of the Aryan Upanishads, and the soul of all the ancient world-faiths."[56]

Olcott was disturbed to see that most Ceylonese Buddhists were sectarians, so he decided to teach them the truths of their religion. Taking as his model "the elementary handbooks so effectively used among Western Christian sects," he compiled a *Buddhist Catechism*.[57] Based on works by European scholars but carrying the imprimatur of a Buddhist priest, this handbook was published in 1881 and is still in print after more than 135 years. As a Westerner who helped resuscitate Buddhism, Olcott is still revered in Sri Lanka, but he would never have got very far without the help of his student and collaborator Anagarika Dharmapala.

Born into a well-to-do merchant family of Colombo, Dharmapala, or Don David Hewavitarane as he was then known, seemed destined for a cushy government job when he decided to accompany Olcott on a tour of the island in 1886. Traveling in a customized double-decker bullock cart, they brought the Buddha's teachings to remote villages and towns. When they halted at monasteries, the hirsute American towered above the tonsured monks who gathered to hear his sermons (translated into Sinhala by Dharmapala). By the time the two men got back to Colombo, Dharmapala had decided to dedicate his life to Buddhism. In 1891 he founded the Maha-Bodhi Society to win control of the temple in North India that was said to mark the spot where the Buddha achieved enlightenment. As editor of the society's journal, he came to the attention of the organizers of the Parliament of Religions, who invited him to Chicago in 1893.

The forced opening of Japanese ports in 1853 and the humiliating treaties that followed helped bring about the downfall of the Takugawa Shogunate and the restoration of imperial rule in 1868. The faction that backed the young Meiji emperor forced him to accept a charter that limited his powers, gave rights to the lower classes, promised reform, and made acquisition of knowledge from abroad a national priority.

During the early years of the Meiji era Buddhism fell into official disfavor. Its critics condemned it as a decadent foreign religion, saddled with superstitions and an impediment to national progress. Bureaucrats promoted the ethnic religion Shinto, which soon became the official state cult. Buddhist thinkers responded by launching the *shin bukkyo* or New Buddhism movement, which stressed Buddhism's Japanese credentials and at the same time followed official Meiji policy by seeking and applying Western knowledge.

Among the most prominent leaders of the *shin bukkyo* movement were the Rinzai Zen master Imakita Kosen (1816–1892) and his student and successor Shaku Soyen (1860–1919). Besides learning Zen in the traditional way, Soyen attended a "Western studies" college in Tokyo, where he received instruction from foreign teachers. He then passed two years in Ceylon as a wandering monk. (While there he briefly met Olcott, who was interested in promoting interactions between different Buddhist schools.) In 1892 Soyen was named one of the Japanese Buddhist delegates to the Chicago Parliament of Religions. Another proposed delegate spoke for them all when he wrote that the Parliament represented "a great opportunity for spreading Buddhism in the West." Japanese Buddhists should rise to the occasion and "wed the *Daijo* [Mahayana] and Western thought," for only Mahayana was equal to the task of spreading the Buddha's teachings throughout the world.[58]

Soyen, Dharmapala, and Vivekananda were just three of more than twenty Asian delegates at the Parliament. Among the others were Virchand Gandhi, the first Jain scholar to travel abroad, and Pung Kwang Yu, a diplomat and Confucian scholar. The visitors from Asia were, for the most part, well received. When Pung was introduced people rose to their feet and "there was wild waving of hats and handkerchiefs." Vivekananda, wearing his trademark orange turban, began his remarks with "Sisters and brothers of America!" and was met by "a peal of applause that lasted for several minutes." Dharmapala was equally striking: "With his black, curly locks thrown back from his broad brow" and with his "long brown fingers emphasizing the utterances of his vibrant voice, he looked the very image of a propagandist," an American observer wrote, adding: "one trembled to know that such a figure stood at the head of a movement to consolidate all the disciples of Buddha and to spread 'the light of Asia' throughout the civilized [i.e. Western] world."[59]

Clearly many Christians were far from pleased by the presence on the platform of charismatic speakers from foreign outposts. The Asian delegates, who differed about many things, were united in their dislike of Christian missionaries. Pung observed that they promoted their scriptures in China without going to the trouble of learning the Confucian classics. Dharmapala said bluntly that they were selfish and intolerant; if they wanted their religion to spread they should emulate the meekness of their prophet. It was left to Kinzo Hirai, a Buddhist layman, to situate missionary activity in the context of European colonialism: "You send your missionaries to Japan, and they advise us to be moral," he said, but if it was "Christian morality to trample upon the rights and advantages of a non-Christian nation" he was glad to remain a barbarous Buddhist.[60]

The Asian delegates were happy to endorse the pluralistic rhetoric of the organizers but each of them said, more or less plainly, that his religion was best. Vivekananda declared that Hinduism was the only ancient religion that was still going strong after thousands of years: "From the high spiritual flights of the Vedanta philosophy, of which the latest discoveries of science seem like echoes," through various forms of popular worship, to "the agnosticism of the Buddhists, and the atheism of the Jains, each and all have their place in the Hindu's religion." The idea that Western science was anticipated by Eastern religions became a cliché during the late nineteenth century (and is still going strong after more than a hundred years). Pung noted that the principles on which science is based "bear a striking resemblance" to the principles discussed in the *Book of Changes* and *Spring and Autumn Annals*. Dharmapala equated the idea of *samsara* with the theory of evolution, quoting from an English book on Darwin to express the Buddhist idea that the cosmos was "a continuous process unfolding itself in regular order in obedience to natural laws."[61]

Many Asian delegates had trouble explaining that a religion could be based on something other than God. Pung spoke at length of the problems involved in translating the word "God" into Chinese. When Confucian teachers spoke of spiritual things they invoked not a deity but "the law of action and reaction, which operates upon matter without suffering loss, and which causes the seasons to come round without deviation." Virchand Gandhi made it clear that "God, in the sense of an extra cosmic personal creator, has no place in the Jain philosophy." He, along with Soyen and Dharmapala, spoke of the inexorable law of karma, which left no room for a creator God. Dharmapala used quasi-scientific terminology to explain this ancient doctrine: "Speaking of deity in the sense of a Supreme Creator, Buddha says that there is no such being. Accepting the doctrine of evolution as the only true one, with its corollary, the law of cause and effect, he condemns the idea of a creator and strictly forbids inquiry into it as being useless."[62] Western scholars of Confucianism, Jainism, and Buddhism had known for decades that these philosophies and religions were nontheistic. The Parliament of Religions was perhaps the first forum in the Western world where the idea of nontheistic religion was presented to a large nonscholarly audience.

In the years that followed the Parliament, Vivekananda, Dharmapala, and Soyen continued to promote their versions of Hinduism and Buddhism in the West. Drawing on the discourses of Western science, philosophy, and literature, they reformulated the teachings of the Upanishads, the *Yoga Sutra*, the Pali Canon, and the Mahayana sutras in ways that got traction with their foreign audiences. The interpretations that they and their followers put forward eventually became the default versions of Hinduism, Vedanta, Yoga, Buddhism, and Zen in the West and have remained so ever since. Reimported back to the East, they had a significant effect on reformist Hinduism and Buddhism in India, Ceylon, and Japan. All three teachers declared that they were presenting timeless truths as enshrined in ancient scriptures, but their teachings were reinterpretations keyed to the modern mind. As such they have played important roles in the development of global spirituality.

After his triumphal appearance at Chicago, Vivekananda remained in the West for three and a half years. His original purpose in going abroad, he wrote to a brother-disciple, was to gather funds to establish an order of activist monks in India who would "go from village to village, disseminating education and seeking in various ways to better the condition of all down to the Chandala [outcaste]." The Brahmo Samaj had had moderate success doing this sort of thing in Bengal, but no one in India was ready to support Vivekananda's efforts. "Therefore," he wrote, "I have come to America," where people were rich "but lacking in spirituality. I give them spirituality, and they give me money."[63]

The longer the Swami stayed in America, the more he came to feel he had work to do among the natives. Having learned that Americans were practical people, he decided to offer them do-it-yourself methods of spiritual growth. In 1895 he told people in New York that every religion had a practical as well as a theoretical side. Western religions were focused on theory, but in India there was a "Science of Religion" that was strong both in theory and in practice. This was yoga, the method of joining the human with the divine.[64] Before leaving for Europe in 1896 he gave dozens of talks on Yoga and Vedanta that later were published as books. One of them, *Raja Yoga*, is one of the most influential works on yoga ever written.

"Raja Yoga" was Vivekananda's name for the system of the *Yoga Sutra*. In his first lecture he stressed that Raja Yoga offers humanity "a practical and scientifically worked out method" for attaining spiritual truth. The method is primarily mental but the body also has a role to play because it is intimately connected with the mind. The core technique of yoga is concentration. If we direct the mind back upon itself, we will be able to see "whether we have souls, whether life is of five minutes or of eternity, whether there is a God in the universe or more." We will know these things through direct personal experience. Just as objective data obtainable by experiments are the basis of the physical sciences, so subjective experiences obtainable by inner practices are the basis of the world's religions. Christianity is founded on the experiences of Christ, Buddhism on the experiences of the Buddha, Hinduism on the experiences of the *rishis*, and so forth. Most modern spokesmen of these religions insisted that the founders' experiences were no longer attainable. Vivekananda denied that this was true. Anything experienced in the past could be experienced in the present. The teachings of yoga made it clear "that religion is not only based upon the experience of ancient times, but that no man can be religious until he has had the same perceptions himself."[65]

All six characteristics of modern spirituality are apparent in Vivekananda's lecture: innerness, anti-institutionalism, individual practice, universal experiences, scientific empiricism, and the role of the body. He worked out the details in classes and lectures in America, Europe, and India over the next six years. His teachings set the pattern for the Western understanding of yoga and Vedanta and also changed the way that people in India approached their spiritual traditions. Vivekananda expanded the idea, proposed earlier by Keshab Sen, that all religions are based on the experiences of saints and sages, and that these experiences are available to everyone. His assertion that "the mind itself has a higher state of existence, beyond reason, a superconscious state" and that "when the mind gets to that higher state, then this [higher] knowledge, beyond reasoning, comes to man" is one of several passages from *Raja Yoga* that William James quoted in *Varieties of Religious Experience*, the book that more than any other popularized the idea that religions are based on the spiritual experiences of their founders.[66]

Like all self-confident interpreters, Vivekananda presented his views as the plain and simple truth of the texts he examined. Recent historians have pointed out that his ideas about Vedanta and yoga sometimes lack a firm textual basis.[67] There is little in the Upanishads to justify his assertion that traditional Vedanta encourages the cultivation of individual subjective experiences. The *Yoga Sutra* offers practical techniques, but it would be a stretch to call them "scientific." Vivekananda's synthesis of Yoga and Vedanta was a child of its time, produced in the West with an international audience in mind. The same is true of Soyen's and Dharmapala's interpretations of Buddhism.

While in Chicago, Soyen befriended the German-American philosopher and publisher Paul Carus. Impressed by the monk, Carus invited him to stay in the United States to help him translate Asian religious texts. Soyen turned down the offer (he had a monastery to look after in Japan) but suggested that Carus invite his student D.T. Suzuki instead. Suzuki came to America in 1897 and stayed eleven years, translating several classic texts, such as the *Daodejing* and *The Awakening of Faith*, and working on an introduction to Mahayana philosophy. In 1905 Soyen returned to the United States and gave lectures (interpreted by Suzuki) in California and on the East Coast. Before returning to Japan, he left his talks and other material with Suzuki, who published edited versions as *Sermons of a Buddhist Abbot*. (Suzuki's contribution was so extensive that he may be considered the book's joint author.)[68] Many of the talks are straightforward presentations of Mahayana doctrine; others clothe Buddhist ideas in Western attire. Like Vivekananda, Suzuki invoked "the doctrines of modern science," with which the Buddha's teachings were "in exact agreement." He also alluded to European philosophy: Buddhism was similar to German Idealism, but in the end it was "not a system of metaphysics, but a religion which is practical more than anything else. What it teaches is the profound spiritual experience of every enlightened man." Founded, like other religions, "in our subjective life," Buddhism tells us that we must "strive, through our own inner and individual efforts and not through any outside agency, to unfold ourselves and bring about enlightenment."[69]

Three of the components of modern spirituality—subjectivity, individual effort, and scientific validation—are manifest in Soyen's American lectures. They also appear in Dharmapala's writings and speeches. "The message of the Buddha that I have to bring to you," he told an audience in New York, "is free from theology, priestcraft, rituals, ceremonies, dogmas, heavens, hells and other theological shibboleths." The Buddha taught "a scientific religion containing the highest individualistic altruistic ethics, a philosophy of life built on psychological mysticism and a cosmology which is in harmony with geology, astronomy, radioactivity and relativity."[70] In another text he called Buddhism "a religion of internal development" that was at the same time a scientific technique: "Just as light is obtained by means of the electric dynamo without the help of oil, wick and match, so man by following the path of the Lord Buddha, which is the path of scientific wisdom, can attain the highest peace, bliss and freedom by individual effort and personal purity of heart." Properly applied, the Buddha's "science of psychology will open the eyes of man to the power of his own potentialities, and he will try to work for the good of others, because it will bring his own development to quicker realization."[71]

Dharmapala's scientific Buddhism was a modern hybrid that had little to do with practices current in Ceylonese monasteries. Few if any monks had firsthand knowledge of the psychological disciplines Dharmapala spoke of.[72] Anxious to revive the practices of *jhana* or meditation, he searched through monastic libraries and in 1893 came across an old meditation manual. He gave a copy to British orientalist T.W. Rhys Davids, who published a Pali-Sinhala edition three years later. Dharmapala used this book in his own practice, becoming, according to scholar Richard Gombrich, "so far as is known, the first Buddhist to learn meditation from a book without recourse to a master." This marked the start of "the fashion for lay meditation" that later became popular among the urban elite in Ceylon and Burma and recently has spread throughout the world in the form of mindfulness meditation.[73]

Turn-of-the-century Buddhists who debated with Christian apologists had to deal with the question of the Buddha's supposed atheism. To Dharmapala, Buddhism's denial of the gods was a mark of its superiority to the West Asian monotheisms: the Buddha "taught that man can get his salvation without the help of angry, bloodthirsty deities. The religion that the Lord gave to the civilized Aryans of ancient India was psychological. No god is needed to get rid of anger, jealousy, ill-will, pride, ignorance." Soyen (as presented by Suzuki) was more interested in winning over Western readers, so he explained that Buddhists accepted God in the sense of "the highest reality and truth," but instead of calling it God they used such terms as *dharmakaya*, the dharma-body of the Buddha. Lest others think he was endorsing the God of monotheism, Soyen added that *dharmakaya* in fact "differs from the Christian God, perhaps in its most essential aspects." Vivekananda never hesitated to utter the word "God" and sometimes drew comparisons between Christian and Hindu theism, but he also made allowance for the atheists and agnostics in his Western audiences. The yogi, he declared in a talk of 1896, "need not believe in any doctrine whatever. He may not believe even in God."[74]

In *Sermons of a Buddhist Abbot*, Suzuki wrote that quarrels between the followers of different religions were for the most part due to divergences in aesthetic, intellectual, and environmental background. "God," "Allah," "Dharmakaya," and so forth were different terms for "the same fact which is felt in the deepest depths of our being." Yet Soyen also said that Buddhism was the supreme religion and that Japanese Mahayana was the supreme form of Buddhism.[75] Vivekananda was a victim of the same inconsistency. In his speeches in the United States and Europe he preached universal religion and castigated those who claimed that their religions were best. But when he addressed his countrymen back home he came out with statements like this: "Our claim is that the Vedanta only can be the universal religion, that it is already the existing universal religion in the world."[76] This sort of cultural cheerleading is innocuous enough—everyone loves to root for the home team—but when it gets mixed up with politics, the results are sometimes explosive.

The rise of reformed religion in nineteenth-century Asia went hand in hand with the rise of nationalism. In India, religious groups such as the Brahmo Samaj and Arya Samaj had secular counterparts in sociopolitical advocacy groups such as the Sarvajanik Sabha and Indian Association. In 1885 a retired British official and Theosophist named Allan Octavian Hume founded the Indian National Congress. After two decades of ineffectual posturing, the Congress became the vanguard of the Indian independence movement. Vivekananda kept aloof from politics but the speeches he gave after returning from the West did more to motivate Indian nationalists than all the orations ever delivered from Congress platforms. "We must go out, we must conquer the world through our spirituality and philosophy," he told an ecstatic crowd in Madras in 1897.[77] A hundred twenty years later, he remains a popular figure in India, but more as a protonationalist than as a spiritual leader. Among his most fervent admirers are members of Hindu right-wing groups, who publicize his evocations of India's greatness but ignore his criticisms of the country's failings. For such hypernationalists, Hinduism is the universal religion because it alone is universally valid. The same claim, *mutatis mutandis*, was made by admirers of Soyen and Dharmapala, with more unfortunate results.

At the Parliament of Religions, Soyen won acclaim for his talk on the theme "Arbitration Instead of War." A decade later he justified Japan's entry into the Russo-Japanese War with the assurance of a seasoned politician: "In the present hostilities, into which Japan has entered with great reluctance, she pursues no egotistic purpose, but seeks the subjugation of evils hostile to civilization, peace, and enlightenment. She deliberated long before she took up arms"—and so forth.[78] More than a hundred thousand people died during this conflict, which marked the emergence of Japan as a military power.

In Ceylon, Dharmapala extolled the uniqueness of Buddhism in terms that Soyen would have endorsed. He was proud that Buddhists did "not believe in persecuting people for the sake of religion" but at the same time blamed the non-Buddhist people of Ceylon for all its problems: "Barbaric vandals" brought "monotheism [Christianity and Islam] and diabolic polytheism [Hinduism]" to the island and introduced "the vulgar practices of killing animals, stealing, prostitution, licentiousness, lying and drunkenness."[79] Given the historical circumstances (colonialism, missionary aggression) a certain amount of such rhetoric was inevitable. But the Sinhala nationalist movement that Dharmapala helped inspire continued even after independence and was one of the main causes of the long civil war (1983–2009) between Sinhala Buddhists and Tamil Hindus that cost tens of thousands of lives and destroyed the country's prosperity.

* * *

During the nineteenth century the elements that make up godless spirituality—atheism, subjectivity, rejection of institutional religion, and individual striving—came together in the West as well as the East. Thinkers such as Schopenhauer, Feuerbach, and Marx were openly atheistic, and novelists such as Stendhal and Émile Zola made no effort to hide their contempt for Christianity. They and many others looked to literature, art, and music to provide a secular framework for truth and value. Among other substitute religions that emerged were the Romantic worship of Nature and the social and economic gospels of Comte and Marx. People who felt starved for supernatural sustenance turned to esotericism and modernized forms of Hinduism and Buddhism. By the end of the century there was a general recognition that a new term was needed for beliefs and practices that overlapped with those of conventional religions but rejected their exclusiveness and dogmas. Many began to use the old term "spirituality" to serve this modern purpose.

All the elements of modern spirituality are found in the surrogate religions of the nineteenth century, sometimes alone or in pairs, sometimes together. The subjective vision of the English Romantic writers also suffuses the essays of the Transcendentalists and the poetry of Whitman. It became the basis of the psychological novel, which flourished in the hands of Eliot, Dostoyevsky, and others. The subjective viewpoint of Hindu and Buddhist philosophy was embraced by European philosophers such as Schopenhauer and promoted by Asian thinkers such as Vivekananda and Suzuki.

Many Western writers of the period—among them Goethe, Emerson, and Kierkegaard—contrasted the superficiality of outward religious observances with the authenticity of inner spiritual states. Keshab Sen, Vivekananda, Dharmapala, Suzuki, and other spokesmen of modernized Hinduism and Buddhism gave ancient Asian psychophysical practices a nineteenth-century reboot. They also helped popularize the post-Darwinian notion that spirituality is compatible with science. This rejection of the traditional distinction between the physical and spiritual modes of knowledge went hand in hand with the idea, prominent in the work of Schopenhauer, Thoreau, and Whitman, that the physical body was intimately related with the spiritual self. By the end of the nineteenth century all the elements of modern godless spirituality were in place.

7 THE DEATH AND AFTERLIFE OF GOD

A century and a half ago, it was just becoming possible for people in the West to admit to themselves and others that they did not believe in God. Many passed through years of torment before they reached that point. Today hundreds of millions of people regard themselves as atheists or agnostics or simply have no interest in religion and have never felt the lack. This is an unprecedented situation. God- or spirit-oriented religions have underlain most human societies. There have always been scoffers and skeptics, but before the end of the nineteenth century there never was a time when disbelief in God was so prevalent as to be unremarkable. More than one nineteenth-century thinker uttered the phrase "God is dead," but it was Nietzsche who seared it into the mind of the West as with an incandescent branding-iron: "God is dead! God remains dead! And we have killed him!"[1] This declaration of 1882 marks the beginning of the post-theistic era.

The gods did not disappear overnight. Religion continued to engage the hearts and minds of most people, even those who rejected traditional beliefs and practices. Some retrofitted the faiths they were born to, trying to harmonize rationality and faith. Others took part in surrogate religions of literature or art or esotericism or psychotherapy. A good number sought salvation through social gospels. But the proxy faiths that attracted the most believers during the nineteenth and twentieth centuries were cults of nationalism.

Between 1872 and 1912 the European powers avoided making war on one another but they engaged in a costly arms race and competed for territory abroad. These modern rivalries, exacerbating ancient hatreds, set the stage for World War I, which laid waste vast tracts of Europe and the Middle East. Among its repercussions were the Russian Revolution and the dismemberment of the Ottoman Empire, both of which had political consequences that are still being felt today.

During the postwar years, writers, artists, social scientists, and philosophers explored the effects of living in a world that had no stable ethical or aesthetic norms or intellectual points of reference. Meanwhile religious thinkers were searching for ways to meet the challenge of secularism. Liberal theologians tried to harmonize religion and post-Darwinian science. Fundamentalists looked for ways to make antique scriptures the basis of modern life. As the world's economy tottered, nationalism took extravagant forms, making another global war inevitable. After the conflict, the European powers struggled to maintain their ascendancy as their colonies threw off the imperial yoke.

During the 1940s and 1950s conventional religions continued to decline. Spirituality, at first a fringe phenomenon, came to the forefront during the 1960s and 1970s. Today in much of Europe and America, millions of people are atheistic, agnostic, or indifferent to religion but practice spiritual disciplines. Spirituality without God, almost an oxymoron a hundred years ago, has become part of modern life.

Self-exceeding and redemption

In July 1881 the thirty-six-year-old philosopher Friedrich Nietzsche rented a room in a farmhouse in Sils Maria, a village in the Swiss Alps. Two years earlier he had resigned his professorship at the University of Basel because of unrelenting ill health. From that point on he spent most of his time in resorts in Italy, France and Switzerland. Whenever he felt up to it, he applied himself to his writing, turning out a series of aphoristic works that combined philosophical reflection with acerbic social criticism. One day in August he went for a walk in the woods near Sils Maria. Stopping near a huge black pyramid-shaped rock, he was struck by a thought that provided a solution to a problem that had troubled him for years: how could life be justified now that "the belief in the Christian God has become unbelievable." The greatest event of the modern era could be summed up in three words: "God is dead." Without God there could be no morality or truth, and life could have no meaning. Or else—and this is the insight that came to him then—it could have only as much meaning as human beings gave it. Later he expressed this in a thought experiment: What if a demon appeared and told you that you would have to relive your life over and over again, re-experiencing "every pain and every joy and every thought and sigh and everything unspeakably small or great … all in the same succession and sequence." Would you "throw yourself down and gnash your teeth and curse the demon"? Or would you answer, "You are a god, and never have I heard anything more divine"? Nietzsche chose the second option. He would love his fate, rejoicing in everything that happened because he accepted life in its entirety.[2]

Son of a Lutheran pastor, Nietzsche lost his faith in God while a student of theology, but for a while he held onto the idea that religion could be the basis of a well-lived life. In 1866 he wrote to a friend that if Christianity meant "belief in an historical event or in an historical person," he would have nothing to do with it, but if it was "simply the need for redemption," he could "value it highly."[3] This theme of redemption without the need of God recurs throughout his works.

For some time, Nietzsche took Schopenhauer as his guide, drawn by his atheism and his belief in the transforming power of art. But eventually he rejected his predecessor's pessimism and life-denial. For Nietzsche art was a means of affirmation and ultimately of salvation: "it is only as an *aesthetic phenomenon* that existence and the world are eternally *justified*," he wrote in *The Birth of Tragedy* (1872). Those who (like Schopenhauer) longed "for a Buddha-like denial of the will" could be "saved by art."[4]

Between the publication of *The Birth of Tragedy* and the illumination at Sils Maria, Nietzsche came to view most European cultural activities as veiled expressions of an underlying Christian morality. This crypto-Christianity magnified the consequences of the death of God. In *The Gay Science*, the madman who cries out "God is dead" elicits only laughter when he gives the news to a group of atheists. They laugh because they do not see the upshot: "Where are we moving to?" the madman exclaims. "Away from all suns? Are we not continually falling? And backwards, sidewards, forwards, in all directions? Is there still an up and a down? Aren't we straying as though through an infinite nothing?" God's murder was the most consequential act in the history of the world and there was only one way God's murderers could be redeemed: by becoming gods themselves.[5]

The death of God opened the way for the birth of the overman. (The German word is *Übermensch*, which sometimes is translated as "superman.") In *Thus Spoke Zarathustra* (1883), the prophet Zarathustra (Nietzsche's spokesman) comes down from the mountain where he had passed ten years to give his wisdom to human beings. On his way he passes a saint engrossed in his devotions. Zarathustra asks himself: "Could it be possible! This old saint in his woods has not yet heard the news that *God is dead!*" With this in mind, he delivers his first sermon: "Behold, I teach you the overman!" During the theistic age, "the sacrilege against God was the greatest sacrilege." Then God died, and "now to desecrate the earth is the most terrible thing." People should stop looking to heaven for the meaning of the earth: "The overman is the meaning of the earth."[6]

But what is the meaning of overman? Sometimes Nietzsche hinted that the overman was the precursor of an entirely new species, as far above the human as the human is above the ape. He also declared that the overman is a product of human self-exceeding. The great question of the age was not "How are human beings to be preserved?" but rather "How shall human being be *overcome*?" Schopenhauer had spoken of the will to life. Nietzsche went a step further. He has his prophet say: "where life is, is there also will; but not will to life, instead—thus

I teach you—will to power!" Human beings had to rise above their transitory values, for "a stronger force grows out of your values and a new overcoming."[7]

The overman and the will to power are what most people think of when they think of Nietzsche. But the terms appear together only in a few late works, particularly *Zarathustra*, and *Zarathustra*, because it is poetic (some would say bombastic) is subject to various interpretations. One of them, encouraged by the World War I German government and followed up by Adolf Hitler, was that the overman, driven by the will to power, is destined to conquer and exploit inferior races. Nietzsche himself made it clear that the overman was the outcome of *self*-conquest and *self*-overcoming. He hinted at this as early as 1880 in *Human, All too Human*: "The man who has overcome his passions has entered into possession of the most fertile ground. ... To sow the seeds of good spiritual works in the soil of the subdued passions is then the immediate urgent task."[8]

This passage provides a glimpse of a spiritual side of Nietzsche that often goes unnoticed. He returned to it in *The Anti-Christ*, the last book he finished before his breakdown in 1889: "A people which still believes in itself still also has its own God." In ancient Greece, the gods "represented a people, the strength of a people." But the God of Christianity had been castrated and made impotent, becoming "the *contradiction of life*, instead of being its transfiguration and eternal *Yes!*" The one good thing that could be said of Christianity was that it had replaced the Hebrew obsession with sin with the longing for redemption. Christ showed that "it is through the *practice* of one's life that one feels 'divine.'" This practice is "the psychological reality of 'redemption.'—A new way of living, *not* a new belief." But in the end Christianity became a conspiracy against health, beauty, and benevolence, indeed "*against life itself*." Nietzsche proposed instead a religion of Dionysus, the god of fruitfulness, wine, and ecstasy. It would be a religion of liberated spirits standing secure in the faith that "in the totality everything is redeemed and affirmed."[9]

In *Daybreak* (1881) Nietzsche praised Buddhism as a religion without gods or priests, a religion in which people had to work out their own salvation: a "*religion of self-redemption*." Even now, he continued, there were "among the various nations of Europe perhaps ten to twenty million people who no longer 'believe in God.'"[10] There is no way of knowing whether this estimate was accurate, but it is certain that during the last quarter of the nineteenth century there was an enormous flight from organized religions throughout Europe and America.

There were many reasons for this. The Industrial Revolution drew people away from villages where everyone knew one another and deposited them in cities where they were more or less anonymous. This encouraged people who were lukewarm about religion (always the majority) to cut their links with the church. Libraries and bookshops offered works on physics, biology, anthropology, sociology, communism, literary criticism, and Biblical criticism that challenged the fundamentals of Christian belief. Readers of this literature reacted in various ways. In his *Candid Examination of Theism* (1878), Canadian biologist George Romanes wrote that Darwin's theory of evolution and the arguments of materialistic philosophers had convinced him of the hollowness of religion but he had to admit that "with this virtual negation of God, the universe to me has lost its soul of loveliness." Quite different was the reaction of American lawyer and humanist Robert Ingersoll: "When I became convinced that the Universe is natural—that all the ghosts and gods are myths, there entered into my brain, into my soul, into every drop of my blood, the sense, the feeling, the joy of freedom."[11]

For some the response was not a one-time conversion to unbelief but a lifelong negotiation. Russian writer Leo Tolstoy was raised in the Russian Orthodox Church but abandoned religion as a student. Such light-hearted apostasy was, he said, the usual practice among people of his social group. It may have seemed normal at the time, but looking back later he realized that it "had never before happened that the rich, ruling and more educated minority" of a country not only rejected "the existing religion but was convinced that no religion at all is any more needed."[12] Tolstoy passed several years in fashionable dissolution and then became an army officer. His sketches and stories about the Crimean War made his literary reputation. Hanging out with fellow writers in St. Petersburg, he thought of himself as a priest of the religion of literature, a role he found both "pleasant and profitable." Between 1863 and 1878 he wrote and published *War and Peace* and *Anna Karenina*, at once taking his place among the greatest literary figures of the day. But at this moment of triumph he experienced a crisis. Tormented by questions about himself, his family, his projects, and his ambitions, he found no answers but felt that the questions "had to be answered at once, and if I did not answer them it was impossible to live." He searched through books on science, philosophy, Eastern religions, and Christianity. Nothing helped for long. He turned his thoughts to God, but the God of Christian theology—a being "detached from the world and from me"—left him cold. He fell into despair and thought about killing himself.[13]

At length he found solace in the God of the peasants, a God of peace, love, and redemption. He returned to the Orthodox Church but remained dissatisfied. The beliefs of the peasantry were less repellant than those of the priesthood but they still contained a great deal of falsehood. He therefore took it upon himself to discover and promote the central truths of Christianity. Basing himself on the Sermon on the Mount, he identified Jesus' five great commandments—avoid anger, be chaste, take no oaths, do not return violence for violence, love and do good to all—and tried to follow them as best he could. He looked on Jesus as a great moral teacher, not a supernatural visitant. God, who was Spirit, Love, and the Source of all, was "in me and I in Him." The right way of approaching this God was prayer—"not public prayer in churches" but private, individual prayer, by which one acknowledged one's "dependence solely on the will of God." Tolstoy wrote this credo in 1901, a short time after a synod of the Orthodox Church had excommunicated him.[14]

Tolstoy was not the only late-nineteenth-century thinker who concluded that the only true religion was that of the free individual. Recall Walt Whitman's comment to Horace Traubel in 1891: "Here is a world of individuals, each with some fresh, peculiar demonstration of it [spirituality]. Whose is to count—or all?" Four years later American reform rabbi Solomon Schindler said in an address to the Free Religious Association: "The happiest state will come to pass ... when each individual will be allowed to formulate his own ideas regarding the universe and his position in and relation to it." The goal was not a single universal religion, but "as many millions of religions as there will be individuals." The same year Vivekananda told an audience in New York: "Would to God that religions multiplied until every man had his own religion, quite separate from that of any other!"[15]

These statements of the early 1890s are evidence of an unparalleled development in the history of religion: the birth of radically individualistic systems of thought and practice. Academic sociologists, who theorized that religion was a purely social phenomenon, sat up and took note. Georg Simmel observed that from the turn of the twentieth century many individuals began to "find satisfaction for their religious needs in mysticism," by which he meant "an indefinite expansiveness of religious emotion," free from dogma and dependence on outer forms. As a sociologist, he found this difficult to understand, since religion, as he saw it, required external form. But he thought it might be different in the future. Formal religion (*Religion*) might eventually be replaced by pure religiousness (*Religiosität*), an "all-embracing, spontaneous process of life" that was not satisfied with external forms or activities.[16] This distinction between religion and religiousness was similar to the religion/spirituality distinction of contemporary anglophone writers, such a American humanist Felix Adler, who wrote that spirituality was "a quality of soul" that had no necessary connection with any religion or philosophy, and Indian philosopher Sri Aurobindo, who said that religion was interesting "only in proportion as it identifies itself with this [inner, affirmative] spirituality."[17] For all these writers, formal religion was a manifestation of something larger: religiousness or spirituality or something else.

Simmel, along with Émile Durkheim and Max Weber, laid the foundations for the academic sociology of religion. All three were concerned with the problems of living in an era when religion had ceased to provide an assured framework of meaning. For each the first step was to determine how religions came into being. Durkheim believed, contra Marx, that it was inconceivable that religious systems, which had played such a crucial role in history, were just "fabrics of illusion." Religions are realities but they are *social* realities, formations of the collective thought of a group that serve to bind the group together. The gods of a given society are simply that society transfigured and expressed in symbolic form. Weber insisted that the nature of a given religion is not "a simple 'function' of the social situation" of a group (Durkheim's position) or a representation of its "ideology" or "material or ideal interest-situation" (Marx's position). What mattered to believers was how their religion met their psychological needs, in particular how it dealt with the questions of justice and salvation. Simmel held that religious entities are forms of social relationships that "when separated from their empirical content, become independent and are projected on substances of their own," as when the son's dependence on the father becomes the theist's worship of a Father-god.[18] To all three thinkers, God and religion were creations of human consciousness within a social framework.

Durkheim, Weber, and Simmel were more interested in description than prescription, but they all proposed remedies for the social ills they diagnosed. Durkheim used the term *anomie* (the lack of agreed-on social norms) to characterize the disjoined state of European life. His solution was the development of "moral individualism"—not an egoistic individualism obsessed with selfish interests but a benign "cult of the individual" that would open the way to a more just social order. Weber spoke of the "disenchantment" of contemporary society, the sense that there are "no mysterious incalculable forces that come into play," and that "one can, in principle, master all things by calculation." This left life devoid of "meanings that go beyond the purely practical and technical," leading to a sense of purposelessness. He offered no clearcut solution. A return to the old religions was possible but retrograde. Simmel wrote about the conflict between the subjective life of the individual and objective cultural forms (religions, philosophies, artworks, inventions). The creators of these forms obtain subjective fulfillment, but the forms, once established, block further creation and inhibit personal growth. This is the "tragedy of culture." The solution is genuine cultivation, in which subjective development accompanies the creation of new objective forms.[19]

The remedies proposed by these three thinkers may be viewed as sociological alternatives to the Christian doctrine of salvation. As academics they were less liable than Comte and Marx to mirror religious dogmas, but they all reverted to religious terminology when they spoke of social redemption. Durkheim sometimes used the Comtian phrase "religion of humanity" as the equivalent of his "moral individualism." The religion of humanity had "everything it needs to speak to its faithful in a no less imperative tone than the [conventional] religions it replaces." Weber declared it was the task of modern intellectuals to translate values into an accessible form, or, in more poetic language, "to sublimate the possession of sacred values into a belief in 'redemption.'" Simmel noted that the collapse of traditional religion opened the way to a singular development: an impulse to replace formal religion by "a religious life that is purely a functional quality of inner life." A "spiritual evolution" was underway that "would make religion into a kind of direct mode of living, not a single melody, so to speak, within the symphony of life, but the key of the entire symphony." Secular life would be permeated with a spiritual consecration that had nothing to do with religion.[20]

Fifteen years before Nietzsche published *Zarathustra*, 26-year-old William James wrote to his friend Oliver Wendell Holmes: "If God is dead, or at least irrelevant, ditto everything pertaining to 'the Beyond.'" James was in Germany recovering from illness and trying to figure out what to do with his life. Although attracted by philosophy, he knew that neither the idealism of Kant nor the utilitarianism of Mill was for him. The world of culture had been undone by Darwin, but it still might be possible to learn from the Stoics the teaching that "Man is his own Providence."[21] A few months later, he returned to the United States and completed his medical studies. His interest in the nervous system led him to psychology and by 1889 he held an endowed chair in the subject at Harvard. The next year he published a textbook, *Principles of Psychology*, that would dominate the field for decades.

The discipline of psychology had been founded in the early nineteenth century by people who hoped that this "science of the soul" would become a means of defending religion from attacks by materialistic science. Starting around 1870 experimental psychologists reformulated the discipline as the science of *mind* and gave their attention to measurable mental and nervous phenomena. James based the *Principles* and *The Varieties of Religious Experience* on empirical data of various sorts and used this data to support his speculations about the nature of consciousness. The *Varieties* became the founding work of the psychology of religion and it remains the bible of those who consider subjective experiences to be the basis of religious belief and practice. There are, as I pointed out in Chapter 1, some problems with this approach. History and anthropology do not confirm that religion has always been based on "the feelings, acts, and experiences of individual men in their solitude." James himself acknowledged that many religious phenomena were "more primordial" than "personal devoutness," but he brushed them aside as magic rather than religion. This was an unconvincing way of getting rid of several millennia of religious history. Another problem was the apparent kinship of religious experiences with psychopathology. James recognized that many religious geniuses had "shown symptoms of nervous instability" and had "been subject to abnormal psychical visitations"—depression, obsessions, and so forth—that usually are regarded as pathological. He felt, as a pragmatist, that if the overall outcome of the experiences was positive, their pathological side could be forgotten.[22] Later psychologists were less indulgent.

Sigmund Freud published *The Interpretation of Dreams* two years before James's *Varieties* came out. When James learned about the Austrian's book, he told a colleague that he suspected "Freud, with his dream theory, of being a regular *halluciné* [crackpot]." Still, he thought it would be best if Freud pushed his theory "to its limits, as undoubtedly it covers some facts, and will add to our understanding of 'functional' psychology."[23] Freud certainly pushed his theory to its limits, introducing a number of ideas that revolutionized the way we look on mental functioning, such as the dynamic unconscious, together with many theoretical constructs that have been abandoned by all but the most fervent of his acolytes. Along the way he formulated a theory of religion that treats beliefs, rituals, and divine beings and forces as products of human wishes and neuroses.

In one of his earliest discussions of religion, Freud wrote that young people often lose their faith after breaking free from parental authority. This led him to conclude that "the roots of the need for religion are in the parental complex" and that "a personal God is, psychologically, nothing but an exalted father."[24] This remained the core of his theory of religion throughout his life. His first full book on the subject, *Totem and Taboo* (1913), was subtitled, startlingly, "Some Points of Agreement between the Mental Lives of Savages and Neurotics." Basing himself on early (and now rejected) theories of totemism, Freud speculated that religion grew out of feelings of remorse that tormented the sons of a primordial father whom they had murdered. Few people outside the tight-knit world of psychoanalysis ever took this seriously.

In *The Future of an Illusion* and *Civilization and Its Discontents*, Freud placed an amended theory of religion at the center of a broad-based critique of Western civilization. The gods are human creations who serve a threefold function: "they must exorcize the terrors of nature, they must reconcile men to the cruelty of Fate, particularly as it is shown in death, and they must compensate them for the sufferings and privations which a civilized life in common has imposed on them." The source of all religious feelings is the sense of helplessness and vulnerability that we all experience as children. Discovering that our fathers are incapable of giving us the security we need, we invent a heavenly Father who has the necessary powers. This act of conjuration has psychological benefits: "By forcibly fixing human beings in a state of psychical infantilism and drawing them into a mass delusion, religion succeeds in saving many of them from individual neurosis." But mass delusion often leads to social conflict and violence. It would be better, Freud thought, to "leave God out altogether and honestly admit the purely human origin of all the regulations and precepts of civilization." Then we will grow up and assume responsibility over our lives.[25]

Despite the enormous differences between James's experience-based approach and Freud's theoretical analysis, the two thinkers agreed that religions are artifacts of psychological activity that answer personal needs. For Freud, religious ideas are illusory fulfillments of "the oldest, strongest, and most urgent wishes of mankind," in particular the desire for security. They survived "because of their incomparable importance for the maintenance of human society." For James, the purpose of religions is to help people come to terms with existential problems. Their truth is their utility: "On account of their extraordinary influence upon action and endurance," they had to be classed "amongst the most important *biological* functions of mankind."[26]

Freud agreed with James that religious experiences were not rare and he did not deny their value to those who had them, but he viewed them in terms of psychopathology and rejected the suggestion that they formed the basis of the historical religions. The significance of an experience for a given individual could not be used to support general claims: "If one man has gained an unshakable conviction of the true reality of religious doctrines from a state of ecstasy which has deeply moved him, of what significance is that to others?" Many fans of James would be surprised to learn that he agreed with Freud on this point: "mystics have no right to claim that we ought to accept the deliverance of their peculiar experiences" or to think the entities they worship are as true for us as they are for them. But James believed that religious experiences could become the basis of "overbeliefs" such as soul and God, and that these beliefs could be transformative. This was the sort of thing Freud scoffed at when he wrote that philosophers (he clearly was thinking of James) had "a tendency to stretch the meaning of words until they retain scarcely anything of their original sense," for instance giving the name God to "some vague abstraction that they have created for themselves," even though God was "now nothing more than an insubstantial shadow."[27] Yet Freud no less than James believed that religion could help individuals become free from psychic pain. A century later their approaches survive in many of the therapies that are important components of modern spirituality. The Freudian approach is subtractive: getting rid of illusory and harmful beliefs. The Jamesian approach is additive: adopting overbeliefs that have pragmatic value.

The vertigo of relativity

The hottest ticket in Paris in May 1913 was for the latest production of the Ballets Russes, *The Rite of Spring*. With music by Igor Stravinsky and choreography by Vaslav Nijinsky, it promised to be as scandalous as Nijinsky's 1912 hit, *The Afternoon of a Faun*, and the Théâtre des Champs-Élysées was packed for the premiere. Theatergoers of Paris were divided between traditionalists, who wanted things sweet and pretty, and modernists, who insisted on novelty for its own sake. Both factions were satisfied by the evening's first offering, the romantic *Les Sylphides*. But from the first notes of *The Rite of Spring*, the audience began to titter. A high-pitched bassoon played a fragment of a folk tune, then wandered here and there, followed meekly by the other wind instruments. As the curtain rose, percussive strings set the rhythm for a dance by an ancient crone and the youths of a Russian village. Soon they were joined by girls in folkloric costumes (not a tutu in sight). Instead of reaching gracefully to the heavens they skittered and whirled and bent toward the ground. Stravinsky's music kept the audience off balance with dissonant chords and a syncopated drumbeat. Hisses and catcalls rang out. Onstage, the head shaman inaugurated a dance of the earth. In the audience the tumult continued. People jeered, cried out, threw punches. In the beginning of the second act, one of the village girls was chosen by fate to be a sacrificial victim. In the presence of the shamans, she danced herself to death. The weirdness of the story, the dissonance of the music, the ungainliness of the dance created an atmosphere that no one in Paris or anywhere else had ever experienced. For the past hundred years, Romanticism had dominated the European art world. *The Rite of Spring* announced start of something new and strange.[28]

The second decade of the twentieth century saw the end of a period of comparative stability and the beginning of an era of political and cultural uncertainty from which we have yet to emerge. World War I shattered Europe's self-confidence and gave the lie to its belief that its qualities and values made it superior to the rest of the world. This loss of self-assurance helped weaken its hold on its African and Asian colonies.

During the same period, the intellectual and cultural foundations of European life began to totter. Einstein's theories of special and general relativity demonstrated that matter and energy are equivalent and that gravity is a property of space–time. Popular presentations of these highly technical theories threw out some astonishing ideas: the movement of time is relative to the observer, time is a fourth dimension. Meanwhile anthropologists were trying to come to terms with a very different sort of relativity. Their fieldwork convinced them that the beliefs and values of every culture had to be viewed within a given framework and that there was no universal standard by which they could be judged. Artists and writers were among the first to play around with these ideas. Avant-garde painters tried to depict the fourth dimension and exchanged their casts of Roman torsos for African ritual masks. Soon people in Paris, London, and New York were plowing through experimental novels and dabbling with sexual freedom. Before long their heads were spinning with what sociologist Peter Berger called the "vertigo of relativity."[29] There seemed to be no solid truths, no certain ethical or aesthetic values. For the most part the denizens of the Main Streets of the world were oblivious of what was going on. But some were deeply concerned. It was no coincidence that the Christian movement known as Fundamentalism took shape around the time that literary and artistic Modernism began to reach the general public.

Before the twentieth century, every artistic era looked up to a transcendent principle. In ages of faith, it was God; during the Enlightenment, Reason; in the Romantic period, Nature or Force. Modernism had no transcendent foundation, no generally accepted standards of beauty and truth. Its artistic landmarks—Stravinsky's *Rite of Spring*, Marcel Duchamp's *Nude Descending a Staircase*, Franz Kafka's *Metamorphosis*, and many others—were like nothing ever seen before. It was as if the Western elite, like Gregor Samsa in Kafka's tale, woke up one morning to find itself trapped in a world that made no sense and from which there was no escape.

Many Modernists saw the advent of the post-theistic world as a chance to devise "spiritual" forms of expression. "When religion, science and morality are shaken, the two last by the strong hand of Nietzsche, and when the outer supports threaten to fall," wrote Russian Modernist painter Wassily Kandinsky, "man turns his gaze from externals in on to himself. Literature, music and art are the first and most sensitive spheres in which this spiritual revolution makes itself felt." Novelist Virginia Woolf said of fellow Modernist James Joyce: "In contrast with those whom we have called materialists [H.G. Wells et al.], Mr. Joyce is spiritual; he is concerned at all costs to reveal the flickerings of that innermost flame which flashes its messages through the brain," disregarding the logical signposts "which for generations have served to support the imagination of a reader when called upon to imagine what he can neither touch nor see."[30]

The spiritualities that Woolf and Kandinsky hinted at were very different from those of Adler and Aurobindo, but all of them shared the defining features of modern spirituality: subjectivity, individuality, the rejection of conventional religion. The same characteristics are found in the work of Modernist poet Wallace Stevens:

> Poetry
> exceeding music must take the place
> Of empty heaven and its hymns

he wrote in *The Man With the Blue Guitar*. Less suggestively but more clearly, he noted in his diary: "After one has abandoned a belief in God, poetry is that essence which takes its place as life's redemption."[31] This is the religion of literature of Balzac and Arnold updated for the post-Nietzschean age.

In the first quarter of the twentieth century, religions around the world were awkwardly poised between two extremes: innovative efforts to harmonize faith with modern life and reactionary attempts to wall off religion from the modern world. Examples of contemporary liberal organizations include the Ahmadiyya Muslim community, which was dedicated to the peaceful propagation of Islam; the Vedanta Society and Ramakrishna Mission, launched by Vivekananda during the 1890s, which promoted Hindu philosophy and community service; the Social Gospel movement of North American Protestants, formalized around 1910, which tried to apply the teachings of Jesus to social problems; and the Association for the Advancement of Buddhism, a reformist movement launched by the Chinese monk Taixu in 1912. Reactionary trends included the Fundamentalist movement among American Protestants, which took form during the second decade of the century; the purist form of Salafi Islam, which developed around the same period; and the Hindutva or Hinduness movement, which was formalized by an Indian writer in 1923.

"Fundamentalism" was first used as a positive self-description by hyper-conservative American Protestants in 1920. They held that nineteenth-century liberal theology had done great harm to the fundamentals of Christianity, such as belief in the inerrancy of the Bible. Around the same time, Pope Pius X issued a series of pronouncements to combat liberal trends in Catholicism. One of them included an Oath against Modernism that all members of the clergy had to swear to. The Salafi movement, which contends that Muslims must follow practices current during the lifetime of Muhammad and the first three generations of his followers, took hold in Arabia after the defeat of the Ottoman empire in World War I. Among the practices Salafists forbade were *dhikr* or meditation, the veneration of saints, and the use of philosophy to interpret Quranic texts. All fundamentalists—Protestant, Catholic, and Muslim—were opposed to any form of life that smacked of modernism and relativism.

By the beginning of the twentieth century, philosophy had ceased to be a major force in public intellectual culture. Two of its traditional areas of interest—the nature of the universe and the nature of human beings—had been usurped by the physical and social sciences. Virtually all philosophers worked in universities, writing technical papers in which they traded blows with other philosophers. At the turn of the century the field was held by Hegelian idealists, who built enormous metaphysical systems out of intangible abstractions. In the Anglo-American world the rising school was the analytic philosophy of Bertrand Russell and others, which was antimetaphysical, naturalistic, and aggressively atheistic. A handful of thinkers bucked both trends, trying in different ways to bring philosophy and spirituality together.

From his youth, the Spanish-born American George Santayana was convinced that works of imagination, such as poetry, art, and religion, were what gave value to life. By means of these activities, humans are in search of an ideal of perfection that some of them call, for lack of a better word, "God." Religion is the worship of this ideal. It operates through two channels: "piety" and "spirituality." The former looks back to the traditions from which we come, the latter "to the end toward which we move." We achieve spirituality in moments of heightened awareness when we view existence "merely as a vehicle for contemplation, and contemplation merely as a vehicle for joy."[32] There are echoes here of the therapeutic philosophies of the Stoics and Epicureans and of the aesthetic gospel of Schopenhauer.

Santayana was one of the most influential English-language philosophers of the first half of the twentieth century. Today he is almost completely forgotten. A similar fate has overtaken three philosophers who published their main metaphysical works between 1914 and 1929: Sri Aurobindo, Samuel Alexander, and Alfred North Whitehead. Starting from different assumptions, each of them concluded that evolution is not a mere biological process but a cosmic movement leading from matter to life and mind and ultimately to a higher spiritual order.

Educated in England, Aurobindo was familiar with nineteenth-century evolutionary theory when he discovered the Upanishads. Like the authors of those texts, he held that Reality was *brahman*, but he also envisaged a hierarchy of conscious powers that emerge in the course of evolution. Mind is the highest power attained so far. Above mind is supermind, a principle that "exists, acts and proceeds in the fundamental truth and unity of things and not like the mind in their appearances and phenomenal divisions." When viewed as the power that manifests the universe, supermind is "the truth of that which we call God," but this "God" has nothing to do with the "personal and limited Deity ... of the ordinary occidental conception." Alexander began his career as an idealist in the Hegelian mold but he came to think that idealism could not account for the evolutionary emergence of new qualities. He theorized that there is a "nisus" or urge within space-time that has "borne its creatures through matter and life to mind," and "will bear them forward to some higher level of existence." He used the word "deity" to signify "the next higher quality to the highest attained," and "God" for "the whole universe engaged in process towards the emergence of this new quality." Trained as a mathematician, Whitehead helped lay the foundations of analytic philosophy with *Principia Mathematica*, coauthored with his former student Bertrand Russell. Around 1920 Whitehead turned to the philosophy of science and then to metaphysics. In *Religion in Making* he wrote that the universe has two opposite movements: "on one side it is physically wasting, on the other side it is spiritually ascending." The ascent is moving with immeasurable slowness to "new creative conditions" in which the physical world as we know it will cease to be. What will remain are the "realm of abstract forms," "creativity," and "God, upon whose wisdom all forms of order depend."[33]

All three of these thinkers used the word "God," but none of them were theists in the ordinary sense of the term and all of them rejected institutional religion. Whitehead wrote that science helped clear the way for the "spirituality of religion" by getting rid of the Church's medieval fantasies about the universe. This made it possible for modern people to participate in "spiritual adventures—adventures of thought, adventures of passionate feeling, adventures of aesthetic experience." He offered few details about what these adventures might be. Alexander too had little to say about the nature of spiritual practice except to suggest that it ought to include "discovery of truth and creation of beauty." Aurobindo, in contrast, wrote more about *yoga* or spiritual practice than about metaphysical theory. "The generalisation of Yoga in humanity," he said in *The Synthesis of Yoga*, would lead to a harmonious development of all the powers of the human being—physical, vital, mental, and supramental—and in the end open the way to "the higher evolution, the second birth, the spiritual existence" on earth.[34]

By the time that Aurobindo, Alexander, and Whitehead published their theories, analytic philosophy had taken possession of the anglophone philosophical world. This logic- and science-based approach left no room for spiritual practice or even metaphysical speculation. Ironically, a key figure of the analytic trend, Austrian philosopher Ludwig Wittgenstein not only laid the groundwork for the atheistic school of logical positivism but also pointed to a "mystical" sphere beyond logic and language.

Wittgenstein went to England in 1908 to study aeronautics but while there fell under the spell of pure mathematics and logic. In 1911 he paid a visit to Cambridge to exchange ideas with Russell, then a leading figure in both fields. At first put off, Russell eventually accepted the eccentric Austrian as his student. The two worked together for about a year. Russell conceded the force of some of Wittgenstein's criticisms and hoped the younger man would "solve the problems I am too old to solve." In 1914 Wittgenstein enlisted in the Austrian army. While serving on the Eastern Front he read Tolstoy's *Gospel in Brief*. Although an unbeliever, he was moved by Jesus' moral teachings. Around the same time he began work on *Tractatus Logico-Philosophicus*, a book that examined the fundamentals of language but, according to Wittgenstein, was basically about ethics, a subject hardly mentioned in the text.[35]

The *Tractatus* is a densely written, difficult work. Briefly stated, its aim is to describe the relationship between language and reality. According to Wittgenstein, a sentence or proposition represents a state of affairs by being a picture or model of it. Some propositions cannot be pictured, however, for instance those having to do with ethics, aesthetics, and religion. The business of science is to raise questions and provide answers about states of affairs, but it can only go so far. "We feel that even when all *possible* scientific questions have been answered, the problems of life remain completely untouched," Wittgenstein wrote at the end of the *Tractatus*. "The solution of the problem of life is seen in the vanishing of the problem." The right approach is "to say nothing except what can be said" and to accept that certain things cannot be spoken of.[36]

Wittgenstein finished the *Tractatus* in 1918. Satisfied he had in principle disposed of all philosophical problems, he spent a decade in nonphilosophical pursuits, such as teaching in an elementary school and designing a house. In 1929 he returned to Cambridge, where he initiated a new approach to philosophy that undermined much of what he had said in the *Tractatus*. The main work of this later period is *Philosophical Investigations*, published posthumously in 1953. In it, as in the *Tractatus*, he attempted to solve philosophical problems by a careful analysis of language. But he rejected his earlier belief that language has a timeless essence. Rather it is embedded in human social practices, which he called "language games." The meaning of an expression is not (as he had said in the *Tractatus*) its relationship to a fixed state of affairs but its varying use in one of many language games. This view took him away from the idea of absolute truth toward a sort of linguistic and philosophical relativism. There is, he said, "not *a* philosophical method, though there are indeed methods, like different therapies."[37]

Similes of therapy and healing are found throughout Wittgenstein's later work. In *Philosophical Investigations* he aphorized: "The philosopher's treatment of a question is like the treatment of an illness." In a manuscript of 1944 he noted: "People are religious to the extent that they believe themselves to be not so much *imperfect* as *sick*." Such tropes bring to mind the therapeutic metaphors of Epicureanism, Stoicism, and Skepticism and the parables of healing in the New Testament. It does not follow that Wittgenstein practiced a therapeutic philosophy or religion. "I am not a religious man," he once told a friend, "but I cannot help seeing every problem from a religious point of view." The sort of problems he spent his life exploring were those created by language. This was the thrust of his philosophical work. But he also struggled with ethical problems and connected his idea of ethical value with subjective experiences, such as an overwhelming feeling he summed up in the phrase: "I wonder at the existence of the world."[38] Wittgenstein was not a mystic but he did not close the door to the mystical side of life.

Wittgenstein's work on logic and language made him the most influential twentieth-century philosopher in the Anglo-American tradition. Most thinkers however have ignored his work on ethics and religion. Taking their cues from Russell's mathematical logic and Wittgenstein's *Tractatus*, members of the Vienna Circle (1924–1936) developed an approach called logical positivism that tried to rid philosophy of metaphysical conundrums through the strict application of logic and the scientific method. They accepted Wittgenstein's observation that propositions that could not be stated clearly were nonsense, but disregarded his further point that "What we cannot speak about we must pass over in silence."[39] Thus they did not hesitate to say that the meaningless idea "God" had no place in intellectual discourse. As English logical positivist A.J. Ayer put it in *Language, Truth and Logic* (1936): "To say that 'God exists' is to make a metaphysical utterance which cannot be either true or false." It followed that "no sentence which purports to describe the nature of a transcendent god can possess any literal significance." The only comfort Ayer could offer theists was to say that theistic assertions, while definitely not valid, "cannot be invalid either." They are just empty verbiage and no purpose would be served by trying to prove them false.[40]

At the time Ayer wrote, most philosophers in Europe and America considered themselves atheists or agnostics. Few felt it necessary to justify their unbelief. Intellectuals in the Anglo-American world were happy to ignore the question of God, which had no bearing on the practical problems of life. Intellectuals on the European Continent were more likely to be concerned by the challenge posed by Nietzsche a half-century earlier: Now that God was dead, now that there was no transcendental basis of truth and value, how could people continue to go about their lives? During the 1940s a school of philosophy arose in France that drew "all of the conclusions inferred by a consistently atheistic point of view."[41] It was known as existentialism and its leading figure was Jean-Paul Sartre.

While still a student, Sartre reflected that there had never been a truly great philosophy of atheism. All the major philosophers were religious in one way or another. What was needed, he thought, was "a philosophy of the human being in a material world," a philosophy that had no use for God.[42] As a young academic in the 1930s, he was captivated by a new philosophical approach called phenomenology. Briefly, phenomenology concerns itself with objects and events—in technical language "phenomena"—as they appear to our consciousness and not as realities in themselves. Edmund Husserl, the founder of the school, suggested that we should "bracket" the question of the existence of the natural world in order to give our attention to the structures of consciousness. His student Martin Heidegger grew critical of this approach. We cannot separate ourselves from the world, he said, because we are from birth involved in a network of preexisting objects and events. If we want to do philosophy we must do it as living beings in the world. It was this that excited Sartre. Philosophy is not about constructing abstract theories. It is about thinking and acting in the physical world.

As Europe lurched toward war at the end of the 1930s, Sartre saw from up close that theoretical philosophy would no longer do. He reflected that at another pivotal moment in the history of the West, the people of Athens turned from Aristotle's metaphysics to the practical philosophies of the Stoics and Epicureans, who "taught them to *live*." In a similar way Sartre turned to Heidegger, who gave him the tools he needed "to understand History and my destiny."[43] Drafted into the army in 1939, he was captured after the fall of France and lodged in a German prison camp. There he read Heidegger's *Being and Time*, a ponderous tome in which the author developed his existential phenomenology (as opposed to the transcendental phenomenology of Husserl). After his release in 1941, Sartre worked on *Being and Nothingness*, his own ponderous presentation of existential phenomenology or existentialism. After the war, he summarized its fundamentals in a lecture that made him the most famous philosopher of the day. The first principle of existentialism, Sartre said, is that the human being "is nothing other than what he makes of himself." The existing human being is more real than any philosophical or theological essence, such as the Platonic idea of the Good or the Christian idea of God. Human beings must define themselves through freely chosen acts. Even if God existed (and Sartre was certain that he did not) it would make no difference. All that was important was for man "to rediscover himself and to comprehend that nothing can save him from himself, not even valid proof of the existence of God."[44] No one would call Sartre a spiritual figure, but his subjective viewpoint, his rejection of established religion, and his insistence on individual engagement made him a harbinger of certain strands of modern nontheistic spirituality.

The two World Wars that made the twentieth century the most violent and destructive in history were largely the consequences of rival nationalisms and imperialisms. Nationalism is a complex subject and it is beyond the scope of this book to examine it in depth. Here we are concerned with the fraught relationship between nationalism and religion. When the nation and religion both are strong, the bond between them is one of mutual interest. A classic example was the partnership between the European imperial powers and the Christian churches. When religion is dominant it suppresses the growth of nationalism, as the papacy did in Italy before 1870. When the nation is strong and religion weak, nationalism often takes the place of religious belief. As German writer Thomas Mann explained in 1918: "The human being is so formed that having lost metaphysical religion, he puts the religious element into the social sphere, elevates social life to religious consecration" and dreams of a better world that never comes.[45] Mann was thinking not only of the national cults that set the European powers at one another's throats in 1914, but also of transnational social gospels such as communism, which in theory are at odds with the nation-state but in practice engender extreme forms of nationalism.

Secular religion took its most radical forms in the communist Soviet Union and the hypernationalistic regimes of Italy, Germany, and Japan. Invoking the Marxist doctrine of the dictatorship of the proletariat, Vladimir Lenin and other Soviet leaders established a cult of the state that penetrated every aspect of life. Atheism was one of its founding principles: "Religion is the opium of the people—this dictum by Marx is the cornerstone of the whole Marxist outlook on religion," Lenin wrote. But he also said (citing Friedrich Engels) that it would be counterproductive for the Communist Party to declare open war on religion. The right way to get rid of it was to hasten the victory of scientific socialism.[46] For many of Lenin's followers this approach was too tame. During the 1920s two antireligious groups coalesced into the League of Militant Atheists, which spearheaded a drive to convert workers and peasants to atheism. Attempts at persuasion gave way to targeted killings of priests and monks and eventually to mass murder. This was just one example of how believers in the godless ideologies of the twentieth century could be just as deadly as religious fanatics.

Italian Fascism and German National Socialism took hold during the economic and political turmoil that followed World War I. Both drew on nineteenth-century ethnic nationalism but stripped it of its democratic veneer. Times were hard and the endangered nation needed powerful leaders. Benito Mussolini and Adolf Hitler became foci of political religions that had many of the features of traditional faiths: sacred texts (*The Doctrine of Fascism, My Struggle*), group rituals (parades, rallies), sacred symbols (the fasces, the swastika), an elite corps with special dress (the Blackshirts, the SS), links to a glorious past (the Roman Empire, the Teutonic Knights), a chosen-people myth with historical enemies (the Slavs, the Jews), and historical injustices that had to be resolved (irredentism, Lebensraum).

Both Mussolini (who in his youth was an outspoken atheist) and Hitler (who was never a devout believer) were happy to cut deals with the Church when it suited their purposes, and the Church was glad to reciprocate. In 1929 Mussolini signed a treaty with the Holy See granting territorial concessions to the Vatican in exchange for its public support. "Italy has been given back to God, and God to

Italy," proclaimed the official Vatican newspaper after the treaty was promulgated.⁴⁷ Four years later, after Hitler came to power, the German government signed a concordat with the Holy See making it obligatory for Catholic priests to swear an oath of loyalty to the state. Later, as Nazism permeated every aspect of life, most German Protestant denominations constituted themselves into the openly pro-Hitler Protestant Reich Church.

In Japan, the leaders of all Buddhist sects, not omitting Zen, supported the country's military expansion during and after World War I. A document issued in July 1937 justified the Japanese invasion of China as an expression of "the great benevolence and compassion of Buddhism" intended to establish "eternal peace in East Asia." Five months later Japanese soldiers annihilated the Chinese defenders of Nanking and took part in unprovoked massacre and mass rape of Chinese civilians. Other abominations followed. The support of the clergy contributed to the rise of the extreme religious nationalism known as Imperial-Way Buddhism. "To venerate the Three Treasures [of Buddhism] means to revere Imperial edicts without question," wrote a backer of this doctrine in 1938. Japanese soldiers and civilians continued to obey the Emperor's edicts until their country was reduced to rubble.⁴⁸

The 1930s and 1940s were a period of darkness for conventional religion, but there were a few scattered patches of light. After Hitler rose to power in 1933, Lutheran pastor Dietrich Bonhoeffer spoke publicly against him and his anti-Semitic policies and was active in the Confessing Church that opposed the pro-Nazi Protestant Reich Church. Later he made contact with the German resistance movement and in 1943 was arrested and imprisoned. While awaiting trial he wrote a series of letters in which he speculated on the future of Christianity in a godless world. "We are moving toward a completely religionless time," he observed in April 1944. People had to confront the possibility that "the Western form of Christianity, too, was only a preliminary stage to a complete absence of religion." If this is what the future held, "what kind of situation emerges for us, for the church?" Could Christ "become the lord of the religionless as well? Are there religionless Christians?"⁴⁹ Bonhoeffer was executed in April 1945. His letters, published six years later, made him a pivotal figure in the development of late-twentieth-century godless Christianity.

Another German theologian who foresaw a post-theistic future was Paul Tillich. Dismissed from his position at the University of Frankfurt after Hitler came to power, he emigrated to the United States, where he became a prominent theologian and well-known writer. In *The Courage to Be* (1952), he tried to salvage the God-idea by proposing a "God above the God of theism." The "God of theological theism," he wrote, is a being among other beings, not Being-in-itself. This God of theism deprives us of our subjectivity, and we are bound to revolt against him, for he is a tyrant on the model of the Axis dictators. Our frustration with this God is "the deepest root of atheism"—an atheism that "is justified as the reaction against theological theism"—and also the root of the anxiety and sense of meaninglessness that are the primary symptoms of the malaise of modern life. To human beings, God is "ultimate concern," something that transcends both subjectivity and objectivity, but in himself God is "being-itself, not *a* being." It therefore is just as "atheistic to affirm the existence of God as it is to deny it." It is no surprise that Tillich's critics complained that he was just as atheistic as the existentialist philosophers by whom he was influenced.[50]

The writings of Bonhoeffer and Tillich served as inspirations for a group of American theologians who formulated a set of teachings that came to be known as Death of God theology. *Time* magazine published an article on this movement and on contemporary religion in general in its issue of April 8, 1966. The cover asked in huge red letters: "Is God Dead?" The author explained that the God whose death was widely reported was the personal God of the Bible. Tillich's impersonal "Ground of Being" and the God whose voice is heard "in the inner murmurings of the heart" might be still alive. But no one knew for sure.[51]

Godlessness and God today

Don Cupitt became a priest in the Church of England in 1960. Five years later he was elected to a fellowship at Emmanuel College, Cambridge, where he taught philosophy of religion for three decades. His early books attracted little attention, but with *Taking Leave of God* (1980) he became well known as a proponent of nontheistic spirituality within a Christian framework. According to Cupitt, "The Christian doctrine of God just is Christian spirituality in coded form, for God is a symbol that represents to us everything that spirituality requires of us and promises to us." Theism—the belief in a creator God—does not matter as much as religious people think: "What matters is spirituality; and a modern spirituality must be a spirituality for a fully-unified, autonomous human consciousness." Striking at the root of Christian belief, Cupitt wrote: "Christ's birth and death have no saving power and are of no religious interest" in themselves. "They become divine and saving only in their subjective appropriation" by believing Christians. The same is true of other points of doctrine. Moses did not receive the Ten Commandments from an objectively existing supernatural being on an objectively existing mountain. What he and other prophets aspired for was to have the will of God "written within one's heart as an immanent or internalized commandment." (One wonders how Cecil B. DeMille would have handled this.) In his life as a priest, Cupitt met many people who were "quietly agnostic or sceptical about Christian supernatural *doctrines*, while nevertheless continuing to practice the Christian *religion* to strikingly good effect." This description could be taken to apply to

Cupitt himself. During the 1990s he stopped presiding over public worship and in 2008 ceased to be a communicant member of the Church of England, but he remains active as a spiritual writer and speaker.[52]

I have a vague recollection of seeing the "Is God Dead?" issue of *Time* on the newsstand in April 1966. My reaction was something like, "Yes, I suppose He is, but who cares?" I have a much clearer recollection of listening again and again to the Beatles' album *Revolver*, which was released a few months later. I was intrigued by lines like "Lay down all thoughts, surrender to the Void," without realizing that this was John Lennon's take on Timothy Leary's take on a Tibetan Buddhist text as translated by an American Theosophist. I was then in my first year of college and thoroughly uninterested in the courses I was taking. To crawl through *Paradise Lost* seemed to be a complete waste of time. More to my taste was a guest appearance by Beat poet Allen Ginsberg, who intoned his adaptation of Shunryu Suzuki's translation of the *Heart Sutra*. The next day in philosophy class, my professor said scornfully that the line "True because not false" was the height of absurdity, but it seemed to make a lot of sense to me.

I dropped out of college after a couple of years and went to New York to learn yoga and meditation. In this I was following the example of the Beatles and hundreds of other Westerners who had begun to get interested in Asian religions. I was fascinated by books like the Upanishads and *Bhagavad Gita*, and bought into the idea, purveyed by Western scholars and Western-oriented swamis, that gods like Krishna and Shiva were just aspects of the formless Brahman or Absolute. (I was shocked when an Indian engineer told me: "You want to know if people who go to temples are worshipping the idols? Believe me, they are.") I took Sanskrit lessons from a Brahmin of Maharashtra. (I was shocked that he kept copies of *Playboy* on his coffee table.) I stayed at a yoga center in New York and a sort of ashram in the Catskills. I was, in short, a spiritual-but-not-religious person who was getting involved in an Eastern religion on the assumption that Eastern religions were not really religions but rather "ways of life."

Around this time the phrase "The New Age" began to make the rounds. I didn't know then that it had a long history, going back at least as far as William Blake. By 1970 it had become a label applied by journalists and marketers to various manifestations of the 1960s counterculture: pop esotericism, dietary fashions, and spiritual (but not religious!) paths such as Sufism, Yoga, and Zen. Living in the recently rebranded East Village, I was right in the middle of this cultural bazaar. I believed that my choices were mine and mine alone, but they also were expressions of widespread trends: superficially, a bundle of lifestyle preferences (long hair, blue jeans, rock music, and so forth); more deeply, a major societal shift that scholars had begun to discuss under the name of "secularization."

Sociologists had been studying the transformation of religious into secular patterns of behavior since the late nineteenth century. By the 1960s the velocity of change was so great that secularization became a special topic of study. In *The Sacred Canopy* Peter Berger defined it as "the process by which sectors of society and culture are removed from the domination of religious institutions and symbols." Although apparent all over the world it was especially evident in the modern West. And because the world was becoming more and more Westernized, it seemed probable that secularization would soon become a universal phenomenon. In 1968 Berger declared in a *New York Times* interview: "by the 21st century, religious believers are likely to be found only in small sects, huddled together to resist a worldwide secular culture." He was obliged to recant after a decade or two. The rise of Islamic fundamentalism, the spread of evangelical Christianity, and the emergence of revivalist movements among Hindus and Buddhists made it obvious that secularization would not be as quick or as complete as previously thought. By 2002 Berger had made a complete U-turn: "Our age is *not* an age of secularization," he wrote. "On the contrary, it is an age of exuberant religiosity, much of it in the form of passionate movements with global outreach."[53] This seems to me as unbalanced as his 1968 prediction.

Secularization unquestionably is on the rise in Europe, Australasia, and even the United States (the most religious of the developed nations). An often-cited survey published by the Pew Research Center in 2012 found that "one-fifth of the U.S. public—and a third of adults under 30—are religiously unaffiliated." These "nones" (people who said they were "none of the above") included 33 million adults who reported no particular religious affiliation and 13 million atheists and agnostics. But most nones were "religious or spiritual in some way," two-thirds saying that they believed in God, more than half feeling "a deep connection with nature and the earth," and more than a third (roughly 17 million people) regarding themselves as "spiritual but not religious."[54] Three years later, according to another Pew survey, the nones had risen from just under 20 to just under 23 percent of the US population. During the same period the percentage belonging to each of the major divisions of American Christianity (evangelical Protestantism, mainline Protestantism, and Catholicism) declined.[55] It would be hard to conclude from these statistics that our age is one of "exuberant religiosity," at least in many parts of the United States.

What about the rest of the world? According to Pew's 2015 report "The Future of World Religions: Population Growth Percentage, 2010–2050," in 2010 more than 1.1 billion people, around 16 percent of the world's population, were unaffiliated with any religion. By 2050 the number of unaffiliated is expected to rise to more than 1.2 billion. Nones will form the largest group in countries such as France, the Netherlands, and New Zealand. In the United States they will constitute 26 percent of the adult population, which means there will be 100 million unaffiliated Americans in 2050. During the 1950s there were around 3 million. The projected growth of 3 to 100 million between 1950 and 2050 makes it look like the nones will soon inherit the earth—but demographers tell a different tale.[56]

The absolute number of nones in the world will increase between now and 2050 but their share of the global population will *drop* from 16 to 13 percent. There is a simple explanation for this. The nones are currently concentrated in regions of low fertility such as Europe, North America, and Australasia. Regions of high fertility and high percentage of youth population, such as Africa and the Middle East, are highly religious, and believers in these regions will increase rapidly between now and 2050. The nones, currently in third place overall (behind Christians and Muslims), will be pushed down one rank by Hindus, who will number almost 1.4 billion in 2050. Meanwhile the two great missionary monotheisms will be contending for the top spot. Muslims, now a half-billion fewer than Christians, will almost have caught up by 2050, accounting for around 30 percent of the world's population.[57] The nones are on the rise but in most parts of the world the monotheists are rising faster. What then is the long-term significance of secularization?

Before 1600 almost everyone was affiliated with a religion. In contemporary language, the percentage of nones was close to zero. Now there are hundreds of millions of people spread throughout the world who live without religion. However you look at it (approvingly, condemningly, indifferently) this is a historically significant development. For millennia the structure of all the world's cultures was based on the assumption of a supernatural order of being that almost everyone accepted. To publicly question this superhuman order meant to cut oneself off from the support of one's family, community, and country. In many cultures the punishment for apostasy was imprisonment or exile or death. Now you can broadcast your disbelief in God on television or YouTube and hardly anyone will care. At least in the Western world: don't try it in Saudi Arabia or Iran or Pakistan or Bangladesh.

In many parts of Asia and Africa, being an atheist can be dangerous. People suspected of harboring unorthodox views in Saudi Arabia and Pakistan are liable to be tried as blasphemers and executed if found guilty (the most likely outcome). Even in comparatively liberal Muslim states such as Egypt and Indonesia, unbelievers live in fear of persecution or social exclusion. In nominally secular countries such as Bangladesh and India, individuals sometimes take it upon themselves to murder "rationalists" or atheists.

The situation is quite different in most parts of Europe and North America, where atheists and agnostics constitute a significant percentage of the population. Indeed, atheism is so prevalent in some countries, Sweden for instance, that people who go to church are considered "slightly weird."[58] Unbelief is especially entrenched among scientists and other academics. According to a 2009 Pew survey, only 33 percent of American scientists believed in God. More tellingly, a 1998 survey of elite scientists (members of the American Academy of Sciences) found that only 7 percent accepted a personal God.[59] Philosophers show similar levels of unbelief. A 2009 survey by the online index PhilPapers found that 73 percent of philosophers in North America, Europe, and Australasia accepted or were inclined to atheism, while only 15 percent accepted or were inclined to theism.[60]

Despite the prevalence of nonbelief, there is still much prejudice against atheists in certain parts of the West, notably the United States. The main cause of this is a nagging fear that atheists cannot be moral. This fear is not supported by sociological data, which indicate that by most positive and negative measures (e.g., altruism on the one hand, alcoholism on the other) nonbelievers are at least as moral as believers. To get this point across to the general population, American humanist organizations have publicized the slogan "MILLIONS ARE GOOD WITHOUT GOD." In Britain the Atheist Bus Campaign put wheels on their motto "THERE'S PROBABLY NO GOD. NOW STOP WORRYING AND ENJOY YOUR LIFE." Throughout the Western world, atheists and humanists are forming communities of likeminded people. Wishing "to do something like church but without God," two British atheists started the Sunday Assembly in 2013.[61] Now the organization has seventy branches in Europe, North America, and Australasia. Smaller groups with similar aims exist on college campuses and in cities and towns throughout the world. Many such groups offer secular alternatives to ceremonies such as weddings and funerals. Others provide places for unbelievers to get together and talk about matters of mutual interest. Some hold their meetings in deconsecrated churches, of which Europe has a huge number.

In the years that followed the September 11 attacks a number of books harshly critical of religion were published in the United States and Britain. The media dubbed the authors of these books the New Atheists. This was a misnomer, since none of their arguments were new. Most of what the writers said were twenty-first-century versions of scientific, philosophical, and historical arguments that have been around since the Enlightenment. If there is anything new about some of the New Atheists it is their willingness to acknowledge the ethical and aesthetic value of the spiritual approach to life. "There is clearly a sacred dimension to our existence, and coming to terms with it could well be the highest purpose of human life," wrote neuroscientist Sam Harris in *The End of Faith* (2004). He added however that there was no need to believe in "untestable propositions" such as God in order to do this. British biologist Richard Dawkins, who savaged all religions in his bestselling *The God Delusion* (2006), remarked in a 2010 television interview: "Spirituality can mean something that I'm very sympathetic to, which is, a sort of sense of wonder at the beauty of the universe, the complexity of life, the magnitude of space, the magnitude of geological time. All those things create a sort of frisson in the breast, which you could call spirituality." He insisted however that spirituality in this sense "shouldn't be confused with supernaturalism."[62]

In Chapter 6 and the first two sections of this chapter I spoke of cultural activities—philosophy, literature, art, psychotherapy—that for many took the place of religions during the nineteenth and twentieth centuries. These activities serve the same purpose for millions of people today. Most contemporary philosophers, writers, artists, and psychotherapists have little explicit interest in spirituality, but some have attempted to bridge the gulf between the secular and spiritual domains. Philosophers such as André Comte-Sponville, Thomas Nagel, and Ronald Dworkin, whose work I discussed in Chapter 1, commend the religious or spiritual approach to life while remaining convinced atheists. Other prominent thinkers have looked for ways to extend philosophical enquiry beyond linguistic and logical analysis. Jürgen Habermas, a leading defender of Enlightenment values, wrote that reason fails to serve its purpose if it does not awaken in the minds of secular people "an awareness of the violations of solidarity throughout the world, an awareness of what is missing, of what cries out to heaven." Michel Foucault, a critic of the Enlightenment project, looked back to Greco-Roman philosophy for examples of "technologies of the self" that could be applied to modern life.[63]

Shortly before his death in 2007, American philosopher Richard Rorty said that he shared with literary critics such as Matthew Arnold and Harold Bloom "the hope for a religion of literature, in which works of the secular imagination replace Scripture as the principle source of inspiration and hope for each new generation." Arnold and Bloom turned mostly to the great names of the past—Homer, Dante, Shakespeare et al.—although Bloom also endorsed Modernist writers such as Joyce and Stevens. Rorty held that all literary canons are temporary and all touchstones (Arnold's term) replaceable. The important thing is the ability of literary works to provide inspiration, by which he meant their power to make people recontextualize their lives.[64]

The religions of art and literature now have votaries on every continent. "One of the most compelling, if uncategorizable, intellectual tendencies of the twentieth century," wrote Mexican novelist Carlos Fuentes in 2002, was that of "religious temperament without religious faith." He was thinking specifically of the famously atheistic film director Luis Buñuel, but also mentioned, almost at random, French writers François Mauriac and Albert Camus and British novelist Graham Green. He might easily have included D.H. Lawrence, Aldous Huxley, Iris Murdoch, and (among living writers) Jonathan Franzen, who wrote of himself as a reader: "fiction is my religion." Similar lists could be made of twentieth-century painters (Piet Mondrian, Robert Motherwell, Mark Rothko), composers (Dmitri Shostakovich, Karlheinz Stockhausen, Philip Glass), and others in different fields. Motherwell exaggerated the importance of his métier when he wrote "it is the artists who guard the spiritual in the modern world," but there is no doubt that artists, writers, and musicians have done much to keep spirituality alive since the death of God.[65]

Few twentieth-century thinkers have had more impact on the way modern people understand themselves than Freud, yet by the end of the century Freudian psychoanalysis had largely been replaced by a smorgasbord of new theories, some of which have a spiritual component. A turning point was the launch of humanistic psychology in the mid-1960s. Abraham Maslow, the chief theoretician of the school, proposed a hierarchy of human needs with physiological well-being at the bottom and self-actualization at the top. Once their basic needs have been assured, people look for ways to achieve their full potential. Maslow was an atheist but he felt that the development of spiritual values was necessary for a complete humanity. "I want to demonstrate," he wrote, "that spiritual values have naturalistic meaning, that they are not the exclusive possession of organized churches, that they do not need supernatural concepts to validate them, that they are well within the jurisdiction of a suitably enlarged science, and that, therefore, they are the general responsibility of all mankind."[66] With statements like this, he helped popularize the "spiritual but not religious" idea.

The contemporary spiritual scene is so vast and so diverse that I would need another book at least as long as this to cover it adequately. Instead I will look briefly at recent manifestations of some of the religious, philosophical, and spiritual systems I have spoken of in earlier chapters. The three main axial-age religions of India are still alive. Hinduism is the faith of more than a billion people, most in India but some in other Asian countries, not to mention America and Europe. Almost all Hindus are theists. The nontheistic philosophies of Mimamsa and Samkhya are either not practiced or practiced within a theistic framework. Most Indian forms of Yoga and Vedanta take the gods of Hinduism for granted. Buddhism, now largely absent from India, is the leading religion in Sri Lanka, Southeast Asia, Japan, Mongolia, and Tibet. Most Buddhist monks and nuns, and virtually all Buddhist laymen and women, are theistic in practice. Many worship the Buddha as a deity. Jainism is the religion of seven million people, most of them in India. Jain monks and nuns follow the five vows of Mahavira but most lay Jains are theistic, worshipping the Tirthankaras and other supernatural beings, including a number of gods borrowed from Hinduism.

From the point of view of nontheistic spirituality, the most interesting manifestations of Hinduism, Buddhism, and Jainism are the hybrid forms that arose during the nineteenth and twentieth centuries. These include, in the Hindu sphere, the Vedanta-Yoga syntheses of Vivekananda and Aurobindo, the neo-Advaita movement based on the teachings of Ramana Maharshi, and various schools of physical yoga, which combine traditional *hathayoga* with Western exercise techniques. In the Buddhist sphere, the work of Dharmapala, Soyen, and Suzuki opened the way for other new–old forms of Buddhist practice, such as the *vipassana* movement launched by S.N. Goenka and others. Among Jain sects, the Shvetambara Terapanthis have revived practices similar to *hathayoga* and *vipassana* and begun to reach out to non-Jains. All these groups present themselves as scientific and universal, although all retain elements of supernaturalism and sectarianism.

During its long history, Confucianism has gone through several periods of official disfavor and suppression. The twentieth century was one such period, perhaps the most intense since the "burning of books and burying of scholars" of the third century BCE. During the revolutions of the twentieth century, Chinese students and workers targeted Confucian culture as a leading cause of the country's backwardness. Many turned to communism as an alternative. After decades of conflict, the Chinese Communist Party took control of the country and founded the People's Republic in 1949. Sixteen years later, during the Cultural Revolution, party chairman Mao Zedong ordered his Red Guards to destroy every trace of Confucianism in the country. Government hostility lasted until 2000, when officials rediscovered Confucius as a guide to social harmony. Current party chairman and president Xi Jinping often quotes Confucius and other classical writers, and the government promotes the study of Chinese culture and language through its Confucius Institutes.

Daoism also suffered during the antitraditionalist movements but now is counted as one of the five religions officially recognized by the Chinese government (the others are Buddhism, Catholicism, Protestantism, and Islam). In practice, the Daoist religion is theistic and spiritistic, incorporating many elements of Chinese folk religion. Philosophical Daoism is widely studied and forms the basis of two popular exercise systems: *qigong* and *taiji quan* (tai chi chuan). Both of these are practiced by millions of people in China and abroad. A newer discipline, Falun Gong, which incorporates elements of *qigong*, Buddhist meditation, and other spiritual practices, was declared "heretical" by the Chinese government in 1999 but survives in other countries.

The global spread of Eastern religions has been a major catalyst in the growth of Western spirituality. Hinduism, Buddhism, and other Asian teachings have gone in and out of style in the West since the early nineteenth century, but until recently few Europeans and Americans became committed practitioners. Starting in the 1960s a sizeable number of Western seekers joined Hindu ashrams in India and Buddhist monasteries in Japan, Sri Lanka, Thailand, and Myanmar, while gurus, roshis, and rinpoches settled in Western cities and established retreats in the countryside. Some transplanted teachers insisted on preserving the old forms, praying, chanting, and burning incense just like they did in the temple back home. More typically Yoga, Zen, and other Asian teachings have been fitted out for smooth sailing on Western seas. Among the ballast jettisoned was literal belief in God, gods, buddhas, bodhisattvas, and so forth.

The growing popularity of yoga, particularly the physical yogas, and meditation, particularly mindfulness meditation, has provoked debate on the authenticity of Eastern techniques as practiced in the modern West. Some traditional followers of Buddhist and Hindu teachings condemn the Western versions as gimcrack knockoffs that have little to do with the Asian originals. Practice without disciplinary guidelines, they warn, can never lead to liberation. There is something to such criticisms. The teachings and methods of traditional Hindu, Jain, Buddhist, and Daoist teachers are based on the insights of thousands of predecessors. Modern followers of these traditions have a great deal to learn from the pathfinders. It is however clear that teachings conceived during the axial age are in some respects unsuitable for the modern world. (Mount Meru is, in fact, not the center of the physical universe.) The philosophical and psychological aspects of the teachings are less exposed to the weathering of time, but if, as claimed, they are based on universal truths, there is no reason to believe that axial-age (or classical or medieval) statements of these truths are the final word.

Some contemporary teachers of yoga and meditation have tried to sever all ties with tradition, presenting their methods as "scientific" techniques of physical or psychological self-improvement. Conservative cultural critics ridicule such offerings as feel-good activities for stressed-out professionals that do not address the problems that cause the stress in the first place. There is something to these criticisms as well. Many modern methods of yoga and meditation have been dumbed-down and commodified. For all that, they often deliver what they promise: improved physical and psychological health and, for some practitioners, a sense of spiritual engagement.[67]

Popularizers of "Eastern spirituality" sometimes speak of practices such as self-observation and detachment from negative emotions as though there was nothing in the Western tradition to compare them to. This shows their ignorance of the Hellenistic thinkers who preached such techniques for more than five hundred years and who had an enormous influence on the history of Western philosophy and religion. Since the late 1950s, some American and European psychologists have drawn on Stoic philosophy while developing such systems as Rational Emotive Behavior Therapy. During the same period, thousands of ordinary readers turned to the writings of Marcus Aurelius and Epictetus for help in dealing with the complexities of modern life. The writings of the Epicureans and Skeptics have been less influential, though the School of Life of British philosopher Alain de Botton could be described as a sort of popular Epicureanism.

The idea that philosophy should be a way of life, dormant in the West since the seventeenth century, was revived by French cultural historian Pierre Hadot (1922–2010) during the last three decades of his life. Drawing on the works of Socrates, the Stoics, the Epicureans, the Skeptics, and the Neoplatonists, not to mention Kierkegaard, Nietzsche, and Wittgenstein, Hadot tried to show that the post-Enlightenment model of the philosopher as an aloof professional thinker was untrue to the ancient Greco-Roman tradition of therapeutic philosophy. At roughly the same time some Austrian, British, and American psychotherapists turned to Kierkegaard, Nietzsche, Sartre, and Wittgenstein to help them develop Existential Psychotherapy and Logotherapy.

The 1960s and 1970s saw an upsurge of interest in Western and Eastern esoteric lore and this led to the development of dozens of systems of occult knowledge and practice. Many of them have given the New Age a bad name, but a few have offered theories and techniques that may have some pragmatic value. A century ago William James observed: "The whole drift of my education goes to persuade me that the world of our present consciousness is only one out of many worlds of consciousness that exist, and that those other worlds must contain experiences which have a meaning for our life also."[68] As a pioneer in "psychical research," he tried to put the study of unusual states of consciousness on a scientific basis. There is no way of knowing what he would have thought of crystal-healing, channeling, and past-life therapy, but if he had decided to examine them (or earlier equivalents), he doubtless would have pursued his investigations with open-mindedness and interest.

The rise and spread of nonreligious spirituality has occasioned much breast-beating on the part of religious writers. Lutheran scholar Martin Marty wrote that the "'spirituality' versus 'religion'" clash was "a defining conflict of our time." This seems a bit over the top. Most spiritual people are happy to acknowledge the religious origins of some of their practices and few religious people would want to deny that their creeds have a spiritual—that is, an inner and individualistic—side. The actual conflict is not between religion and spirituality but between the exclusivist and pluralist approaches to life. When the Pew survey charting the rise of the nones was published in 2012, liberal theologian Stanley Hauerwas viewed it as "a crucial development," showing that "America produces people that say, 'I believe Jesus is Lord, but that's just my personal opinion.'" No grounds for conflict there. When Bryan Fischer, a spokesman for the American Family Association, was shown the same survey he declared it was a sign that "the foundations of our culture are crumbling."[69]

The American Family Association is a Fundamentalist organization that maintains "that God has communicated absolute truth to mankind, and that all people are subject to the authority of God's Word [i.e., the Christian Bible] at all times." According to a recent survey, American Fundamentalists are holding their own even as mainstream denominations decline.[70] Other sorts of fundamentalism are on the rise across the world. Salafism is deeply entrenched in Arabia and Egypt and expanding in South Asia. Hindu "vigilante" groups operate almost without constraint in northern India.[71] Ultraconservative Judaism is well established in Israel and Buddhist fundamentalism has recently reared its head in Sri Lanka and Myanmar. Wherever it occurs, fundamentalism is a reaction against modernity and its uncertainties. Clinging to unquestionable scriptures and traditions gives fundamentalists a sense of security in a rapidly changing world. Paradoxically, they are quick to adopt new technologies, such as television, the internet, and, in some cases, advanced weaponry.

In the course of this book I have had some hard things to say about theistic religions, particularly in regard to their links with violence. But religious activism is not always bad. Many devout people have been at the forefront of the struggle *against* violence. Mahatma Gandhi and Martin Luther King, Jr., are notable examples. Social scientists have begun to collect data supporting the assumption that religious activities have positive effects on psychological and physical health. Anthropologist Tanya Luhrmann noted for example: "Religious attendance—at least, religiosity—boosts the immune system and decreases blood pressure. It may add as much as two to three years to your life." She cited in particular a study that showed that "attachment to God significantly decreased stress and did so more effectively than the quality of a person's relationships to other people." She added however that the cause of the correlation between religiosity and health "is not entirely clear."[72]

Other studies of the effects of religion on health are more equivocal. In a review of current literature, atheism researcher Karen Hwang noted that "the majority of research studies on religion and health outcomes have reported a 'small, robust' association" between religiosity and personal well-being, but added that there is "no empirical evidence" to support the idea that lack of religion "must carry a corresponding health detriment." Getting along with God can be good for you but being an unbeliever is not necessarily unhealthy. The question of the relationship between religion and societal health is even harder to settle. Owing to the complexity of social life it is almost impossible to pin down causal factors. Still, after reviewing recent literature, sociologist Phil Zuckerman concluded: "we can say this with relative surety: theism doesn't seem to help, nor is atheism a detriment."[73]

Moving away from statistics to the testimony of cultural history, it is evident that countless masterpieces of art, music, and literature were created by people who believed in God. Few examples of unbeliever art can compete with Angkor Wat, the Shiva Nataraja, Bach's *B-minor Mass*, and—yes—*Paradise Lost*. It would however be wrong to think that artists belonging to nontheistic traditions were inferior to their theistic peers. Confucian calligraphers, Daoist landscape artists, and Buddhist architects, painters, and sculptors created countless masterpieces in East, Central, and South Asia, while openly atheistic writers, from Stendhal to Salman Rushdie, produced some of the most memorable literature of the modern West.

I believe that nontheistic spirituality offers a way to keep some of the good effects of religion while getting rid of many of its abominations. One of the reasons different religions come to blows is incompatible beliefs about supernatural beings. All theistic religions make assertions that are not open to discussion because they are based on sources that are said to be divinely inspired. If your god or prophet says one thing and my god or prophet says another, and both of us feel that the question is vital to our survival, conflict is inevitable. The only way out is for everyone to honor or at least tolerate the beliefs of others. This is only possible when both sides adopt a pluralistic attitude.

Many modern thinkers have stressed the importance of pluralism in matters of religion. It's a simple fact, wrote British theologian John Hick in 1985, that there is "a plurality of saving human responses to the ultimate divine Reality." We therefore need a pluralistic approach to religious phenomena that "enables us to recognize and be fascinated by the manifold differences between the religious traditions, with their different conceptualizations, their different modes of religious experience, and their different forms of individual and social response to the divine." Remaining true to the traditions they belong to, people can participate in "the growing network of inter-faith dialogue and the interactions of faith-communities."[74] Hick's approach was imbued with modern values (he was a Kantian as well as a Christian) but it may also be viewed as an echo of one of the greatest voices of antiquity. Two thousand two hundred years ago, the Indian emperor Ashoka caused this edict to be inscribed in stone for the edification of his subjects:

> There should be growth in the essentials of all religions. Growth in essentials can be done in different ways, but all of them have as their root restraint in speech, that is, not praising one's own religion, or condemning the religion of others without good cause. And if there is cause for criticism, it should be done in a mild way. But it is better to honor other religions for this reason. By so doing, one's own religion benefits, and so do other religions, while doing otherwise harms one's own religion and the religions of others. Whoever praises his own religion, due to excessive devotion, and condemns others with the thought "Let me glorify my own religion," only harms his own religion. Therefore contact between religions is good. One should listen to and respect the doctrines professed by others.[75]

In a world tormented by the disease of religious conflict, it would be hard to find a better prescription.

* * *

Over the last hundred fifty years, atheism has become more and more widespread but at the same time spirituality has flourished. This unusual conjunction has encouraged the growth of nontheistic spiritualities. After the death of God, agnostic and atheistic thinkers—physical and social scientists, philosophers, psychologists—took the lead in explaining the nature of the world and the human being. Agnostic and atheistic writers, artists, and musicians developed new forms of expression to reinterpret life. Followers of religions struggled to adapt to the changing conditions. Some expanded the boundaries of their beliefs, others drew back into fundamentalism.

All the characteristics of modern spirituality—subjectivity, rejection of institutional religion, individual practice—are found together or separately in the works of many of the most important thinkers and creators of the modern era. To the writers and artists of the Modernist movement, the expression of the creator's subjective states was an essential aspect of the work of art. Philosophers such as Santayana, Aurobindo, and Husserl stressed the importance of the subjective point of view. Psychologists from James to Maslow and beyond made subjective consciousness a primary focus of their studies. Sociologists such as Durkheim, Simmel, and Weber viewed modern life as an interaction between the subjective individual and the social world. Subjectivity also emerged as a topic in theology, with God being conceived as a product of human mental states.

Organized religion was in decline well before Nietzsche announced the death of God. Few important players in modern thought and art were committed members of traditional religions. Many unbelievers embraced surrogate faiths. Some of them, for example, the religions of art and literature, contributed to the growth of civilized values. Others, notably nationalism and revolutionary socialism, became in practice life-destroying creeds.

The idea that thought has to be embodied in action was an important feature of the philosophy of Nietzsche and was given full expression in the existentialism of Sartre. Some recent philosophers have tried to recover the meditative practices of ancient Greece and Rome. Others have been inspired by Eastern philosophies and religions. Techniques of meditation and physical self-discipline are now elements of a global movement of practical spirituality. The wide diffusion of spiritual paths, theistic as well as nontheistic, has resulted in some loss of focus. It remains to be seen whether spirituality without God will continue to provide ways of personal growth for nonreligious people or whether it will be reabsorbed by conventional religion or snuffed out by military or environmental disaster.

EPILOGUE: SPIRITUAL BUT STILL RELIGIOUS?

While I was working on this book, a visiting friend suggested that I accompany him and his wife and daughter on a visit to a temple not far from where I live. I was happy to accept. It was a pleasant morning and the countryside we drove through was fresh and green. When we reached the temple my friend quickly transformed himself from Western-appareled mathematician to dhoti-clad devotee. Leaving my sandals in the car, I followed him and the others as they joined the line of pilgrims.

The temple is more than a thousand years old. Its main claim to fame is to have been mentioned in verses by a ninth-century Tamil saint whose poems form part of the canon of South Indian Vaishnavism. Half a millennium later a poet-philosopher wrote several works while living on a hilltop near the temple. When my friend was a boy, he used to recite passages from one of these works at home. Recently he brushed up his Sanskrit so he could study them word by word.

Like most South Indian temples this one consists of a central sanctum and a number of secondary shrines. The sanctum was closed, so we visited the shrines—or rather the others worshipped while I looked on and listened and absorbed the atmosphere. On the walls of one of the exterior shrines I noticed some numbers written in charcoal. I had seen this sort of thing before and offered my theory that they were lottery ticket numbers. "No," my friend's daughter corrected me. "They're seat numbers for the secondary school leaving examination." She had recently passed this with distinction. I doubt whether she scrawled her seat number on the wall of her local temple, but I wouldn't be surprised if she'd prayed to the family's God for good results.

After we had *darshan* of the presiding deity we climbed a flight of steps that led to a shrine to Hayagriva—Vishnu with horse's head—who is worshipped as the god of learning. On the verandah some children sat with open notebooks as their parents helped them write the letters of the Tamil alphabet. In this way they inaugurated their studies. I found the ritual touching. I also reflected that in fifteen or twenty years some of these kids may be writing the code that runs our electronic devices.

In this book about nontheistic spiritualities I have looked primarily at the works of writers and teachers who did not believe in God. An agnostic, I feel more at ease with Buddha, Lucretius, Spinoza, and Emerson than with Plato, Jesus, Rumi, and Nichiren. But as I worked I realized I had as much to learn from theistic as from nontheistic teachers. You don't have to be a Christian to appreciate the Sermon on the Mount or a Muslim to be knocked out by the *Masnavi*. For some followers of Buddhism, *vajrayana* visualization is a better means of mental discipline than *vipassana* meditation. Speaking for myself, I could never succeed in visualizing a deity I didn't believe in, but I certainly don't believe those who do such exercises are wasting their time.

While gathering material and writing the book, I found that my respect for religious people rose while my interest in the contents of theistic religions declined. While traveling I saw Buddhist monks doing their alms rounds in Laos, Muslims praying in mosques in Morocco, Christians and Jews visiting sacred sites in Israel, and I always was struck by their dignity. I feel a sort of envy for people who belong to theistic communities and at the same time am glad I don't belong to one myself. To belong to a theistic community means to enjoy the support of an all-powerful, all-wise Entity and the companionship of one's fellow devotees. But all this comes at a price. To be a paid-up member of the community, one has to accept a set of beliefs that are, at best, imperfect human attempts to represent something that is by definition more than human. Eventually the representation takes the place of the something, and one is stuck with a bunch of human, all-too-human beliefs. Left to themselves, people could put such beliefs to productive use, but theistic communities are rarely content to leave people to themselves. Everyone must subscribe to the community's dictates. Surrender to the group-mind helps certain people achieve worthwhile goals, but it sometimes prepares the way for unthinking participation in herd behavior and even violence.

Critics of modern spirituality often condemn it for its subjective and individualistic focus: Spiritual people are solipsistic navel-gazers with no community spirit. If everyone was "spiritual but not religious" society would collapse. And so forth. An influential statement of such ideas is found in *Habits of the Heart*, a 1984 study by sociologist Robert N. Bellah and his colleagues. Basing himself on observations by nineteenth-century French historian Alexis de Tocqueville, Bellah wrote: "We are concerned that this individualism may have grown cancerous—that it may be destroying those social integuments that Tocqueville saw as moderating its more destructive potentialities, that it may be threatening the survival of freedom itself." Bellah examined the lives of some famous American individualists, such as Benjamin Franklin and Walt Whitman, but devoted most of his book to two hundred participants in a study he and his colleagues carried out. One of his subjects gained some notoriety as a proponent of "purely private spirituality." Bellah dubbed her Sheila Larson and described her condescendingly as "a young nurse who has received a good deal of therapy." He quoted her as saying: "My faith has carried me a long way. It's Sheilaism. Just my own little voice." This passage was enough to make "Sheilaism" an ironic buzzword among conservative critics for more than a decade.[1]

Bellah worried that Sheila's "radically individualistic religion" raised the possibility "of over 220 million American religions, one for each of us." The result, he thought, would be social breakdown. Ninety years before Bellah's prognosis, Walt Whitman, Solomon Schindler, and Swami Vivekananda—none of whom had "received a good deal of therapy"—looked forward to a world in which each individual followed his or her own religion. They did not imagine that this would mean the end of society. Neither in fact did Sheila. One of the tenets of Sheilaism, she said, was for all of us "to take care of each other."[2]

It certainly is not the case that everyone interested in self-development is unconcerned with others or with society as a whole. Most people I know who follow spiritual paths belong to intentional communities. They have a personal practice but also take part in work that is useful to others. In this they follow the lead of the founders of the traditions I have written about in this book. All of them stressed the importance of personal effort but also spoke of the need to balance the demands of individual and community life. The Buddha told his followers to be lights unto themselves but also said that friendship, companionship, and comradeship constituted "the entire holy life."[3] Classical Confucians viewed the life of the individual within a social framework but also said that the preservation of the social structure depended on self-cultivation. Hellenistic philosophers underlined the need of personal self-development but also stressed the importance of communities of learning and practice. The same search for balance between the claims of the community and the individual is apparent in the annals of medieval Sufism, Neo-Confucianism, Japanese Zen, and most of the other traditions we have studied.

With the start of the modern era in the West, the individual human being began to play a greater role than in any traditional culture. As the Christian consensus began to crumble, arch-individualists such as Emerson, Whitman, and Kierkegaard paved the way for an inner spirituality unfettered by institutional constraints. Yet all of them were members of communities that provided them with a framework within which they did their work. Around the same time, the founders of the nineteenth-century social gospels—Comte, Marx, and others—proclaimed that individuals had to surrender themselves to the common good. Their thought set the stage for the sociopolitical revolutions of the twentieth century, which had disastrous results. At the cusp of this era, Tolstoy wrote in his diary:

> There can only be one permanent revolution—a moral one; the regeneration of the inner man.
>
> How is this revolution to take place? Nobody knows how it will take place in humanity, but every man feels it clearly in himself. And yet in our world everybody thinks of changing humanity, and nobody thinks of changing himself.[4]

This is just as true today as it was in 1900.

Life in the first quarter of the twenty-first century is far more complex than it was in Tolstoy's time. The internet and social media have added imponderables that even Bellah could not anticipate. One thing seems clear, however. Many of the most "cancerous" aspects of contemporary life—demagoguery, fake news, hate crimes, terrorism—have more to do with dysfunctional societies than with individual self-absorption. Attempts by governmental and voluntary organizations to solve these problems make little headway. In contrast, most people who practice spiritual disciplines not only gain some degree of personal fulfillment but also become more compassionate, more productive members of their communities.

To my mind the danger is not that individuals practicing spiritual disciplines will destroy whatever "integuments" may be holding society together but that society will reabsorb all nonconforming individuals into its undifferentiated mass. It is remarkable, and disheartening, that many of those who call themselves "spiritual but not religious" end up becoming as intolerantly religious as any fundamentalist Muslim or Christian.

Kierkegaard, an extremely nonfundamentalist Christian, waged a lifelong battle against the Danish state church and, in more general terms, against what he called "the crowd." He viewed the conflict between the individual and the crowd in black-and-white terms: "There is a view of life that holds that truth is where the crowd is" and another view "that holds that wherever the crowd is, untruth is." He himself insisted that "The crowd is untruth" and that the link between the two was so strong that if people who had found some truth came together in a crowd, "untruth would promptly be present there." The instruments of the crowd, in particular the press, could never "run down the lies and the errors." (Fake news was just as slippery in nineteenth-century Copenhagen as it is in twenty-first-century Washington.) The only suggestion he could offer was for individuals to form themselves into voluntary communities instead of amorphous crowds. The crowd, he said, is a collection of numbers summing up to zero. The community on the other hand is "a sum of ones" and also "more than a sum."[5]

Both Tolstoy and Kierkegaard were theists, but they were my kind of theists: dedicated to individual effort, at odds with institutions, suspicious of the mob. They are theists I can learn from, though I still respond better to the ideas of nontheists such as Nagarjuna and Nietzsche. Finally, however, the crucial distinction is not between nontheists and theists, but between people who are open-minded and people who think they have all the answers. The universe is large and full of surprises. The answers served up by the closed-minded today will look ridiculous tomorrow.

NOTES

Prologue: A religion is born

1 Supreme Court of India, Civil Appeal No. 12 of 2016.

1 Introduction: Religion and spirituality, gods and godlessness

1 Traubel, *With Walt Whitman*, vol. 7, 430; Chadwick, "Samuel Johnson," 83; Traubel, "Collect," 81.
2 Chadwick, "Paine versus Spirituality," 2.
3 Plato, *Alcibiades I*, 127D–128D, in Jowett, *Dialogues*, vol. 2, 497–498. This is one of two passages (the other is Plato, *Apology*, 29D–30B) discussed by Michel Foucault in connection with *epimeleia heautou* or "care of the self" (Foucault, *Hermeneutics of the Self*, 4–8, 51–57). That phrase does not occur in either Greek passage but inflected forms of the verb *epimeleomai* ("to take care of") along with the reflexive pronoun occur in both.
4 Pater, *Coleridge's Writings*, 126; Hutton, "Spirituality without God," 9; Whitman, *Democratic Vistas*, in *Complete Prose Works* (1892), 233. (The passage first occurred in the 1876 edition of *Democratic Vistas*, included in *Two Rivulets*.)
5 Santayana, *Philosophy of Santayana*, 190.
6 Sen, *Discourses and Writings*, 71; Dharmapala, *Arya Dharma*, 25; Nivedita, *Religion and Dharma*, 74; Olcott, *Catechism*, 90.
7 Mead, "On the Track of Spirituality," 250–255; "Spiritual Tendencies," 177.
8 Aurobindo, *Complete Works*, vol. 1, 450.
9 Dexter, "Wanted: A New Messiah," 234.
10 Gallop, "Americans' Spiritual Searches Turn Inward"; Grossman, "Millennials 'more spiritual than religious.'"
11 I have relied primarily on Adler, "In Search of the Spiritual"; Bender, "Religion and Spirituality"; Hanegraaff, "New Age Religion"; Heelas, "Spiritual Revolution"; Heelas and Woodhead, *The Spiritual Revolution*; Hollywood, "Spiritual but Not Religious";

Huss, "Spirituality"; McMahan, "Enchanted Secular"; Rose, "The Term 'Spirituality'"; Schmidt, "Aspiring Side of Religion"; Schmidt, *Restless Souls*; Shek, "Spirituality of the Chinese People"; and Zinnbauer et al., "Religion and Spirituality." I have also consulted Bender, *New Metaphysicals* and Roof, *Spiritual Marketplace*. It is worth noting the national origin of my authorities: American (8), British (2), Dutch (1), Israeli (1), Chinese (1). Few academics in South and East Asia have written about spirituality as such. Shek's critical review of literature is an exception, but he laments the paucity of Chinese studies of spirituality and excuses himself from the task of relating Chinese beliefs and values to spirituality.

12 Schneiders, "Religion vs. Spirituality," 163; Sheldrake, *Spirituality*, 2.
13 James, *Letters*, vol. 2, 149; *Varieties*, 338–340, 344, 398.
14 Schopenhauer, *Two Essays*, 11.
15 Paley, *Natural Theology*, 20.
16 Shankara, *Brahma-sutra-bhasya* 3.2.38, in Gambhirananda, *Brahma-Sutra-Bhasya*, 640.
17 I leave out of consideration the colorful details in reincarnation narratives and the fascinating but still anecdotal material in Ian Stevenson's *Twenty Cases Suggestive of Reincarnation*.
18 Hick, "Soul-Making Theodicy," 306.
19 Küng, *On Being a Christian*, 431.
20 1 Samuel 15:3 (New International Version). See also Deuteronomy 20:13–14 and Numbers 15:35.
21 Confucius, *Analects* 8.18, in Lau, *Analects*, 121; Lin Yutang, *My Country*, 101.
22 James, *Varieties*, 29, 328, 402.
23 Broad, "Arguments for the Existence of God," 156–167.
24 Alston, "Religious Experience as Perception of God," 28–29.
25 Alston, *Perceiving God*, 3.
26 Swinburne, *Existence of God*, 303–310.
27 Davies, *Mind of God*, 16, 58, 232.
28 Monod, *Chance and Necessity*, 145, 180. For a more recent discussion of "fine-tuning," see Fred Adams, "Not-So-Fine Tuning of the Universe."
29 Sperry, "Modified Concept of Consciousness," 532–533.
30 Monod, *Chance and Necessity*, 29.
31 Chalmers, "Problem of Consciousness," 203, 210.
32 Dennett, "Facing Backwards," 35.
33 Nietzsche, *Twilight of the Idols*, 121.
34 Steiner, *Real Presences*, 3.
35 Steiner, *Real Presences*, 181, 229, 132.
36 Humanist Manifesto I (1933); Dewey, letter to Charles Witzell, in Hickman, "Secularism, Secularization," 25; Dewey, *Common Faith*, 3, 27–28, 42, 51.
37 Schleiermacher, *On Religion*, 282.
38 James, *Varieties*, 399–400.

39   Dewey, letter to Max Otto, in Hickman, "Secularism, Secularization," 22; *Common Faith*, 32.
40   Comte-Sponville, "Les athées n'ont pas moins d'esprit" (page 2); *Atheist Spirituality*, ix–xi. (*L'esprit de l'athéisme* was published in English under the unfortunate title *The Little Book of Atheist Spirituality*. For the convenience of English-speaking readers I cite this translation rather than the French original.)
41   Comte-Sponville, *Atheist Spirituality*, 140; "Les athées n'ont pas moins d'esprit" (page 2); "Un certain silence," 10.
42   Nagel, *Secular Philosophy and the Religious Temperament*, 6.
43   Nagel, *Secular Philosophy and the Religious Temperament*, 6–14; *Mortal Questions*, 2.
44   Dworkin, *Religion without God*, 1–10.
45   Dworkin, *Religion without God*, 2, 65, 155–156.
46   Batchelor, *Confession*, 176–179.
47   Batchelor, *Confession*, 40, 131; "Secular Buddhist," 1.
48   Gyatso, "Many Faiths, One Truth"; *Beyond Religion*, xiii–xv, 17.
49   Gyatso, *Beyond Religion*, 107–109, 124, 185.

2 Theistic and nontheistic religions in the ancient world

1   Nakamura, *Comparative History*, 3–4.
2   Jaspers, *Origin and Goal*, 1–2. In this translation the German *Achsenzeit* is rendered "axial period."
3   *Theogony of Dunnu*, in Dalley, *Myths from Mesopotamia*, 279–281. For the sake of readability I have removed Dalley's brackets and question marks indicating conjectural readings. I have also Americanized the spelling of "Plough."
4   Malinowski, *Magic, Science, and Religion*, in Otto and Strausberg, *Defining Magic*, 169.
5   Frankfort et al., *Before Philosophy*, 93, 197.
6   *Shatapatha Brahmana* 2.3.1.5, in Eggeling, *Satapatha Brahmana*.
7   *Rig Veda* 10.71.4, in Doniger, *Rig Veda*, 61.
8   *Rig Veda* 8.48.3, in Doniger, *Rig Veda*, 134.
9   *Doctrine of the Mean*, in Chan, *Source Book*, 104.
10 *Chhandogya Upanishad*, book 6, in Roebuck, *The Upanishads*, 171–179.
11 *Rig Veda* 10.121, 10.129, in Doniger, *Rig Veda*, 27–28, 25–26.
12 *Shatapatha Brahmana* 10.5.4.15-16 and 11.2.3.1, in Eggeling, *Satapatha Brahmana*.
13 *Maitri Upanishad* 4.4, in Roebuck, *Upanishads*, 359.
14 *Chhandogya Upanishad* 6.12, in Roebuck, *Upanishads*, 178.
15 *Kena Upanishad*, books 3–4, in Roebuck, *Upanishads*, 266–68.
16 *Katha Upanishad* 2.22, in Roebuck, *Upanishads*, 280.

17 *Digha Nikaya* 2, in Walsh, *Long Discourses*, 93–97; Kalupahana, *Ethics in Early Buddhism*, 19.

18 *Kalpa Sutra* 5, in Jacobi, *Jaina Sutras*, vol. 22, 262–265.

19 *Majjhima Nikaya* 36, 10, in Nanamoli and Bodhi, *Middle Length Discourses*, 340, 145–155.

20 Hanh, *Heart of the Buddha's Teaching*, 225, 231, 222.

21 *Anguttara Nikaya* 3.61, in Nyanaponika and Bodhi, *Anguttara Nikaya*, Part I, 28–29.

22 *Majjhima Nikaya* 100, in Nanamoli and Bodhi, *Middle Length Discourses*, 821; *Digha Nikaya* 1, in Walsh, *Long Discourses*, 77.

23 *Dhammapada* 276, in Kaviratna, *Dhammapada*, 109.

24 *The Shoo King [Shujing]* (trans. Legge), in Creel, *Chinese Thought*, 17; Confucius, *Lunyu* 7.5, in Lau, *Analects*, 86. To avoid confusion, I have amended "Chou" to "Zhou" in the quotations from Creel and Lau.

25 *Daxue* 1.6, 1.5, in Gardner, *The Four Books*, 5–6; Confucius, *Lunyu* 1.1, in Lau, *Analects*, 59.

26 Confucius, *Lunyu* 12.1, in Lau, 112.

27 Confucius, *Lunyu* 14.28, 7.26, in Lau, 128, 89.

28 Confucius, *Lunyu* 9.12, 6.22, in Lau, 107, 84.

29 Mencius, *Mengzi* 6A:2, 7A:4, 6A:7, in Chan, *Source Book*, 52, 79, 55–56.

30 Xunzi, *Xunzi*, chapter 23, in Chan, 128.

31 Mencius, *Mengzi* 6B:15, in Chan, 78.

32 Xunzi, *Xunzi*, chapter 17, in Chan, 116–117.

33 Confucius, *Lunyu* 15.29, in Lau, 136.

34 *Daodejing* 38, in Chan, 158. To avoid confusion I have changed Chan's "Tao" to "Dao."

35 *Daodejing* 1, 25, 15, 6, 28, in Chan, 139, 152, 147, 142, 154. To avoid confusion I have changed Chan's "Tao" to "Dao."

36 *Daodejing* 55, 51, in Chan, 165, 163. To avoid confusion I have changed Chan's "Tao" to "Dao."

37 *Daodejing*, 37, 2, in Chan, 158, 140.

38 *Daodejing*, 32, 66, 7, 47, in Chan, 156, 170, 143, 162. A different translation of the last passage formed the basis of George Harrison's "The Inner Light."

39 *Daodejing* 4, in Chan, 141; *Zhuangzi*, section 2, in Chan, 181.

40 *Zhuangzi*, sections 18, 3, in Watson, Basic *Writings*, 115, 45–46.

41 *Zhuangzi*, sections 22, 17, 6, 2, 26, in Watson, 15, 101, 74, 35, 139.

42 *Zhuangzi*, section 6, in Watson, 74.

43 Xenophanes, fragments B15, B23, B26, B25, in Barnes, *Presocratic Philosophers*, 71–72, 65; Whitmarsh, *Battling the Gods*, 61; *Isha Upanishad* 4, in Roebuck, *Upanishads*, 7.

44 Heraclitus, fragments B30, B90, in Barnes, 45; Heraclitus, fragment B32, in Curd, "Presocratic Philosophy."

45 *To Helios*, in Evelyn-White, *Homeric Hymns*.
46 Euripides, *Troades*, 1021–1023, in Shapiro, *Trojan Women*, 61 (see also note on pages 95–96); Euripides, fragment 286, in "Euripidean Fragments and Bellerophon's Atheism."
47 Protagoras, fragments DK 80B4 and 80B1, in Taylor and Lee, "The Sophists."
48 Plato, *Theaetetus*, in Jowett, *Dialogues*, vol. 4, 206; Xenophon, *Memorabilia* 1.1.11-16, in Nadler, *Spinoza's Ethics*, viii.
49 Plato, *Phaedrus* 229d-230a, in Waterfield, *Phaedrus*, 6.
50 Plato, *Apologia* 38a, 30b, in *Five Dialogues* 41, 34.
51 Plato, *Apologia* 27–42; *Phaedo* 67e, 117c, in *Five Dialogues*, 32–44, 104, 153.
52 Berlin, *Sense of Reality*, 168–169; Epicurus, fragment 54, in *Essential Epicurus*, 97.
53 Diogenes Laertius, *Lives*, 6.1, 6.2, in Hicks, *Lives*.
54 Diogenes Laertius, *Lives*, 6.2, in Hicks, *Lives*; Tertullian, *Ad Nationes*, 2. 2.
55 Diogenes Laertius, *Lives*, 6.1, 2.8, in Hicks, *Lives*.
56 Epicurus, Letter to Monoeceus, in *Essential Epicurus*, 65, 67.
57 Epicurus, Letter to Herodotus, in *Essential Epicurus*, 41.
58 Epicurus, Letter to Pythocles, in *Essential Epicurus*, 49.
59 Epicurus, Letter to Monoeceus, in *Essential Epicurus*, 62.
60 Epicurus, *Principal Doctrines* 27, in *Essential Epicurus*, 73.
61 Zeno quoted in Baltzly, "Stoicism."
62 Diogenes Laertius, *Lives*, 9.11, in Hicks, *Lives*.
63 Sextus Empiricus, *Pyrrhoneioi hypotyposeis* 1.12, 28–29, in *Outlines of Scepticism*, 6, 10–11.
64 Sextus Empiricus, *Pyrrhoneioi hypotyposeis* 3.218, in *Outlines of Scepticism*, 200.
65 Sextus Empiricus, *Pyrrhoneioi hypotyposeis* 3.12, in *Outlines of Scepticism*, 146.
66 *The Epic of Creation* [*Enuma Elish*], in Dalley, *Myths*, 233–274.
67 *Ahunavaiti Gatha*, Yasna 28.4.
68 Exodus 20:3 (*New International Version*).
69 Hosea 13:4.
70 Deuteronomy 6.4. This verse forms part of the Jewish profession of faith known after its first two words as Shema Yisrael.
71 Biblical scholars give the name Deutero-Isaiah or Second Isaiah to the author of the second part of the book of *Isaiah*.
72 Isaiah 48:10, 40:2, 45:5, 54:5, 49:6.
73 Job 5:7, 21:7,13; 28:11–12; 28:28.
74 Ecclesiastes 8:15, 9:5; 12:13.

3 Defending and debating tradition

1 *Samkhyakarika* 70, 59, 64, in Larson, *Classical Samkhya*, 273–276; Gaudapada, *Bhashya* to *Samkhyakarika*, in Mainkar, *Samkhyakarika*, 37.

2   *Samkhyakarika* 1, 65, 68, in Larson, 255, 275.

3   See Nicholson, *Unifying Hinduism,* 67–83 and Larson, *Classical Samkhya,* 91–95.

4   *Samkhya Sutra* 1.92, 95, 5.1–12, in Ballantyne, *Sankhya Aphorisms,* 113–115. 312–321.

5   *Yogasutra* 1.2–3, in Miller, *Yoga,* 29.

6   *Yogasutra* 1.23–4, 4.31–34, in Miller, 35, 82–83.

7   *Vaisheshika Sutra* 1.1.5, 5.2.1–23, in Radhakrishnan and Moore, *Source Book,* 387, 393–394.

8   Prashastapada, *Padarthadharmasamgraha,* with commentary by Sridhara, Chapter 5, in Radhakrishnan and Moore, 401.

9   Kumarila Bhatta, *Slokavartika,* 1.47–49, in Radhakrishnan and Moore, 498–499.

10 Shankara, *Brahmasutra Bhashya,* comment on 1.2.14, in Gambhirananda, *Brahma Sutra Bhasya,* 128.

11 Shankara, *Upadeshasahasri* 10, 15, 38, in Deutsch, *Essential Vedanta,* 166–176.

12 Jinasena, *Mahapurana* 4, in Embree et al., *Sources,* 80–83.

13 Siddhasena Divakara, *Sanmati Tarka* 1.23, in Radhakrishnan and Moore, *Source Book,* 270.

14 Amritchandra Suri, *Purushartha Siddhyupaya* 148, in *Purushartha Siddhyupaya,* 95.

15 Ashvaghosa, *Buddhacarita,* part 3, canto 18: 29, 20, 24, in Johnston, *Buddhacarita,* 30–33 of separately numbered Part III.

16 *Heart Sutra,* in Conze, *Buddhist Texts,* 152.

17 Gyatso, *Meaning of Life,* 35–37.

18 Nagarjuna, *Mulamadhyamakakarika* 24.18, in Garfield, *Fundamental Wisdom,* 304–305.

19 *Twelve Gate Treatise,* chapter 10, in Cheng, *Nagarjuna's Twelve Gate Treatise,* 93–100. The *Twelve Gate Treatise* (Chinese: *Shi'ermen lun*) purports to be the Chinese translation of a lost Sanskrit original written by Nagarjuna. The authorship of the text and of the commentary that accompanies it is disputed. In any event the text is very much in the spirit of Nagarjuna. Compare the passage under discussion here to Nagarjuna, *Mulamadhyamakarika,* 12.1, in Garfield, *Fundamental Wisdom,* 202.

20 Vasubandhu, *Abhidharmakosa* 2.64, in de la Valée Poussin, *Abhidharmakosa,* 311–313.

21 Vasubandhu, *Trimsika-karika,* 28–30, in Conze, *Buddhist Texts,* 210–211.

22 Hsuan-tsang [Xuanzang], *Treatise of the Establishment of the Doctrine of Consciousness-Only,* Chapters 3 and 10, in Chan, *Source Book,* 382, 394–395.

23 Shantideva, *Bodhicaryavatara,* "Perfection of Understanding" 118–125, in Santideva, *Bodhicharyavatara,* 127–128.

24 Shantarakshita, *Tattvasamgraha* 2.87, in Santaraksita, *Tattvasangraha,* 94.

25 Sima Qian, *Historical Records,* 30–31, 75–77. I have conflated Sima Qian's two accounts of these events.

26 Yang Hsiung [Yang Xiong], quoted in Chan, *Source Book,* 290; Wang Ch'ung [Wang Chong], *A Treatise on Death* 62, in Chan, 300.

27 *Huai-Nan Tzu* [*Huainanzi*], in Chan, 308.
28 Kuo Hsiang [Guo Xiang], commentary on the *Chuang Tzu* [*Zhuangzi*], sections 14 and 9, in Chan, 328–329. Compare *Bhagavad Gita* 2:15–23.
29 Seng-Chao [Sengzhao], *Chao lun* [*Zhao lun*], chapter 2, in Chan, 350–351.
30 Tao-husan, *Continued Biographies of Excellent Monks*, in Broughton, *Anthology*, 62; Sasaki, *Record of Linji*, 118.
31 *Treatise on the Two Entrances and Four Practices*, in McRae, *Seeing through Zen*, 29.
32 See Suzuki, *Lankavatara Sutra*, 192–193, 203 and Broughton, *Bodhidharma Anthology*, 72.
33 *Treatise on the Essentials of Cultivating the Mind*, in McRae, 40.
34 *Platform Sutra* 12, 31, in Red Pine, *Platform Sutra*, 10, 24.
35 *Record of Linji*, Discourses 18 and 1, in Sasaki, *Record of Linji*, 25, 4.
36 *Record of Linji*, Discourse 18, in Sasaki, 20–22.
37 *Record of Linji*, Discourses 20, 22, 10, in Sasaki, 29, 32, 7–8.
38 *Platform Sutra* 35–37, in Red Pine, *Platform Sutra*, 28–33.
39 Li Ao, *Recovery of Nature* 2, in Chan, 457.
40 Cicero, *De Finibus* 5.1–3, in Thayer, LacusCurtus.
41 Cicero, *De Natura Deorum*, book 1, in Cicero, *The Nature of the Gods*, 69–70.
42 Cicero, *De Natura Deorum*, book 1, in Cicero, *The Nature of the Gods*, 70.
43 Cicero, *Tusculanae Disputationes* 5.81–2, in Mitsis, "Stoicism," 264; Cicero in Mitsis, 263.
44 Lucretius, *De Rerum Natura*, books 1 and 3, in Lucretius, *Nature of the Universe*, 12, 67.
45 Lucretius, *De Rerum Natura*, books 2, 5, 6, in Lucretius, 64, 133, 159, 168.
46 Lucretius, *De Rerum Natura*, book 2, in Lucretius, 44.
47 Horace, *Odes* 1.11; Catullus, *Carmina* 5, line 6; Ovid, *Ars Amores* 1.637.
48 Pliny, *Naturalis Historia* 2.5, in Pliny, *Natural History*, 179.
49 Seneca, *Epistulae morales* 123, 41, in Seneca, *Letters from a Stoic*, 231, 86.
50 Seneca, *De Consolatione ad Helviam*, in *Dialogues and Letters*, 11, 6; *Epistulae morales* 123, in *Letters from a Stoic*, 227; *Epistulae morales* 110, in *Dialogues and Letters*, 104.
51 Seneca, *De Tranquillitate Animi*, in *Dialogues and Letters*, 33; *Epistulae morales* 24, in *Dialogues and Letters*, 87–89.
52 Beard, "How Stoical Was Seneca?"
53 Musonius, *Lectures & Sayings*, 36, 86, 37, 39.
54 Musonius, *Lectures & Sayings*, 87.
55 Epictetus, *Diatribai* 2.14, 1.14, in *Discourses*, 107, 38–39.
56 Epictetus, *Diatribai* 1.1, in *Discourses*, 6.
57 Epictetus, *Diatribai* 3.23, 3.3, 4.1, in *Discourses*, 172, 147, 188.
58 Marcus Aurelius, *Ta eis heauton*, 9.28, 2.11, in *Meditations*, 123, 20.
59 Marcus Aurelius, *Ta eis heauton*, 3.10–11, in *Meditations*, 32.

60 Marcus Aurelius, *Ta eis heauton*, 8.49, 6.13, 3.16, 2.12, in *Meditations*, 111, 70–71, 34, 21.
61 Lucian, *Hermotimus* 46–47, 86, in *Selected Dialogues*, 109, 127.
62 Sextus Empiricus, *Pyrrhoneioi hypotyposeis*, 3.280, 1.206, in *Outlines of Scepticism*, 216, 50.
63 Sextus Empiricus, *Pyrrhoneioi hypotyposeis*, 1.23, 3.2, in *Outlines of Scepticism*, 9, 143.
64 Epictetus, *Diatribai* 1.15.2, in *Discourses*, 40.

4 The triumph of theism

1 Shelley, "A Refutation of Deism," in *Selected Prose*, 57.
2 *Bhagavad Gita*, chapter 11, in Johnson, *Bhagavad Gita*, 49–53.
3 Chapters 1, 2, and 5 of the *Shwetashwatara* are meditative-ascetic; chapters 3, 4, and 6 are primarily devotional. Chapters 2, 3, 5, 6, 8, 13, 14 (part), 15 (part), 16, 17 (part), and 18 of the *Gita* are primarily disciplinary on the lines of Yoga, Samkhya, and Vedanta. The remaining 6 full and 3 part chapters (leaving out chapter 1) are primarily devotional.
4 *Shwetaswatara Upanishad* 3.3,5, in Roebuck, *Upanishads*, 302; *Bhagavad Gita* 11.16, in Johnson, 50.
5 *Shwetaswatara Upanishad* 3.8; 6.15, in Roebuck, 303, 314; *Bhagavad Gita* 18.64–66, in Johnson, 80.
6 John 1:14 (New International Version).
7 *Samyutta Nikaya* 22.87, in Bodhi, *Connected Discourses*, 939.
8 *Lotus Sutra*, chapters 18, 24, 25, in Watson, *Lotus Sutra*, 232, 296, 303, 306.
9 *Lotus Sutra*, chapter 3, in Watson, 73–74.
10 *Samyutta Nikaya* 48.10–51, in Bodhi, *Connected Discourses*, 1671–1695; Nagarjuna, *Ratnavali*, 5.
11 Jaini, *Path of Purification*, 162–163; "Navakar Mantra," in Vijay, *Guidances of Jainism*.
12 Matthew 22:36–39 (New International Version).
13 Romans 1.16; Romans 10.9.
14 John 1:1.
15 John 20:31.
16 Lucian, *The Death of Peregrinus* 13, in *Selected Dialogues*, 77.
17 *Sunan an-Nasa'i* 2047.
18 Caesarius of Heisterbach and Arnau Amalric, cited in Pegg, *Most Holy War*, 77; Pegg, xiv, 188–189.
19 Todd, "Top UBC psychologist uncovers roots."
20 Hitchens, *God is not Great*, 13; Dawkins, *God Delusion*, 343.
21 Cavenaugh, *Myth*, 4; Armstrong, *Fields*, 13, 233.

22 Freud, *Civilization*, 48–50.
23 Alcorta and Sosis, "Ritual, Religion, and Violence," 7; Girard, *Violence and the Sacred*, 26; Burkert, *Homo Necans*, 3.
24 Arendt, *Eichmann in Jerusalem*, 287.
25 Reich, Haslam, and Rath, "Making a Virtue of Evil," 1337, 1333.
26 Williams, "Religion, Value Orientations, and Intergroup Conflict," 647.
27 Juergensmeyer, *Terror*, 217. Cf. Gorski and Türkmen-Dervisoglu, "Religion, Nationalism, and Violence," 193–210; Hall, "Religion and Violence," 2.
28 Jeurgensmeyer, *Terror*, 161–162.
29 Nichiren, letter to Konichi-bo, from *Major Writings of Nichiren Daishonin*, vol. 4, 155.
30 Harada, quoted in Victoria, *Zen War Stories*, 67.
31 Wirathu, quoted in Campbell, "Extremist Buddhist Network."
32 *Bhagavad Gita*, 2.31, in Johnson, 9.
33 Vivekananda, *Complete Works*, vol. 3, 32.
34 Panditaradhya, *Sivatattvasamaru*, verse 275, in Rao and Roghair, *Siva's Warriors*, 12.
35 Rao and Roghair, *Siva's Warriors*, 12; Aurobindo, *Complete Works*, vol. 20, 187.
36 Brass, *Production*, 15, 33–34.
37 Ajju Chouhan, quoted in Gahlot, "Filmmaker's View."
38 Hume, *Natural History*, Section 9.
39 Assmann, *Price*, 8–30.
40 Avraham Stern, "Ideology of the Lehi"; Yigal Amir, in Schmemann, "Assassination in Israel."
41 Matthew 5:39.
42 Chrysostom, *Homilies on the Statutes*, 1.32, in Schaff, *Nicene and Post-Nicene Fathers*, series 1, vol. 9, 476.
43 Chrysostom, *Homilies Against the Jews*, 3.1–2.
44 Augustine, *City of God* 18.54, in Dods, *City of God*, 603.
45 Shenoute, quoted in Gaddis, *There Is No Crime*, 151.
46 Pope Urban II, speech at Council of Clermont (1095), and Raymond of Agiles, *Historia Francorum*, both quoted in Bainton, *Christian Attitudes*, 111–113.
47 Montaigne, *Complete Works*, 392–393, 971–972.
48 Natalie Zemon Davis, "Rites of Violence," 65, 90.
49 Bray, *A Time to Kill*, in Juergensmeyer, *Princeton Reader*, 57.
50 Quran 15:94, 22.39, 2.217, 9.29 (Sahih International Version).
51 *Sahih Muslim* 32.3 ("Book of Jihad and Expeditions").
52 *Riyad as-Salihin* 12.1 ("Book of Jihad").
53 Qutb, *Milestones*, 63–86; Streusand, "What Does Jihad Mean?"; Suroor, "Islam and its Interpretations."

54 Firestone, *Jihad*, 5.
55 Toft, "Religion and Political Violence," 4–5.
56 Hamid, "What Makes a Terrorist."
57 Wood, "What the ISIS Really Wants"; Callimachi, "ISIS Enshrines a Theology of Rape."
58 "Al-Shabab statement."
59 Al-Ma'arri, in Nicholson, *Literary History*, 318–319, and in Nicholson, *Studies in Islamic Poetry*, 177; "Syria Violence Claims Head of Ancient Arab Poet."
60 Al-Razi, in Stroumsa, *Freethinkers*, 96–98; Paul Kraus and Schlomo Pines, quoted in Stroumsa, 98.
61 Al-Ghazali, quoted in Nicholson, *Literary History*, 380.
62 Al-Hallaj, "Release into Reality," in Jacobs, *Element Book*, 57–58.
63 Nicholson, *Literary History*, 402–403.
64 Rumi, *Masnavi*, in Ernst, *Sufism*, 168; Rumi, quatrain 587, in Moyne and Barks, *Unseen Rain*, 31.
65 Lu Hsiang-shan [Lu Jiuyuan] and Chu Hsi [Zhu Xi], in Creel, *Chinese Thought*, 212–213, 208.
66 Wang Yangming, in Creel, *Chinese Thought*, 214. To avoid confusion I have altered Creel's "Chu Hsi" to the pinyin form, Zhu Xi.
67 Wang Yangming, in Chan, *Source Book*, 677.
68 *Gateless Gate,* case 6 and commentary by Mumon Ekai [Wumen Hukai], *teisho* by Yamada, in Yamada, *Gateless Gate*, 36–38.
69 *Gateless Gate*, case 1 and commentary by Mumon [Wumen], in Yamada, 11; Wumen quoted in Yamada, *Gateless Gate*, Appendix I, 262. In Japanese the word for "no" is "Mu" not "Wu."
70 Dogen, in Tanahashi, *Essential Dogen*, 10, 56, 53, 11, 135.
71 Bassui, in Braveman, *Mud and Water*, 184, 202, 55–56.
72 Jaini, *Path of Purification*, 309–310; "Minor Divisions and Subdivisions of the Svetambaras."
73 Kabir, sakhi, in Vaudeville, *Weaver*, 179; Kabir, *Bijak*, sabda 10, in Vaudeville, "Sant Mat," 33; Kabir, sakhi 2.8, in Vaudville, Kabir-Vani, 5.
74 Kabir, *Bijak*, sabda 98, in Hess and Singh, 74.
75 Raidas, in Callewaert and Friedlander, *Raidas*, 159–160, 164, 118, 110, 122.
76 Nanak, *Adi Granth*, in McLeod, *Guru Nanak*, 193.
77 Tegh Bahadur, *Adi Granth*, *shalok* 57, in Kaur Singh, 170.
78 Boccaccio, *Decameron*, 83.
79 Montaigne, *Complete Works*, 452.
80 Montaigne, *Complete Works*, 453.
81 Luther, "Open Letter to the German Nobility."
82 Calvin, *Institutes of the Christian Religion*, 1.7.5, in Popkin, *History of Scepticism*, 10.
83 Ginzburg, *Cheese and Worms*, 4.

5 The coming of modernity and the decline of God

1. Wootton, *Invention of Science*, 11.
2. Cowell, "After 350 Years, Vatican Says Galileo Was Right."
3. Montaigne, *Complete Works*, 960–962; Wesley, *Works*, vol. 3, 245.
4. Galileo, *The Assayer*, in Popkin, *Philosophy of the Sixteenth and Seventeenth Centuries*, 65.
5. Newton, *Principia*, in Ariew and Watkins, *Modern Philosophy*, 289; Newton, *Opticks*, in Ariew and Watkins, 292–293.
6. Newton, *Opticks*, in Ariew and Watkins, 292.
7. Descartes, *Discourse on Method*, 41–44.
8. Descartes, *Discourse*, 55–57, 51.
9. Descartes, *Discourse*, 63.
10. Descartes, *Discourse*, 63–66.
11. Williams, "Descartes," 91.
12. Hobbes, *Leviathan*, 447.
13. Hobbes, *English Works*, vol. 4, 383.
14. Hobbes, *Leviathan*, 71. Hobbes italicized "religion" twice.
15. Hobbes, *Leviathan*, 366.
16. Nadler, *Spinoza: A Life*, 120, 154.
17. Spinoza, *Complete Works*, 3,6.
18. Nadler, *Spinoza: A Life*, 295–296.
19. Spinoza, *Complete Works*, 558, 393.
20. Spinoza, *Complete Works*, 388–390, 504.
21. Spinoza, *Complete Works*, 391, 457, 493, 504, 508.
22. Spinoza, *Complete Works*, 217, 321.
23. Spinoza, *Complete Works*, 277–278.
24. Spinoza, *Complete Works*, 365.
25. Spinoza, *Complete Works*, 358, 377–378.
26. Raphson, translated in Suttle, "Raphson, Joseph," 1342.
27. William Nicholls, in Hudson, *English Deists*, 155.
28. Locke, *Letter Concerning Toleration*.
29. Locke, *Letter Concerning Toleration*.
30. Voltaire, *Philosophical Dictionary*, "Ancients and Moderns."
31. Wang Fu-chih [Wang Fuzhi], in Chan, *Source Book*, 697, 694.
32. Voltaire, *Philosophical Dictionary*, "China."
33. Hakuin, in Waddell, *Essential Teachings*, 44–45, 26–27.
34. Hakuin, in Waddell, 102, 62–64.

35 Vidyaranya, *Panchadasi*, 229.
36 Vijnanabhiksu, *Samkhyapravacanabhasya*, in Nicholson, *Unifying Hinduism*, 88–89, 96.
37 Paltu Sahib, in Ezekiel, *Saint Paltu*, 29, 8, 39.
38 Prannath, *Kiyamat-nama*, trans. in Growse, *Mathura*, 236–237.
39 Bakhtawar, *Suni Sar*, trans. in Wilson, *Religious Sects*, 308; Bakhtawar, *Suni Sar*, trans. in Growse, *Mathura*, 240.
40 Schimmel, *Pain and Grace*, 75.
41 Sultan Bahu, in Elias, ed. and trans., *Death Before Dying*, 85; Sachal Samarst, in Advani, *Sachal Samarst*, 19.
42 Guyon, *Moyen court*, 82–83.
43 Guyon, *Moyen court*, 190.
44 Wesley, *Works*, vol. 3, 309; vol. 5, 201; vol. 6, 348.
45 Chauncy, "Enthusiasm described and caution'd against."
46 Wesley, *Works*, vol. 5, 168, 3.
47 Schleiermacher, *Religion*, 277.
48 Meslier, *Œuvres complètes*, vol. 1, 3; vol. 3, 185.
49 Voltaire, *Philosophical Dictionary*, "Faith."
50 Voltaire, *Œuvres complètes*, vol. 10, 281, 522.
51 Israel, *Radical Enlightenment*, 11–12, vi.
52 D'Holbach, *System of Nature*, vol. 1, chapter 1; vol. 2, chapter 1.
53 D'Holbach, *System of Nature*, vol. 2, chapters 9 and 13.
54 D'Holbach, *Le bon-sens*, ii–iii.
55 Kors, *D'Holbach's Coterie*, 41. See Kors's discussion on 41–42.
56 Hume, *Natural History*, 1.
57 Hume, *Natural History*, 9–10, 70.
58 Hume, *Dialogues*, 17.
59 Hume, *Dialogues*, 19, 55.
60 Hume, *Dialogues*, 86, 89, 100, 102.
61 Kant, *Prolegomena*, 10, 7.
62 Kant, *Critique*, 110, 117.
63 Kant, *Philosophische Enzyklopädie*, 9–12.
64 Kant, *Prolegomena*, 111.

6 Secularizing the sacred

1 Biré, *Journal d'un bourgeois de Paris*, vol. 4, 24–28.
2 Abrams, *Natural Supernaturalism*, 68.
3 Goethe, "Prometheus," in *Selected Poetry*, 11, 13; *Faust*, Part I, lines 3432–3460, in *Faust*, 148.

4   Goethe, in Bielschowsky, *Life of Goethe*, vol. 2, 157.
5   Wordsworth, "Lines Composed a Few Miles Above Tintern Abbey..."
6   Shelley, *Queen Mab*.
7   Shelley, *Hymn to Intellectual Beauty*.
8   Coleridge, *Aids*, 122, 336.
9   Menand, *Metaphysical Club*, 247; Marsh, "Preliminary Essay," in Coleridge, *Aids*, xxxvii.
10 Coleridge, *Aids*, 13; Emerson, *Journals and Notebooks*, vol. 3, 164, 173, 312.
11 Emerson, *Selected Essays*, 214, 206, 224.
12 Emerson, *Selected Essays*, 290–291, 239.
13 Emerson, *Journals and Notebooks*, vol. 8, 96.
14 Thoreau, *Journal*, vol. 2, 472.
15 Thoreau, *Walden*, 221.
16 Thoreau to H. G. O. Blake, 7 December 1856, in *Correspondence*, 444–445.
17 Whitman, *Leaves of Grass* (1856), 167–177, 95, 128. In his letter to Blake, Thoreau mentioned that he was reading the second (1856) edition, so I quote from that edition here. "Poem of the Body" was later expanded into "I Sing the Body Electric."
18 Whitman, Leaves of Grass, 1860, 186.
19 Whitman, *Leaves of Grass* (1855), 10.
20 Schopenhauer, *Two Essays*, 13; Schopenhauer, *Essays and Aphorisms*, 118.
21 Schopenhauer, *World as Will and Representation*, 23, 124, 127.
22 Schopenhauer, *World as Will and Representation*, 336.
23 Schopenhauer, *World as Will and Representation*, 40, 200–201, 419.
24 Schopenhauer, *Essays and Aphorisms*, 100, 217.
25 Kierkegaard, *Concluding Unscientific Postscript*, 172.
26 Kierkegaard, *Concluding Unscientific Postscript*, 398, 514, 246.
27 Kierkegaard, *Concluding Unscientific Postscript*, 254.
28 Hoffmann, *Musical Writings*, 97.
29 Carlyle, *Essay on Burns*, 73; Vigny, *Œuvres complètes*, vol. 2, 1058.
30 Balzac, *Œuvres complètes*, vol. 24, 405.
31 Stendhal, *Red and Black*, 342. Stendhal's aphorism is cited in this form by Nietzsche in *Ecce Homo*, 28. The source is a pamphlet attributed to the dramatist Prosper Mérimée (1803–1870), which notes that Stendhal "had a feeling of anger and resentment toward Providence: 'What excuses God,' he said, 'is that God does not exist'" (Duckett, *Dictionnaire*, 508).
32 Arnold, *Stanzas from the Grande Chartreuse*; Arnold, *Culture & Anarchy*, xvi, 10.
33 Arnold, *Literature & Dogma*, 11, 39, 37; Arnold, "Study of Poetry."
34 Eliot, letter of 1876, in Dolin, *George Eliot*, 190.
35 Nietzsche, *Twilight*, 80; Mallock, review of Eliot, *Impressions of Theophrastus Such*, 290.

36 Spencer, *First Principles*, 148.
37 Darwin, in *Charles Darwin's Natural Selection*, 224; Darwin, letter to Asa Gray, May 22, 1860.
38 Stephen, *Agnostic's Apology*, 12.
39 Feuerbach, *Essence of Christianity*, 34; Marx, *Collected Works*, vol. 3, 175–176.
40 Comte, *System of Public Polity*, vol. 4, 320, 282.
41 Spencer, *Principles of Ethics*, vol. 1, 245–246, 277.
42 Spencer, "Retrogressive Religion," 4, 24.
43 "Society for Psychical Research," 251–252.
44 Lévi, *Haute magie*, vol. 1, 63–64.
45 "Preamble and By-Laws of the Theosophical Society," in Ransom, *Short History*, 81.
46 Blavatsky, letter of February 16, 1875, in Lavie, *Theosophical Society*, 40–41.
47 Blavatsky, *Isis Unveiled*, vii.
48 Evans, *Hours with the Ghosts*, 266.
49 Blavatsky, *Isis Unveiled*, 61.
50 Charles Bonney and Archbishop of Canterbury, in Barrows, *World's Parliament*, 67, 20–22.
51 Hastings, in Wilkins, *Bhagvat-Geeta*, 13.
52 "The Trust Deed of the Brahma Samaj," in Roy, *Essential Writings*, 105.
53 Tagore, *Autobiography*, 164.
54 Sen, *Lectures in India*, 490, 484, 397.
55 Olcott, *Old Diary Leaves*, 394–405; Dayananda, "Humbuggery of the Theosophists," in Singh, *Life and Teachings*.
56 Olcott, *Old Diary Leaves*, second series, 168–169.
57 Olcott, *Old Diary Leaves*, second series, 299.
58 Shimaji Mokurai, in *Japan Weekly Mail*, December 31, 1892, reproduced in "Japan," 5.
59 Barrows, *World's Parliament*, 88, 101, 95.
60 Hirai, "The Real Position of Japan Toward Christianity," in Seager, *Dawn*, 401.
61 Vivekananda, *Complete Works*, vol. 1, 6; Pung, "Confucianism," in Burrows, *World's Parliament*, 437; Dharmapala, "The World's Debt to Buddha," in Seager, *Dawn*, 417.
62 Pung, "Confucianism," in Burrows, ed., *World's Parliament*, 376, 412; Gandhi, "The Philosophy and Ethics of the Jains," in Seager, *Dawn*, 373; Dharmapala, "The World's Debt to Buddha"; in Seager, *Dawn*, 417.
63 Vivekananda, *Complete Works*, vol. 6, 254–255.
64 Vivekananda, *Complete Works*, vol. 6, 41, 308.
65 Vivekananda, *Complete Works*, vol. 1, 124–131.
66 Vivekananda, *Complete Works*, vol. 1, 183; James, *Varieties*, 310.
67 See for example Rambachan, *The Limits of Scripture*.
68 Suzuki, "Translator's Preface," in Soyen, *Sermons*, iv–v.

69 Soyen, *Sermons*, 122, 75, 130–131.
70 Dharmapala, *Return to Righteousness*, 27.
71 Dharmapala, *Arya Dharma*.
72 Rhys Davids, *Yogacharya's Manual*, v. In giving the text to Rhys Davids, Dharmapala "expressed the hope that I [Rhys Davids] should be able to make some more out of it than either he, or the members of the Order in Ceylon, where the practice of Jhana [meditation] had quite died out, could do."
73 Gombrich, *Theravada Buddhism*, 187–189.
74 Dharmapala, "Arya Dharma"; Soyen, *Sermons*, 25, 32, 47; Vivekananda, *Complete Works*, vol. 1, 111.
75 Soyen, *Sermons*, 138, 156–157, 80.
76 Vivekananda, *Complete Works*, vol. 3, 250.
77 Vivekananda, *Complete Works*, vol. 3, 277.
78 Soyen, *Sermons*, 201.
79 Dharmapala, "Arya Dharma," 39; Dharmapala, quoted in Seneviratne, *Work of Kings*, 30.

7 The death and afterlife of God

1 Nietzsche, *Gay Science*, 120. Nietzsche was anticipated by Gérard de Nerval (epigraph to *Le Christ aux oliviers*, 1844) and by William James (see below).
2 Nietzsche, *Ecce Homo*, 69; *Gay Science*, 199, 194.
3 Nietzsche, *Selected Letters*, 12–13.
4 Nietzsche, *Birth of Tragedy*, 32, 39.
5 Nietzsche, *Gay Science*, 119–120.
6 Nietzsche, *Zarathustra*, 5–6.
7 Nietzsche, *Zarathustra*, 232, 89–90.
8 Nietzsche, *Human, All Too Human*, 323. This passage is part of the supplement entitled *The Wanderer and His Shadow*, published in 1880.
9 Nietzsche, *Twilight of the Idols and Anti-Christ*, 138–141, 158, 114.
10 Nietzsche, *Daybreak*, 96.
11 Romanes, *Candid Examination*, 113–114; Ingersoll, *Works*, vol. 4, 65.
12 Tolstoy, "What is Religion," in *Last Steps*, 151.
13 Tolstoy, *Confession*, 6, 11, 43.
14 Tolstoy, "Reply to the Synod's Edict," in *Last Steps*, 148–149.
15 Traubel, *With Walt Whitman*, vol. 7, 430; Schindler, in Schmidt, *Restless Souls*, 118; Vivekananda, *Complete Works*, vol. 4, 37.
16 Simmel, in *Simmel on Culture*, 87–88.
17 Adler, *Essentials*, 1–2; Aurobindo, *Complete Works*, vol. 25, 181.
18 Durkheim, *Elementary Forms*, 66, 351; *Sociology and Philosophy*, 25; Weber, *From Max Weber*, 269–270; Simmel, *Essays*, 113.

19 Durkheim, *Sociology and Philosophy*, 29; Weber, *From Max Weber*, 139; Simmel, in *Simmel on Culture*, 55–58.
20 Durkheim, *On Morality and Society*, 48–49; Weber, *From Max Weber*, 280; Simmel, in *Simmel on Culture*, 88.
21 James, letter of May 15, 1868, in Parry, *Thought and Character*, 93–97.
22 James, *Varieties*, 29, 11.
23 James, letter of September 19, 1909, in Parry, *Thought and Character*, 199.
24 Freud, "Leonardo da Vinci and a Memory of his Childhood," in *Freud Reader*, 474.
25 Freud, *Future*, 22; *Civilization*, 22; *Future*, 53.
26 Freud, *Future*, 38, 36; James, *Varieties*, 391 (my emphasis).
27 Freud, *Future*, 35–36; James, *Varieties*, 328, 389–398; Freud, *Future*, 41.
28 Stravinsky, *Rite of Spring*.
29 Berger and Luckmann, *Social Construction*, 5.
30 Kandinsky, *Concerning the Spiritual in Art*, 44; Woolf, *Common Reader*, 190–191.
31 Stevens, *Collected Poems*, 167; *Opus Posthumous*, quoted in Bloom, *Wallace Stevens*, 27.
32 Santayana, *Philosophy of Santayana*, 131, 190, 374.
33 Aurobindo, *Complete Works*, vol. 21, 153, 141; Alexander, *Space Time and Deity*, vol. 2, 346, 429; Whitehead, *Religion in the Making*, 160.
34 Whitehead, *Science and the Modern World*, 189, 207; Alexander, *Space Time and Deity*, vol. 2, 301; Aurobindo, *Complete Works*, vol. 23, 30.
35 Russell, letter to Ottoline Morrell, 1911; Wittgenstein, letter to Ludwig von Ficker, 1919; both in Monk, *Wittgenstein*, 41, 178.
36 Wittgenstein, *Tractatus*, 88–89.
37 Wittgenstein, *Philosophical Investigations*, §133.
38 Wittgenstein, *Philosophical Investigations*, §255; *Culture and Value*, 51; comment to M.O'C. Drury, in Malcolm, *Wittgenstein*, vii; "Lecture on Ethics," 8.
39 Wittgenstein, *Tractatus*, 89.
40 Ayer, *Language, Truth and Logic*, 120–121.
41 Sartre, *Existentialism is a Humanism*, 53.
42 Sartre, conversation with Simone de Beauvoir, 1974, in Beauvoir, *Adieux*, 548.
43 Sartre, *War Diaries*, 185–186.
44 Sartre, *Existentialism is a Humanism*, 22, 53–54.
45 Mann, *Reflections*, 237.
46 Lenin, *Religion*, 18.
47 *Osservatore Romano*, quoted in Duggan, *Force of Destiny*, 484.
48 Statement dated July 28, 1937 issued by Myowa-kai, quoted in Victoria, *Zen and Japanese Militarism*, 226; Shio Benkyo, quoted in Victoria, 219.
49 Bonhoeffer, *Writings*, 119.
50 Tillich, *Courage to Be*, 184–7, 47; from *Systematic Theology*, vol. 1, in Pojman and Rea, *Philosophy of Religion*, 52.

51 Elson, "Toward a Hidden God."
52 Cupitt, *Talking Leave*, Kindle locations 487, 378, 2035, 2019, 204.
53 Berger, *Sacred Canopy*, 107; "A Bleak Outlook," 3; "Globalization and Religion," 10.
54 Pew Research Center, "'Nones' on the Rise," October 9, 2012.
55 Pew Research Center, "America's Changing Religious Landscape," May 12, 2015.
56 Pew Research Center, "The Future of World Religions," April 2, 2015.
57 Pew Research Center, "The Future of World Religions," April 2, 2015.
58 Brown, "The Twentieth Century," 234.
59 Pew Research Center, "Scientists and Belief"; Larson and Witham, "Leading Scientists still Reject God."
60 The Philpapers Surveys.
61 Pigott, "Doing Church Without God."
62 Harris, *End of Faith*, 16; Dawkins, interview on Al-Jazeera, *One on One*, at 4:00-4:30.
63 Habermas, "Awareness," 19; Foucault, *Hermeneutics of the Subject*, 46-53.
64 Rorty, *Achieving Our Country*, 132-136.
65 Fuentes, *This I Believe*, 21; Franzen, *Farther Away*, 291; Motherwell, *Collected Writings*, 30.
66 Maslow, *Religions, Values, and Peak Experiences*, 17.
67 Thousands of articles have been published on the physical and psychological effects of meditation and yoga. See, for example, Goyal et al., "Meditation Programs" and Field, "Yoga Clinical Research Review."
68 James, *Varieties*, 400.
69 Marty, "Me, my church and I," 47; Hauerwas and Fischer quoted in Worthen, "One Nation Under God?"
70 American Family Association, "Our Mission"; Pew Research Center, "America's Changing Religious Landscape."
71 Ananthakrishnan, "Supreme Court to states."
72 Luhrmann, "Benefits of Church."
73 Hwang, "Atheism, Health, and Well-Being," 526, 533; Zuckerman, "Atheism and Societal Health," 507.
74 Hick, *Problems of Religious Pluralism*, in Peterson et al., ed., *Philosophy of Religion*, 563-570.
75 Asoka, Twelfth Rock Edict.

Epilogue: Spiritual but still religious?

1 Bellah et al., *Habits*, xlviii, 248, 221.
2 Bellah et al., *Habits*, 235, 221.
3 *Samyutta Nikaya* 3:18, in Bodhi, *Connected Discourses*, 180.
4 Tolstoy, "Three Methods of Reform," in *Some Social Remedies*, 29.
5 Kierkegaard, *The Point of View*, 106-110; *Kierkegaard's Journals and Notebooks*, vol. 7, 37.

BIBLIOGRAPHY

Abrams, M. H. *Natural Supernaturalism*. New York: Norton, 1973.
Adams, Fred. "The Not-So-Fine Tuning of the Universe." *Nautilus* 44 (January 19, 2017), available online at http://nautil.us/issue/44/luck/the-not_so_fine-tuning-of-the-universe.
Adler, Felix. *The Essentials of Spirituality*. New York: James Pott, 1905.
Adler, Jerry. "In Search of the Spiritual." *Newsweek*, August 29, 2005, available online at http://www.newsweek.com/search-spiritual-117833.
Advani, Kalyan. *Sachal Samarst*. New Delhi: Sahitya Akademi, 1997.
Ahunavaiti Gatha, Yasna 28, trans. C. Bartholomae, available online at Avesta.org, http://www.avesta.org/yasna/.
Alcorta, Candace, and Richard Sosis. "Ritual, Religion, and Violence: An Evolutionary Perspective." In Michael Jerryson, Mark Juergensmeyer, and Margo Kitts, eds., *The Oxford Handbook of Religion and Violence*, 1–19. Oxford: Oxford University Press, 2013.
Alexander, Samuel. *Space Time and Deity*, 2 vols. London: Macmillan, 1920.
"Al-Shabab Statement on Deadly Campus Assault in Kenya." *Washington Post*, April 4, 2015, available online at https://www.washingtonpost.com/world/africa/al-shabab-statement-on-deadly-campus-assault-in-kenya/2015/04/04/4577ce52-dad9-11e4-8103-fa84725dbf9d_story.html?hpid=z5.
Alston, William. *Perceiving God*. Ithaca, NY: Cornell University Press, 1991.
Alston, William. "Religious Experience as Perception of God." In Michael Peterson, William Hasker, Bruce Reichenbach, and David Basinger, eds., *Philosophy of Religion: Selected Readings*, 20–29. Oxford: Oxford University Press, 2001.
American Family Association. "Our Mission," available online at http://www.afa.net/who-is-afa/our-mission/.
Amritchandra Suri. *Shri Amritchandra Suri's Purushartha Siddhyupaya*, trans. Vijay Jain. Dehradun, India: Vikalp Printers, 2012.
Ananthakrishnan, G. "Supreme Court to States: Pick Officers to Stop Cow Vigilantism," *Indian Express*, September 7, 2017, available online at http://indianexpress.com/article/india/supreme-court-to-states-pick-officers-to-stop-cow-vigilantism-4831833/.
Arendt, Hannah. *Eichmann in Jerusalem*. New York: Viking Press, 1964.
Ariew, Roger, and Eric Watkins, eds. *Modern Philosophy: An Anthology of Primary Sources*. Indianapolis, IN: Hackett, 2009.
Armstrong, Karen. *Fields of Blood*. London: The Bodley Head, 2014.
Arnold, Matthew. *Culture & Anarchy*. New York: Macmillan, 1908.
Arnold, Matthew. *Literature & Dogma*. New York: Macmillan, n.d.
Arnold, Matthew. *Stanzas from the Grande Chartreuse*, available online at Poetry Foundation, http://www.poetryfoundation.org/poem/172861.

Arnold, Matthew. "The Study of Poetry," available online at Poetry Foundation, http://www.poetryfoundation.org/learning/essay/237816.
Asoka. Twelfth Rock Edict, trans. Ven. S. Dhammika, available online at Livius.com, http://www.livius.org/sources/content/ashoka-s-rock-edicts/.
Assmann, Jan. *The Price of Monotheism*, trans. Robert Savage. Stanford, CA: Stanford University Press, 2010.
Augustine. *The City of God*, trans. Marcus Dods. Peabody, MA: Hendrickson Publishers, 2009.
Aurobindo, Sri. *Complete Works of Sri Aurobindo*, 36 vols. Pondicherry: Sri Aurobindo Ashram, 1997–2017.
Ayer, Alfred Jules. *Language, Truth and Logic*. London: Penguin, 1971.
Bainton, Roland. *Christian Attitudes toward War and Peace*. Eugene, OR: Wipf and Stock, 2008.
Ballantyne, James, trans. *The Sankhya Aphorisms of Kapila*. London: Trübner, 1885.
Baltzly, Dirk. "Stoicism," available online at Stanford Encyclopedia of Philosophy, http://plato.stanford.edu/entries/stoicism/.
Balzac, Honoré de. *Œuvres complètes de H. de Balzac*, vol. 24. Paris: Calman Lévy, 1882.
Barnes, Jonathan. *The Presocratic Philosophers*. London: Routledge, 1982.
Barrows, John, ed. *The World's Parliament of Religions*, vol. 1. Chicago: The Parliament Publishing Company, 1893.
Batchelor, Stephen. *Confession of a Buddhist Atheist*. New York: Spiegel & Grau, 2010.
Batchelor, Stephen. "A Secular Buddhist." Sea of Faith Conferences 2013, available online at http://www.sofn.org.uk/sofia/110batchelor.pdf.
Beard, Mary. "How Stoical Was Seneca?," *New York Review of Books*, October 9, 2014, available online at http://www.nybooks.com/articles/archives/2014/oct/09/how-stoical-was-seneca/.
Beauvoir, Simone de. *La cérémonie des adieux suivi par entretiens avec Jean-Paul Sartre*. Paris: Gallimard, 1981.
Bellah, Robert, Richard Madsen, William M. Sullivan, Ann Swidler, and Steven M. Tipton. *Habits of the Heart*. Berkeley: University of California Press, 2007.
Bender, Courtney. "Religion and Spirituality: History, Discourse, Measurement" (January 24, 2007), available online at Social Science Research Council, religion.ssrc.org/reforum/Bender.pdf.
Bender, Courtney. *The New Metaphysicals: Spirituality and the American Religious Imagination*. Chicago: University of Chicago Press, 2010.
Berger, Peter. "A Bleak Outlook Is Seen for Religion," *New York Times* (February 25, 1968), page 3, available online at http://nyti.ms/234GnK7.
Berger, Peter. *The Sacred Canopy*. New York: Anchor Books, 1990.
Berger, Peter. "Globalization and Religion," *Hedgehog Review* 4 (Summer 2002): 7–20.
Berger, Peter, and Thomas Luckmann. *The Social Construction of Reality*. New York: Anchor Books, 1967.
Berlin, Isaiah. *The Sense of Reality*. New York: Farrar, Straus and Giroux, 1997.
Bielschowsky, Albert. *The Life of Goethe*, 3 vols., trans. William Cooper. New York: Haskell House, 1969.
Biré, Edmond. *Journal d'un bourgeois de Paris pendent la Terreur*, vol. 4. Paris: Perrin et Cie, n.d.
Blavatsky, Helena Petrovna. *Isis Unveiled*. Pasadena, CA: Theosophical University Press Online Edition, n.d., available online at http://www.theosociety.org/pasadena/ts/tup-onl.htm.
Bloom, Harold. *Wallace Stevens*. Broomall, PA: Chelsea House, 2003.
Boccaccio, Giovanni. *The Decameron*, trans. G. H. McWilliam. London: Penguin, 1972.
Bodhi, Bhikkhu, trans. *The Connected Discourses of the Buddha*, 2 vols. Boston: Wisdom Publications, 2000.

Bonhoeffer, Dietrich. *Writings*. Maryknoll, NY: Orbis, 1998.
Brass, Paul. *The Production of Hindu-Muslim Violence in Contemporary India*. Seattle: University of Washington Press, 2003.
Braverman, Arthur, trans. *Mud and Water: The Collected Teachings of Zen Master Bassui*. Boston: Wisdom Publications, 2002.
Broad, Charlie Dunbar. "Arguments for the Existence of God," *The Journal of Theological Studies* 40, no. 158 (April 1939): 156–167.
Broughton, Jeffrey. *The Bothidharma Anthology*. Berkeley: The University of California Press, 1999.
Brown, Callum. "The Twentieth Century." In Stephen Bullivant and Michael Ruse, eds., *The Oxford Handbook of Atheism*, 229–244. Oxford: Oxford University Press, 2013.
Burkert, Walter. *Homo Necans*, trans. Peter Bing. Berkeley: University of California Press, 1983.
Callewaert, Winnand, and Peter Friedlander. *The Life and Works of Raidas*. Delhi: Manohar, 1992.
Callimachi, Rukmini. "ISIS Enshrines a Theology of Rape," *New York Times* (August 13, 2015), available online at https://www.nytimes.com/2015/08/14/world/middleeast/isis-enshrines-a-theology-of-rape.html?_r=0.
Campbell, Charlie. "How an Extremist Buddhist Network Is Sowing Hatred across Asia," *Time* (August 8, 2014), available online at http://time.com/3090990/how-an-extremist-buddhist-network-is-sowing-hatred-across-asia/.
Carlyle, Thomas. *Essay on Burns*. Boston: Heath, 1897.
Cavanaugh, William. *The Myth of Religious Violence*. Oxford: Oxford University Press, 2009.
Chadwick, John W. "Samuel Johnson: A Correction—Thomas Paine," *The Conservator* 1, no. 11 (January 1891): 83.
Chadwick, John W. "Paine versus Spirituality." *The Conservator* 2, no. 1 (March 1892): 2–3.
Chalmers, David. "Facing Up to the Problem of Consciousness," *Journal of Consciousness Studies* 2, no. 3 (1995): 200–219.
Chan, Wing-Tsit, ed. *A Source Book in Chinese Philosophy*. Princeton, NJ: Princeton University Press, 1969.
Chauncy, Charles. "Enthusiasm described and caution'd against," available online at Evans Early American Imprint Collection, http://quod.lib.umich.edu/e/evans/N03978.0001.001?rgn=main;view=fulltext.
Cheng, Hsueh-li, trans. *Nagarjuna's Twelve Gate Treatise*. Dordrecht, Holland: D. Reidel, 1982.
Chrysostom, John. *Homilies Against the Jews*, available online at PreteristArchive.com, http://www.preteristarchive.com/ChurchHistory/0386_chrysostom_adversus-judeaus.html.
Cicero. *De Finibus*, available online at Bill Thayer, LacusCurtius, http://penelope.uchicago.edu/Thayer/E/Roman/Texts/Cicero/de_Finibus/5*.html.
Cicero. *The Nature of the Gods*, trans. Horace McGregor. London: Penguin, 1972.
Coleridge, Samuel Taylor. *Aids to Reflection and Confessions of an Inquiring Spirit*. New York: Cosimo, 2005.
Comte, Auguste. *System of Public Polity*, vol. 4, trans. Richard Congreve. London: Longmans Green, 1877.
Comte-Sponville, André. "Les athées n'ont pas moins d'esprit que les autres." *Psychologies*, available online at http://www.psychologies.com/Culture/Savoirs/Philosophie/Interviews/Andre-Comte-Sponville-Les-athees-n-ont-pas-moins-d-esprit-que-les-autres.
Comte-Sponville, André. "Un certain silence." *Le point références* (May–June 2013): 9–11.
Comte-Sponville, André. *The Little Book of Atheist Spirituality*. New York: Viking, 2007.
Conze, Edward, ed. *Buddhist Texts Through the Ages*. Oxford: Bruno Cassirer, 1954.

Cowell, Alan. "After 350 Years, Vatican Says Galileo Was Right." *New York Times* (October 31, 1992), available online at http://www.nytimes.com/1992/10/31/world/after-350-years-vatican-says-galileo-was-right-it-moves.html.

Creel, Herrlee. *Chinese Thought from Confucius to Mao Tsê-tung*. Chicago: University of Chicago Press, 1953.

Cupitt, Don. *Talking Leave of God*. London: SCM Press (Kindle edition), 2001.

Curd, Patricia. "Presocratic Philosophy." In *Stanford Encyclopedia of Philosophy*, available online at http://plato.stanford.edu/entries/presocratics/.

Dalai Lama, *see* Gyatso, Tenzin.

Dalley, Stephanie, ed. and trans. *Myths from Mesopotamia*. Oxford: Oxford University Press, 2000.

Darwin, Charles, "Letter to Asa Gray." May 22, 1860, available online at Darwin Correspondence Project, University of Cambridge, https://www.darwinproject.ac.uk/letter/DCP-LETT-2814.xml.

Darwin, Charles. *Charles Darwin's Natural Selection*, ed. Robert C. Stauffer. Cambridge: Cambridge University Press, 1975.

Davies, Paul. *The Mind of God*. New York: Simon & Schuster, 1992.

Davis, Natalie Zemon. "The Rites of Violence: Religious Riot in Sixteenth-Century France," *Past & Present* 59 (1973): 51–91.

Dawkins, Richard. *The God Delusion*. London: Black Swan, 2007.

Dawkins, Richard. "Interview on Al-Jazeera." *One on One* (January 9, 2010), available online at http://www.aljazeera.com/programmes/oneonone/2010/01/201015101057987686.html.

De la Vallée Poussin, Louis, trans. *L'Abhidharmakosa de Vasubandhu*. Paris: Paul Geuthner, 1923.

Dennett, Daniel. "Facing Backwards on the Problem of Consciousness." In Jonathan Shear, ed., *Explaining Consciousness—The Hard Problem*, 33–36. Cambridge, MA: MIT Press, 1997.

Descartes, René. *Discourse on Method*, trans. John Veitch. In *The Rationalists*. New York: Anchor Books, 1974.

Deutsch, Eliot, ed., *The Essential Vedanta*. Bloomington, IN: World Wisdom, 2004.

Dewey, John. *A Common Faith*. New Haven, CT: Yale University Press, 1967.

Dexter, Byron. "Wanted: A New Messiah," *The American Mercury* 9 (October 1926): 233–241.

Dharmapala, Anagarika. *Return to Righteousness*. Colombo: Ministry of Education and Cultural Affairs, 1965.

Dharmapala, Anagarika. *The Arya Dharma of Sakya Muni, Gautama Buddha*. Calcutta: Maha Bodhi Book Agency, 1989, available online at http://www.arfalpha.com/selfdiscipline/selfdiscipline.htm.

D'Holbach, Baron de. *Le bon-sens, ou, Idées naturelles opposes aux idées surnaturelles*. London: n.p., 1772.

D'Holbach, Baron de. *System of Nature*. 2 vols., available online at Project Gutenberg, http://www.gutenberg.org/files/8909/8909-h/8909-h.htm and http://www.gutenberg.org/files/8910/8910-h/8910-h.htm.

Diogenes Laertius. *Lives of Eminent Philosophers*, trans. R. D. Hicks. Cambridge, MA: Harvard University Press, 1925, available online at Perseus Digital Library, http://www.perseus.tufts.edu/hopper/text?doc=Perseus:text:1999.01.0258.

Dolin, Tim. *George Eliot*. Oxford: Oxford University Press, 2005.

Doniger [O'Flaherty], Wendy, trans. *The Rig Veda*. New Delhi: Penguin, 1994.

Duckett, M. W., ed. *Dictionnaire de la conversation et de la lecture*, Supplément, vol. 1. Paris: Didot, 1864.

Duggan, Christopher. *The Force of Destiny: A History of Italy since 1796*. New York: Houghton Mifflin, 2007.
Durkheim, Émile. *Sociology and Philosophy*, trans. D. F. Pocock. London: Cohen & West, 1953.
Durkheim, Émile. *On Morality and Society*, trans. Mark Traugoff. Chicago: University of Chicago Press, 1973.
Durkheim, Émile. *The Elementary Forms of the Religious Life*, trans. Karen Fields. New York: The Free Press, 1995.
Dworkin, Ronald. *Religion without God*. Cambridge, MA: Harvard University Press, 2013.
Eggeling, Julius, trans. *Satapatha Brahmana*. Vols. 12, 24, 26, 37, 47 of *Sacred Books of the East*, available online at Internet Sacred Text Archive, http://www.sacred-texts.com/hin/sbr/index.htm.
Elias, Jamal, trans. *Death Before Dying: The Sufi Poems of Sultan Bahu*. Berkeley: University of California Press, 1998.
Elson, John. "Toward a Hidden God." *Time* (April 8, 1966), available online at http://content.time.com/time/magazine/article/0,9171,835309,00.html.
Embree, Ainslie, ed. *Sources of Indian Tradition*, vol. 1. New Delhi: Penguin, 1992.
Emerson, Ralph Waldo. *The Journals and Miscellaneous Notebooks of Ralph Waldo Emerson*, 16 vols. Cambridge, MA: Harvard University Press, 1960–1982.
Emerson, Ralph Waldo. *Selected Essays*. New York: Penguin, 1982.
Epictetus. *Discourses and Selected Writings*, trans. Robert Dobbin. London: Penguin, 2008.
Epicurus. *The Essential Epicurus*, trans. Eugene O'Connor. Amherst, NY: Prometheus Books, 1993.
Ernst, Carl. *The Shambhala Guide to Sufism*. Boston: Shambhala, 1997.
"Euripidean Fragments and Bellerophon's Atheism." *Sententiae Antiquae* (August 16, 2015), available online at https://sententiaeantiquae.com/2015/08/16/euripidean-fragments-and-bellerophons-atheism/.
Euripides. *The Trojan Women*, trans. Alan. Shapiro. Oxford: Oxford University Press, 2009.
Evans, Henry Ridgely. *Hours with Ghosts or Nineteenth-Century Witchcraft*. Chicago: Laird and Lee, 1897.
Evelyn-White, Hugh, trans. *The Homeric Hymns and Homerica*. London: William Heinemann, 1914, available online at Perseus Digital Library, http://www.perseus.tufts.edu/hopper/text?doc=Perseus%3Atext%3A1999.01.0138%3Ahymn%3D31.
Ezekiel, Isaac. *Saint Paltu: His Life and Teachings*. Beas, India: Radha Soami Satsang, 1979.
Feuerbach, Ludwig. *The Essence of Christianity*, trans. Marian Evans [George Eliot]. New York: Calvin Blanchard, 1855.
Field, Tiffany. "Yoga Clinical Research Review," *Complementary Therapies in Clinical Practice* 17 (2001): 1–8.
Firestone, Reuven. *Jihad: The Origin of Holy War in Islam*. Oxford: Oxford University Press, 1999.
Foucault, Michel. *The Hermeneutics of the Subject*, trans. Graham Burchell. New York: Picador, 2004.
Frankfort, Henri, Henriette Antonia Frankfort, John A. Wilson, and Thorkild Jacobsen. *Before Philosophy*. Baltimore, MD: Penguin, 1973.
Franzen, Jonathan. *Farther Away*. London: Fourth Estate, 2012.
Freud, Sigmund. *The Future of an Illusion*, trans. James Strachey. New York: Norton, 1961.
Freud, Sigmund. *The Freud Reader*, ed. Peter Gay. New York: Norton, 1989.
Freud, Sigmund. *Civilization and its Discontents*, trans. David McLintock. London: Penguin, 2002.
Fuentes, Carlos. *This I Believe*, trans. Kristina Cordero. London: Bloomsbury, 2005.

Gaddis, Michael. *There Is No Crime for Those Who Have Christ*. Berkeley: University of California Press, 2005.

Gallop, George. "Americans' Spiritual Searches Turn Inward." February 11, 2003, available online at http://www.gallup.com/poll/7759/americans-spiritual-searches-turn-inward.aspx.

Gahlot, Mandakini. "Filmmaker's View." October 8, 2015, available online at Aljazeera.com http://www.aljazeera.com/programmes/peopleandpower/2015/10/indias-hindu-fundamentalists-151008073418225.html.

Gambhirananda, Swami, trans. *Brahma-Sutra-Bhasya of Shankaracharya*. Mayavati, India: Advaita Ashrama, 1996.

Gardner, Daniel, trans. *The Four Books: The Basic Teachings of the Later Confucian Tradition*. Indianapolis, IN: Hackett, 2007.

Garfield, Jay, trans. *The Fundamental Wisdom of the Middle Way: Nagarjuna's Mulamadhyamakarika*. New York: Oxford University Press, 1995.

Ginzburg, Carlo. *The Cheese and the Worms*, trans. John and Anne Tedeschi. Baltimore: Johns Hopkins University Press, 1992.

Girard, René. *Violence and the Sacred*, trans. Patrick Gregory. Baltimore: Johns Hopkins University Press, 1979.

Goethe, Johann Wolfgang von. *Faust*, Parts 1 & 2, trans. A.S. Kline. N.p.: Poetry in Translation, 2003.

Goethe, Johann Wolfgang von. *Selected Poetry*, ed. and trans. David Luke. London: Penguin, 2005.

Gombrich, Richard. *Theravada Buddhism*. London: Routledge, 2006.

Gorski, Philip, and Gülay Türkmen-Dervisoglu. "Religion, Nationalism, and Violence: An Integrated Approach," *Annual Review of Sociology* 39 (2013): 193–210.

Goyal, Madhav, et al. "Meditation Programs for Psychological Stress and Well-being," *JAMA Internal Medicine* 174 (2014): 357–368.

Grossman, Cathy Lynn. "Survey: 72% of Millennials 'More Spiritual Than Religious.'" *USA Today* (October 14, 2010), available online at http://usatoday30.usatoday.com/news/religion/2010-04-27-1Amillfaith27_ST_N.htm.

Growse, Frederic Salmon. *Mathura: A District Memoir*. New Delhi: Asian Educational Services, 1979.

Guyon, Madame [Jeanne]. *Le moyen court et autres écrits spirituels*. Grenoble: Jérôme Millon, 1995.

Gyatso, Tenzin [Dalai Lama]. *The Meaning of Life*, trans. Jeffrey Hopkins. Boston: Wisdom, 1992.

Gyatso, Tenzin [Dalai Lama]. "Many Faiths, One Truth." *New York Times* (May 24, 2010), available online at http://www.nytimes.com/2010/05/25/opinion/25gyatso.html?_r=0.

Gyatso, Tenzin [Dalai Lama]. *Beyond Religion*. Boston: Houghton Mifflin Harcourt 2011.

Habermas, Jürgen. "An Awareness of What is Missing." In Jürgen Habermas et al., *An Awareness of What is Missing*, trans. Ciaran Cronin, 15–23. Malden, MA: Polity, 2010.

Hall, John. "Religion and Violence from a Sociological Perspective." In Michael Jerryson, Mark Juergensmeyer, and Margo Kitts, eds., *The Oxford Handbook of Religion and Violence*, 1–9. Oxford: Oxford University Press, 2013.

Hamid, Nafees. "What Makes a Terrorist." *New York Review of Books*, NYR Daily, August 23, 2017, available online at http://www.nybooks.com/daily/2017/08/23/what-makes-a-terrorist/.

Hanegraaff, Wouter. "New Age Religion." In Linda Woodhead, ed., *Religions in the Modern World*, 287–304. London: Routledge, 2002.

Hanh, Thich Nhat. *The Heart of the Buddha's Teaching*. London: Rider, 1999.

Harris, Sam. *The End of Faith*. New York: Norton, 2004.
Heelas, Paul. "The Spiritual Revolution: From 'Religion' to 'Spirituality.'" In Linda Woodhead, ed., *Religions in the Modern World*, 412–436. London: Routledge, 2002.
Heelas, Paul, and Linda Woodhead. *The Spiritual Revolution*. Malden, MA: Wiley-Blackwell, 2005.
Hess, Linda, and Shukhdev Singh, trans. *The Bijak of Kabir*. Delhi: Motilal Banarsidass, 1986.
Hick, John. "Religious Pluralism." In Michael Peterson, William Hasker, Bruce Reichenbach, and David Basinger, eds., *Philosophy of Religion: Selected Readings*, 560–570. Oxford: Oxford University Press, 2001.
Hick, John. "Soul-Making Theodicy." In Michael Peterson, William Hasker, Bruce Reichenbach, and David Basinger, eds., *Philosophy of Religion: Selected Readings*, 301–315. Oxford: Oxford University Press, 2001.
Hickman, Larry A. "Secularism, Secularization and John Dewey." In A. G. Rud, James Garrison, and Lynda Stone, eds., *John Dewey at 150*, 18–29. West Lafayette, IN: Purdue University Press, 2009.
Hitchens, Christopher. *God Is Not Great*. London: Atlantic Books, 2008.
Hobbes, Thomas. *The English Works of Thomas Hobbes*, vol. 4. London: John Bohn, 1811.
Hobbes, Thomas. *Leviathan*. Oxford: Oxford University Press, 1998.
Hoffmann, Ernst Theodor Amadeus. *E.T.A. Hoffmann's Musical Writings*, trans. Martyn Clarke. Cambridge: Cambridge University Press, 2003.
Hollywood, Amy. "Spiritual but Not Religious." *Harvard Divinity Bulletin* 38, nos. 1 & 2 (Winter/Spring 2010), available online at https://bulletin.hds.harvard.edu/articles/winterspring2010/spiritual-not-religious.
Hudson, Wayne. *The English Deists: Studies in Early Enlightenment*. London: Routledge, 2016.
Humanist Manifesto I (1933), available online at American Humanist Association, http://americanhumanist.org/Humanism/Humanist_Manifesto_I.
Hume, David. *The Natural History of Religion*. 1889 edition, available online at Online Library of Liberty, http://oll.libertyfund.org/titles/hume-the-natural-history-of-religion.
Hume, David. *Dialogues Concerning Natural Religion*. Cambridge: Cambridge University Press, 2007.
Huss, Boas. "Spirituality: The Emergence of a New Cultural Category and Its Challenge to the Religious and the Secular." *Journal of Contemporary Religion* 29, no. 1 (2014): 47–60.
Hutton, Richard Holt. "Spirituality without God." *The Spectator* (January 13, 1866): 37–39, available online at http://archive.spectator.co.uk/page/13th-january-1866/9.
Hwang, Karen. "Atheism, Health, and Well-Being." In Stephen Bullivant and Michael Ruse, eds., *The Oxford Handbook of Atheism*, 525–536. Oxford: Oxford University Press, 2013.
Ingersoll, Robert. *The Works of Robert G. Ingersoll*, vol. 4. New York: Dresden, 1902.
Israel, Jonathan. *Radical Enlightenment: Philosophy and the Making of Modernity 1650-1750*. Oxford: Oxford University Press, 2001.
Jacobi, Hermann, trans. *Jaina Sutras*. Vols. 22 and 45 of *Sacred Books of the East*. Delhi: Motilal Banarsidass, 1999.
Jacobs, Alan, ed. *The Element Book of Mystical Verse*. Shaftesbury, Dorset: Element, 1997.
Jaini, Padmanabh. *The Jaina Path of Purification*. Delhi: Motilal Banarsidass, 1998.
James, William. *The Letters of William James*, vol. 2. Boston: The Atlantic Monthly Press, 1920.
James, William. *The Varieties of Religious Experience: A Study in Human Nature*. London: Routledge, 2002.
"Japan." *Journal of the Maha-Bodhi Society* 1, no. 11 (March 1893): 5.
Jaspers, Karl. *The Origin and Goal of History*, trans. Michael Bullock. New Haven, CT: Yale University Press, 1965.

Johnson, Edward Hamilton, trans. *Asvaghosa's Buddhacarita*. Delhi: Motilal Banarsidass, 1995.
Johnson, W. J., trans. *The Bhagavad Gita*. Oxford: Oxford University Press, 1994.
Juergensmeyer, Mark. *Terror in the Mind of God*. Berkeley: University of California Press, 2000.
Juergensmeyer, Mark, and Margo Kitts. *Princeton Readings in Religion and Violence*. Princeton, NJ: Princeton University Press, 2011.
Kalupahana, David. *Ethics in Early Buddhism*. Delhi: Motilal Banarsidass, 2008.
Kandinsky, Wassily. *Concerning the Spiritual in Art*. N.p.: The Floating Press, 2008.
Kant, Immanuel. *Philosophische Enzyklopädie*. In *Gesammelte Schriften*, vol. 29, 1–45. Berlin: Walter de Grunter, 1980.
Kant, Immanuel. *Critique of Pure Reason*, trans. Paul Guyer and Allen Wood. Cambridge: Cambridge University Press, 1998.
Kant, Immanuel. *Prolegomena to any Future Metaphysics*, trans. Gary Hatfield. Cambridge: Cambridge University Press, 2004.
Kaur Singh, Nikky-Guninder. *The Name of My Beloved: Verses of the Sikh Gurus*. San Francisco: HarperSanFrancisco, 1996.
Kaviratna, Harishchandra, trans. *Dhammapada: Wisdom of the Buddha*. Pasadena, CA: Theosophical University Press, 2001.
Kierkegaard, Søren. *Concluding Unscientific Postscript to the Philosophical Crumbs*, trans. Alastair Hannay. Cambridge: Cambridge University Press, 2009.
Kierkegaard, Søren. *The Point of View*, ed. and trans. Howard Hong and Edna Hong. Princeton, NJ: Princeton University Press, 2009.
Kierkegaard, Søren. *Kierkegaard's Journals and Notebooks*, vol. 7, ed. Niels Jørgen Cappelørn, Alastair Hannay, Bruce H. Kirmmse, David D. Possen, Joel D. S. Rasmussen, Vanessa Rumble, and K. Brian Söderquist. Princeton, NJ: Princeton Univesity Press, 2014.
Kors, Alan Charles. *D'Holbach's Coterie*. Princeton, NJ: Princeton University Press, 2015.
Küng, Hans. *On Being a Christian*, trans. Edward Quinn. Garden City, NY: Doubleday, 1976.
Larson, Edward, and Larry Witham. "Leading Scientists Still Reject God." *Nature* 394 (23 July 1998): 313, available online at https://www.nature.com/nature/journal/v394/n6691/full/394313a0.html.
Larson, Gerald James. *Classical Samkhya*. Delhi: Motilal Banarsidass, 1979.
Lau, Din-cheuk, trans. *The Analects (Lun yü)*. London: Penguin, 1979.
Lavie, Jeffrey. *The Theosophical Society: The History of a Spiritualist Movement*. Boca Ratan, FL: BrownWalker, 2012.
Lenin, Vladimir Ilyich. *Religion*. London: CPGB-ML, 2012.
Lévi, Éliphas. *Dogme et rituel de la haute magie*, vol. 1. Paris: Germer Baillière, 1861.
Locke, John. *A Letter Concerning Toleration*, trans. William Popple. Adelaide: eBooks@Adelaide, 2014, available online at https://ebooks.adelaide.edu.au/l/locke/john/l81t/complete.html.
Lucian. *Selected Dialogues*, trans. Desmond Costa. Oxford: Oxford University Press, 2005.
Lucretius. *On the Nature of the Universe*, trans. R. E. Latham. London: Penguin, 2005.
Luhrmann, Tanya Marie. "Benefits of Church." *New York Times* (April 20, 2013), available online at http://www.nytimes.com/2013/04/21/opinion/sunday/luhrmann-why-going-to-church-is-good-for-you.html?_r=0.
Luther, Martin. "Open Letter to the Christian Nobility of the German Nation Concerning the Reform of the Christian Estate (1520)," available online at http://web.stanford.edu/~jsabol/certainty/readings/Luther-ChristianNobility.pdf.
Mainkar, Trimbak Govind, trans. *Samkhyakarika of Isvarakrsna*. Delhi: Chaukhamba Sanskrit Pratishthan, 2004.
Malcolm, Norman. *Wittgenstein: A Religious Point of View?* London: Routledge, 1997.

Mallock, William Hurrell. Review of George Eliot, *Impressions of Theophrastus Such*. *Edinburgh Review* 150 (October 1879): 287–302.
Mann, Thomas. *Reflections of a Nonpolitical Man*. New York: Ungar, 1983.
Marcus Aurelius. *Meditations*, trans. Gregory Hayes. New York: The Modern Library, 2002.
Marsh, James. "Dr. Marsh's Preliminary Essay." In Samuel Taylor Coleridge, *Aids to Reflection and Confessions of an Inquiring Spirit*, xxiii–lxxvi. New York: Cosimo, 2005.
Marty, Martin. "Me, My Church and I," *The Christian Century* 122 (January 25, 2005): 47.
Marx, Karl, and Fredrich Engels. *Collected Works*, vol. 3, trans. Clemens Dutt. Moscow: Progress Publishers, 1975.
Maslow, Abraham. *Religions, Values, and Peak Experiences*. Seattle: Stellar, 2014.
McLeod, William Hewat. *Guru Nanak and the Sikh Religion*. Delhi: Oxford University Press, 2001.
McMahan, David. "The Enchanted Secular." *The Eastern Buddhist* 43, nos. 1 & 2 (2012): 205–223.
McRae, John. *Seeing through Zen*. Berkeley: University of California Press, 2003.
Mead, George Robert Stowe. "On the Track of Spirituality." *The Theosophical Review* 41, no. 243 (November 1907): 250–257.
Menand, Louis. *The Metaphysical Club*. New York: Farrar, Straus and Giroux, 2002.
Meslier, Jean. *Œuvres complètes*, 3 vols. Paris: Anthropos, 1974–1984.
Miller, Barbara Stoler, trans. *Yoga: Discipline of Freedom: The Yoga Sutra Attributed to Patanjali*. New York: Bantam Books, 1998.
"Minor Divisions and Subdivisions of the Svetambaras," available online at Jain World, http://www.jainworld.com/book/historyofjainism/ch11c.asp.
Mitsis, Philip. "Stoicism." In Christopher Shields, ed., *The Blackwell Guide to Ancient Philosophy*, 253–267. Malden, MA: Blackwell, 2003.
Monk, Ray. *Ludwig Wittgenstein: The Duty of Genius*. London: Penguin, 1991.
Monod, Jacques. *Chance and Necessity*, trans. Austryn Wainhouse. New York: Vintage Books, 1972.
Montaigne, Michel de. *The Complete Works*, trans. Donald Frame. New York: Everyman's Library, 2003.
Motherwell, Robert. *Collected Writings*. Berkeley: University of California Press, 1999.
Moyne, John, and Coleman Barks. *Unseen Rain: Quatrains of Rumi*. Boston: Shambhala, 2001.
Musonius. *Lectures & Sayings*, trans. Cynthia King. N.p.: William P. Irvine, 2011.
Nadler, Steven. *Spinoza: A Life*. Cambridge: Cambridge University Press, 2001.
Nadler, Steven. *Spinoza's Ethics: An Introduction*. Cambridge: Cambridge University Press, 2006.
Nagarjuna. *The Precious Garland Ratnavali*, available online at The Zen Site, http://www.thezensite.com/ZenEssays/Nagarjuna/Garland_of_Ratnavali.html.
Nagel, Thomas. *Mortal Questions*. Cambridge: Cambridge University Press, 1979.
Nagel, Thomas. *Secular Philosophy and the Religious Temperament*. Oxford: Oxford University Press, 2010.
Nakamura, Hajime. *A Comparative History of Ideas*. Delhi: Motilal Banarsidass, 1992.
Nanamoli, Bhikhu, and Bhikhu Bodhi. *The Middle Length Discourses of the Buddha*. Boston: Wisdom Publications, 1995.
Nichiren. Letter to Konichi-bo, 1276. In *Major Writings of Nichiren Daishonin*, available online at http://nichiren.info/gosho/LetterKonichibo.htm.
Nicholson, Andrew. *Unifying Hinduism*. Ranikhet, India: Permanent Black, 2011.
Nicholson, Reynold. *Studies in Islamic Poetry*. Cambridge: Cambridge University Press, 1921.
Nicholson, Reynold. *A Literary History of the Arabs*. London: Routledge, 1993.
Nietzsche, Friedrich. *Twilight of the Idols and The Anti-Christ*, trans. Reginald John Hollingdale. London: Penguin, 1990.

Nietzsche, Friedrich. *The Birth of Tragedy*, trans. Shaun Whiteside. London: Penguin, 1993.
Nietzsche, Friedrich. *Human, All too Human*, trans. Reginald John Hollingdale. Cambridge: Cambridge University Press, 1996.
Nietzsche, Friedrich. *Selected Letters*, trans. Christopher Middleton. Indianapolis, IN: Hackett, 1996.
Nietzsche, Friedrich. *Daybreak*, trans. Reginald John Hollingdale. Cambridge: Cambridge University Press, 1997.
Nietzsche, Friedrich. *The Gay Science*, trans. Josefine Nauckerhoff. Cambridge: Cambridge University Press, 2001.
Nietzsche, Friedrich. *Ecce Homo*, trans. Reginald John Hollingdale. London: Penguin, 2004.
Nietzsche, Friedrich. *Thus Spoke Zarathustra*, trans. Adrian del Caro. Cambridge: Cambridge University Press, 2006.
Nivedita, Sister [Margaret Noble]. *Religion and Dharma*. London: Longmans, Green, 1915.
Nyanaponika Thera, and Bhikhu Bodhi, trans. *Anguttara Nikaya: Discourses of the Buddha*. Kandy, Sri Lanka: Buddhist Publication Society Online Edition, 2010.
Olcott, Henry Steel. *The Buddhist Catechism*. Colombo: Ministry of Cultural Affairs, n.d.
Olcott, Henry Steel. *Old Diary Leaves* [first series]. New York: G.P. Putnam's Sons, 1895.
Olcott, Henry Steel. *Old Diary Leaves* [second series]. London: The Theosophical Publishing Society, 1900.
Otto, Bernd-Christian, and Michael Strausberg. *Defining Magic: A Reader*. Abingdon, Oxon: Routledge, 2014.
Paley, William. *Natural Theology*. New York: American Tract Society, 1881.
Parry, Ralph Barton. *The Thought and Character of William James*. Nashville, TN: Vanderbilt University Press, 1996.
Pater, Walter. "Coleridge's Writings." *Westminster Review*, N.S. 29 (January 1866), 106–132.
Pegg, Mark Gregory. *A Most Holy War*. Oxford: Oxford University Press, 2008.
Pew Research Center. "Scientists and Belief," November 5, 2009, available online at http://www.pewforum.org/2009/11/05/scientists-and-belief/.
Pew Research Center. " 'Nones' on the Rise," October 9, 2012, available online at http://www.pewforum.org/2012/10/09/nones-on-the-rise/ [press release], http://www.pewforum.org/files/2012/10/NonesOnTheRise-full.pdf [full report].
Pew Research Center. "The Future of World Religions: Population Growth Projections, 2010–2050," April 2, 2015, available online at http://www.pewforum.org/2015/04/02/religious-projections-2010-2050/.
Pew Research Center. "America's Changing Religious Landscape," May 12, 2015, available online at http://www.pewforum.org/files/2015/05/RLS-08-26-full-report.pdf.
Philpapers Surveys, available online at http://philpapers.org/surveys/results.pl?affil=Target+faculty&areas0=0&areas_max=1&grain=fine.
Pigott, Robert. "Doing Church Without God." *BBC News* (November 1, 2013), available online at http://www.bbc.com/news/uk-24766314.
Pine, Red, trans. *The Platform Sutra: The Zen Teaching of Hui-Neng*. Berkeley: Counterpoint, 2006.
Plato. *The Dialogues of Plato*, vol. 2, trans. Benjamin Jowett. New York: Oxford University Press, 1892.
Plato. *The Dialogues of Plato*, vol. 4, trans. Benjamin Jowett. London: Oxford University Press, 1931.
Plato. *Five Dialogues*, trans. George Maximilian Antony Grube. Indianapolis, IN: Hackett, 2002.
Plato. *Phaedrus*, trans. Robin Waterfield. Oxford: Oxford University Press, 2002.

Pliny. *Natural History,* vol. 1, trans. H. Rackham. Cambridge, MA: Harvard University Press, 1867.
Pojman, Louis, and Michael Rea, eds. *Philosophy of Religion: An Anthology.* Independence, KY: CenageBrain, 2013.
Popkin, Richard Henry. *The Philosophy of the Sixteenth and Seventeenth Centuries.* New York: Simon and Schuster, 1966.
Popkin, Richard Henry. *The History of Scepticism.* Oxford: Oxford University Press, 2003.
Qutb, Sayyid. *Milestones.* Birmingham: Maktabah Booksellers and Publishers, 2006.
Radhakrishnan, Sarvepalli, and Charles Moore, eds. *A Source Book in Indian Philosophy.* Princeton, NJ: Princeton University Press, 1973.
Rambachan, Anantanand. *The Limits of Scripture: Vivekananda's Reinterpretation of the Vedas.* Delhi: Sri Satguru Publications, 1995.
Ransom, Josephine. *A Short History of the Theosophical Society.* Madras, India: Theosophical Publishing House, 1938, available online at http://www.teozofija.info/Teozofsko_gibanje/Ransom_History1_E.htm.
Rao, Velcheru Narayana, and Gene Roghair, trans. *Siva's Warriors: The Basava Purana of Palkuriti Somanatha.* Princeton, NJ: Princeton University Press, 1990.
Reicher, Stephen, S. Alexander Haslam, and Rakshi Rath. "Making a Virtue of Evil: A Five-Step Social Identity Model of the Development of Collective Hate." *Social and Personal Psychology Compass* 2/3 (2008): 1313–1344.
Rhys Davids, Thomas William, ed. *Yogavacara's Manual of Indian Mysticism as Practised by Buddhists.* London: Pali Text Society, 1896.
Riyad as-Salihin, available online at Sunnah.com, https://sunnah.com/riyadussaliheen/12.
Roebuck, Valerie, trans. *The Upanishads.* Delhi: Penguin, 2000.
Romanes, George John. *A Candid Examination of Theism.* Boston: Houghton, Osgood, 1878.
Roof, Wade Clark. *Spiritual Marketplace.* Princeton, NJ: Princeton University Press, 1999.
Rorty, Richard. *Achieving Our Country.* Cambridge, MA: Harvard University Press, 1998.
Rose, Stuart. "Is the Term 'Spirituality' a Word that Everyone Uses but Nobody Knows What Anyone Means by It?" *Journal of Contemporary Religion* 16, no. 2 (2001): 193–207.
Roy, Rammohan. *The Essential Writings of Raja Rammohan Roy*, ed. Bruce Carlisle. Delhi: Oxford University Press, 1999.
Sahih Muslim, available online at Sunnah.com, https://sunnah.com/muslim/32/3.
Santaraksita. *The Tattvasangraha of Santaraksita,* vol. 1, trans. Ganganatha Jha. Baroda, India: Oriental Institute, 1937.
Santayana, George. *The Philosophy of Santayana*, ed. Irwin Edman. New York: Modern Library, 1942.
Santideva. *The Bodhicharyavatara,* trans. Kate Crosby and Andrew Skilton. Oxford: Oxford University Press, 1995.
Sartre, Jean-Paul. *War Diaries: Notebooks from a Phoney War 1939–40,* trans. Quintin Hoare. London: Verso, 1999.
Sartre, Jean-Paul. *Existentialism Is a Humanism,* trans. Carol Macomber. New Haven, CT: Yale University Press, 2007.
Sasaki, Ruth Fuller, trans. *The Record of Linji.* Honolulu: University of Hawaii Press, 2009.
Schaff, Philip. *Nicene and Post-Nicene Fathers*, series 1, vol. 9. Grand Rapids, MI: Christian Classics Ethereal Library, n.d.
Schimmel, Annemarie. *Pain and Grace.* Leiden: Brill, 1976.
Schleiermacher, Friedrich. *On Religion: Speeches to Its Cultured Despisers,* trans. John Oman. London: Kegan Paul, 1893.

Schmemann, Serge. "Assassination in Israel." *New York Times* (November 5, 1995), available online at http://www.nytimes.com/1995/11/06/world/assassination-israel-overview-stunned-israel-mourns-honors-its-fallen-leader.html.
Schmidt, Leigh. *Restless Souls: The Making of American Spirituality*. New York: HarperCollins, 2005.
Schmidt, Leigh. "The Aspiring Side of Religion," *Spiritus* 7, no. 1 (2007): 89–92.
Schneiders, Sandra Marie. "Religion vs. Spirituality: A Contemporary Conundrum," *Spiritus* 3, no. 2 (2003): 163–185.
Schopenhauer, Arthur. *Two Essays*. London: George Bell and Sons, 1889.
Schopenhauer, Arthur. *Essays and Aphorisms*, trans. Reginald John Hollingdale. London: Penguin, 1970.
Schopenhauer, Arthur. *The World as Will and* Representation, vol. 1, trans. Judith Norman, Alistair Welchman, and Christopher Janaway. Cambridge: Cambridge University Press, 2010.
Seager, Richard. *The Dawn of Religions Pluralism: Voices from the World's Parliament of Religions*. La Salle, IL: Open Court, 1993.
Sen, Keshub Chunder. *Keshub Chunder Sen's Lectures in India*. London: Cassell, 1901.
Sen, Keshub Chunder. *Discourses and Writings*. Calcutta: Brahmo Tract Society, 1904.
Seneca. *Letters from a Stoic: Epistulae Morales ad Lucilium*, trans. Robin Campbell. London: Penguin, 2004.
Seneca. *Dialogues and Letters*, trans. C. D. N. Costa. London: Penguin, 2005.
Seneviratne, H. L. *The Work of Kings*. Chicago: University of Chicago Press, 1999.
Sextus Empiricus. *Outlines of Scepticism*, trans. Julia Annas and Jonathan Barnes. Cambridge: Cambridge University Press, 2000.
Sheldrake, Philip. *A Brief History of Spirituality*. Malden, MA: Blackwell, 2007.
Shelley, Percy Bysshe. *Hymn to Intellectual Beauty*, available online at Poetry Foundation, http://www.poetryfoundation.org/poem/174390.
Shelley, Percy Bysshe. *Queen Mab*. Adelaide: ebooks@Adelaide, 2014, available online at https://ebooks.adelaide.edu.au/s/shelley/percy_bysshe/queen_mab/complete.html.
Shelley, Percy Bysshe. *Selected Prose*. London: Watts, 1915.
Shek, Daniel. "The Spirituality of the Chinese People: A Critical Review." In Michael Harris Bond, ed., *Oxford Handbook of Chinese Psychology*, 343–366. Oxford: Oxford University Press, 2010.
Sima Qian. *Historical Records*, trans. Raymond Dawson. Oxford: Oxford University Press, 1994.
Simmel, Georg. *Essays on Religion*, trans. Horst Jürgen Helle. New Haven, CT: Yale University Press, 1997.
Simmel, Georg. *Simmel on Culture: Selected Writings*, ed. David Frisby and Mike Featherstone. London: Sage, 1997.
Singh, Bawa Chhajju. *Life and Teachings of Swami Dayanand Saraswati*. Lahore: n.p., 1903, extract available online at Blavatsky Study Center, http://www.blavatskyarchives.com/dayanandahumbuggery.htm.
"Society for Psychological Research." In "Notes and Comments." *Psychological Review* 4 (May 1882): 251–254.
Soyen, Shaku. *Sermons of a Buddhist Abbot*, trans. D. T. Suzuki. Chicago: Open Court, 1906.
Spencer, Herbert. "Retrogressive Religion," *The Nineteenth Century* 16 (July 1884): 3–26.
Spencer, Herbert. *Principles of Ethics*, vol. 1. New York: Appleton, 1893.
Spencer, Herbert. *First Principles*. Cambridge: Cambridge University Press, 2009.
Sperry, Roger Wolcott. "A Modified Concept of Consciousness," *Psychological Review* 76, no. 6 (1969): 532–536.

Spinoza, Baruch. *Complete Works*, trans. Samuel Shirley. Indianapolis, IN: Hackett, 2002.
"Spiritual Tendencies." *U.L.T.* 4, no. 23 (December 1915): 177–178.
Steiner, George. *Real Presences*. Chicago: University of Chicago Press, 1989.
Stendhal. *The Red and the Black*, trans. Burton Raffel. New York: Modern Library, 2004.
Stephen, Leslie. *An Agnostic's Apology*. New York: G.P. Putnam's Sons, 1908.
Stern, Avraham. "The Ideology of the Lehi," available online at http://www.saveisrael.com/stern/saveisraelstern.htm.
Stevens, Wallace. *The Collected Poems of Wallace Stevens*. New York: Knopf, 1971.
Stevenson, Ian. *Twenty Cases Suggestive of Reincarnation*. Charlottesville: University Press of Virginia, 1974.
Stravinsky, Igor. *The Rite of Spring*. Performance by Joffrey Ballet, 1987, available online at YouTube, https://www.youtube.com/watch?v=jF1OQkHybEQ&list=PLiLVo7MRLxI5IHMF4qQNjbwJzfITfzkbj.
Streusand, Douglas. "What Does Jihad Mean?" *Middle East Quarterly* (September 1997), 9–17, available online at http://www.meforum.org/357/what-does-jihad-mean.
Stroumsa, Sarah. *Freethinkers of Medieval Islam*. Leiden: Brill, 1999.
Sunan an-Nasa'i, available online at Sunnah.com, https://sunnah.com/nasai.
Supreme Court of India, Civil Appeal No. 12 of 2016, January 5, 2016, available online at Court Verdict, http://courtverdict.com/supreme-court-of-india/sri-aurobindo-ashram-trust-and-ors-vs-r-ramanathan-and-ors.
Suroor, Hasan. "Islam and its Interpretations." *The Hindu* (September 29, 2014), available online at http://www.thehindu.com/opinion/lead/islam-and-its-interpretations/article6455101.ece.
Suttle, Gary. "Raphson, Joseph (1648–1715)." In Bron Taylor, ed., *Encyclopedia of Religion and Nature*. London: Continuum, 2008.
Suzuki, Daisetsu Teitaro. "Translator's Preface." In Shaku Soyen, *Sermons of a Buddhist Abbot*, iii–vi. Chicago: Open Court, 1906.
Suzuki, Daisetsu Teitaro, trans. *Lankavatara Sutra*. Delhi: Motilal Banarsidass, 1999.
Swinburne, Richard. *The Existence of God*. Oxford: Oxford University Press, 2004.
"Syria Violence Claims Head of Ancient Arab Poet." *Reuters* (February 12, 2013), available online at http://www.reuters.com/article/2013/02/12/us-syria-crisis-statue-idUSBRE91B13420130212.
Tagore, Devendranath. *The Autobiography of Maharshi Devendranath Tagore*, trans. Satyendranath Tagore and Indira Devi. London: Macmillan, 1914.
Tanahashi, Kazuaki, and Peter Levitt, trans. *The Essential Dogen*. Shambhala: Boston, 2013.
Taylor, C. C. W., and Mi-Kyoung Lee. "The Sophists." In *Stanford Encyclopedia of Philosophy*, available online at http://plato.stanford.edu/entries/sophists/.
Tertullian, *Ad Nationes*, available online at The Tertullian Project, http://www.tertullian.org/works/ad_nationes.htm.
Thoreau, Henry David. *The Journal of Henry David Thoreau*, 14 vol. Boston: Houghton Mifflin, 1906.
Thoreau, Henry David. *The Correspondence of Henry David Thoreau*. New York: New York University Press, 1958.
Thoreau, Henry David. *Walden*. Princeton, NJ: Princeton University Press, 2004.
Tillich, Paul. *The Courage to Be*. New Haven, CT: Yale University Press, 2000.
Todd, Douglas. "Top UBC Psychologist Uncovers Roots of Religion—and Himself." *Vancouver Sun* (November 22, 2008), available online at http://blogs.vancouversun.com/2008/11/22/top-ubc-psychologist-uncovers-roots-of-religion-and-himself/.
Toft, Monica Duffy. "Religion and Political Violence." In Michael Jerryson, Mark Juergensmeyer, and Margo Kitts, eds., *The Oxford Handbook of Religion and Violence*, 1–9. Oxford: Oxford University Press, 2013.

Tolstoy, Leo. *A Confession*. Grand Rapids, MI: Christian Classics Ethereal Library, n.d.
Tolstoy, Leo. *Some Social Remedies*. Christchurch, Hants: The Free Age Press, 1900.
Tolstoy, Leo. *Last Steps: The Late Writings of Leo Tolstoy*, ed. Jay Parini. Penguin: London: 2009.
Traubel, Horace. "Collect," *The Conservator* 1. no. 11 (January 1891): 81.
Traubel, Horace. *With Walt Whitman in Camden*, vol. 7. Carbondale, IL: Southern Illinois University Press, 1992.
Vaudeville, Charlotte, ed. *Kabir-Vani*. Pondicherry: Institut Français d'Indologie, 1982.
Vaudeville, Charlotte. "*Sant Mat*: Santism as the Universal Path to Sanctity." In Karine Schomer and William Hewat McLeod, eds., *The Sants*, 21–40. Delhi: Motilal Banarsidass, 1987.
Vaudeville, Charlotte. *A Weaver Named Kabir*. Delhi: Oxford University Press, 1997.
Victoria, Brian. *Zen and Japanese Militarism: A Critical Inquiry into the Roots of "Imperial-Way Zen."* Dissertation. Temple University, 1995.
Victoria, Brian. *Zen War Stories*. London: Routledge, 2012.
Vidyaranya. *A Hand-Book of Hindu Pantheism: The Panchadasi of Sreemut Vidyaranya Swami*, vol. 1, trans. Nandalal Dhole. Calcutta: Heeralal Dhole, 1899.
Vigny, Alfred de. *Œuvres complètes*, vol. 2. Paris: Gallimard, 1948.
Vijay, Bhadrabahu. *Guidances of Jainism*. Mehsana, India: Shri Vishwa Kalyan Prakashan Trust, n.d., available online at http://www.jainworld.com/pdf/GUIDLINE.pdf.
Vivekananda, Swami. *Complete Works of Swami Vivekananda*, 8 vols. Mayavati, India: Advaita Ashrama, 1989.
Voltaire, *Œuvres complètes de Voltaire*, vol. 10. Paris: Furne, 1836.
Voltaire, *A Philosophical Dictionary*, trans. William F. Fleming. Adelaide: eBooks@Adelaide, 2014, available online at https://ebooks.adelaide.edu.au/v/voltaire/dictionary/index.html.
Waddell, Norman, trans. *The Essential Teachings of Zen Master Hakuin*. Boston: Shambhala, 1994.
Walsh, Maurice, trans. *The Long Discourses of the Buddha*. Boston: Wisdom Publications, 1995.
Watson, Burton, trans. *The Lotus Sutra*. New York: Columbia University Press, 1993.
Watson, Burton, trans. *Zhuangzi: Basic Writings*. New York: Columbia University Press, 2003.
Weber, Max. *From Max Weber: Essays in Sociology*, trans. Hans Heinrich Gerth and Charles Wright Mills. New York: Oxford University Press, 1958.
Wesley, John. *The Works of the Rev. John Wesley*, 10 vol. New York: J. & J. Harper, 1826–1830.
Whitehead, Alfred North. *Science and the Modern World*. New York: Pelican Mentor, 1948.
Whitehead, Alfred North. *Religion in the Making*. New York: Fordham University Press, 1996.
Whitman, Walt. *Leaves of Grass* [second edition]. Brooklyn, NY: Fowler & Wells, 1856.
Whitman, Walt. *Complete Prose Works*. Philadelphia: David McKay, 1892.
Whitman, Walt. *Leaves of Grass: The First (1855) Edition*. New York: Penguin, 1986.
Whitman, Walt. *Leaves of Grass, 1860*. Iowa City: University of Iowa Press, 2009.
Whitmarsh, Tim. *Battling the Gods*, New York: Knopf, 2015.
Wilkins, Charles, trans. *The Bhagvat-Geeta, or Dialogues of Kreeshna and Arjoon*. London: C. Nourse, 1785.
Williams, Bernard. "Descartes." In Bryan Magee, ed., *The Great Philosophers*, 78–95. Oxford: Oxford University Press, 1987.
Williams, Robin M. "Religion, Value Orientations, and Intergroup Conflict." In Eleanor Macoby, Theodore Newcomb and Eugene Hartley, eds., *Readings in Social Psychology*, 647–653. New York: Henry Holt, 1958.
Wilson, Horace. "Sketch of the Religious Sects of the Hindus." *Asiatic Researches* [Calcutta] 17 (1832): 169–313.
Wittgenstein, Ludwig. "A Lecture on Ethics." *The Philosophical Review* 74 (January 1965): 3–12.
Wittgenstein, Ludwig. *Tractatus Logico-Philosophicus*, trans. David Pears and Brian McGuinness. London: Routledge, 1974.

Wittgenstein, Ludwig. *Philosophical Investigations*, trans. Gertrude Elizabeth Margaret Anscombe. Oxford: Basil Blackwell, 1986.

Wittgenstein, Ludwig. *Culture and Value*, trans. Peter Winch. Oxford: Blackwell Publishers, 1998.

Wood, Graeme. "What the ISIS Really Wants." *The Atlantic* (March 2015), available online at http://www.theatlantic.com/magazine/archive/2015/03/what-isis-really-wants/384980/.

Woolf, Virginia. *The Common Reader*. First Series. London: The Hogarth Press, 1975.

Wootton, David. *The Invention of Science*. New York: HarperCollins, 2015.

Wordsworth, William. "Lines Composed a Few Miles Above Tintern Abbey...," available online at Poetry Foundation, http://www.poetryfoundation.org/poem/174796.

Worthen, Molly. "One Nation Under God?" *New York Times* (December 22, 2012), available online at http://www.nytimes.com/2012/12/23/opinion/sunday/american-christianity-and-secularism-at-a-crossroads.html?_r=0.

Yamada, Koun, trans. *The Gateless Gate: The Classic Book of Zen Koans*. Boston: Wisdom Publications, 2004.

Yutang, Lin. *My Country and My People*. London: Heinemann, 1936.

Zinnbauer, Brian J., Kenneth I. Pargament, Brenda Cole, Mark S. Rye, Eric M. Butter, Timothy G. Belavich, Kathleen M. Hipp, Allie B. Scott, Jill L. Kadar. "Religion and Spirituality." *Journal for the Scientific Study of Religion* 36, no. 4 (December 1997): 549–564.

Zuckerman, Phil. "Atheism and Societal Health." In Stephen Bullivant and Michael Ruse, eds., *The Oxford Handbook of Atheism*, 497–510. Oxford: Oxford University Press, 2013.

INDEX

Abbasid Caliphate 102, 124, 127, 133
Abrams, M. H. 171
Adler, Felix 206
Advaita 76–7, 131
   Neo-Advaita 155
   see also Vedanta
agnosticism 9, 166, 183
ahimsa 115; see also nonviolence
Ahmadiyya Muslim community 212
Ahura Mazda 64, 101
Ajivikas 42–3, 45
Akbar 155
Akhenaten 64
Albigensian Crusade 119
Alcorta, Candace 113
Alexander the Great 58
Alexander, Samuel 214
Allah 66
Alston, William 20
Amitabha 89, 108
Anaxagoras 56
Anaximander 54–5
Anaximenes 54–5
Antisthenes 59
apatheia 61
Apelles 63
aponia 60
Aquinas, Thomas 58, 133
Arendt, Hannah 114
arguments against the existence of God
   in *Buddhacharita* 78
   of Jinasena 77
   of Mimamsa 76
   of Samkhya 74
   of Shantideva and Shantarakshita 81
   social scientific 21

arguments for the existence of God 14, 15–21
   common consent argument 15
   cosmological argument 15–16
   of Descartes 144
   Kant on 15, 167
   moral arguments 16–19
   of Nyaya–Vaisheshika 75
   ontological argument 15, 144
   from religious experience 19–21
   from scripture 15
   teleological argument (argument from design) 16, 75, 163, 166
Aristippus 59
Aristotle 55, 58–9, 124
   and medieval philosophy 124, 133, 135, 139
Armstrong, Karen 113
Arnold, Matthew 169, 181, 212, 225
art of living 10, 99
Arya Samaj 192
Ashoka 231
Ashur 64, 65
Ashvaghosa 78
Assmann, Jan 118
ataraxia 60, 61, 62, 135
atheism
   did not exist in medieval Europe 134–5
   history of term 9
   and Hobbes 140, 145
   in India 73, 82
   of Marx 184, 218
   and morality 18, 224
   Nagel on 28
   New Atheists 224

in nineteenth century Europe 169,
    180, 204
  positive and negative 9
  religious 28
  of Samkhya 74, 156
  of Sartre 216–17
  of Schopenhauer 179
  in seventeenth-century Europe 150
  Tillich on 220
  in twenty-first century 223–4, 230
atman 40, 77
atomic theory
  of Epicurus 60, 61
  Indian 75
  of Leucippus and Democritus 55
  of Lucretius 92, 143
Augustine of Hippo 58, 119
  City of God 119
Augustus Caesar 93
Aurangzeb 132, 133, 156
Aurobindo, Sri 213–14, 226
  mind and supermind 214
  on spirituality 12, 206
  on yoga 214
Avalokita/Avalokiteshwara 79, 85, 105
avatar 104–5, 131
Avesta 37
Avignon 134
axial age/period 35, 39, 47, 53, 64, 66,
    68–9, 75, 98, 101, 241
Ayer, A. J. 216

Bablylon 63, 64, 66
Babylonia 35, 37, 66
Bacchus 104; *see also* Dionysus
Baghdad 123, 124, 125, 127
Baha'ism 71
Bakhtawar 157
Balzac, Honoré de 180
Bangladesh 117, 223
Barhaspatya Sutras 82
Bassui Tokusho 130, 135, 154
Batchelor, Stephen 29–30
  Confession of a Buddhist Atheist 29
Beard, Mary 94
Beatles, the 52, 221
Beauvoir, Simone de 179
Beckett, Samuel 24
Beethoven, Ludwig van 180

Bellah, Robert N. 234–5, 236
Berger, Peter 211, 222
Berlin, Isaiah 58
Bhagavad Gita 84, 103, 104, 116, 246
  first English translation 190
bhakti 106–7, 116
  nirgun bhakti 103, 131
Bible, the
  Ecclesiastes 68
  Emerson on 174, 175
  Job 68
  John, Gospel of 105, 110
  King James Bible 68
  New Testament 118
  Spinoza on 147
  Wesley on 161
  wisdom literature 68
  on witchcraft 141
Blavatsky, Helena Petrovna 188–9, 192
  Isis Unveiled 188
Bloom, Harold 225
Blount, Charles 150
Boccaccio, Giovanni 134
Bodhidharma 86
bodhisattva(s) 78, 81, 82, 88, 105
body, the 13, 76, 200
  Hobbes on 145, 148
  mind-body dualism 144, 148
  Musonius on 94
  Schopenhauer on 178
  Thoreau on 176
  three bodies of the Buddha 80
  Whitman on 176
Bonhoeffer, Dietrich 219
Botton, Alain de 228
Brahe, Tycho 139
brahman 40, 41, 54, 69, 76, 77, 101
Brahmanas 40
  Shatapatha Brahmana 37, 40
Brahmo Samaj 191, 192, 196
Brass, Paul 117
Bray, Michael 120
breathing exercises/breath control 8, 53,
    69, 75, 81, 87, 99
Broad, C. D. 20
Bronze Age 34, 37, 38, 47, 101, 137
Bruno, Giordano 137, 150, 179
Buddha, the 29, 35, 42, 43–5
  Buddha-in-embryo 86

Buddha-nature 86, 87, 88, 89, 99, 128, 129
  deified 78, 226
  dharma-body of 80, 105, 198
  images of 105
  life of historical Buddha 44
Buddhacharita 78
Buddhism 26, 73, 170
  Chan 86–9, 99, 128, 129, 153–4
  in China 84–90, 108
  four noble truths 44
  Imperial-Way 219
  in Japan 108, 115–16, 129–30, 193, 219; *see also* Zen
  Mahayana 78–81, 194
  and Neo-Confucianism 128
  Olcott on 193
  persecution of, in China 89
  Pure Land 89, 108, 129, 154
  Schopenhauer and 178, 179
  skillful means 81
  Suzuki on 197
  in twenty-first century 226
  and violence 116, 219, 229
  Zen Buddhism, *see* Zen
Buddhist philosophy 79–81, 85
  idea of Emptiness 79, 80, 82, 85
  Middle Way (Madhyamaka) 79, 80–2, 85
  Yogachara 80–1, 85, 86
Buddhist *suttas/sutras* 73, 86
  Brahmajala Sutta 46
  Heart Sutra 79
  Lankavatara Sutra 86
  Lotus Sutra 104, 105, 106, 108–9
  Mahasaccaka Sutta 44
  Perfection of Wisdom sutras 79
  Platform Sutra 87
  Samannaphala Sutta 41
Buñuel, Luis 225
Burkert, Walter 113
Byzantium 119

Calvin, John 136
Camus, Albert 24, 28, 179
Carlyle, Thomas 180
Carneades 90
Cathars 111, 119
Catholicism 102, 134, 143, 159, 171, 213

Catullus 92
Cavanaugh, William 113
Ceylon, *see* Sri Lanka (Ceylon)
Chadwick, John 7
Chaitanya 156
Chalmers, David 23
Chan Buddhism 86–9, 99, 128, 129, 153–4
  gongan 88, 128, 129, 153–4
  Linji and Caodong schools 129
  of seventeenth century 153
  see also Zen
Charvaka 73, 76, 82, 83, 98
Chauncy, Charles 161
China
  Bronze Age 38, 47
  falls behind the West 152
  Han dynasty 83–4
  middle empires 103
  Ming dynasty 152
  in nineteenth century 155
  Qing dynasty 153
  in seventeenth and eighteenth centuries 140
  Shang dynasty 38, 46
  Song dynasty 127
  Tang dynasty 151
  three teachings in 72, 83
  Zhou dynasty 47
Chinese philosophy 84–5, 89, 127–8, 152–3
Christian Science 186
Christianity 67, 69, 71, 72
  Catholicism 102, 134, 143, 159, 171, 213
  Death of God theology 220
  early history of 110–11
  evangelicalism 11, 19, 141, 159, 160
  Fundamentalist movement 212, 229
  Kierkegaard on 179
  in Medieval Europe 134
  missionaries 190, 194
  Nietzsche on 203
  Orthodox 159, 205
  Protestantism 102, 124
  in Roman Empire 98, 102, 111, 118
  and violence 115
Chrysostom, John 118–19
Cicero 15, 90–1
  On the Nature of the Gods 90
Clement of Alexandria 54

Coleridge, Samuel Taylor 174, 179
  Aids to Reflection 174
colonialism 140, 155, 190, 194
Communist Party 218, 227
Comte, Auguste 182, 184, 200
  Religion of Humanity 184
Comte-Sponville, André 27, 225
  L'esprit de l'athéisme 27
Confucianism 26, 48–50, 69, 89, 99, 115
  during Han Dynasty 84
  key terms 48, 49
  Neo-Confucianism, *see*
    Neo-Confucianism
  in twentieth and twenty-first
    centuries 227
Confucius 19, 35, 47–9, 57
  Analects 48
  on Duke of Zhou 47
  The Great Learning 48
consciousness 22–3
  in Charvaka 82
  to James 229
  and phenomenology 217
  in Samkhya 74–5
  in Yogachara Buddhism 80–1, 85
Constantine 111, 118
Constantinople, fall of 135, 152
Copernicus, Nicolaus 139
Crookes, William 187
Cupitt, Don 220
Cynic philosophers 59, 61, 62
Cyrenaic philosophers 59
Cyrus of Persia 66
Czech Republic 18

Dalai Lama, *see* Gyatso, Tenzin
Damascus 126
Dao 101
  to Confucius 50
  in Daoism 50–2
  to Wang Fuzhi 153
Daodejing 50, 51, 52, 84
Daoism 26, 50–3, 69, 115
  during Han dynasty 84
  philosophical and religious 50, 107
  in the twenty-first century 227
  Xuanzue or Neo-Daoism 84
Dara Shikoh 156
Darwin, Charles 16, 169–70, 183

Davies, Paul 22
Davis, Natalie Zemon 120
Dawkins, Richard 112, 224
Dayananda Saraswati 192
deism 9, 162
Delhi Sultanate 130, 132
Democritus 55–6, 60
Denmark 18
Dennett, Daniel 23
Derrida, Jacques 24, 83
Descartes, René 26, 27, 140, 143–4
  Discourse on the Method 143
  Spinoza and 146, 148
Destiny 43, 75; *see also* Fate
Dewey, John 25–6
  A Common Faith 25
dharma 8
dharma-body 80, 105, 198
Dharmapala, Anagarika 11, 190, 194, 197,
    198, 253
  and nationalism 199–200
Diagoras 56, 63, 90
Dickens, Charles 186
Diderot, Denis 163
Dikshita, Appayya 155
Diogenes 59, 109
Dionysus 64, 101, 104
Dogen, Eihei 129–30
Dong Zhongshu 84
Dostoyevsky, Fyodor 169
  The Brothers Karamazov 182
Duchamp, Marcel 211
Durkheim, Émile 21, 113
  on individual/individualism 206, 207
  on religion 206
  and religion of humanity 207
Dworkin, Ronald 28–9, 225
  Religion without God 28

Eddy, Mary Baker 186
Edwards, Jonathan 160
Egypt, ancient 37, 64
Einstein, Albert 211
Eisai, Myoan 129
Eliot, George 169, 182, 200
Ellis, Albert 228
Emerson, Ralph Waldo 169, 174–5, 191
Emptiness 79, 80, 82, 85, 157
England 150

English Civil War 145
enlightenment, in Buddhism 30, 44, 87, 105, 129
Enlightenment, the 26, 159–60, 211, 225
Enuma Elish 63
Epictetus 61, 95–6, 99, 228
Epicureanism 26, 91, 141, 217
   in Greece 60–1
   in Rome 72, 91
Epicurus 58, 60, 91
Erasmus, Desiderius 136
esotericism, Western 185–9
Euhemerus 60
Euripides 56
   Bacchae 104
evangelicalism 11, 19, 141, 159, 160
Evans, Henry R. 188
evil, problem of 17, 63, 77, 79, 166
evolution
   biological 183
   Dharmapala on 195
   spiritual 207, 213
experience, religious (spiritual, mystical), *see* religious (spiritual, mystical) experience

faith
   in Buddhism 105–6
   Kant on 167
   Kierkegaard on 179
   Locke on 150
   reason and 134, 161, 162, 179
   Schleiermacher on 11, 161
   in Zen 154
Fascism 218
Fate
   to Epictetus 95
   and free will 92
   to Stoics 61
   see also Destiny
Fatimid Caliphate 102
Fénelon, François 160
Feuerbach, Ludwig 200
   Essence of Christianity 182, 184
fideism 166, 179
Fischer, Bryan 229
Foucault, Michel 24, 225, 239
Franklin, Benjamin 164
Franzen, Jonathan 225

Frazer, James 21, 185
free will
   in Christianity 17
   and fate 92
   to Lucretius 92
French Revolution 170, 171
Freud, Sigmund 21, 24, 179, 208–10, 225
   Civilization and its Discontents 209
   The Future of an Illusion 209
   Totem and Taboo 209
Fuentes, Carlos 225
fundamentalism 213, 229
Fundamentalist movement 212, 229

Galileo Galilei 139–40, 142, 159
Gandhi, Mohandas (Mahatma) 229
Gandhi, Virchand 194, 195
Gaofeng Yuanmiao 154
Gaudapada 72
Genghis Khan 127
genius (term) 180
gentleman (*junzi*) 48
Ghazali, al- 125
Gibbon, Edward 164
Girard, René 113
Gnosticism 33
Gobind Singh, Guru 132
God
   to Ajivikas 43
   Alexander on 214
   arguments against, *see* arguments against the existence of God
   arguments for, *see* arguments for the existence of God
   Arnold on 181
   Aurobindo on 214
   belief in, in twenty-first century 223
   Blavatsky on 189
   Buddha on 45
   to classical Yoga 75
   to Confucianism 49, 195
   Cupitt on 220
   to Daoism 52
   Emerson on 175
   Epictetus on 95
   Freud on 209
   Guyon on 160
   Hobbes on 144, 145
   incarnation of 104

    Indian theories of 73
    Jainism on 43, 195
    James on 210
    logical positivists on 216
    Musonius on 94
    Santayana on 213
    Sartre on 217
    to Skeptics 63, 97
    Spinoza on 148
    Stendhal on 180
    Tolstoy on 205
    in *Twelve Gate Treatise* 79
    to Vaisheshika 75
    Vivekananda on 198
    Voltaire on 153, 162–3
    to West Asian monotheisms 65
    Whitehead on 214
    Whitman on 177
    see also Ishwara
gods
    to the Epicureans 60, 92
    to Mimamsa 76
    nature of, in Cicero 90
    Sextus Empiricus on 97
Goenka, S.N. 226
Goethe, Johann Wolfgang von 169, 171–2, 191
    Faust 172
    on Spinoza 149
Gosala, Makkhali 42, 43
Greece
    Bronze Age 38, 54
    mystery religions 39
    philosophy in 54–63
Guanyin 85
Gunaratna 130
Guo Xiang 84
Gupta Empire 103
Gurney, Edmund 187
Guyon, Jeanne 11, 158–9, 160
    A Short and Very Easy Method of Prayer 159
Gyatso, Tenzin (14th Dalai Lama) 30
    Beyond Religion 30
    on dependent arising and God 79

Habermas, Jürgen 225
Hadot, Pierre 228
Hakuin Ekaku 154
Hall, G. Stanley 187
Hallaj, Mansur al- 125
Han Yu 89
Hanh, Thich Nhat 45
happiness
    Antisthenes on 59
    Aristotle on 58
    Cicero on 91
    Epicurus on 60–1
    Greek Stoics on 61–2
    d'Holbach on 164
    Seneca on 93
    Spinoza on 146, 149
Harris, Sam 224
Haslam, Alexander 114
Hastings, Warren 190
Hauerwas, Stanley 229
Heaven (Tian) 8, 47, 49
    in Daoism 52
    Xunzi on 49
Hebrew scriptures
    immorality of 18
    see also Bible, the
Hegel, Georg Wilhelm Friedrich 177
Heidegger, Martin 217
Hellenistic philosophy 58–63, 69
henotheism 65
Heraclitus 55
Hesiod 54
Hick, John
    on pluralism 231
    on soul-making theodicy 17
Hicks, Elias 7
Hinduism 8, 67, 71, 102, 106, 152, 155, 191, 192, 194, 195, 227
    caste system 18, 131–2
    in contemporary India 226
    Hindu–Muslim violence 117
    hypernationalist view 199
    ishta devatas in 110
    and violence 116, 123
Hirai, Kinzo 194
Hitchens, Christopher 112
Hitler, Adolf 218
Hobbes, Thomas 11, 120, 140, 144–5, 150, 161
    Leviathan 145
Hoffmann, E. T. A. 180
Holbach, Baron d' 162, 163–5

Common Sense 164
System of Nature 163
Holocaust of the Jews 114
Holy Roman Empire 133
Homer 38, 54
Homeric Hymns 55
Hongren 87
Horace 92
Hosea 65
Huangdi 101; *see also* Yellow Emperor
Huang-Lao cult 84, 104
Huayan 86
Huike 86–7
Huineng 87, 89, 153
Hulagu Khan 127
Humanism 25
    Nagel on 28
Hume, Allan Octavian 199
Hume, David 164–7
    Dialogues concerning Natural Religion 165–6
    Natural History of Religion 117–18, 165
Hus, Jan 134
Huxley, Thomas Henry 9, 183
Hwang, Karen 230

Ibn ʿArabi 126
Iceland 18
India
    Delhi Sultanate 130, 133
    falls behind the West 152
    Mughal Empire 133, 155, 156, 158
    Upanishadic period 39–41
    Vedic period 37–8, 47
Indian philosophy
    atheistic and skeptical 82–3, 157
    Buddhist 78–82
    Jain 77–8, 130
    Vedic schools 73–7, 155–6
Indra 41, 64, 101
Industrial Revolution 169, 204
Ingersoll, Robert 6, 205
Iran, Avestan 37
Iron Age 101
Isaiah, Second 66
Ishwara
    to Advaita Vedanta 76
    to atheistic Samkhya 74
    to classical Yoga 75
    to different schools of Indian philosophy 82–3
Islam 67, 69, 71, 111
    Hindu-Muslim violence 117
    Salafi 212–13, 229
    Sunni-Shia divide 122
    and violence 115, 121–3
    Wahhabism 121
Islamic State of Iraq and Syria (ISIS) 115, 122, 123
Israel, Jonathan 163
Israel (modern) 229
Israel, Kingdom of 65

Jacobsen, Jens Peter 182
Jainism 26, 42–3, 73, 115
    Buddha on 45
    devotional literature 106
    Jain philosophy 77–8, 130
    Jain sutras 73
    methods of practice 78
    in twenty-first century 226
James, William 14, 187, 229
    psychology of 208, 209–10
    on religion 209
    and religious experience 20, 26
    Varieties of Religious Experience 20, 197, 208
Japan 152
    Buddhism in 108
    Confucianism in 89
    Kamakura period 108, 115, 129
    military expansion 219
    in seventeenth and eighteenth centuries 140
    Tokugawa era 154
Jaspers, Karl 35
Jayarasi 82
Jefferson, Thomas 163
Jerusalem 65, 115
Jesus 65, 101, 104, 105, 110
    as the messiah 105, 110
    Sermon on the Mount 118
Jews 65–9
    Holocaust 114
    Jesus and 110
    massacres (pograms) of 118, 119
    movement to resettle in Palestine 118
    see also Judaism

jihad 121
Jinasena 77, 83
Josiah 65, 66
Joyce, James 24, 212
Judah, Kingdom of 65, 66
Judaism 66, 67, 69, 110, 118, 229; *see also* Jews
Juergensmeyer, Mark 115
Julian the Apostate 98
Jung, Carl 24
junzi 48
Justinian 98

Kabir 131, 157
Kafka, Franz 24, 211
Kandinsky, Wassily 24, 212
Kant, Immanuel 24, 166–8, 177
    and Hume 167
    moral argument for God 16
    on rational arguments for God 15
karma 17, 40, 79
    in Ajivism 43
    Buddha on 45
    to Buddhists 69, 78
    to Jains 42, 69
    rebirth and 17
Khusrau, Amir 130
Kierkegaard, Søren 179, 180
    and the crowd 236
King, Martin Luther 229
Klee, Paul 24
Korea 89
Kosen, Imakita 194
Krishna 103, 116
Kublai Khan 127
Kumarajiva 85
Kumarila Bhatta 76, 83
Küng, Hans 17

La Mettrie, Julien Offray de 163
Lankavatara Sutra 86
Laozi 50, 107, 108
Leibniz, Gottfried 17
Lenin, Vladimir 218
Leucippus 55
Lévi, Éliphas 187
li (principle) 85, 127, 128, 153
li (propriety) 48, 49, 50
Li Ao 89

Linji Yixuan 88, 89, 153
Lipsius, Justus 135, 146
Livy 120
Locke, John 120, 140, 150–1, 168, 175
    Letter Concerning Toleration 150
logic 55
    Aristotle's syllogism 58
    syllogism in Indian philosophy 75
Logos 55, 92, 93, 95, 101
    in Gospel of John 105, 110
Lonka Shaha 130
Lotus Sutra 104, 105, 106, 108–9
Lu Jiuyuan 127
Lucian 96, 97
    Hermotimus 96
    Passing of Peregrinus 111
Lucretius 91–2, 98
    On the Nature of Things 91, 135
Luhrmann, T. M. 230
Luther, Martin 136
Łyszczyński, Kazimierz 150

Ma'arri, Abul 'Ala, al- 123–4
magic 8, 36
Mahavira 35, 42, 78, 106
    and Buddha 44
Mahler, Gustav 24
Malinowski, Bronisław 36
Mandate of Heaven 46
Mann, Thomas 218
Mao Zedong 227
Marcus Aurelius 61, 96, 228
Marduk 37, 63, 64, 65, 101
Marsh, James 174
Marty, Martin 229
Marx, Karl 21, 184, 200
    on religion 184, 218
Mary (mother of Jesus) 101, 110
Maslow, Abraham 13, 225–6
Maurya Empire 72
Mead, G. R. S. 12
meditation 8, 69, 81
    mindfulness 44–5, 198, 227
    revival of, in Ceylon 198, 253
    vipassana 226
Menand, Louis 174
Mencius 49, 89
Menocchio 137
Meslier, Jean 161–2

Mesmer, Franz 185
Mesopotamia, ancient 37, 63
Milgram experiment 114
Mimamsa 26, 73, 76, 226
   arguments against existence of God 76
mindfulness meditation 44–5, 198, 227
Mithraism 72
moksha 40, 42
Molinos, Miguel de 159, 160
Mondrian, Piet 225
Mongol Empire 127, 130, 133
Monod, Jacques 22–3
   Chance and Necessity 22
monolatrism 65
monotheism 9, 64, 98
   and violence 117, 123
Montaigne, Michel de 120, 135–6, 141
   Essays 135, 136
Motherwell, Robert 225
Mouzi 84
Mughal Empire 132, 133, 155, 156, 158
Muhammad 111, 121
Müller, Max 185
Musonius Rufus, Gaius 94
Mussolini, Benito 218
Myers, Frederic 186
mystery religions 39, 64, 109
mystical experience, *see* religious
     (spiritual, mystical) experience

Nadler, Steven 150
Nagarjuna 79, 85, 106, 157, 244
   *Fundamental Wisdom of the Middle
     Way* 79, 244
Nagel, Thomas 27–8, 225
   *Secular Philosophy and the Religious
     Temperament* 28
Nakamura, Hajime 34
Nanak, Guru 132
National Socialism (Nazism) 218
nationalism
   in Asia 199
   and religion 217–18
Nature
   to Epicureans 61
   to Galileo 142
   to Lucretius 91–2
   Spinoza on 148
Nausiphanes 60

Nebuchadnezzar 66
Neo-Confucianism 89, 103, 127–8, 152–3
   and Buddhism 128
Neolithic Age 101
Neo-Platonism 97
Nepal 44
Nero 93, 94
Nerval, Gérard de 253
New Age, the 221, 228
New Thought 186
Newton, Isaac 140, 142, 159
nibbana, see *nirvana*
Nichiren 108–9, 116
Nietzsche, Friedrich 24, 179, 202–4, 251
   The Anti-Christ 204
   The Birth of Tragedy 203
   Daybreak 204
   The Gay Science 203
   on George Eliot 182
   "God is dead" 201, 202
   overman 203
   Thus Spoke Zarathustra 203
   will to power 204
nirgun devotees 131; see also *sants*
nirguna, and *saguna* 76, 104
nirvana 44, 45, 81
Nivedita, Sister 11
nones, rise of 71, 222
nontheism (term) 9
nonviolence 42, 115–16, 175
Norenzayan, Ara 112
Nyaya 16, 73, 75, 83, 98

Ockham, William of 134
Olcott, Henry Steel 11, 194
   and Dayananada 192
O'Neill, Eugene 24, 211
Ottoman Empire 152
   dismemberment of 201
Ovid 92

Paganism 33
Paine, Thomas 7
Pakistan 117
Paley, William 16
Paltu Sahib 156
Panditaradhya 117
Panjab 158
pantheism 9, 149, 172, 173

Schopenhauer on 179
parapsychology 187
Parliament of Religions, World's 189, 192, 193, 194, 195, 199
Parmenides 55
Parshvanatha 42
Patanjali 74
Pater, Walter 11
Paul (apostle) 66, 110
phenomenology 217
philosophy
   Chinese, see Chinese philosophy
   Greek 54–8
   Hellenistic 59–63, 69
   Indian, see Indian philosophy
   as love of wisdom 54, 68
   Roman 72, 90–7, 98, 99
   twentieth century Western 213–17
pietism 11, 19, 141, 159, 160
Platform Sutra 87
Plato 10, 15, 58, 109, 124, 167
   Euthyphro 18, 29
   Theaetetus 56
pleasure
   to Cyrenaics 59
   to Epicureans 60–1, 91–2
Pliny the Elder 93
Plotinus 58, 98
pluralism 231
polytheism 9, 64, 117
prakriti 72, 74, 75
pramanas 76, 82
Prannath 157
pratitya-samutpada 45
Priestly, Joseph 164
Protagoras 56
Protestant Reformation, see Reformation, Protestant
Protestantism 102, 124
psychology
   of nineteenth and twentieth centuries 186, 208–10
   Stoic 93, 95
psychotherapies 210, 225, 228
Pung Kwang Yu 194, 195
Punjab 132, 158
Puranas 106
purusha 72, 74, 75
Pyrrho 62

quietism 11, 19, 141, 158, 159, 160
Quimby, Phinias 186
Quran 66, 121

Rabin, Yitzhak 118
Raidas 131
Rama 116
Ramakrishna Paramahamsa 192
Ramana Maharshi 226
Ramayana 116
Rameses II 37
Raphson, Joseph 149
Rath, Rakshi 114
Rawandi, Ibn al- 124
Razi, Abu Bakr al- 124–5, 133
Realism (literary) 169, 180–2
reason, and faith 134, 161, 162, 179
rebirth, and karma 17
Reformation, Protestant 11, 103, 135
   and Wars of Religion 120, 136
Reicher, Stephen 114
relativity
   cultural 211
   in physics 211
religion 7–8
   hard to define 5, 7
   and morality 164
   and nationalism 217–18
   pragmatic value of 14
   Religion of Humanity 184, 207
   religious activitiy, main types 8
   and spirituality 6, 7, 9, 206
   true religion and superstition 147
   in twenty-first century 222
   and violence 111–23
religious (spiritual, mystical) experience
   as basis of religious life 141, 196, 208, 209
   Freud on 209
   James on 20, 26, 208, 210
   regarded as source of religions 14
Renaissance, European 26, 135
Renaissance, Carolingian 133
revelation 4, 73, 111, 136, 150, 154, 174–5
Rhys Davids, T. W. 198, 253
Rig Veda 38, 39–40, 103
Robespierre, Maximilien 170–1
Roman philosophy 72, 90–7, 98, 99
Romanes, George 205

Romanticism/Romantic movement 11, 19, 169, 171
Rome
   Empire 67, 72, 102
   philosophy of, *see* Roman philosophy
   Republic 72, 91, 92, 93
Rorty, Richard 225
Rothko, Mark 225
Rousseau, Jean-Jacques 11, 164
Roy, Rammohan 191
Rumi, Jalal ad-Din 126
Rushdie, Salman 230
Russell, Bertrand 213, 215
Russia 152

Sachal Sarmarst 158
sacrifice 8, 37, 101
Sadananda 155
sage, the
   to Cicero 91
   in Confucianism 48, 49
   in Daoism 51, 53
   to Guo Xiang 84
   to Sengzhao 85
   in Stoicism 61, 91
   to Wang Yangming 128
saguna, and *nirguna* 76, 104
Salafism 212, 213
samanas/sramanas 41, 53
Sambandar 117
Samkhya 26, 72–3, 74, 155, 226
   Samkhya Karika 72–3, 74
   Samkhya Sutra 74, 156
   theistic and atheistic 74
samsara 40, 44
Santayana, George 11, 213
sants, the 131–2, 156
Sartre, Jean-Paul 24, 179, 216–17
Schimmel, Annemarie 158
Schindler, Solomon 206, 235
Schleiermacher, Friedrich 11, 26, 172
   On Religion 161
Schopenhauer, Arthur 169, 177–9, 200
   on Hegel 177
   Nietzsche and 203
   on ontological argument 15
secularization 221–2
   of the sacred 169–80
Semler, Johann 161
Sen, Keshab Chandra 11, 191–2, 196
Seneca the Younger 61, 93–4
Sengzhao 85
Sennacherib 65
Servetus, Michael 136
Sextus Empiricus 62–3, 83, 135
   Outlines of Pyrrhonism 62–3, 97
Shabaab, Al- 123
Shah Jahan 156
Shaivism 155
   and violence 117
shamanism 33
Shambuka 116
Shangdi 38, 47, 101, 153
Shankara 17, 76
Shantarakshita 81, 83
   Compendium on Reality 81
Shantideva 81, 83
   Way of the Bodhisattva 81
Shelley, Percy Bysshe 102, 173–4
Shenoute 119
Shenxiu 87
Shingon 109
Shinto 33, 67, 193
Shiva 101, 117, 137, 155
siddhas, in Jainism 43
Siddhasena Divakara 77
Sidgwick, Henry 186
Sikhism 71, 132
   Guru Granth Sahib 133
Simmel, Georg 205–7
   on religion 206, 207
   on spiritual evolution 207
   tragedy of culture 207
Skepticism 141
   Academic 62, 90
   during European Renaissance 136
   Pyrrhonian 62, 97
Smith, Adam 164
Society for Psychical Research 186
   American 187
sociology
   nineteenth century 182, 183, 184
   twentieth century 206–7
Socrates 9, 10, 56, 57, 62
Song dynasty 133
Sosis, Richard 113
soul (*psyche*) 57, 69
Soyen, Shaku 194, 195, 197, 198, 199

and nationalism 199
Sermons of a Buddhist Abbot 197
Spain 133
Spencer, Herbert 183–4
Spener, Philipp 160
Sperry, R. W. 22–3
Spinoza, Baruch 9, 11, 26, 120, 146–9, 150, 161, 163
   and atheism 26, 140, 150
   Ethics 146–9, 182
   on God 148, 149
   Principles of Cartesian Philosophy 146
   Theologico-Political Treatise 9, 146
   Treatise on the Emendation of the Intellect 146
Spiritism 186
spiritual
   "spiritual but not religious" 2, 12, 222, 226, 234, 236
   term "spiritual" in English 10, 11, 12
   term "*spirituel*" in French 10, 11, 160
spiritual experience, *see* religious (spiritual, mystical) experience
spiritualism 186, 188, 189
spirituality
   aim and raison d'être 13
   Aurobindo on 12, 206
   characteristics of 6, 12–13, 69, 149, 175, 196, 231
   history of term 6–7, 9–11, 200
   New Atheists and 224
   and religion 6, 7, 9, 206
   Santayana on 11, 213
   theistic and nontheistic 31
   without God (godless) 5, 25–31, 33, 150, 200, 202
sramanas, see *samanas*
Sri Lanka (Ceylon) 116, 192–3, 226, 229
   civil war 200
Steiner, George 24
Stendhal (Marie-Henri Beyle) 169, 180, 200, 230, 251
Stephen, Leslie 183
Stern, Avraham 118
Stevens, Wallace 212
Stoicism 91, 208, 217, 228
   in Greece 61–2
   Neostoicism of Lipsius 135, 146
   premeditation of evil 62, 94
   psychology 95

   rediscovery in Europe 135
   in Rome 92, 93–6, 98
Strauss, David 182
Strauss, Richard 24
Stravinsky, Igor 210, 211
   The Rite of Spring 210, 211
substance
   Descartes on 144
   Hobbes on 145
   Spinoza on 148, 149
Sufism 121, 125–6, 158
Sultan Bahu 158
sutras
   Buddhist, *see* Buddhist *suttas/sutras*
   in Vedic philosphies 73
Suzuki, D. T. 20, 190, 197, 198
Suzuki, Shunryu 221
Sweden 18
Swedenborg, Emmanuel 185
Swinburne, Richard 20
Syria 123

Tagore, Devendranath 191
Tagore, Rabindranath 191
Taishang Laojun 107
Takugawa Shogunate 193
Tang Dynasty 72
tantra 106, 107
Tegh Bahadur, Guru 132, 156
Teile, Cornelis 185
tekhné tou biou 10; *see also* art of living
Tendai 108, 109
Terrorism 114, 115, 118, 120, 122–3
Thales 54–5
theism
   Buddha on 45
   Nagel on 28
   triumph of 101–37
   and violence 111
Theodorus the Atheist 59, 63, 90
Theodosius I 98
Theosophical Society 187–9
Thoreau, Henry David 175–6, 191
Tian 47, 49; *see also* Heaven (Tian)
Tiantai 86, 108
Tillich, Paul 219–20
Tirunavukkarasar 117
Tocqueville, Alexis de 234
Tolstoy, Leo 206–7, 215
   on moral revolution 236

Transcendentalism 11, 174–6
Traubel, Horace 6, 7
Tylor, Edward 21, 185

Umayyad Caliphate 67
unconscious mind
   Freud's dynamic unconscious 208
   and Buddhist storehouse consciousness 80–1
United States 11, 12, 18, 120, 155, 174, 188, 222, 224
Upanishads 69, 73
   Chhandogya 39
   Isha 54
   Kena 41
   Maitri 40
   Shwetashwatara 104–5, 246
   to Vedanta 76

Vaisheshika 73, 75
Vallabhacharya 156
Vanini, Lucilio 150, 179
Vasubandhu 80
   Thirty Verses 80, 85
   Treasury of Abhidharma 80
Vedanta 16, 73, 76–7, 83, 170
   advaita 76–7, 131, 155
   dvaita 76
Vedas 37
   to Mimamsa 76
   to Mimamsa and Vedanta 73
   Rig Veda, see Rig Veda
Vesalius, Andreas 139
Vidyaranya 155
Vienna Circle 216
Vietnam 89
Vigny, Alfred de 180
Vijayanagara Empire 103
Vijnanabhikshu 156
violence, religion and 111–23
vipassana 226
Vishnu 104–5, 155
Vivekananda, Swami 20, 116, 190, 192, 194, 195–7, 206, 212, 226, 235
   on God 198
   on Hinduism 194
   and nationalism 199
   Raja Yoga 196

Voltaire 151, 153, 162–3
   Candide 17
   Philosophical Dictionary 162

Wahhabism 121
Wang Chong 84
Wang Fuzhi 153
Wang Yangming 128, 152
Weber, Max 206–7
   disenchantment 207
   and redemption 207
   on religion 206
Wesley, John 11, 141, 160–1
Whitehead, Alfred North 214
Whitman, Walt 6, 11, 206, 235
   Leaves of Grass 176
will, Schopenhauer on 178
will to power 204
Williams, Bernard 144
Williams, Robin M. 114
witchcraft 141
Wittgenstein, Ludwig 214–16
   Philosophical Investigations 215
   Tractatus Logico-Philosophicus 215
Woolf, Virginia 212
Wootton, David 139
Wordsworth, William 169, 172–3, 181
World War I 122, 201, 211, 213
World War II 114, 116
worship 8, 102
wu wei 51
Wumen Huikai 128–9, 130
   Gateless Gate 128
Wycliffe, John 134

Xenophanes 54
Xi Jinping 227
xiushen 10, 48, 127
Xuanxue 84
Xuanzang 85
Xunzi 49–50

Yahweh 64, 65–6, 101
   to second Isaiah 66
yakshas 46
Yang Xiong 84
Yellow Emperor 84, 101, 104, 107
Yoga
   Aurobindo on 214
   classical philosophy of 73, 74–5

eight limbs 75
in the West 227
Yoga Sutra 74, 87, 197
Yogachara Buddhism 80–1, 85, 86
Yutang, Lin 19

Zen 86, 103, 129–30
  in the eighteenth century 154
  kensho 154
  koan 88, 129, 154
  Rinzai 129, 130, 154, 194
  Soto 129, 154
  and war 116, 129
  in the West 227
  see also Chan Buddhism

Zeno of Citium 61
Zeno of Elea 55
Zeus 38, 101
Zhang Daoling 107
Zhaozhou Congshen 129
Zheng He 152
Zhiyi 108
Zhou, Duke of 46
Zhu Xi 127–8, 152, 154
Zhuang Zhou 35, 50, 52, 53, 107
Zhuangzi 50, 52, 53, 84
Zola, Émile 200
Zoroaster 35, 64, 65
Zoroastrianism 64–5
Zuckerman, Phil 230